THE 47TH ANNUAL
BRIGHAM YOUNG UNIVERSITY
SIDNEY B. SPERRY SYMPOSIUM

THOU ART THE
CHRIST,
the SON of the LIVING GOD
THE PERSON AND WORK OF JESUS IN THE NEW TESTAMENT

Edited by Eric D. Huntsman,
Lincoln H. Blumell, and Tyler J. Griffin

BYU   DESERET BOOK

Published by the Religious Studies Center, Brigham Young University, Provo, Utah, in cooperation with Deseret Book Company, Salt Lake City.

Visit us at rsc.byu.edu.

Printed in the United States of America.

DESERET BOOK is a registered trademark of Deseret Book Company.

Visit us at DeseretBook.com.

Cover and interior design by Emily Strong.

ISBN: 978-1-9443-9453-0

Library of Congress Cataloging-in-Publication Data

Names: Sperry Symposium (47th : 2018 : Brigham Young University), author. |
    Huntsman, Eric D., 1965- editor. | Blumell, Lincoln H. (Lincoln Harris),
    1975- editor. | Griffin, Tyler J. (Tyler Jay), 1973- editor.
Title: "Thou art the Christ, the son of the living God" the person and work
    of Jesus in the New Testament / edited by Eric D. Huntsman, Lincoln H.
    Blumell, and Tyler J. Griffin.
Description: Provo, Utah : Religious Studies Center, Brigham Young University ;
    Salt Lake City : Deseret Book, [2018] | Includes index.
Identifiers: LCCN 2018012938 | ISBN 9781944394530 (alk. paper)
Subjects: LCSH: Jesus Christ--Mormon interpretations--Congresses. | Bible.
    New Testament--Congresses.
Classification: LCC BX8643.J4 S66 2018 | DDC 232--dc23 LC record available at
    https://lccn.loc.gov/2018012938

Contents

JESUS IN THE NEW TESTAMENT

Introduction

While Jesus and his disciples were at or near Caesarea Philippi, Peter shared his witness that Jesus was "the Christ, the Son of the living God" (Matthew 16:16; parallels Mark 8:29; Luke 9:20). Martha had a similar divine testimony, proclaiming at Lazarus's death, "I believe that thou art the Christ, the Son of God, which should come into the world" (John 11:27). In much the same way, a standard part of Latter-day Saint discourse includes bearing testimony that "Jesus is the Christ," but what do we mean when we say that is Jesus is *the Christ*? Since the earliest days of Christianity, believers have sought to better understand who Jesus was and what he came to do. Over millennia, both theologians and scholars have called this search for understanding Jesus and his role Christology.[1]

The 2018 Sidney B. Sperry Symposium takes up these questions from a Latter-day Saint perspective, bringing together both biblical scholarship and Restoration insights and application. Technically Christology is "the study of Christ" and has historically encompassed Jesus's relationship to God the Father, how divine and how human he was, and the way his ministry, saving death, and glorious resurrection reveal his role in our salvation. These are not insignificant matters. At the beginning of his famous Intercessory Prayer, Jesus proclaimed, "And this is life eternal, that they might know thee the only true God, and Jesus Christ, whom thou hast sent" (John 17:3; emphasis added). In light of this, attaining eternal life—the kind of immortal, glorified life that the Father and the Son share—is dependent not only upon our learning *about* them but also upon our coming to actually *know* them. Shortly before this, Jesus had taught, "I am the way, the truth, and the life: no man cometh unto the Father, but by me. If ye had known me, ye should have known my Father also: and from hence-forth ye know him, and have seen him" (John 14:6–7). Accordingly, before we can come to know the Father, we must first know the Son.

Since 1973, this symposium series has honored the legacy of Sidney Branton Sperry (1895–1977), a lifelong religious educator who became one of the first Latter-day Saints to receive formal training in biblical studies. He earned an MA from the University of Chicago Divinity School in 1926 and then a PhD in oriental languages and literature, also from Chicago, in 1931. Each year the speakers at the symposium and contributors to the associated published volume not only strive to emulate the examples of Sperry and other well-trained but faithful LDS scholars, they also endeavor to raise our scholarly and spiritual standards in response to a mandate given by Spencer W. Kimball (1895–1985), twelfth president of The Church of Jesus Christ of Latter-day Saints. On October 1, 1976, President Kimball spoke as part of Brigham Young University's centennial celebration. In that address, he charged that moving forward we must be "bilingual," saying, "As LDS scholars you must speak with authority and excellence to your professional colleagues in the language of scholarship, and you must also be literate in the language of spiritual things."[2]

Accordingly, as this year's symposium participants have attempted to better unfold what the New Testament authors and books taught about Jesus, we have felt an obligation to explore these vital texts with sound scholarship, rigorous methodology—and continued faith. As we have sought to bring new insights from biblical scholarship to a wider Latter-day Saint audience, we have kept in mind our continuing obligation to foster conviction and deepen testimony. We also feel that becoming more "bilingual" is an obligation of our listeners and readers. To that end, we have been willing to stretch our audience, introducing new terms and ways of speaking about Jesus Christ and his work. To aid with what is sometimes a new language for our readers, we have provided an appendix of christological titles and a glossary of terms that we hope will be helpful to those who read and study this volume's contents. Because there are different ways of approaching the same task—and because the topic divides fairly well into discussions of doctrine, scriptural analysis, and history—we have divided this volume into three sections, each with slightly different aims and different kinds of writing but all contributing to the same end: to come to know more about our Lord Jesus Christ even as we seek to *know* him better.

Beyond those whose contributions appear in this volume as written works, we are grateful to those who presented in this year's symposium. We express special thanks to those whose efforts helped produce this year's symposium and this collection. These include Beverly Yellowhorse and support staff of the College of Religious Education and the blind reviewers who carefully vetted each submission and made helpful suggestions for all of the papers. Thomas Wayment, Devan Jensen, Shirley Ricks, Brent Nordgren, Emily Strong, and the staff of BYU's Religious Studies Center deserve particular mention for continuing to bring new levels of professionalism and scholarship to this series. In addition, we are grateful for the efforts of Nicholas Frederick, who reviewed and assisted with much of this volume.

Coming to Christ

We are pleased to have as our keynote speaker this year Sister Neill F. Marriott, second counselor in the Young Women General Presidency from 2013 to 2018. A gifted and inspiring speaker, Sister Marriott is known for her personal and powerful way of testifying of Jesus. To open our symposium, she is speaking on the topic of "Becoming Better Disciples of Jesus Christ," and she and her publisher, Deseret Book, have graciously agreed to allow us to reprint a chapter by the same name from her recent book, *Seek This Jesus*. We wanted to begin with Sister Marriott because her witness is that of one who knows Jesus Christ, not just someone who knows something about him. While her original published story was geared toward the women of the Church, its message reaches all of us as she teaches through her own experiences, starting as a young woman seeking to come to Christ at a Protestant revival. In her words, "I have sought the Savior Jesus Christ for much of my life, and I believe, in my own weak and limited way, I have found him. He is my hope, my refuge, my teacher, my Redeemer. There is no other place to go for lasting help, direction, joy, and peace."

Sister Marriott's words comprise a homily, or a religious discourse intended for edification rather than simply intellectual instruction. We have a strong and valued homiletic tradition in the Church, where preachers of sermons, speakers at conferences, and writers find ways to relate the gospel and its teachings to real life—not only to teach but also to apply doctrine and, most of all, to inspire faith. As editors, we felt that stressing the value of coming to Christ and reviewing essential doctrines about him were important before embarking on a detailed study of New Testament teachings about him. To that end, this section of our volume includes essays from Robert Millet and Andrew Skinner, two senior, respected LDS scholars and both former deans of Religious Education. It concludes with the address of our other plenary speaker this year, Camille Fronk Olson, a former chair of ancient scripture, who uses the testimonies of Peter, Martha, and Mary as valuable patterns for how we can come to "believe and be sure" that Jesus is the Christ, the Son of the Living God.

Jesus in the New Testament

Camille Olson's address provides a bridge into the main, exegetical section of the volume. Exegesis is the careful and formal analysis of a scriptural text that seeks to understand its original meaning before seeking appropriate, contemporary application. Employing the historical-critical method and other scholarly tools in this endeavor, LDS exegesis attempts to do this while keeping in mind the teachings and contributions of Restoration scripture and teaching, recognizing that different readings of the same text can often be valuable. In this case, such effort can help us better understand and appreciate what the New Testament teaches about Jesus Christ. While gospel study often harmonizes our picture of Jesus, the reality is that the four Gospels and other New Testament writings actually present different portraits of Christ. Just as the Gospels have been described as different facets of a diamond or varied stones in a mosaic,[3] the essays in this section combine to reveal what we hope readers will find to be a rich stained glass window, each pane providing different, and perhaps even new, answers to the questions of who Jesus was and what he did for us.

Scholars and students of the New Testament over the years have sought to answer these questions by focusing on texts that emphasize Jesus's divinity or humanity, his premortal existence or his postresurrection glory, the nature of his relationship to God his Father, and his ministry or his sacrifice. Scholars in the twentieth century tended to view early Christian Christology as something that evolved or developed over time. For instance, some of the earliest texts seemed to suggest that Jesus in some way more fully became God's Son with his resurrection, while Mark's might imply that Jesus was appointed to do God's work at his baptism. While Matthew and Luke clearly present a Jesus who was divinely conceived and miraculously born, John proclaims that as the divine Word, Jesus was in the presence of God in the beginning. Nevertheless, more recent analyses of the texts show that these ideas are present in both early and late passages.

Latter-day Saints certainly have no problem with the proposition that New Testament authors fully understood who Jesus was and what he accomplished but might have emphasized or taught different aspects at different times. As a result, this section of the volume will present treatments of the Gospels, the writings of Paul, and the books of Hebrews and Revelation that will hopefully bring to light new insights about these texts and their presentations of Jesus Christ. By looking at the Savior in new ways, we may deepen our understanding of him and strengthen our faith in his saving work.

Christology after the New Testament

The final section of this volume is primarily historical. While these essays reveal how Christians in the period after the apostles sometimes struggled to understand the nature and work of Jesus Christ, they also seek to increase our appreciation of their sincerity and their desire to worship God and his Son. Such an appreciation can make us less critical of their efforts even as it leads us to be more understanding of people of different beliefs in our own day. From a Latter-day Saint perspective, of course, these essays make us grateful for the understanding and clarity that the restored gospel gives us, but we may also find ourselves wanting to be more thoughtful as we seek to reaffirm what we know about Christ and how we know it.

Our final contribution this year is about Christology in Joseph Smith's New Translation of the Bible, commonly known as the Joseph Smith Translation. By ending with the work of the Church's founding prophet, we hope to conclude with a reflection on how Restoration readings of the texts are important in helping us know and worship a *revealed* Jesus, one who is known not only from early scripture but also through revelation to prophets and apostles, one who is an inspiration to saints and sinners. Indeed, coming not only to know Jesus but also to become more like him through his atonement is the desired end: "Beloved, now are we the sons [and daughters] of God, and it doth not yet appear what we shall be: but we know that, when he shall appear, we shall be like him; for we shall see him as he is" (1 John 3:2).

Eric D. Huntsman
Lincoln H. Blumell
Tyler J. Griffin
Beverly Yellowhorse
2018 Sperry Symposium Committee

Notes

1. For some important scholarly treatments of the subject, see Raymond E. Brown, *An Introduction to New Testament Christology* (New York: Paulist Press, 1994); Ben Witherington, *The Christology of Jesus* (Minneapolis: Augsburg Fortress, 1990); Thomas P. Rausch, *Who Is Jesus? An Introduction to Christology* (Wilmington, DL: Michael Glazier, 2003); N. T. Wright, *The Challenge of Jesus: Rediscovering Who Jesus Was and Is* (Downers Grove: InterVarsity Press, 2015).

2. Spencer W. Kimball, "Second Century Address," *BYU Quarterly* 16, no. 4 (1976): 446.

3. Roger R. Keller, "Mark and Luke: Two Facets of a Diamond," in *Sperry Symposium Classics: The New Testament*, ed. Frank F. Judd Jr. and Gaye Strathearn (Provo, UT: Religious Studies Center; Salt Lake City: Deseret Book, 2006), 92–107; Richard Holzapfel, *A Lively Hope* (Salt Lake City: Bookcraft, 1999), 1–8.

COMING TO CHRIST

1

Becoming True Disciples of Jesus Christ

Neill F. Marriott

When I was fifteen years old, my parents and I attended an Easter revival service at our Protestant church in Louisiana. We had a guest minister who gave a sermon, which I don't remember, and then introduced the last hymn, entitled "Just As I Am," which I vividly remember. The first verse says:

> *Just as I am, without one plea,*
> *But that Thy blood was shed for me,*
> *And that Thou bidd'st me come to Thee,*
> *O Lamb of God, I come! I come!"*
> ("Just As I Am," Charlotte Elliott, 1835)

Each of the five verses ends with the words "O Lamb of God, I come! I come!"

As I sang, I wanted to come unto Christ. Our minister stopped the hymn momentarily and invited any and all to come down to the altar as we sang the last verse, to witness that we were coming to Christ. So, as the last verse was being sung, several members of our congregation began to slowly walk down to the altar railing. I walked to the altar too.

When the hymn ended, we milled around for a moment. The minister heartily shook our hands, and then my parents and I went home. *Was that it?* I thought. *Did I come to Christ?* It felt like I had only gotten as far as the altar.

That walk did have a form of godliness—we walkers were witnessing as best we knew—but it denied the power needed to enter a binding covenant with God. The preacher did his best too, but he simply didn't have the authority to offer us an ordinance and covenant with the Lord. And we didn't have the ability to enter such a covenant without the sanction of godly power—priesthood power.

I was to learn some years later that to truly come unto Christ, we must come by the strait and narrow way, by the Lord's authorized ordinances and covenants. True it is that many believing people the world over are living by the light of Christ and doing good. They are following Jesus Christ with all their hearts, and they will be blessed. However, our conversion to the Lord must go farther than the altar and even farther than good deeds and loving service if it is to open an eternal path back to the Father's presence. He is a God of order, and His kingdom is orderly in its commandments, justice, mercy, forgiveness, and organization. It is not randomly created by men, even well-meaning believers or highly educated teachers. God's true church is established by our Eternal Father and his Son, Jesus Christ, according to eternal law.

Soon after the resurrection and ascension of Jesus, the apostle Peter taught, "Let all . . . know assuredly, that God hath made that same Jesus, whom ye have crucified, both Lord and Christ." The listeners were stricken in their hearts and asked Peter and the others, "Men and brethren, what shall we do? Then Peter said unto them, Repent, and be baptized every one of you in the name of Jesus Christ for the remission of sins, and ye shall receive the gift of the Holy

Ghost" (Acts 2:36–38). And they subsequently obeyed Peter's teachings with gladness. As I ponder my own desire that each of us come unto Christ, I ask, "Sisters and brothers, what shall we do?" True disciples follow the Savior's commandments and teach his truths.

I have watched examples, heard testimonies, and felt of sisters' faith from Brazil to Botswana. Women of the Church carry a circle of influence with them wherever they go. I've even described it as a hula hoop that circles around us and is constantly touching those nearby. Are we radiating goodness and charity to others? We can. The Lord's Church needs Spirit-directed women who use their unique gifts to nurture, to speak up, and to defend gospel truth. Our inspiration and intuition are necessary parts of building the kingdom of God, which really means doing our part to bring salvation to God's children.

Women in the workplace and mothers in the home, if watching for opportunities to teach truth, will find ample time to speak of faith in Jesus Christ and his restored gospel. Surely a mother's prayer to teach her children the gospel will be answered swiftly. Surely colleagues in a work environment will be uplifted and even blessed by a converted, faithful sister's words and actions.

As the apostle Peter was charged, "When thou art converted, strengthen thy brethren" (Luke 22:32), so we must become converted ourselves and then reach out to strengthen others. In that regard, the background of the word convert is exquisitely right. It comes from the Latin con, which means "with," and vert, which means "to turn." We come unto Jesus Christ with the action of turning to him—and that means turning away from the world and worldliness.

As I ponder the embarking on this journey of conversion, I picture a bayou behind my parents' home in Louisiana, where my father built a house for wood ducks and positioned it on a ten-foot pole. From the back porch we could watch the freshly hatched ducklings launch themselves from the door of their little home. The mother duck circled below in the water, watching and calling as duckling after duckling jumped off the edge and plummeted straight into the water.

It wasn't always a pretty sight: baby ducks falling out of the duck house and landing unceremoniously in the small stream. It wasn't entirely safe, either, because once in the water, the ducklings had to evade predators. Nevertheless, their focus and desire was to get to the mother, and that required leaving the nest. They embarked from the house and immediately began moving through the bayou, purposefully following the mother duck.

When we decide to follow Jesus Christ, do we continue with our allegiance past the planning stage or the baptismal day? The ducklings, driven by instinct, commit to their way of life by leaping into the bayou. Our commitment, on the other hand, as spirit sons and daughters of God is made thoughtfully as we take upon us sacred ordinances and covenants that draw us close to our Heavenly Father and put upon us responsibilities that we promise to fulfill.

The wood ducklings instinctively understand that in order to survive, they must not get casual in their daily living and must look steadily to their leader. Occasionally we would see some of the young ducks swim away from the parent. Hawks circled, above, and snatched up the ducklings before they could return to the protection of the family group.

Are we, like the ducklings, following experienced leaders, or are we putting ourselves in danger by being too casual in our attention to prophets of God? A true disciple will follow the prophet, knowing he will lead us to do what the Lord wants of us at the present time.

Another danger that threatens our faithful discipleship is to look beyond the mark, to look past gospel doctrine and think that we have a special calling to achieve more than is required by our covenants with the Lord. A few ducklings would paddle ahead of the family group, often to their demise. When this attitude is found in humans, pride—that is, putting our own plans ahead of God's will—is at its center. Are we looking for "something more" than the doctrines of Christ? There is no happiness beyond the mark. As Elder Quentin L. Cook has taught, "Jesus Christ is the mark!"[1] Are we intrigued by someone who takes a different stand than the prophets' on such things as how to seek God or administer the laws of the kingdom? Such "wolves in sheep's clothing" do exist, and we must be firmly determined to continue on the strait way and give them no heed.

A third danger is to turn back to ungodly ways after we have once left them behind. We may put our hand "to the plow" and then be tempted to step off the path of righteousness and return to former habits (see Luke 9:62). Using the analogy of the ducklings, once they have leapt from the nest, they cannot go back because they will not actually be able to fly for eight to ten more weeks. Once they are on the ground or in the water, they are committed to stay there until they are mature. We, unlike the ducklings, are free to "go back," and the choice is ever before us. Will we commit wholeheartedly to Christ, seeking his will and adding more and more light of his truth to ourselves, or will we follow the path of least resistance, diminishing in gospel understanding and capacity to recognize and follow the promptings of the Holy Ghost? President Ezra Taft Benson elaborated on the sort of tests we will encounter and spoke of our present day: "There is a real sifting going on in the Church, and it is going to become more pronounced with the passing of time. It will sift the wheat from the tares, because we face some difficult days, the like of which we have never experienced in our lives."[2] In order to gain eternal happiness, we must be steadfast in retaining our commitment, our conversion to God—in other words, "enduring to the end." And it follows that we, as ever-growing, ever-learning disciples of Jesus Christ, will seek to bring others to this same happiness.

When we ask ourselves, "What shall we do?" let's ponder this question: "What does the Savior do continually for us?" He nurtures. He creates. He encourages growth and goodness.

The Savior's creation of the earth, under the direction of his Father, was a mighty act of nurturing. He provided a place for us to be born into mortality, so that we can be tested in our obedience to him and develop faith in his atoning power. All of us need a spiritual and physical haven of belonging as we grow in the gospel. We, sisters and brothers of all ages, can create this haven as we help build his king-dom; it is even a holy place.

We build the kingdom when we nurture others; however, the first child of God we must build up in the restored gospel is our-selves. Emma Smith, wife of the Prophet Joseph, said, "I desire the Spirit of God to know and understand myself, that I might be able to overcome whatever of tradition or nature that would not tend to my exaltation."[3] Sometimes we go on "automatic pilot" as we live our daily lives. Do we have personal habits or traditions that limit our faith or our ability to nurture faith in others? Are we even aware of those limitations? How can we learn all that we need to know and do?

The few moments we spend partaking of the ordinance of the sacrament is a time of powerful connection to the Godhead. Here is a sacred gift for each of us. Knowing, as King Benjamin taught, that God has all wisdom and all power both in heaven and in earth (see Mosiah 4:9), we can turn with full confidence to him during this sacred time of covenant. "What do I need to change in my life, Father?" could be a powerful part of our prayer during the sacrament. Sunday after Sunday we have this opportunity, a priesthood ordi-nance, to point us to our baptismal covenant and other covenants and to open a channel of guidance through the Holy Ghost from God the Father and the Lord, Jesus Christ, to us.

There was a time in my life when, as the deacons passed the sanctified bread and the sanctified water, I looked around the chapel, paying attention to someone's new haircut or outfit. What a waste of opportunity! One Sunday I honestly felt these words summarily impressed upon my thoughts: "Bow your head." I was so surprised that I immediately bowed my head. It felt right; my thoughts moved from earthly things to the Savior's payment for my sins.

Our attitude about the symbols of the Savior's sacrifice and atonement will inevitably influence others. Adam, one of our grown sons, admitted that as a child he liked to cause mischief during sac-rament meeting. (I might even call it havoc!) He then said, "But somehow, I didn't feel like misbehaving when I saw you with your head bowed and your eyes closed during the passing of the sacrament. Even though I knew I could get away with misbehaving since you wouldn't see me, I just didn't want to." He also spoke of his father's solemn attitude as he presided on the stand. Honestly honoring Jesus Christ has an effect on those around us, even without words.

However, our words carry much influence too. We serve when we testify of our faith. When David and I were serving as missionaries in Brazil, my Portuguese was primitive. Especially at the outset, I could hardly cobble together one strong sentence. I sounded something like this: "You nice. Church true. I happy." If nothing else, my attempts got attention, and then the missionaries could fill in the gaps! But as I limped along, sharing my grammatically pathetic testimony, I began to realize something: the power of a testimony isn't in the grammar. It isn't in the well-turned phrase. And it isn't in the pronunciation. The power and authority of our testimonies is in the Spirit that accompanies them. The Holy Ghost is a perfect translator of wholehearted faith in any language, even in broken Portuguese sentences. I believe that as we speak truth, the light of the Spirit illuminates the humble hearts of listeners and testifies to their souls that Jesus is the Christ.

We, as daughters of God, have an essential part in the work of salvation. As we participate in the ordinances of baptism and the temple endowment, we are armed with power from God and can be significant in nurturing others' faith in the Redeemer.

I remember a lovely sister missionary from a remote town in Brazil. She, the only Church member in her family, worked under the direction of a zone leader who came from a long-established LDS family of Utah. The zone leader had had all the support possible throughout his life to be the great leader he was in the mission. However, he recognized the delegated priesthood power in this sister's testimony of the Savior, and he asked her to teach in zone meetings, to strengthen the elders and demonstrate how to bring souls to Christ.

As women, we can participate in the holy work of bringing God's spirit children into the world to gain a physical body, have earthly experience, and be eternally sealed in a family unit. We make a difference—a major difference—by teaching a pattern of faith, especially within a family. Our daughter Paige, mother of five, says she asks herself often, "How would Mom or Dad teach truth in this moment?" Mothers' gospel teachings affect generations.

President Russell M. Nelson reminds us, "Attacks against the Church, its doctrine, and our way of life are going to increase. Because of this, we need women who have a bedrock understanding of the doctrine of Christ and who will use that understanding to teach and help raise a sin-resistant generation. . . . We need women who have the courage and vision of our Mother Eve."[4]

As we faithfully covenant with Father in Heaven, in the name of his Son, he will make us builders of his kingdom, and we will be his true disciples.

I have sought the Savior Jesus Christ for much of my life, and I believe, in my own weak and limited way, I have found him. He is my hope, my refuge, my teacher, my Redeemer. There is no other place to go for lasting help, direction, joy, and peace. Through toil and trouble, as well as reward and delight in my life, he stands bright and loving, constant in his mercy and grace. As I try to follow his commandments, even though I often fail, I still know of his love. I know of his steadiness. I know of his kindly wisdom. This knowledge began with years of seeking him, singing of him, and feeling his love on rare but real occasions. By the power of authorized priesthood ordinances and covenants restored to the earth through the Prophet Joseph Smith, I have gained more knowledge of God and felt his grace pour down upon me and my family through the gift of the Holy Ghost, especially in times of grief and pain. I have a testimony of the callings of modern-day prophets; I know, by the witness of the Spirit, these are men of God who continue to reveal God's word to the world.

My keenly felt need for the Redeemer and his true Church grows as I see my weaknesses and reach for divine help. Here is the sweetest, deepest love I've ever known, a love that draws me in and binds me to him. This love is not just for me; it is continually flowing out to all on earth, for we are all children of God. I have felt this flow and seen his image in the countenances of others who also know of his love.

I testify that the resurrected Savior, Jesus Christ, lives today. I trust, because of his atoning sacrifice for our sins, mistakes, and faults, that he will heal all our wounds and lead all who will humbly follow him and his ways back to Heavenly Father and to eternal life. Truly, as prophets and apostles have said, God be thanked for the matchless gift of his divine Son!

NEILL F. MARRIOTT *served as the second counselor in the general presidency of the Young Women organization of The Church of Jesus Christ of Latter-day Saints from April 2013 to April 2018.*

Notes

Originally published as Neill Marriott, "Becoming True Disciples of Jesus Christ," chapter 7 of *Seek This Jesus* (Salt Lake City: Deseret Book, 2017). Reprinted by permission.

1. Quentin L. Cook, "Valiant in the Testimony of Jesus," *Ensign*, November 2016.

2. *The Teachings of Ezra Taft Benson* (Salt Lake City: Bookcraft, 1988), 107.

3. *Daughters in My Kingdom: The History and Work of Relief Society* (Salt Lake City: The Church of Jesus Christ of Latter-day Saints, 2011), 12.

4. Russell M. Nelson, "A Plea to My Sisters," *Ensign*, November 2015.

2

One Eternal God

The Latter-day Saint Doctrine
of the Father and the Son

Robert L. Millet

The work of the salvation of souls is a work in which each member of the Godhead is intimately involved and to which they are eternally committed. Elohim, who is God the Eternal Father; Jesus Christ, who is the Only Begotten Son of God in the flesh; and the Holy Ghost, who is the representative and witness of the Father and the Son—these three are perfectly united and forevermore linked in bringing to pass the immortality and eternal life of the children of God (Moses 1:39). The highest of eternal rewards in the world to come—exaltation in the celestial kingdom—comes only to those who worship the Father and the Son and have enjoyed the revelations and cleansing powers of the Holy Ghost.

This volume represents a study of the life and divine ministry of the Son of God, as taught in the New Testament. As Latter-day Saints, we also rejoice in the fact that the restored gospel provides vital insights into the relationship of the first two members of the

Godhead, as well as the Savior's central role in the plan of salvation. These Restoration truths are essential for properly understanding the person and work of Jesus Christ and will serve as an important interpretive framework as the contributions in this volume examine how he is presented in the various writings of the New Testament.

The Relationship of the Father and the Son

Few passages in the New Testament have touched my heart more than the gentle invitation from Jesus to "come unto me, all ye that labour and are heavy laden, and I will give you rest. Take my yoke upon you, and learn of me; for I am meek and lowly in heart: and ye shall find rest unto your souls. For my yoke is easy, and my burden is light" (Matthew 11:28–30). Four centuries later the last great Nephite prophet-editor expanded upon this glorious truth. Moroni brought the Book of Mormon to a close by inviting its readers to "come unto Christ, and be perfected in him, and deny yourselves of all ungodliness; and if ye shall deny yourselves of all ungodliness, and love God with all your might, mind, and strength, then is his grace sufficient for you, that by his grace ye may be perfect in Christ" (Moroni 10:32). There it is: the eternal mission of the Church of Jesus Christ (compare D&C 20:59), the invitation to all humankind to come unto the Holy Messiah and enjoy perfection—wholeness, maturity, or spiritual completion in him.

While postapostolic Christianity endlessly debated the nature and relationship of the Father and the Son, the Prophet Joseph Smith (1805–1844) declared simply: "I have always declared God to be a distinct personage, Jesus Christ a separate and distinct personage from God the Father, and that the Holy Ghost was a distinct personage and a Spirit; and *these three constitute three distinct personages and three Gods.*"[1] The New Testament, especially the Gospel of John, clearly teaches that Jesus the Son is subordinate to God the Father. This is also the doctrine taught in the scriptures of the Restoration. Those scriptures teach the following:

- God the Father is greater than Christ (John 14:28).
- There is only one that is good, that is, the Father (Matthew 19:16–17).
- Jesus came to do the will of the Father in all things (John 6:38; 3 Nephi 27:13–14).
- The gospel or glad tidings is the "gospel of God," meaning the Father (Romans 1:1; 15:16; 1 Thessalonians 2:2, 8; 1 Peter 4:17).
- The Father sent the Son to atone for all of humanity (John 3:16; 2 Nephi 2:8).
- Jesus came in his Father's name (John 5:43).
- The Father sanctified the Son (John 10:36).
- Jesus had power given to him by the Father to redeem earth's inhabitants from their sins (Helaman 5:11).
- The Father "raised [the Son] up from the dead, and gave him glory; that [our] faith and hope might be in God" (1 Peter 1:21).
- God the Father will also raise us from the dead (2 Corinthians 4:14).
- The Father, through the Son, is reconciling the world to himself (2 Corinthians 5:18–20; 2 Nephi 10:24).
- Christ is our Advocate and Intercessor, the Mediator between God and man (1 Timothy 2:5–6; D&C 45:3–5).
- God was in Christ, manifesting himself to the world (Hebrews 1:3; John 14:9).
- Christ's doctrine is not his, but the Father's (John 7:16).
- Jesus works through the power of the Father (John 5:26, 57; Helaman 5:10–11).
- The Holy Ghost proceeds forth from the Father (John 15:26).
- We are born again by the power of God the Father (1 Peter 1:3).
- We are made perfect by the Father (Hebrews 13:21; 1 Peter 5:10).

- The Father sends the "earnest of the Spirit," the Holy Spirit of Promise, to certify to us that we are on course to inherit eternal life (2 Corinthians 1:21–22; 5:5; Ephesians 1:13–14).
- The Father has committed all judgment to the Son (John 3:35; 5:21–22, 26–27; 2 Nephi 9:41).
- Christ loves, serves, and worships the Father (John 20:17).
- Christ worked out his own salvation by worshipping the Father; all men and women must do the same (D&C 93:12–13, 16–17, 19–20).
- Christ is the revealer of and the Way to the Father (Luke 10:22; John 14:6).
- Christ glorifies the Father (John 17:1, 4).

These scriptural passages affirm that the Son was and is subordinate to the Father. We obviously could now take the time—which we will not—to consider all the passages that state that the Father and the Son are one; that Christ received a fullness of the glory and power of the Father in the resurrection;[2] and that Jesus possesses in perfection every divine quality, attribute, or endowment, just as his Father does. The point to be made here is that there is in fact a hierarchy among the members of the Godhead.

"Our Father in heaven . . . is the Father of all spirits," wrote President John Taylor, "and who, with Jesus Christ, his first begotten Son, and the Holy Ghost, are one in power, one in dominion, and one in glory, *constituting the first presidency of this system, and this eternity.*"[3] Of that royal presidency, the Prophet Joseph Smith explained that it is "the province of the Father to preside as the Chief or President, Jesus as the Mediator, and the Holy Ghost as the Testator or Witness."[4] Elder Bruce R. McConkie (1915–1985), a prolific author and member of the Twelve from 1972 to 1985, put it this way: "In the ultimate and final sense of the word, there is only one true and living God. He is the Father, the Almighty Elohim, the Supreme Being, the Creator and Ruler of the universe. . . . Christ is God; he alone is the Savior. The Holy Ghost is God; he is one with the Father and the Son. But these two are the second and third members of the Godhead. The Father is God above all, and is, in fact, the God of the Son."[5] The early brethren were taught in the School of the Elders that "God is the only supreme governor and independent being in whom all fullness and perfection dwell; who is omnipotent, omnipresent [by means of his Holy Spirit], and omniscient; without beginning of days or end of life; and that in him every good gift and every good principle dwell; that he is the Father of lights; in him the principle of faith dwells independently, and *he is the object in whom the faith of all other rational and accountable beings center for life and salvation.*"[6]

The plan of salvation is the Father's plan. It is the *gospel of God* (Romans 1:1; 15:16; 1 Thessalonians 2:2, 8; 1 Peter 4:17). It became known as the gospel of Jesus Christ as Jehovah became the chief proponent, advocate, and expositor of that gospel (Mosiah 4:4). "In that great concourse of spirit intelligences," Elder James E. Talmage (1862–1933), a member of the Twelve and the author of the classic *Jesus the Christ*, explained, "the Father's plan whereby His children would be advanced to their second estate, was submitted and doubtless discussed. The opportunity so placed within the reach of the spirits who were to be privileged to take bodies upon the earth was so transcendently glorious that those heavenly multitudes burst forth into song and shouted for joy" (Job 38:7).[7] It was then that Jehovah the Firstborn meekly consecrated himself to the Father's plan of salvation and said simply, "Father, thy will be done, and the glory be thine forever" (Moses 4:1–2). This simple phrase speaks volumes; it confirms that the plan of salvation was the plan of the Father, that Elohim was the originator and designer of the plan, and that it had been taught and discussed with the spirit children of God for who knows how long. And as it was long before Christ came to earth, so it was as he completed his earthly mission. From the cruel cross of Calvary, "Jesus, when he had cried again with a loud voice, saying,

Father, it is finished, *thy will is done*, yielded up the ghost" (Joseph Smith Translation, Matthew 26:54; emphasis added).

In the apostle Paul's glorious defense of the resurrection, he states that every person comes forth from the dead "in his own order: Christ the firstfruits; afterward they that are Christ's at his coming" (1 Corinthians 15:23). He then went on to explain that the Savior will eventually deliver up the kingdom to the Father and thereby "put all enemies under his feet. . . . But when he saith all things are put under him, it is manifest [clear, plain, evident] that he [God the Father] is excepted." And now note what follows: "And when all things shall be subdued unto him [the Father], *then shall the Son also himself be subject unto him that put all things under him, that God may be all in all*" (1 Corinthians 15:24–25, 27–28; emphasis added).

In his Messiah series, Elder Bruce R. McConkie stated: "Jesus' Father is greater than he! Are they not one? Do they not both possess all power, all wisdom, all knowledge, all truth? Have they not both gained all godly attributes in their fullness and perfection? Verily, yes, for the revelations so announce and the Prophet [Joseph Smith] so taught. And yet our Lord's Father is greater than he, greater in kingdoms and dominions, greater in principalities and exaltations. One does and shall rule over the other everlastingly. Though Jesus is himself God, he is also the Son of God, and as such the Father is his God as he is ours."[8]

Speaking as it were in the language of Jesus, the Prophet Joseph asked: "What did Jesus do? why I do the things I saw my Father do when worlds came rolling into existence. I saw my Father work out his kingdom with fear and trembling, and I must do the same; and when I get my kingdom I shall present it to my Father, so that he obtains kingdom upon kingdom, and it will exalt his glory, so that Jesus treads in his tracks to inherit what God did before."[9] Or, as Parley P. Pratt (1807–1857), one of the original members of this dispensation's Quorum of the Twelve, wrote: "The difference between Jesus Christ and his Father is this: one is subordinate to the other and does nothing of himself independently of the Father, but does all things in the name and by the authority of the Father, being of the same mind in all things."[10]

Recovering the Father

When Philip asked Jesus to show them the Father, Jesus responded, "Have I been so long time with you, and yet hast thou not known me, Philip? he that hath seen me hath seen the Father; and how sayest thou then, Shew us the Father?" (John 14:9) Yet while we come to know the Father through the Son, without a proper understanding of their relationship, postapostolic Christianity has arguably lost a clear understanding of both. For the most part, the great christological debates of the fourth and fifth centuries were concerned with the nature of Christ and his relationship to the Father, but there was less discussion of the Father himself.

This is especially tragic, given that one of the major thrusts of the Lord Jesus Christ, as he taught in both the Old World and the New, was to reveal and make known the Father. Elder Jeffrey R. Holland, a member of the Twelve since 1994, taught that "in all that Jesus came to say and do, including and especially in His atoning suffering and sacrifice, *He was showing us who and what God our Eternal Father is like*, how completely devoted He is to His children in every age and nation. *In word and in deed Jesus was trying to reveal and make personal to us the true nature of His Father, our Father in Heaven.*" Elder Holland went on to explain how many Christians

> feel distant from the Father, even estranged from Him, if they believe in Him at all. And if they do believe, many moderns say they might feel comfortable in the arms of Jesus, but they are uneasy contemplating the stern encounter of God. . . . Jesus did not come to improve God's view of man nearly so much as He came *to improve man's view of God* and to plead with them to love their Heavenly Father as He has always and will always love them. The plan of God, the power of God,

the holiness of God, yes, even the anger and the judgment of God they had occasion to understand. But the love of God, the profound depth of His devotion to His children, they still did not fully know—until Christ came.[11]

The Savior himself was extremely clear regarding the order of prayer: we are to pray to God the Father, in the name of Christ the Son (see John 14:13–14; 15:16; 16:23–24, 26; 3 Nephi 18:19, 23, 30; 19:6–8; D&C 14:8; Moses 7:59). Those prayers are most focused and spiritually effectual when we do so by the power of the Holy Ghost. To say that we are to pray to our Father in heaven in the name of the Son is *not* to say that our prayers somehow go *through* Christ. No, the scriptures speak otherwise. Christ is our Mediator with the Father, our Intercessor in the courts of glory, but we pray directly to God our Father. The mighty prophet Enoch, some three thousand years before Christ came to earth, was commanded to pray to the Father in the name of the Only Begotten Son. "Forasmuch as thou art God, and I know thee, and thou hast sworn unto me, and commanded me that *I should ask in the name of thine Only Begotten*; thou hast made me, and given unto me a right to thy throne, and not of myself, but through thine own grace" (Moses 7:59; emphasis added).

Why did Jesus need to pray? To begin with, during his mortal ministry he set aside much of the power and glory he had enjoyed before he came into the world (John 17:5). Paul, perhaps quoting an even earlier Christian hymn, wrote that Jesus "made himself of no reputation, and took upon him the form of a servant, and was made in the likeness of men: and being found in fashion as a man, he humbled himself, and became obedient unto death, even the death of the cross" (Philippians 2:7–8). Other translations render the above passage as "*emptied himself*, taking the form of a slave" (New American Bible; emphasis added; see also New Revised Standard Version). By choice Jesus did not turn the stones to bread, although he certainly possessed the power to do so (Luke 4:3–4). By choice Jesus did not cast himself down from the pinnacle of the temple and anticipate divine deliverance, although he had the power to do so (Luke 4:9–12). By choice our Lord did not call down legions of angels to deliver him in the Garden of Gethsemane, although he indeed possessed the power to do so (Matthew 26:51–54). And by choice the Master of ocean and earth and skies did not come down from the cross and bring an end to the pain and suffering, the ignominy and irony of his crucifixion and death, although the power to do just that was within his grasp (Matthew 27:39–40; Luke 23:39).

By setting aside the fullness of power and glory that he possessed, he was able to know mortality in its fullness, to know by experience what it felt like to be hungry, thirsty, tired, snubbed, ridiculed, excluded; in short, he chose to endure the throes and toils of this estate so he might then be in a position to succor his people (Alma 7:11–13; D&C 62:1). Thus when he felt the need for reassurance, he prayed to his Father in Heaven. When he needed answers or perspective, he prayed. When he needed the sacred sustaining influence of the Father in his darkest hours, he prayed earnestly (Luke 22:44). Because of the Spirit, which conveys the mind of God (1 Corinthians 2:16),[12] he was in the Father, as the Father was in him. They were one (John 10:30; 14:10; 17:21–23; D&C 50:43), and by his praying and through his example, he showed us how we could be one with them.

Then what of the risen Lord among the Nephites? Why would Jesus, now a glorified, immortal, and resurrected Being, now possessing and manifesting the fullness of the glory and power of the Father (Matthew 28:18; D&C 93:16), spend so much of his time among the Nephites on his knees in prayer? Was there some truth he did not know, some godly attribute he did not possess, some energy or strength he lacked? Was there some approval of the Father, some encouragement or permission he needed? I rather think not. The descendants of Lehi might have cried out *Emmanuel,* "God is with us." Jesus prayed frequently as an example to the saints and to all men and women of the need to communicate with God—often, regularly, consistently, intensely, reverently. Building on these truths, we therefore ask further whether there are not other purposes of prayer, both in time and in eternity. Jesus prayed to the Father because he loved the Father and because it was a reverential way of speaking to his Father, who is forever worthy of the reverence of his children. Jesus prayed to the Father because *they enjoyed communion.*

Finally, we ask: Do we worship the Holy Ghost? Do we pray to him? It is true that he is the third member of the Godhead, the messenger and representative of the Father and Son, and the one who bears witness of both. He is one with the Father and the Son and possesses all the qualities and attributes that they do. There is evidence in holy writ that the Holy Ghost is God (Acts 5:3, 4, 9), but to my knowledge there is no scripture or prophetic statement that encourages us or even suggests that we should worship him or pray to him. Many of our more conservative Protestant brothers and sisters (for example, Pentecostals) occasionally pray to or "in" the Holy Spirit, but this is not a part of the restored gospel.

"Becoming" the Children of God

Jesus Christ "came unto his own, and his own received him not. But as many as received him, *to them gave he power to become the sons of God,* even to them that believe on his name" (John 1:11–12; emphasis added). We find that same language used by the Savior in our own dispensation. He declared that "as many as receive me, to them will I give power to become the sons of God, even to them that believe on my name" (D&C 11:30; compare 34:1, 3). We might ask: What does it mean to say that if we accept the Savior we will be given *power to become* the sons and daughters of God? Aren't we already his spirit children? Isn't he the Father of our spirits? And of course the answer is yes; God is the Father of our spirits (Numbers 16:22; 27:16; Hebrews 12:9).

The verses cited above, however, speak of those persons who accept Jesus Christ and his gospel *being given the power to become* the children of God. What power is this? It is the power of redemption, the power of regeneration, the power of the Lord's atonement, the power that derives from the gospel of Jesus Christ, the "power of God unto salvation" (Romans 1:16). To say this another way, those who come unto Christ by covenant and through ordinances become the sons and daughters of God *by adoption*. They are adopted into the royal family of God. Or as King Benjamin pointed out, they become the children of Christ (Mosiah 5:7; compare 27:23–26). This is essentially the testimony that Joseph Smith and Sidney Rigdon bore in the Vision of the Glories, when they attested that by and through Christ "the worlds are and were created, and *the inhabitants thereof are begotten sons and daughters unto God*" (D&C 76:24; emphasis added). It is thus the power not just to regain a lost former position but to inherit, through Christ, a new exalted status.

It was never intended, however, that men and women remain children forever, even children of Jesus Christ. After persons have received the appropriate formative ordinances (baptism and confirmation), have chosen to forsake evil, have begun to have dross and iniquity burned out of the souls as though by fire, have become alive to the things of the Spirit and thus been born again, they qualify to enter the house of the Lord. These higher ordinances give them "power to become the sons of God, meaning the Father. They thus become joint heirs [co-inheritors] with Christ who is [the Father's] natural heir. *Those who are sons of God in this sense are the ones who become gods in the world to come* (D&C 76:54–60). *They have exaltation and godhood because the family unit continues in eternity.*"[13]

Becoming One with the Father and the Son

In his moving Intercessory Prayer, offered shortly before Gethsemane and with a view to the wrenching ordeal of Calvary, Jesus pled, "For their sakes I sanctify myself, that they also might be sanctified through the truth. Neither pray I for these alone, but for them also which shall believe on me through their word; *That they all may be one*; as thou, Father, art in me, and I in thee, *that they also may be one in us*: that the world may believe that thou hast sent me (John 17:19–21; emphasis added). This indeed is the intent and purpose of Christ's great atonement, that we can become one with him and one with our Eternal Father in Heaven.

As the children of God, we are charged to become like God, like his Son Jesus Christ. "But as he which hath called you is holy," the apostle Peter wrote, "so be ye holy in all manner of conversation; because it is written, Be ye holy; for I am holy" (1 Peter 1:15–16). Elder D. Todd Christofferson, a member of the Twelve since 2008, taught: "If we yearn to dwell in Christ and have him dwell in us, then holiness is what we seek, in both body and spirit. We seek it in the temple, whereon is inscribed 'Holiness to the Lord.' We seek it in our marriages, families, and homes. We seek it each week as we delight in the Lord's holy day. We seek it even in the details of daily living: our speech, our dress, our thoughts."[14]

Another way of putting this is to say that we strive to be holy in the same way that the Father and the Son are holy and wholly united, so that we may be one with them as they are one—"united in purpose, in manner, in testimony, in mission. We believe Them to be filled with the same godly sense of mercy and love, justice and grace, patience, forgiveness, and redemption."[15] And we become one with them through obtaining and cultivating the Spirit of God. The early elders of this dispensation were blessed to learn that "all those who keep the commandments shall grow up from grace to grace, and become heirs of the heavenly kingdom, and joint heirs with Jesus Christ; *possessing the same mind, being transformed into the same image or likeness, even the express image of him who fills all in all*; being filled with the fullness of his glory, and become one in him, as the Father, Son and Holy Spirit are one." Hence, through "the love of the Father, the mediation of Jesus Christ, and the gift of the Holy Spirit, [we] are to be heirs of God, and joint heirs with Jesus Christ."[16]

To repeat, the work of redemption, the labor of salvation, is an endeavor undertaken by all three members of the Godhead—the Creator, the Redeemer, and the Witness or Testator.[17] The Father, Son, and Holy Ghost, while three Beings and three Gods, are one

(John 10:30; 17:21; 2 Nephi 31:21; Alma 11:44; 3 Nephi 11:27; 28:10; Mormon 7:7; D&C 20:28). As the essays in this volume explore the crucial, divine role of Jesus Christ in the Father's plan, the Latter-day Saint doctrine of the Father and the Son reminds us that our Lord did not do it alone. Rather, he carried out his sacred assignment in harmony with the other members of the Godhead in a powerful example of selflessness and unity. Coming to know him is to come to know the Father, and this is done in and by the power of the Holy Ghost. The Savior's call to his Latter-day Saints is forever to "be one; and if ye are not one ye are not mine" (D&C 38:27). Such is our opportunity and our great challenge, our glory or our condemnation.

ROBERT L. MILLET *is professor emeritus of ancient scripture and a former dean of Religious Education at Brigham Young University.*

Notes

1. Address by Joseph Smith, 16 June 1844, Joseph Smith Collection, Church History Library; see also *Teachings of Presidents of the Church: Joseph Smith* (Salt Lake City: The Church of Jesus Christ of Latter-day Saints, 2007), 41–42; emphasis added.
2. See Joseph Fielding Smith, *Doctrines of Salvation*, comp. Bruce R. McConkie (Salt Lake City: Bookcraft, 1955), 2:269.
3. John Taylor, "The Living God," *Times and Seasons*, 15 February 1845, 809.
4. *Teachings: Joseph Smith*, 42.
5. Bruce R. McConkie, *A New Witness for the Articles of Faith* (Salt Lake City: Deseret Book, 1985), 51.
6. *Lectures on Faith* (Salt Lake City: Deseret Book, 1985), 10; emphasis added.
7. James E. Talmage, *Jesus the Christ* (Salt Lake City: Deseret Book, 1972), 8; see also John Taylor, *The Mediation and Atonement of Our Lord and Savior Jesus Christ* (Salt Lake City: Deseret News, 1892), 93. Note the

following from Elder Bruce R. McConkie: "Although we sometimes hear it said that there were two plans—Christ's plan of freedom and agency, and Lucifer's of slavery and compulsion—such teaching does not conform to the revealed word. Christ did not present a plan of redemption and salvation, nor did Lucifer present his own plan. There were not two plans up for consideration; there was only one; and that was the plan of the Father: originated, developed, presented, and put in force by him. Christ, however, made the plan his own by his willing obedience to its terms and provisions. . . . Always it is the Father's plan; always the Son is the obedient co-worker." Bruce R. McConkie, "Who Is the Author of the Plan of Salvation?" *Improvement Era*, May 1953, 322–23.

8. Bruce R. McConkie, *The Mortal Messiah* (Salt Lake City: Deseret Book, 1981), 4:79.

9. "Conference Minutes," *Times and Seasons*, 15 August 1844, 614.

10. Parley P. Pratt, *Key to the Science of Theology* (Salt Lake City: Deseret Book, 1978), 20–21; see also a statement by Joseph F. Smith, in *Messages of the First Presidency*, comp. James R. Clark (Salt Lake City: Bookcraft, 1970), 4:329.

11. Jeffrey R. Holland, "The Grandeur of God," *Ensign*, November 2003, 70–72.

12. *Lectures on Faith*, 60.

13. Bruce R. McConkie, *Doctrinal New Testament Commentary* (Salt Lake City: Bookcraft, 1971), 2:474; see also "The Father and the Son: A Doctrinal Exposition by The First Presidency and The Twelve," in *Messages of the First Presidency*, 5:29.

14. D. Todd Christofferson, "The Living Bread Which Came Down from Heaven," *Ensign*, November 2017, 38.

15. Jeffrey R. Holland, "The Only True God and Jesus Christ Whom He Hath Sent," *Ensign*, November 2007, 40.

16. *Lectures on Faith*, 60–61.

17. *Teachings: Joseph Smith*, 42.

3

In Praise of the Resurrection of Jesus Christ
The Culmination of His Saving Work

Andrew C. Skinner

The New Testament, in concert with Restoration scripture, clarifies, solidifies, and expands our understanding of the resurrection of Jesus Christ as the culmination of his salvific mission and ministry. The apostle Paul pointedly noted to the Corinthian saints that "if Christ be not raised, your faith is vain; ye are yet in your sins. Then they also which are fallen asleep in Christ are perished. If in this life only we have hope in Christ, we are of all men most miserable" (1 Corinthians 15:17–19). Here and in his powerful discourse that followed, he taught important truths about the resurrection that connect it not only with overcoming physical death but with the wider fruits of the atonement of Jesus Christ. Our English word *resurrection* derives ultimately from the Latin *resurgere* and means to "rise back up," reflecting the meaning of the Greek noun for resurrection (*anastasis*). This Latin root is closely related to another English word, *resurge*, meaning to "surge back again," and connotes movement and power—apt images associated with resurrection. To be resurrected is, in some sense, to rise again with power. In 1986, Howard W. Hunter (1907–1995), an apostle of Jesus Christ and later the fourteenth president of the Church, declared that "the doctrine of the Resurrection is the single most fundamental and crucial doctrine in the Christian religion. It cannot be overemphasized, nor can it be disregarded."[1]

The profundity of this statement is affirmed when we understand that the resurrection of Jesus Christ is the ultimate triumph over the effects of the fall resulting from Adam and Eve's transgression (1 Corinthians 15:25–26; 2 Nephi 2:18–26). Because the fall affects all of Adam and Eve's posterity, the resurrection of Jesus Christ does the same. Because he was the first to overcome the grave, all humankind will be resurrected (1 Corinthians 15:22). Furthermore, the resurrection of Jesus Christ stands at the core of our Heavenly Father's eternal plan in additional, vital ways: first, the resurrection constitutes redemption, in and of itself without any conditions attached; second, it is a literal, bodily resurrection, providing us the means to obtain a true fullness of joy; third, it imposes a permanent judgment on all individuals—realities which are, perhaps, not always immediately associated with the doctrine of resurrection. So important is the resurrection that without it "the gospel of Jesus Christ becomes a litany of wise sayings and seemingly unexplainable miracles."[2] Understanding that the resurrection of Jesus Christ is central to the fulfillment of the Father's plan yields valuable insights into the entire New Testament and provides a vital interpretive lens through which we may see how the other contributions in this volume explore and explain what it truly means to say that Jesus is the Christ.

Jesus Christ, "the firstfruits of them that slept"

The apostle Paul articulated a foundational doctrine when he testified, "But now is Christ risen from the dead, and become the firstfruits of them that slept" (1 Corinthians 15:20). Jesus of Nazareth was the "firstfruits" of the resurrection because he was the first of all human beings to rise with power from the dead (1 Corinthians 15:20), it being impossible for death to keep its hold on him (Acts 2:24). He had testified during his mortal ministry that just as his Father had life in himself so he had given his Son the power of life within himself (John 5:26). It is in this sense that we understand the apostle Peter's declaration that "Him [Jesus Christ] God [the Father] raised up the third day" (Acts 10:40). The Father passed on to his Son his divine attribute of "life in himself," life independent of external forces (John 5:26). Jesus himself said, "No man taketh it [my life] from me, but I lay it down of myself. I have power to lay it down, and I have power to take it again. This commandment have I received of my Father" (John 10:18).

Not only was Jesus the firstfruits of the resurrection, but his resurrection made it possible for all others to be resurrected. The apostle Paul explained that "since by man came death, by man came also the resurrection of the dead. For as in Adam all die, even so in Christ shall all be made alive . . . Christ the firstfruits; afterward they that are Christ's at his coming" (1 Corinthians 15:21–23). The name Adam is a Hebrew word, 'adam, and simply means "man." Therefore, Christ is referred to as the second Adam, as Paul further explained: "And so it is written, The first man Adam was made a living soul; the last Adam [Christ] was made a quickening spirit. . . . And as we have borne the image of the earthy [man], we shall also bear the image of the heavenly [being]" (1 Corinthians 15:45–59). Thus, just as the actions of the first Adam gave life and provided a physical body for all members of the human family, so the actions of the second Adam gave life again and provided a second physical body for all members of the human family.

Joseph Fielding Smith (1876–1972), tenth president of the Church, taught that Jesus's "atonement for sin and death is the force by which we are raised to immortality."[3] Whether an individual has been righteous or not makes no difference; all will be resurrected. Such is the power of the resurrection. When Jesus was resurrected, foreordained laws were put into operation whereby the spirit bodies of all individuals who have lived or will yet live on earth are reunited with tangible physical bodies, never to be separated again (Alma 11:42–45). President Smith continued, "Jesus Christ did for us something that we could not do for ourselves, through his infinite atonement. On the third day after the crucifixion he took up his body and gained the keys of the resurrection, and thus has power to open the graves for all men, but this he could not do until he had first passed through death himself and conquered."[4]

This is important doctrine, for it means that priesthood keys are associated with the resurrection. No mortal, not even the President of The Church of Jesus Christ of Latter-day Saints, yet possesses these keys, as Spencer W. Kimball (1895–1985), twelfth president of the Church, noted. The keys of resurrection are conferred after one has been resurrected. Those keys are then used to resurrect others. Jesus was the prototype. Having obtained the keys of resurrection himself (after his own experience with resurrection), he then possessed power to resurrect all others.[5] Before Jesus was resurrected, only his Father, our Father in Heaven, possessed the keys of resurrection. But as the lyrics of the hymn "Rejoice the Lord Is King," by Charles Wesley (1707–1788), declare, after he had purged our stains and risen triumphantly from the tomb, "The keys of death and hell, to Christ the Lord are giv'n."[6] After he was resurrected, Jesus acquired the keys of resurrection which could then be given to others.

Redemption from Sin and Death

Paul concluded his discourse to the Corinthians on resurrection with the exclamation, "Death is swallowed up in victory. O death, where is thy sting? O grave, where is thy victory? The sting of death is sin; and the strength of sin is the law. But thanks be to God, which giveth us the victory through our Lord Jesus Christ" (1 Corinthians 15:54–57). The Book of Mormon prophet Jacob had earlier described Christ's twin victory over the grave (physical and spiritual) as an escape "from the grasp of [an] awful monster; yea, that monster, death and hell, which

I call the death of the body, and also the death of the spirit," an escape that came "by the power of the resurrection of the Holy One of Israel" (2 Nephi 9:10, 12). Similarly, Alma the Younger, in a sermon to the church at Zarahemla asked, "Were the bands of death broken, and the chains of hell which encircled them about, were they loosed? . . . And now I ask of you on what conditions are they saved? Yea, what grounds had they to hope for salvation? What is the cause of their being loosed from the bands of death, yea, and also the chains of hell?" (Alma 5:9–10). The answer is resurrection!

In this sense, salvation from sin and death are indeed redemption: redemption in the sense of rescuing—literally "buying back" or freeing—captives from the grave and eternal hell. Resurrection, the reuniting of spirit and physical body, reconstitutes or forms again the soul of every individual, for "the spirit and the body are the soul of man" (D&C 88:15). The reuniting of the spirit and physical body is declared by the Lord to be "the redemption of the soul" (D&C 88:16). Therefore, redemption that comes from or is provided through resurrection is far more significant than we sometimes give credit to. For what the scriptures are saying is that resurrection by itself is redemption. Even without repentance, every person who is resurrected is the recipient of redemption. Though some are occasionally prone to regard redemption as only being saved from our sins (because of a misreading of Alma 11:40–41), resurrection is nevertheless actual redemption. Note the language of verses 40–41: "And he shall come into the world to redeem his people; and he shall take upon him the transgressions of those who believe on his name; and these are they that shall have eternal life, and salvation cometh to none else. Therefore, the wicked remain as though there had been no *redemption* made, *except* it be the loosing of the bands of death; for behold, the day cometh that all shall rise from the dead and stand before God, and be judged according to their works" (emphasis added).

Though this text tells us that eternal life comes only to those who have their transgressions remitted by Jesus Christ, the "loosing of the bands of death," or resurrection, is still a powerful type of redemption. In fact, the next three verses of Alma 11 emphasize the magnificence of the "loosing of the bands of death" by pointing out that "all shall be raised from this temporal death" (Alma 11:42); that the reuniting of the spirit and body of individuals will be "in its perfect form" and "to its proper frame" (Alma 11:43); and that this perfect reuniting of limb and joint is part of the law of restoration that operates for "both the wicked and the righteous" (Alma 11:44). Both categories of people will never die again; their spirits and physical bodies will never be divided or separated again (Alma 11:45). So complete and detailed is this restoration that not even "a hair of the head" shall be lost, "but *all things* shall be restored to their proper and perfect frame" (Alma 40:23; emphasis added). Such is the power of the resurrection and such is reason for praising its effects on us because of the sacrifice of Jesus Christ.

But there is even greater reason for praise of the resurrection. It saves, rescues, reclaims, and redeems every individual from the eternal grasp or influence of Lucifer (except, of course, those who rebel against the Father's plan and the Son's mercy, and become sons of perdition). Again, this redemption from Satan's clutches is not dependent on an individual's repentance. The prophet Jacob is clear that resurrection alone is redemption, without any action on the part of mortals, and that the resurrection promised to all persons is part of the infinite atonement of Jesus Christ. In language that resonates with praise and exultation, the profound power of the resurrection is again laid out:

> For as death hath passed upon all men, to fulfil the merciful plan of the great Creator, there must needs be a power of resurrection, and the resurrection must needs come unto man by reason of the fall; and the fall came by reason of transgression; and because man became fallen they were cut off from the presence of the Lord.
>
> Wherefore, it must needs be an infinite atonement—save it should be an infinite atonement this corruption could not put on incorruption. Wherefore, the first judgment which

came upon man must needs have remained to an endless duration. And if so, this flesh must have laid down to rot and to crumble to its mother earth, to rise no more.

O the wisdom of God, his mercy and grace! For behold, if the flesh should rise no more our spirits must become subject to that angel who fell from before the presence of the Eternal God, and became the devil, to rise no more.

And our spirits must have become like unto him, and we become devils, angels to a devil, to be shut out from the presence of our God, and to remain with the father of lies, in misery, like unto himself; yea, to that being who beguiled our first parents, who transformeth himself nigh unto an angel of light, and stirreth up the children of men unto secret combinations of murder and all manner of secret works of darkness. (2 Nephi 9:6–9)

If there had been no resurrection provided for the human family, the spirits of every individual would have succumbed to a path of inevitable spiritual entropy and dissolution, spiraling downward to become just like the father of destruction and ruin for eternity and, just like his followers in our premortal existence, become sons of perdition. (The word *perdition* derives from Latin, *perdere*, meaning "destruction.") Without the redeeming rescue of the resurrection, every spirit child of our heavenly parents would have become devils—no matter how they had lived in mortality, even if they had tried to be moral and upright. But because of the resurrection, "All beings who have bodies have power over those who have not. . . . The devil has no body, and herein is his punishment."[7]

Resurrection is universal—it redeems all people (except sons of perdition) and all creation from the degeneration that the physical universe displays. It redeems the earth from decay and wickedness and is part of the process by which this planet becomes sanctified and the designated abode of those souls who inherit the celestial glory (D&C 88:17–20).

Much later, the prophet Moroni described the other towering result of the resurrection's redemptive effect: "And because of the redemption of man, which came by Jesus Christ, they are brought back into the presence of the Lord; yea, this is wherein all men are redeemed, because the death of Christ bringeth to pass the resurrection, which bringeth to pass a redemption from an endless sleep, from which sleep all men shall be awakened by the power of God when the trump shall sound; and they shall come forth, both small and great, and all shall stand before his bar, being redeemed and loosed from this eternal band of death, which death is a temporal death" (Mormon 9:13; emphasis added).

Because of the resurrection, brought about by Jesus Christ, every single member of the human family is redeemed from physical death as well as from the first spiritual death inaugurated by the fall. The first spiritual death is overturned. Every person is restored to the presence of God to be judged. Thus, resurrection is both redemption and restoration. Samuel the Lamanite is a second witness to the stunning verity that both physical death and the first spiritual death are swallowed up in the resurrection:

> For behold, he surely must die that salvation may come; yea, it behooveth him and becometh expedient that he dieth, to bring to pass the resurrection of the dead, that thereby men may be brought into the presence of the Lord.
>
> Yea, behold, this death bringeth to pass the resurrection, and redeemeth all mankind from the first death—that spiritual death; for all mankind, by the fall of Adam being cut off from the presence of the Lord, are considered as dead, both as to things temporal and to things spiritual.
>
> But behold, the resurrection of Christ redeemeth mankind, yea, even all mankind, and bringeth them back into the presence of the Lord. (Helaman 14:15–17)[8]

A Tangible, Physical Resurrection and a Fullness of Joy

The Gospels, particularly Luke and John, end with clear demonstrations that Jesus rose from the tomb with a tangible, physical body. Mary Magdalene, the first to see the Risen Lord, appears to have touched him, for when he told her, "Touch me not" (Greek, *mē mou haptou*), he actually meant "Do not keep touching me," or, as Joseph Smith's New Translation renders it, "Hold me not." While the first witnesses in Luke received proof from the empty tomb and the angels, the two disciples on the road to Emmaus not only saw and heard the Risen Lord, they ate with him and received bread from his tangible hands (Luke 24:13–32). Shortly thereafter, when the resurrected Jesus Christ appeared to the eleven remaining apostles, he declared to them, "Behold my hands and my feet, that it is I myself: handle me, and see; for a spirit hath not flesh and bones, as ye see me have," and after they had presumably touched him, he ate broiled fish and honeycomb in their presence (see Luke 24:36–43). The experience of the eleven in John's account is even more explicit. First ten of them, and then the late-arriving Thomas, felt the wounds in his hands and his side and felt his breath as he bid them to receive the Holy Ghost (John 20:19–27). This experience led Thomas to declare, "My Lord and my God" (John 20:28), and experiences like this no doubt constituted what Luke called the "many infallible proofs" (Greek, *pollois tekmēriois*, or "sure signs or tokens") by which Christ showed himself alive after his passion.

The corporality of Jesus's raised body demonstrates that the resurrection was literal and physical and not just a spiritual raising of some kind. As mentioned before, Alma the Younger taught, "The soul shall be restored to the body, and the body to the soul; yea, and every limb and joint shall be restored to its body" (Alma 40:23). This permanent reuniting of spirit and physical body inseparably connected is, according to modern revelation, the only way that we can receive a fullness of joy (D&C 93:33; 138:17). As the LDS Church's he *may know according to the flesh* how to succor his people according to their infirmities" (Alma 7:12; emphasis added).

To learn to obey physical laws, individuals must possess a physical body. To comply with gospel ordinances and performances, a physical body is required—a requirement so important in fact that ordinances performed by proxy are obligatory for those who have died without them. But a physical body is also necessary to learn to listen to and act on the voice of the Spirit, or Holy Ghost. President Boyd K. Packer (1924–2015), a member of the Twelve from 1970 and then acting president and president of that body, said, "Our physical body is the instrument of our spirit."[10] A physical body is necessary in the world to come. Becoming like God means becoming creators in eternity, since God is a Creator. In this mortal sphere, "The Father and the Son have entrusted [everyone] with a portion of Their creative power" through the gift of a physical body. How individuals use that power "will determine in large measure whether additional creative power will be [theirs] in the life to come."[11] Only those "who obtain a glorious resurrection from the dead," said Joseph Smith, "are exalted far above principalities, powers, thrones, dominions and angels, and are expressly declared to be heirs of God and joint heirs with Jesus Christ, all having eternal power"[12]—part of which is the power of eternal creation which comes only by having a physical, resurrected body.

Freedom and Empowerment

Perhaps we can now more fully appreciate Joseph Smith's statement that "the great principle of happiness consists in having a body."[13] Evidence of the truth of this assertion is quite striking and grounded in doctrine presented in the New Testament.

During the waning days of World War I, while pondering two key passages from the New Testament that concern life after death (1 Peter 3:18–20; 4:6), President Joseph F. Smith experienced a detailed vision of the spirits of the dead residing in the spirit

"Proclamation on the Family" states, the plan of God the Fatl one "by which His children could obtain a physical body ar earthly experience to progress toward perfection and ultimate ize their divine destiny,"[9] which is to be exalted, inherit all th possesses, and indeed be like God himself (D&C 76:58).

This is true for women as well as for men, as indica Abraham's creation account:

> We will go down, for there is space there, and we will take oi these materials, and we will make an earth whereon these may dwell; And we will prove them herewith, to see if they will do all things whatsoever the Lord their God shall command them; . . . And the *Gods* [plural] organized the earth. . . . And the *Gods* took counsel among *themselves* and said: Let *us* go down and form man [humankind] in *our* image, after *our* like- ness; and we will give them dominion over the fish of the sea, and over the fowl of the air, and over the cattle, and over all the earth, and over every creeping thing that creepeth upon the earth. So the *Gods* went down to organize man [human- kind] in *their* own image, in the image of the *Gods*, . . . male and female. (Abraham 3:24–25; 4:25–27; emphasis added)

Central to God's plan for each individual is the possessioi physical body in mortality and in eternity. A body is necessa become like Deity precisely because God possesses a physical (D&C 130:22). Thus, no one can be tested and proven and ultim become like God without a body. A physical body is essential to s tual development and eternal progression. Individuals are tested and by their physical body. There are lessons that must be lea and experiences that must be had "according to the flesh" (1 N 19:6). This was true for Jesus as well as for all other individuals: " he will take upon him death, that he may loose the bands of d which bind his people; and he will take upon him their infirmi that his bowels may be filled with mercy, according to the flesh, i world. We emphasize that the vision came by his pondering of New Testament passages. He saw the yearning of the righteous to receive back their physical bodies. "For the dead had looked upon the long absence of their spirits from their bodies as a bondage" (D&C 138:50). These righteous spirits were in that part of the spirit world called paradise, a place and condition of happiness, "a state of rest, a state of peace," a place where they rested "from all their troubles and from all care, and sorrow" (Alma 40:12). They were not residing in that realm called spirit prison, where the spirits of the wicked were confined (Alma 40:13). And yet the righteous spirits still regarded their existence without their bodies as a prison. They knew they could only experience a fullness of joy when "their sleeping dust was to be restored unto its perfect frame, bone to his bone, and the sinews and the flesh upon them, the spirit and the body to be united never again to be divided, that they might receive a fulness of joy" (D&C 138:17).

In this regard, Melvin J. Ballard commented on the condition of departed spirits: "I grant you that the righteous dead will be at peace, but I tell you that when we go out of this life, leave this body, we will desire to do many things that we cannot do at all without the body. We will be seriously handicapped, and we will long for the body; we will pray for that early reunion with our bodies. We will know then what advantage it is to have a body."[14]

President Smith went on to describe the righteous spirits assembled together, "awaiting the advent of the Son of God into the spirit world, to declare their *redemption* from the bands of death, . . . declaring liberty to the captives who had been faithful" (D&C 138:16, 18; emphasis added). They knew true freedom could only come from the Son of God.

Jesus Christ's appearance in the world of spirits was an important part of his work of salvation. It was the partial fulfillment of Isaiah's messianic prophecy quoted by Jesus himself in the Nazareth synagogue at the beginning of his public ministry: "And when he had opened the book [scroll], he found the place where it was written, The Spirit of the Lord is upon me, because he hath anointed me to preach the gospel to the poor; he hath sent me to heal the brokenhearted, to preach deliverance to the captives, and recovering of sight to the blind, to set at liberty them that are bruised, To preach the acceptable year of the Lord" (Luke 4:17–19; see Isaiah 61:1–2).

Indeed, Jesus did proclaim liberty to the captives in the spirit world as he taught the righteous spirits there. And by his resurrection he completely fulfilled his promise of providing liberty and deliverance and the opening of the prison to all those in the spirit world, including the wicked. He bridged the great gulf that separated the righteous from the wicked and made it possible for the wicked to hear the gospel, repent, and be resurrected as soon as their sins were removed. Through his teachings and subsequent resurrection, Jesus empowered the righteous to enter the Father's presence. In the words of President Smith's revelation, "the Lord taught [them], and *gave them power* to come forth, after his resurrection from the dead, to enter into his Father's kingdom, there to be crowned with immortality and eternal life" (D&C 138:51; emphasis added). This too is cause for praise.

Resurrection and Judgment

After Jesus healed the lame man at the Pool of Bethesda, he delivered a powerful discourse about the relationship between the Father and the Son. Among the things that he taught was, "For the Father judgeth no man, but hath committed all judgment unto the Son" (John 5:22). This role as judge, however, is closely connected to the resurrection that he brings about. Jesus continued, "Verily, verily, I say unto you, The hour is coming, and now is, when the dead shall hear the voice of the Son of God: and they that hear shall live. For as the Father hath life in himself; so hath he given to the Son to have life in himself; And hath given him authority to execute judgment also, because he is the Son of man" (John 5:25–27). Much of this judgment manifests itself in the very nature of the resurrection, as Jesus indicated: "And [they] shall come forth; they that have done good, unto the resurrection of life; and they that have done evil, unto the resurrection of damnation" (John 5:29).

Practically speaking, this means that there is a partial judgment at the time a person is resurrected. Each individual will be resurrected with the type of body they will possess in eternity—a celestial, terrestrial, or telestial body, or a body not fit for any kingdom of glory, but only for outer darkness. The apostle Paul illustrated this doctrine by using an analogy. Just as "all flesh is not the same," there being different kinds of bodies in nature such as men, beasts, fish, birds, and so on (1 Corinthians 15:39), so there are different types of flesh or bodies in the resurrection of humankind, bodies with different capabilities and potentials. "There are also celestial bodies, and bodies terrestrial: but the glory of the celestial is one, and the glory of the terrestrial is another. There is one glory of the sun, and another glory of the moon, and another glory of the stars: for one star differeth from another star in glory" (1 Corinthians 15:40–41).

Individuals receive the kind of resurrected body they are entitled to receive based on obedience to God's laws. "And the degree of glory gained by each person shall be that which his [or her] resurrected and immortal body can abide."[15] Thus, "in the resurrection, some are raised to be angels, others are raised to become Gods," as Joseph Smith said. Therefore, the doctrines of the resurrection and the degrees of glory are inextricably linked. In fact, our expanded understanding of the degrees of glory came about as a direct result of Joseph Smith's and Sidney Rigdon's contemplation of the very passages in John in which Jesus had connected resurrection and judgment. As they worked on the inspired revision of the Bible known as the New Translation, or Joseph Smith Translation, and read and thought specifically about John 5:29, they received the vision now known as Doctrine and Covenants 76. In it they testified:

> We, Joseph Smith, Jun., and Sidney Rigdon, being in the
> Spirit on the sixteenth day of February, in the year of our
> Lord one thousand eight hundred and thirty-two—

> By the power of the Spirit our eyes were opened and our understandings were enlightened, so as to see and understand the things of God— . . .
>
> For while we were doing the work of translation, which the Lord had appointed unto us, we came to the twenty-ninth verse of the fifth chapter of John, which was given unto us as follows—
>
> Speaking of the resurrection of the dead, concerning those who shall hear the voice of the Son of Man:
>
> And shall come forth; they who have done good, in the resurrection of the just; and they who have done evil, in the resurrection of the unjust.
>
> Now this caused us to marvel, for it was given unto us of the Spirit.
>
> And while we meditated upon these things, the Lord touched the eyes of our understandings and they were opened, and the glory of the Lord shone round about. (D&C 76:11–12, 15–19)

Hence, "knowledge of degrees of glory and kinds of salvation is in fact an amplification and explanation of the doctrine of resurrection."[16] Resurrection precedes our inheritance of a kingdom of glory, and the degree of glory resurrected beings inherit depends on the kind of body they are resurrected with. Celestial glory is reserved for those "whose bodies are celestial" (D&C 76:70), resulting from their obedience to divine will. Those resurrected with terrestrial bodies receive a terrestrial inheritance. They differ from inheritors of the celestial kingdom as the moon differs from the sun (1 Corinthians 15:41). "In effect they bask, as does the moon, in reflected glory, for there are restrictions and limitations placed on them. They 'receive of the presence of the Son, but not of the fulness of the Father' (D&C 76:77), and to all eternity they remain unmarried and without exaltation. (D&C 132:17.)"[17]

Those who inherit a telestial glory differ from those in the celestial and terrestrial kingdoms just as stars differ from the sun and moon in luminosity. But they also differ from each other as "one star differeth from another star in glory," meaning that those who inherit the telestial kingdom will not all be alike in glory. They will differ from one another. But more significantly, "they shall be servants of the Most High; but where God and Christ dwell they cannot come, worlds without end" (D&C 76:112). There is no upward movement between kingdoms of glory because of the type of resurrected body the inhabitants of each kingdom receive. They can only enjoy that glory their resurrected body is made for. Doctrine and Covenants 88:28–32 attests to this principle:

> They who are of a celestial spirit shall receive the same body which was a natural body; even ye shall receive your bodies, and your glory shall be that glory by which your bodies are quickened.
>
> Ye who are quickened by a portion of the celestial glory shall then receive of the same, even a fulness.
>
> And they who are quickened by a portion of the terrestrial glory shall then receive of the same, even a fulness.
>
> And also they who are quickened by a portion of the telestial glory shall then receive of the same, even a fulness.
>
> And they who remain shall also be quickened; nevertheless, they shall return again to their own place, to enjoy that which they are willing to receive, because they were not willing to enjoy that which they might have received.

Closely related to the partial judgment that occurs when a person is resurrected and that determines the kind of body they receive is an established order of resurrection—dictating who is resurrected when. This, too, is predicated upon an individual's obedience to our Heavenly Father's will and laws. The most righteous of all, Jesus Christ, was resurrected first (1 Corinthians 15:20). The most wicked of all (of those who have before lived on the earth) will be resurrected last, which means the sons of perdition (D&C 88:102). The following rough chart may help to illustrate the order of the resurrection (including supporting scriptures).

Time	Characteristic	Scriptural support
First to be resurrected after Christ—righteous who lived from Adam to Christ	CELESTIAL prophets, believers, "all those who have kept commandments"	Mosiah 15:21–26 Matthew 27:52–53 Alma 40:16–20 D&C 133:54–55
"Morning of the first resurrection," at the Second Coming— those living from Christ to Millennium	CELESTIAL "just men made perfect"	D&C 88:95–98 D&C 76:50–70
"Afternoon of the first resurrection," second trump at Christ's coming	TERRESTRIAL "received not the testimony of Jesus in flesh"	D&C 88:99 D&C 76:71–80
Last resurrection— after "the thousand years are ended," third trump	TELESTIAL "found under condemnation"	D&C 88:100–101 D&C 76:81–85
Last of the last, fourth trump	PERDITION "filthy still"	D&C 88:102 D&C 76:43–44 D&C 43:18

The resurrection occurs at different times depending on the kind of body people will inherit. It is a grave error to suppose an individual can treat lightly the commandments of God or opportunities to repent and expect to be resurrected with a celestial body. The prophet Alma's caution applies specifically to this situation:

> And it is requisite with the justice of God that men should be judged according to their works; and if their works were good in this life, and the desires of their hearts were good, that they should also, at the last day, be restored unto that which is good.
>
> And if their works are evil they shall be restored unto them for evil. Therefore, all things shall be restored to their proper order, every thing to its natural frame—mortality raised to immortality, corruption to incorruption—raised to endless happiness to inherit the kingdom of God, or to end-less misery to inherit the kingdom of the devil, the one on one hand, the other on the other. (Alma 41:3–4)

Alma emphasizes that the law of restoration can only mean "to bring back again evil for evil, or carnal for carnal, or devilish for devilish—good for that which is good; righteous for that which is righteous; just for that which is just" (Alma 41:13). The profoundest demonstration of that principle is the resurrection and the order in which it unfolds.

Witnesses of the Resurrection

The veracity of the doctrines we have discussed depends on the his-toricity of the resurrection. The book of Acts indicates that the sin-gle most important qualification needed for one to fill the office of apostle in the early church was that of being an eyewitness of Jesus's resurrection (Acts 1:8, 22; 2:32; 3:15; 4:20, 33; 5:32; 10:39; 13:31; 26:16). The evidence for the existence of a multiplicity of ancient witnesses to the resurrection of Jesus of Nazareth is overwhelming. This is all the more impressive when we realize that these early witnesses stepped forward to testify of the resurrection in a cultural and social environment that was, at best, not accepting of their assertions and, at worst, hostile—the environment of Greco-Roman culture.

Among the Jews, one of the most prominent of the several sects in Jesus's day, the Sadducees, denied there was a bodily resurrection. Even more than that, according to Jewish historian Josephus of the first century AD, the Sadducees maintained that at death "the soul perishes along with the body."[18] Yet one of the clearest statements of belief in the resurrection of the physical body, outside the New Testament in the era known as the intertestamental period, comes from the Jewish apocryphal text, 2 Maccabees, where a martyr about to die puts out his tongue, stretches forth his hands and says, "I got these from Heaven, and because of his laws I disdain them, and from him I hope to get them back again" (2 Maccabees 7:1 Revised Standard Version). Another martyr is brought forward, maltreated, and tortured. When he is near death he says, "One cannot but choose to die at the hands of men and to cherish the hope that God gives of being raised again by him." But then he says to his executioner, "But for you there will be no resurrection to life" (2 Maccabees 7:14 RSV), meaning, it is assumed, that the wicked will have no resurrection to eternal life, only damnation (see Revelation 20:13–15).

Indeed, the Pharisees and their historical precursors believed in a bodily resurrection. The Mishnah—which is the codification of Jewish oral tradition in the Pharisaic mold, developed from 200 BC to AD 200—states: "All Israelites have a share in the world to come . . . and these are they that have no share in the world to come: he that says that there is no resurrection of the dead" (Sanhedrin 10:1). But what many of the Pharisees could not believe, or refused to believe, is that God had come to earth in the person of Jesus of Nazareth and that he alone was the source of the universal resurrection. Some non-Jews believed that death was the end of everything. Others thought of an afterlife as a "shadowy existence in Hades."[19] Still others, like Platonists, believed that death was a release of the spirit from its mortal prison, which was the physical body, or some variation of that outlook. However, all except the Pharisees and the

Christians agreed that there was no resurrection of the physical form. The death of the body was final. Thus, Christianity was born into an environment where its central tenet, bodily resurrection, was recognized almost universally in Greek and Roman thought as false—even odd.[20]

Hence, Paul described the challenging environment the apostles faced in their teaching and witnessing: "For the Jews require a sign, and the Greeks seek after wisdom: But we preach Christ crucified [and resurrected], unto the Jews a stumbling-block, and unto the Greeks foolishness" (1 Corinthians 1:22–23). And yet nothing could shake the certitude of apostolic witnesses. They went forward—driven by what they had seen, and heard, and handled (Luke 24:39) as illustrated by John's witness: "That which was from the beginning, which we have heard, which we have seen with our eyes, which we have looked upon, and our hands have handled, of the Word of life; . . . declare we unto you, that ye also may have fellowship with us: and truly our fellowship is with the Father, and with his Son Jesus Christ. And these things write we unto you, that your joy may be full" (1 John 1:1–4).

The result was the spread of the central message of the faith, the good news that Jesus Christ was resurrected, and the subsequent organization of the Church based on priesthood leadership who fully embraced that message. Writing near the end of the first century AD, Clement of Rome (died AD 99) gives us a sense of the powerful, unrelenting, apostolic witness going forth:

> The apostles received the Gospel for us from the Lord Jesus Christ; Jesus Christ was sent forth from God. So then Christ is from God, and the Apostles are from Christ. Both therefore received a charge, and having been fully assured through the Resurrection of our Lord Jesus Christ and confirmed in the word of God with full assurance of the Holy Ghost, they went forth with the glad tidings that the kingdom of God should come. So preaching everywhere in country and town, they appointed their firstfruits, when they had proved

them by the Spirit, to be bishops and deacons unto them that should believe.[21]

Modern New Testament scholar, Bruce M. Metzger, offered this assessment of the witness of the early apostles concerning the resurrection of Jesus Christ:

> The evidence for the resurrection of Jesus Christ is overwhelming. Nothing in history is more certain than that the disciples believed that, after being crucified, dead, and buried, Christ rose again from the tomb on the third day, and that at intervals thereafter he met and conversed with them. The most obvious proof that they believed this is the existence of the Christian church. It is simply inconceivable that the scattered and disheartened remnant could have found a rallying point and a gospel in the memory of him who had been put to death as a criminal, had they not been convinced that God owned him and accredited his mission by raising him from the dead. . . .
>
> Fifty-some days after the crucifixion the apostolic preaching of Christ's resurrection began in Jerusalem with such power and persuasion that the evidence convinced thousands.[22]

Those who were witnesses of the resurrection of Jesus of Nazareth knew that the worst that could happen to them, or any disciple, because of their testimony of the resurrection of Jesus Christ was physical death. But such a happening mattered little, for just as Jesus was raised after his death, so would all others be raised by the power of the resurrection. As Paul testified: "If the Spirit of him who raised Jesus from the dead dwells in you, he who raised Christ Jesus from the dead will give life to your mortal bodies also through his Spirit which dwells in you" (Romans 8:11 RSV). This is the essence of the early Church's message, affirmed by many special witnesses.

These many witnesses testified that the resurrection of Jesus Christ was a literal physical event. Yet, to them it was more than just another aspect of Jesus's ministry. It was the apex and *sine qua non* of the atonement because it brought to all the human family redemption, judgment, empowerment, and eternal freedom. It was the singular event demonstrating that Jesus was God's anointed and Chosen Son. These truths, presented in the New Testament and clarified and expanded by Restoration scripture, are *why* God sent his Only Begotten Son into the world—to bring to pass the immortality and eternal life of humankind, the ultimate work and glory of the Father and the Son (Moses 1:39). This is the doctrinal lens through which Latter-day Saints may understand all the teachings about Jesus and his work in the New Testament. As the crowning fruit of the atonement, the resurrection is the Savior's great gift to the human family. It is a singular reason to praise him.

ANDREW C. SKINNER *is a professor of ancient scripture and former dean of religious education at Brigham Young University.*

Notes

1. Howard W. Hunter, "An Apostle's Witness of the Resurrection," *Ensign*, May 1986, 16.
2. Hunter, "An Apostle's Witness," 15.
3. Joseph Fielding Smith, *Doctrines of Salvation*, comp. Bruce R. McConkie (Salt Lake City: Bookcraft, 1970), 1:128.
4. Smith, *Doctrines of Salvation*, 1:128.
5. Spencer W. Kimball, in Conference Report, April 1977, 69. According to President Brigham Young, those keys of resurrection first acquired by the Savior are then further given, extended, or delegated to others who have died and been resurrected. "They will be ordained, by those who hold

the keys of the resurrection, to go forth and resurrect the Saints, just as we receive the ordinance of baptism, then the keys of authority to baptize others." *Discourses of Brigham Young*, selected and arranged by John A. Widtsoe (Salt Lake City: Deseret Book, 1971), 398.

6. "Rejoice the Lord Is King," *Hymns*, no. 66.

7. *Teachings of the Presidents of the Church: Joseph Smith* (Salt Lake City: The Church of Jesus Christ of Latter-day Saints, 2007), 211.

8. There is, of course, a second spiritual death that awaits those who do not repent when given the opportunity. Again, Samuel declared that if individuals have not repented, "there cometh upon them again a spiritual death, yea, a second death, for they are cut off again as to things pertaining to righteousness" (Helaman 14:18).

9. "The Family: A Proclamation to the World," *Ensign*, November 1995, 102.

10. Boyd K. Packer, *Let Not Your Heart Be Troubled* (Salt Lake City: Bookcraft, 1991), 211.

11. David A. Bednar, "Ye Are the Temple of God," *Ensign*, September 2001, 16.

12. *Teachings: Joseph Smith*, 222.

13. *Teachings: Joseph Smith*, 221.

14. Bryant S. Hinckley, *Sermons and Missionary Services of Melvin Joseph Ballard* (Salt Lake City: Deseret Book, 1949), 240–42.

15. Bruce R. McConkie, *Doctrinal New Testament Commentary* (Salt Lake City: Bookcraft, 1970), 2:398.

16. McConkie, *Doctrinal New Testament Commentary*, 2:397.

17. McConkie, *Doctrinal New Testament Commentary*, 2:400.

18. Josephus, *Jewish Antiquities* 18.16.

19. N. T. Wright, "The Resurrection of Resurrection," in *Easter: Exploring the Resurrection of Jesus*, ed. Sarah Murphy (Washington, DC: Biblical Archaeology Society, 2010), 17, PDF.

20. See also the summary of Richard D. Draper, "The Reality of the Resurrection," *Ensign*, April 1994, 32–34, and the sources he cites on page 40.

21. 1 Clement 42:1–4.

22. Bruce M. Metzger, *The New Testament, Its Background, Growth, and Content* (Nashville: Abingdon Press, 1965), 126–27.

4

We Believe and Are Sure

Camille Fronk Olson

The examples of those disciples who walked with Jesus during his mortal ministry can inspire our understanding of who he is and what he came to earth to do. They knew Jesus personally as a master and friend, but they also came to recognize him as the Son of God and Savior of the World. These first-century men and women illustrate that this knowledge comes incrementally, in a process seasoned with multiple stumbles and periods of blindness that nonetheless leads to an unshakeable testimony of the person and mission of Jesus Christ.

Because of the rich detail recorded about them in the New Testament, Peter the Galilean fisherman and Martha and Mary of Bethany provide particularly insightful evidence for the process of becoming trusted and effective disciples of Christ. Their testimonies of Jesus Christ came in stages: Their faith in him was initially incomplete, and their attempts to demonstrate devotion to him were at first ill conceived. Yet as they learned and practiced each saving truth that

Jesus taught and exemplified, their faith, testimony, and service became steadfast in that aspect of the gospel. Eventually, they became stalwart, inspired, and selfless disciples who courageously stood for truth and righteousness in all places and circumstances, providing us with models as we strive to come to better know and follow Jesus Christ.

Peter's Testimony of Who Jesus Is

While Jesus was with his disciples up north in Caesarea Philippi, he asked them who others thought he was. Apparently, neither Jesus nor others had made any clear or at least public announcements, claims, or general assumptions of his true identity at that time. People were circulating a variety of possibilities, including proposals that he was John the Baptist returned to life or one of the Old Testament prophets. Jesus then asked those present, "But whom say ye that I am?" In the Marcan account, Peter answered, "Thou art the Christ" (Mark 8:29; parallel Luke 9:20). Matthew's account of the incident adds an important phrase to Peter's testimony: "Thou art the Christ, the Son of the living God" (Matthew 16:16). All three Synoptic accounts verify that Peter knew who Jesus was—the Anointed Servant of God—to which Matthew added the Son of God.

How did Peter gain his testimony? Scriptural evidence suggests that he and others first *believed* that Jesus was divinely sent and then acted upon that belief. For example, while still working in his fishing business in Galilee, Peter was engaged in the arduous task of cleaning his nets after a disappointing night of unsuccessful fishing. Jesus entered Peter's boat and asked Peter to row them back into the water so Jesus could teach them. Peter's respect for Jesus is evident from his obedience and reference to Jesus as "Master." But when he directed Peter to launch his newly cleaned nets back into the sea, Peter complained because he believed that further attempts to catch fish that day were futile. Even under a shadow of doubt, Peter acted on a belief in this Jesus, saying, "Nevertheless at thy word I will let down the net" (Luke 5:5). When the nets broke from the weight of such a huge catch of fish, Peter fell before Jesus's knees in reverence crying, "Depart from me; for I am a sinful man, O Lord" (5:6–8).

Later in the Savior's ministry, after witnessing and participating in the miraculous feeding of the five thousand, the Twelve left Jesus on the shore and began to row back home in a boat. Caught in a storm that kept them battling the winds and waves during most of the night, they saw what appeared to be a spirit coming toward them on the water. Jesus immediately called out, "Be of good cheer: it is I; be not afraid" (Mark 6:49–50; parallel Matthew 14:26–27; John 6:19–20). To the shared account, Matthew adds the additional detail that Peter, believing but not knowing with certainty, responded, "Lord, if it be thou, bid me come unto thee on the water" (Matthew 14:28). Peter desired to know for certain who this Jesus was. Jesus told him, "Come." Acting on his desire to know, Peter climbed over the side of the boat and began walking toward Jesus but soon fell beneath the stormy seas when fear seized him. Jesus immediately pulled him out of the water and encouraged him to strengthen his faith: "O thou of little faith, wherefore didst thou doubt?" (14:29–31). By acting on imperfect faith, with a desire to believe, Peter created a bigger space for his testimony to take root and expand.

In yet another instance that acting on belief is an important step in the process of gaining a testimony of who Jesus is, Peter was unafraid to ask Jesus for help in understanding his parables and other teachings. Even when Jesus prefaced his clarification of a teaching with a note of disappointment in Peter, "Are ye also yet without understanding?" in response to Peter's request, Peter was vigilant in his efforts to learn from Jesus and was courageous in his continued queries for help (Matthew 15:15–17).

After these and other sincere manifestations of willingness to act on a belief that Jesus was come from God, at Caesarea Philippi Peter could finally declare that Jesus was God's Chosen or Anointed One, declaring, "Thou art the Christ, the Son of the living God" (Matthew 16:16). Once Peter had progressed in his testimony to know who Jesus was, Jesus then confirmed the truth by clarifying how Peter had received this knowledge, declaring, "Flesh and blood hath not revealed it unto thee, but my Father which is in heaven" (Matthew 16:17). "Flesh and blood" at the time included the mortal Jesus; Jesus did not tell Peter this truth about his identity. Just as in our day, only through the Father-sent Spirit is divine truth revealed.

The Bread of Life sermon and the responses to it in John 6:26–71 provide another example of Peter proclaiming a firm testimony of who Jesus is, even when he and others did not yet fully understand what he had come to do.[1] In this discourse, Jesus proclaimed that he was the bread come down from heaven, symbolically answering the christological question of who he was. In the process he revealed how those who came to know this truth would be saved. "And this is the will of him that sent me, that every one which seeth the Son, and believeth on him, may have everlasting life: and I will raise him up at the last day" (6:40). He also intimated what he had come to do, alluding to his salvific death when he declared, "Except ye eat the flesh of the Son of man, and drink his blood, ye have no life in you. Whoso eateth my flesh, and drinketh my blood, hath eternal life; and I will raise him up at the last day" (6:53–54). Only the day before, the multitude had benefited from the miracle of the loaves and the fishes and were eager to accept him as their king (6:15). Now, Jesus's declaration that he must die contradicted the messianic expectations of not only the crowd but even many of his own disciples, who complained, "*This is an hard saying; who can hear it?*" (6:60; emphasis added). Because they could not properly understand who he was or what he had come to do, they could not accept his mission of sacrificing his "flesh and blood" to save them.

While Peter and the Twelve may not yet have fully understood that Christ had come to die, nevertheless their firm witness of who Jesus was gave them the faith to continue with him in the face of other doubt. When "many . . . went back, and walked no more with him" (John 6:66), Jesus asked the Twelve, "Will ye also go away?" (6:67). Peter's response was simply, "Lord, to whom shall we go? thou hast the words of eternal life. *And we believe and are sure that thou art that Christ, the Son of the living God"* (6:68–69; emphasis added). Peter exemplified the power of remaining loyal to the truth that he had received, even when it wasn't complete. In a similar way, Peter's example can encourage our loyalty to what we know to be true when we are faced by "hard sayings," such as those messy questions and problems that often accompany policies, politics, history, and doubts.

Incomplete but Growing Testimonies

In spite of Peter's powerful spiritual witness of Jesus's identity, events immediately following his declaration at Caesarea Philippi show that he was still very much uncertain and confused about what Jesus came to do. His incomplete testimony needed to grow, moving him to a better appreciation for what Jesus had come to do. For instance, on at least three different occasions in the Synoptic Gospels, Jesus foretold his apostles of his upcoming death at the hands of evil men and his subsequent rising from the grave. Beginning there at Caesarea Philippi, he prophesied, "The Son of man must suffer many things, and be rejected of the elders, and of the chief priests, and scribes, and be killed, and after three days rise again" (Mark 8:31; parallels Matthew 16:21; Luke 9:22).[2] After the Transfiguration, he repeated the prophecy (Mark 9:31). Finally, a third time, as he accompanied the Twelve up to Jerusalem, he repeated "what things should happen unto him" (Mark 10:32–33). The responses of the Twelve collectively and of Peter specifically indicate that they did not yet understand that of necessity Jesus came to suffer, die, and rise again. Moments after bearing his Spirit-filled witness of Jesus as the Christ, Peter "rebuked" the very Son of God, declaring to him, "Be it far from thee, Lord: this shall not be unto thee" (Matthew 16:21–23; cf. Mark 8:31–33). After the second time that Jesus foretold of his suffering, death, and resurrection, the Twelve "understood not that saying, and were afraid to ask him" (Mark 9:31–32). They perceived him as their master and king, but not yet as their great high priest and spiritual Savior.

The placement of these three predictions of his upcoming passion in Mark 8–10 falls between the story of him healing in stages a blind man in Bethsaida (Mark 8:22–26) and the story of him healing the blind Bartimaeus near Jericho (Mark 10:46–52) and underscores the uncertainty of the disciples' knowledge. Because physical blindness easily serves as a metaphor for a lack of spiritual understanding, the way these two very different healing miracles frame the experiences of Peter and the Twelve encourages us to see them as part of a process toward greater knowledge and conversion. As their vision of Jesus sharpens and deepens in stages, so does ours in our own walk of discipleship.

In Bethsaida, after spitting on the blind man's eyes and putting his hands on him, Jesus asked the man if he could see. The man answered, "I see men as trees, walking" (Mark 8:24). He was beginning to see, but not clearly; things were blurry and confusing, much like Peter's testimony. So Jesus again put his hands on the man's eyes and this time "he was restored, and saw every man clearly" (8:25). Certainly Jesus could have healed the blind man instantly and completely, so Jesus's healing him in stages provides a model or pattern to how Peter, the other disciples, and we ourselves can receive spiritual understanding and a complete testimony of the Savior incrementally. In the incident at Caesarea Philippi immediately preceding this healing, Peter had come to know *who* Jesus was, but he did not yet understand, or accept, *what* he had come to do—suffer, die, and rise again for our salvation.

In Mark 8–10, between the two stories of blind men being healed and interwoven among the accounts of the three passion predictions, we also find reminders that Peter and the other apostles were unsure and lacking in understanding even after Peter had witnessed that Jesus is the Christ. Consider these episodes: On the Mount of Transfiguration, Peter proposed making three tabernacles to honor Moses, Elias, and the transfigured Jesus because Peter "[knew] not what to say; for they were sore afraid" (Mark 9:5–6). There on the holy mountain, Jesus in glory told them again about his impending resurrection after death. When they returned from the mountain, however, Peter, James, and John were still "questioning one with another what the rising from dead should mean" (9:9–10). Shortly afterward, the Twelve could not cast out an unclean spirit. Jesus responded to the situation: "O faithless generation, how long shall I be with you? how long shall I suffer you? bring him to me" (9:14–29). And when some of the people brought young children to Jesus to bless them, his disciples rebuked the people because they thought the children were a nuisance and detracted from Jesus's work. Peter and his associates were clearly confused by the Savior's displeasure toward their inaccurate assumption and by his words in response: "Whosoever shall not receive the kingdom of God as a little child, he shall not enter therein" (Mark 10:13–16). Their spiritual blindness for what Jesus came to do was again apparent.[3]

After these instances, just outside of Jericho Jesus at last came to the blind man named Bartimaeus, who sat by the side of the road begging. When he heard Jesus of Nazareth was passing by, he called out to him for mercy (Mark 10:46–48). His plea, "Thou Son of David, have mercy on me," highlights the man's belief that Jesus was the promised messianic fulfillment that David's seed would reign forever (2 Samuel 7:12–16). In response to the man's sincere pleas, the scripture reads, "Jesus stood still" (Mark 10:49). He did not immediately reply to the blind man's prayer. Instead, he asked others to call the man to come to him; Jesus required Bartimaeus to act on his belief even when he could not see. Then Bartimaeus, "casting away his garment, rose, and came to Jesus," who asked him to repeat what he desired from him. "Lord, that I might receive my sight" (10:50–51). After Bartimaeus asked for help multiple times, when he could easily have felt that he was being ignored or rejected, the Savior asked him to come—to act—when none of his physical senses confirmed he had a reason to hope. In that moment of *acting* on a belief or hope, Jesus told him, "Thy faith hath made thee whole. And immediately he received his sight, and followed Jesus in the way" (10:52).

Like the blind man healed in stages, Peter's testimony had expanded from belief to acknowledgment of who Jesus was and eventually to what he came to do. Bartimaeus's faith was similarly rewarded and strengthened as he acted on the incomplete faith he then possessed.[4] In the process, Bartimaeus learned that the Lord is not merely a physical healer but a spiritual healer—his faith was made "whole." Nevertheless, while he still needed to act on his faith, his healing came more quickly, and Jesus restored his physical sight completely in an instant. Bartimaeus then left his "garment" or cloak behind when he came to Jesus. Understanding that Jesus Christ is the Atoning One, Bartimaeus's covering (from the Hebrew root *kpr* come the words *covering* and *atonement*) was made perfect in what the Savior came to do, but not through physical evidences of protection and cover. With this complete covering, Bartimaeus "followed Jesus in the way"; he authentically walked the gospel path of a disciple of Christ.

Martha's Testimony of the Resurrection and the Life

Martha of Bethany provides another example of this progressive conversion process. Four days after her brother Lazarus died and was buried in a tomb, Martha met Jesus as he came to visit and console her and her sister Mary. Martha's words reflect her knowledge of the Savior's healing power: "Lord, if thou hadst been here, my brother had not died. But I know, that even now, whatsoever thou wilt ask of God, God will give it thee." To which Jesus declared to her, "Thy brother shall rise again." Martha's next statement of knowledge indicates that she also knew, at least in part, the doctrine of resurrection: "I know that he shall rise again in the resurrection at the last day" (John 11:21–24).

Martha's understanding of and belief in the resurrection, together with her active dialoging with Jesus on spiritual matters, contrast markedly with Luke's depiction of her in her home near Jerusalem, where, while serving Jesus, she became "cumbered about much serving" (Luke 10:39–40). In that setting, Martha complained to Jesus that he didn't care about her. She was focused on what *she* was doing to help others and was ignorant of how her sister served or her profound need for the Savior's sacrifice. Certainly, she had the beginning of a testimony. Her belief and respect for Jesus were evident in the care and effort she made to host him in her home. Like Peter and his associates, however, she did not understand or appreciate the purpose for his coming. The Lord's poignant response to her incomplete testimony provides a hint of where she was spiritually blind: "Martha, Martha, thou art careful and troubled about many things: But one thing is needful" (10:41–42). His correction prompted in her a much stronger witness and commitment to selflessly serve. According to John, days before the crucifixion, Martha served a meal to her brother Lazarus, her sister Mary, Jesus, and other disciples. The setting is almost identical to the Luke incident, but Martha herself had changed. She still served, but this time in ways that focused the attention on Jesus and his imminent sacrifice (John 12:1–9).[5]

In John's account, the words of the Lord deepened Martha's belief after watching her brother die, leading Jesus to respond by teaching her more truth: "I am the resurrection and the life: he that believeth in me, though he were dead, yet shall he live: And whosoever liveth and believeth in me shall never die. Believeth thou this?" To this Martha responded as steadfastly as did Peter after the Bread of Life discourse: "Yea, Lord: *I believe that thou art the Christ, the Son of God, which should come into the world*" (John 11:25–27; emphasis added). Her firm response contrasts with the response of her sister, Mary, who also patiently nurtured an incomplete conversion to the Savior. She initially declared the same faith in his healing powers after Lazarus's death as did her sister: "Lord, if thou hadst been here, my brother had not died" (11:32). Yet whereas Mary had sat, eagerly listening, at the feet of Jesus in Luke, in John's story she is overwhelmed with grief, leading Jesus to groan with compassion and weep as well (11:33–34).

Both sisters reverenced his power as healer, teacher, and master, but experiencing profound grief at the loss and burial of their brother may have ignited Mary's and Martha's faith and anticipation for what Jesus came to do eternally when he raised Lazarus from the dead. As witnesses of their brother's return to life after he had been dead four days, the sisters learned a deeper meaning in the Savior's words "I am the resurrection and the life." Mary in particular, with her grief over Lazarus changed to joy at his restoration to life, is then presented as one of very few disciples whose testimony expanded to embrace knowledge *before* he went to Calvary that his mission included dying for us all.

Arriving at a Complete and Sure Witness

The Gospels present Mary of Bethany and another woman as coming to an understanding that Jesus would soon die, even before the male disciples gained that knowledge. Six days before Jesus's crucifixion, Mary, the sister of Martha, anointed Jesus's feet with an expensive ointment while Judas Iscariot rebuked her for such extravagance. Jesus defended Mary's generosity. "Let her alone," he said, "against the day of my burying hath she kept this," or as is found in the Joseph Smith New Translation: "For she hath preserved this ointment until now, that she might anoint me in token of my burial" (John 12:3–7). On a similar occasion a few days later, an unnamed woman in Bethany brought "an alabaster box of ointment of spikenard very precious" to anoint the Savior's head. Again, there were those who protested the "waste" of the expensive oil. Once more, Jesus defended the woman's gift. "Why trouble ye her? she hath wrought a good work on me. . . . She hath done what she could: she is come aforehand to anoint my body to the burying" (Mark 14:3–9; parallel Matthew 26:6–12).

Although connected to the burial customs of the day, the act of anointing had powerful precedents in Jewish history. From the beginning of the kingdom of Israel, prophets had anointed Saul, then David, and then Solomon to serve as God's chosen sovereign for his people (1 Samuel 10:1; 16:13; 2 Samuel 5:3; 1 Kings 1:39). Thereafter, the rightful king of Judah and the kings of Israel were ritually anointed with oil to designate those chosen to rule. Beginning with Aaron, priests were anointed with oil to commemorate their authority to minister (Exodus 40:13–15). At least in some instances, leading prophets, too, were anointed for their upcoming responsibility (1 Kings 19:16; Isaiah 61:1; Psalm 105:15).[6] This practice of anointing prophets, priests, and kings is a type of anointing the "King of kings" (1 Timothy 6:15), the "High Priest of good things to come" (Hebrews 9:11), and the awaited Prophet foretold by Moses (Deuteronomy 18:15–19; Acts 3:22). The titles "Messiah" (Hebrew, *māšîaḥ*) and "Christ" (Greek, *christos*) both mean "the Anointed One." The anointing or anointings that Jesus received before his passion, while explicitly performed in preparation for his death and burial, might also have been implicit testimonies that Mary and the unnamed woman knew that Jesus was, in fact, the Anointed One.[7]

Other women from Galilee had followed and ministered to Jesus of their substance since he made them whole in both body and spirit (Luke 8:1–3).[8] These were in Jerusalem at the time that Jesus died, having followed him there from Galilee. While some of them may not have had the exact insight that Mary of Bethany and the unnamed woman who anointed him had, their faith and love were enough to lead them to the horrible crucifixion, where the Synoptics portray them watching the scene somewhat from a distance (Mark 15:40–41; parallels Matthew 27:55–56; Luke 23:49), and John shows at least some of them "[standing] by the cross of Jesus" (John 19:25). Although these women did not yet know that Jesus would of a certainty rise from the grave, by their actions they witnessed that he had indeed come to die. And they stood by him in his agony.

When Jesus was dead and taken to a sepulchre to be buried, these same women "followed after, and beheld the sepulchre, and how his body was laid. And they returned, and prepared spices and ointments; and rested the sabbath day" (Luke 23:55–56; cf. Mark 15:47). Some of these same women, coming to the tomb to anoint the body—which they were not allowed to do since the body was removed from the cross—were the first to discover that the tomb was empty and hear the witnesses of angels that the Lord had risen (Mark 16:1–5; parallels Matthew 28:1–8; Luke 24:1–11). According to John, Mary Magdalene, one of the women from Galilee who had also stood at the foot of the cross, became the first person to see the resurrected Christ (John 20:11–18). By following Jesus, despite hardship, grief, or distance, these women began to embrace the reality that the Messiah came to lose his life that we may live. When their devotion led them to prepare him more completely for his burial, they received further witnesses and soon gained testimonies that he also conquered death for us.[9]

Peter and the Beloved Disciple received a similar clarification and deepening of testimony after the resurrection. When they ran to see the empty tomb for themselves in response to the women's declaration, the two apostles were surprised, "for as yet they knew not" or, perhaps better said, they had not yet understood (Greek, ēdeisan) "the scripture, that he must rise again from the dead" (John 20:3–10). Their continued misunderstanding quickly dissipated after Jesus finally appeared to *them* after his death and invited *them* to touch the prints in his hands, side, and feet (20:19–29; cf. Luke 24:36–43). As the first fruits of the resurrection, he "opened their understanding, that they might understand the scriptures," which prophesy, "Thus it [is necessary for] Christ to suffer, and to rise from the dead the third day: and that repentance and remission of sins should be preached in his name among all nations, beginning at Jerusalem" (Luke 24:44–47). Finally, they began to grasp what he, the Messiah and the Son of God, had come to earth to do.

After the resurrection, the disciples' testimonies grew dramatically, empowered by the receipt of the gift of the Spirit. The testimony of Peter and his fellow apostles is recorded multiple times in the first eight chapters of Acts.[10] Their fearless defense of the mission of Jesus Christ underscores their expanding understanding that he who died lives again to grant us the gift of salvation. For example, the high priest–led Sanhedrin in Jerusalem commanded the apostles to cease teaching in Jesus's name but quickly arrested them anew when they found the apostles openly testifying of Christ at the temple

(Acts 5:17–28). In response to the council's threats and warnings, the apostles unflinchingly responded, "We ought to obey God rather than men. The God of our fathers raised up Jesus, whom ye slew and hanged on a tree. Him hath God exalted with his right hand to be a Prince and a Saviour, for to give repentance to Israel, and forgiveness of sins. And we are his witnesses of these things; and so is also the Holy Ghost, whom God hath given to them that obey him" (Acts 5:29–32).

In the years following the Lord's postresurrection ministry to the New Testament disciples, other believers in addition to the apostles lived Christ-centered lives to courageously spread the gospel. Men and women of faith were among those that persecutors threatened, arrested, and even slayed in their attempts to halt the spread of power in the name of Jesus Christ (see Acts 9:1–2).

"That ye might believe that Jesus is the Christ, the Son of God"

The New Testament thus provides us powerful examples of how true conversion is wrought. The authors of the four Gospels believed in Jesus Christ and recorded the words and deeds of Jesus so that countless others could learn truths about him (see Luke 1:1–4). Specifically, John wrote his testimony of the gospel so that "[we the readers] might believe that Jesus is the Christ, the Son of God; and that believing ye might have life through his name" (John 20:31). For John, it wasn't enough to know who Jesus is. He wanted us to also know that Jesus came to give us life, and to "have it more abundantly" (John 10:10).

Witnesses of Jesus Christ in the New Testament such as Peter, Martha, and Mary began their journey to full conversion with an imperfect understanding and limited vision of what Jesus came to earth to do. Incremental learning over time while putting into practice what we learn is often the pattern that we follow to achieve a firm reverence and appreciation for our dependence on him. Like them, we often find ourselves faced by "hard sayings" and circumstances that seem incongruent with our perspective of God's purposes. We may easily relate to those disciples who "walked no more after [Jesus]," being offended by his words. Like Martha, we may think that Jesus no longer cares about us when we are so often overburdened, overwhelmed, and underappreciated. That is why it is tempting to give up and renounce the witness of God's truth we have already received. The world is ready to support our despair as it carefully and sophisticatedly articulates reasons to abandon what we know because of what we don't know.

As we seek to "come unto Christ, and be perfected in him" (Moroni 10:32), we must come to better know what it means that he is the Son of God and the Savior of the World. This knowledge is rarely perfect or certain in our early walk of discipleship. Nevertheless, the examples of Peter, Martha, Mary, and the women from Galilee show us how we can push forward from hope to belief to more sure knowledge. These New Testament witnesses call us to similarly come to know Jesus and what he has done for us. If we will stay steadfast in the gospel knowledge that we know from experience to be true and refuse to be offended by what we do not understand, we can and will proceed through incremental and often imperfect jumps and starts to finally see what only Christ can show us and become what only he can make of us. That full conversion embraces the gospel of repentance, forgiveness, and everlasting life made possible only through the mercy, merits, grace, and sacrifice of Jesus Christ. We then can stand with Martha and Peter of old, as witnesses at all times and places, to declare "We believe and are sure." This is the promise and enabling power Jesus Christ came to earth to offer.

CAMILLE FRONK OLSON *is a professor emerita and former chair of ancient scripture at Brigham Young University.*

Notes

1. See Eric D. Huntsman, "The Bread of Life Sermon," in *Celebrating Easter*, ed. Thomas A. Wayment and Keith J. Wilson (Provo, UT: Religious Studies Center, 2006), 87–111.

2. For a discussion on why Mark's Gospel is a particularly meaningful source for understanding Peter, see Eric D. Huntsman, "The Petrine *Kērygma* and the Gospel according to Mark," in *The Ministry of Peter the Chief Apostle* (Provo, UT: Religious Studies Center; Salt Lake City: Deseret Book, 2014), 169–77.

3. For additional scriptural evidence of Peter's incomplete testimony, see Jared W. Ludlow, "Stand Down and See the End," in *Ministry of Peter the Chief Apostle*, 67–90; and Brent L. Top, "Fallible but Faithful," in *Ministry of Peter the Chief Apostle*, 1–12.

4. Eric D. Huntsman sees Bartimaeus as having a "full understanding" of who Jesus is and why he had come from the beginning of his story as contrasted to the blind man healed in stages. Huntsman, *Miracles of Jesus* (Salt Lake City: Deseret Book, 2014), 103. For a lovely discussion on how healing physical blindness can symbolize the Savior's power to heal spiritual blindness, see pages 87–103.

5. For an in-depth analysis of Martha's transformation as a disciple, see Camille Fronk Olson, *Mary, Martha, and Me: Seeking the One Needful Thing* (Salt Lake City: Deseret Book, 2006), 155–64.

6. See Eric D. Huntsman, *God So Loved the World* (Salt Lake City: Deseret Book, 2011), 44–45, 133–35.

7. See Camille Fronk Olson, "Mary and Martha," in *Women of the New Testament* (Salt Lake City: Deseret Book, 2014), 163–64.

8. See also stories of other Galilean women whose lives were touched and forever changed through their interactions with Jesus, which Luke relates in the same context in Luke 7–8—that is, the woman who loved much, the widow of Nain, the woman who touched the hem of the Savior's robe, the daughter of Jairus and her mother, and Mary the mother of Jesus. These women may also have been among those Galilean women who

followed Jesus to the cross and the tomb; see "Women of Galilee," in Olson, *Women of the New Testament*, 177–213.

9. See Camille Fronk Olson, "They Ministered unto Him of Their Substance: Women and the Savior," in *To Save the Lost: An Easter Celebration*, ed. Richard Neitzel Holzapfel and Kent P. Jackson (Provo, UT: Religious Studies Center, 2009), 61–80.

10. For a fuller discussion of what Peter's testimony grew to become, see Terry B. Ball, "'Whom Say Ye That I Am?': Peter's Witness of Christ," in *Ministry of Peter the Chief Apostle*, 13–26.

JESUS IN THE NEW TESTAMENT

5

Matthew's Portrayal of Jesus

Son of David, a New Moses, and Son of God

Tyler J. Griffin

Although the Gospel of Matthew appears at the beginning of the New Testament, many scholars believe that the Gospel of Mark was written first.[1] Yet while Matthew follows the basic order and storyline of Mark, Matthew weaves new material into it, especially many teachings of Jesus, some of which are shared with the Gospel of Luke and others that are unique to the First Gospel. Some aspects of Matthew's Gospel, such as his influential Sermon on the Mount and his references to the church (Matthew 16:18; 18:17), the only ones in any of the Gospels, made his treatment of the ministry and mission of Jesus particularly important to early Christians.[2] These factors and the way its author frequently used Jewish scripture helped make Matthew a natural bridge between the Old and New Testaments, and this may have led to Matthew's Gospel being placed first in the canon.[3] An important result of this Gospel's prominent placement is that Matthew's presentation of Jesus is the first that most Bible readers encounter.

As a result, even though Matthew is often harmonized and blended with Mark and Luke as one of the Synoptic Gospels, its unique perspective of Jesus of Nazareth is fundamental to our understanding of Christology—that is, the way early and contemporary Christians understand who Jesus was and how he helped bring about salvation. Before analyzing Jesus Christ through the Matthean lens, we will first analyze that lens to more fully appreciate its structure, methods, potential purposes, and likely audience. We will then consider how Matthew's Gospel went beyond Mark's by beginning with a story of Jesus's divine conception and miraculous birth. Written to show how Jesus was the "Christ, the son of David, the son of Abraham" (Matthew 1:1), this infancy narrative also introduced the image of Jesus as the New Moses, ideas that were developed in the rest of the Gospel. In addition to demonstrating that Jesus was the "Son of the living God," Matthew also placed emphasis on Jesus's role as the Son of Man, one who would not only suffer and die for us but also rise from the dead and one day return in glory. These aspects of Matthew's presentation of Jesus are important to Latter-day Saint readers, whose own understanding of these elements of Jesus's person and work are often strengthened by Restoration scripture and testimony. As we study the Matthean Jesus, our own testimonies of Christ can then deepen as we come to know him better.

Matthew, a Jewish Gospel?

Tradition attributes authorship of this Gospel to Matthew the publican, or tax collector, whom Jesus called to follow him and who was later named an apostle (Matthew 9:9; 10:3).[4] Despite this attribution, the author of Matthew was also well acquainted with Jewish scripture, traditions, and various messianic expectations of his day. In fact, his familiarity with and use of such material led to Matthew's Gospel being described "as the most Jewish book of the New Testament."[5]

With over sixty quotations from the Old Testament, along with many other allusions, Matthew quotes the Old Testament at least twice as often as any other Gospel writer.[6] In particular, Matthew lists at least thirteen specific instances where Jesus said or did something that expressly fulfilled a prophecy that would have been familiar to a Jewish audience (Matthew 1:22–23; 2:5–6, 15, 17–18, 23; 4:14–16; 8:17; 12:17–21; 13:14, 35; 21:4–5; 27:9–10, 35).[7] As an example, Matthew's first fulfillment statement declares Jesus's miraculous birth as fulfilling Isaiah 7:14 where a "virgin" conceives and bears a son who would be called Emmanuel, "God *with us*" (Matthew 1:22–23; emphasis added).[8] After introducing this name in the first chapter, Matthew forms an *inclusio*, or literary bookend, with the final verse in the Gospel: "Teaching them to observe all things whatsoever I have commanded you: and, lo, *I am with you alway*, even unto the end of the world. Amen" (Matthew 28:20; emphasis added). Every sermon, miracle, and interaction between these two bookends shows Jesus fulfilling his Emmanuel role.

In spite of Matthew's supposed Jewishness, he also displays greater harshness toward the Jewish leaders than any other Gospel writer. For example, Matthew records a long string of Jesus's scathing rebukes of the scribes and Pharisees in Matthew 23. He also lists Jesus's harsh judgments and prophecies of destruction (Matthew 24). Nevertheless, while Matthew's Jesus does not hold back his criticism of certain Jewish leaders and behaviors, he never speaks negatively about the law of Moses. Matthew's portrayal of Jesus shows him upholding key Jewish traditions such as "Go not into the way of the Gentiles" (10:5), "I am not sent but unto the lost sheep of the house of Israel" (15:24), Jesus facilitating Peter to pay the temple tax (17:24–27), and "Pray ye that your flight be not in the winter, neither on the Sabbath day" (24:20). Unlike the other Synoptics, in Matthew's account Jesus is never accused of breaking certain traditions of the elders (e.g., plucking grain on the Sabbath, eating with unwashed hands, not fasting, etc.). Instead, Matthew shows Jesus being questioned about why he allows his *disciples* to do these things but is never confronted for personally breaking these traditions of the law himself. On at least one occasion, Jesus appears to have defended certain traditions that would have been reverenced by many in a Christian-Jewish audience due to centuries of tradition (see Matthew 23:3). Unlike Luke's Sermon on the Plain, Matthew's Sermon on the Mount appears to emphasize the importance of the law: "Think not that I am come to destroy the law, or the prophets: I am not come to destroy, but to fulfil. For verily I say unto you, Till heaven and earth pass, one jot or one tittle shall in no wise pass from the law, till all be fulfilled" (5:17–18).

Nevertheless, despite the common description that "Matthew was written to persuade the Jews that Jesus was the promised Jewish Messiah,"[9] our understanding of the Gospel's original audience may need to be slightly more nuanced. Matthew's inclusion of gentiles who recognize Jesus—such as the magi or wise men who worship Jesus as the true King of Israel at the beginning (Matthew 2:11) and the centurion at the foot of the cross who acknowledges him as the Son of God at the end (27:54)—and the Risen Lord's final directive that his eleven remaining disciples take the gospel to all the world (28:16–20) might suggest that it was also directed to a mixed Jewish-gentile Christian audience.[10] Matthew's apparent hostility toward Jewish leaders might partially have been the result of first-century Jewish Christians struggling with the emerging rabbinic leadership of the Jewish community after the destruction of Jerusalem and the temple in AD 70. The early Christian community, consisting of both Jewish and gentile Christians, may also have been struggling to combine the seemingly exclusive promises made to the house of Israel in the past with their newfound Christian faith. Nevertheless, the Jewish aspects of Matthew provide particular insight into how Jesus's earliest disciples may have gradually come to understand how he was in fact their Messiah—one who was not only the kingly successor to David and a prophet like Moses but also the actual Son of God who came to suffer, die, and rise again and who would come again in glory.

Bring Forth a Son

When it comes to actually beginning his Gospel, Matthew does not follow Mark's lead in commencing his story with an account of the ministry of John the Baptist leading up to Jesus's baptism. For Mark, Jesus was the Son of God because the Father declared it so when he proclaimed after the baptism, "Thou art my beloved Son, in whom I am well pleased" (Mark 1:11). Jesus's divine identity was then confirmed as he acted and taught with authority throughout his ministry. Nevertheless, the Marcan proclamation by the Father could be interpreted in such a way as to promote an adoptionist Christology—that is, a belief that Jesus was a fully human figure who was adopted by the Father at the baptism, much as the royal kings of Judah had been "adopted" as the Lord's representatives at their coronations (see Psalm 2:7).[11] Perhaps to counter such a misunderstanding, Matthew decided, and no doubt was inspired, to begin his Gospel with a narrative account of Jesus's divine conception and miraculous birth. In addition to establishing Jesus's unique conception, Matthew could also have been using his birth narrative to make additional connections with the Old Testament.[12] According to noted biblical scholar Raymond Brown (1928–98), this "conception christology" was the focus of a prologue (Matthew 1–2) that answered important questions such as *who* was Jesus (1:1–17), how did he come into being (1:18–25, Jesus's genealogy), where did he go (2:1–12, Bethlehem, where he was recognized by the magi), and from whence did he come (2:13–23, back from Egypt, where his family had gone to escape Herod).[13]

In addressing the question of who Jesus was, Matthew's work begins with two words, *biblos geneseōs*,[14] an important phrase that echoes Genesis 2:4 (the generations of the heavens and the earth), 5:1 (the generations of Adam), and 6:9 (the generations of Noah). As Brown further notes, Matthew begins his Gospel account as an inversion of the Genesis account; where Adam's genealogy lists his descendants, Jesus's lists his ancestors.[15] Abraham holds a prominent place in Matthew's description of Jesus's identity.[16] Matthew's first verse ends by declaring that Jesus was "the son of Abraham." The genealogy list immediately following that declaration begins with Abraham as the first ancestor mentioned (Matthew 1:2).[17] Eric Huntsman, a BYU professor of ancient scripture, notes that, "while much of Jesus's genealogy focuses on his role as the Son of David and the king of Israel, the reference to Abraham can also be seen as expanding his role as a blessing to all nations and peoples. . . . Although overall [Matthew's] gospel comes from the perspective of a Jewish author writing for a Jewish audience, he also seems to have been writing when a growing number of gentiles were coming into the Church, and there are important references to gentiles in his Gospel."[18] Huntsman also observes that Old Testament genealogies serve "an important function in establishing kinship, confirming a family's position in the House of Israel, and validating claims to important royal or priestly positions."[19] Unlike Luke (Luke 3:23–38),[20] Matthew follows the Old Testament pattern of fathers *begetting* sons. In addition to the men, Matthew included five women in this list: Tamar (Matthew 1:3), Rahab and Ruth (1:5), Uriah's wife (1:6), and Mary (1:16).[21] Perhaps Matthew included Mary with this list of women because they, too, were seen as either sinners or outcasts. Or maybe Matthew was simply showing how gentiles would also have a part in Jesus's work and ministry, since they appear in his ancestry.[22]

Nevertheless, perhaps the clearest statement of *who* Jesus is in the opening chapter of Matthew comes during the angelic annunciation to Joseph, in which he is told, "Fear not to take unto thee Mary thy wife: for that which is conceived in her is of the Holy Ghost" (Matthew 1:20), a statement that makes clear that Joseph the carpenter was not the actual father of Mary's expected child. Rather, the conception had come about by divine agency. For Latter-day Saints, this divine agency is clarified through Restoration scripture, which clarifies that Mary, a precious and chosen vessel, conceived and was overshadowed "*by the power* of the Holy Ghost" (see Alma 7:10; emphasis added). The angel then continued with Joseph, "And she shall bring forth a son, and thou shalt call his name Jesus: for he shall save his people from their sins" (Matthew 1:21). The word *for* in this context implies that the reason Joseph should name him Jesus is *because* he will save. While there is no logical connection between salvation and the name Jesus in English or *Iēsous* in Greek, there is a correlation in Hebrew, where the name *Yehôshua* is taken to mean "Yahweh is salvation."[23] Matthew underscores this connection of Jesus with YHWH, the Lord of the Old Testament, with the first formula quotation from Isaiah: "Now all this was done, that it might be fulfilled which was spoken of the Lord by the prophet, saying, Behold, a virgin shall be with child, and shall bring forth a son, and they shall call his name Emmanuel, which being interpreted is, *God with us*" (Matthew 1:22–23; emphasis added).

The Son of David

Matthew, more than any other Gospel writer, emphasized a royal Christology—a belief that a Davidic king would rise up, be anointed to take the throne, and restore Israel's kingdom again. David himself, like Saul before him, had been anointed king of Israel (see 1 Samuel 10:1; 16:13; 2 Samuel 5:3). David was the greatest of Israel's kings and clearly held a significant place of honor for biblical authors, with his name appearing more than any other name in the Bible (1,085 times).[24] Despite his later personal failings, David remained faithful to the Lord and received a covenant and promise from the Lord that he would always have a descendant to reign in the house of Israel, with God promising to be his father (see 2 Samuel 7:12–16). Because David, his successors, the high priests, and some prophets were all anointed, each could be referred to by the title "messiah" (Hebrew, *māšîaḥ*; Greek, *christos*), which means literally "anointed one." David's ruling line lapsed following the destruction of Jerusalem and the exile of Zedekiah in 586 BC, but royal psalms and prophecies held out the hope for a restoration of both the kingdom and the Davidic throne. As a result, in the intertestamental period prophecies and hopes for a restored Davidic kingdom led to the expectation of a future anointed king who would be a particular messiah or even "*the* Messiah."[25]

Matthew presents Jesus as this Davidic Messiah more clearly than any of the other Gospels. For instance, he uses the title "son of David" for Jesus nine times (see Matthew 1:1; 9:27; 12:23; 15:22; 20:30–31; 21:9, 15; 22:42). In contrast, the title "son of David" appears only three times each in Mark and Luke and is absent in John, the idea appearing only once in that Gospel as "the seed of David."[26] Because royal succession was patrilineal, Matthew's infancy narrative focused on Joseph, unlike Luke's, which was largely told from the perspective of Mary. Jesus's genealogy is that of Joseph, his foster father (see Matthew 1:16), and in the annunciation to Joseph, the angel specifically identifies the carpenter as "Joseph, thou son of David" (1:20). In order to legally claim Jesus as his own son, thereby making Jesus an heir to the Davidic throne, Joseph accepts Mary's baby when he is born, giving him a name (1:25) and thereby adopting him into the Davidic line.[27] Matthew's Davidic focus can also be seen in how he organized his genealogy of Jesus into three sets of fourteen generations in a manner that emphasizes Jesus's descent through David's line (from Abraham down to David, from David to the Babylonian captivity, and from the exile down to Christ; 1:2–17). While the number fourteen has little meaning to an English or Greek reader in a genealogical context, in Hebrew, the name David was associated with the number fourteen because of an alphanumeric Hebrew code known as *gematria*. The numerical values of the Hebrew consonants *dalet-vav-dalet* add up to fourteen.[28] It is possible that Matthew purposely organized the pedigree in such a way that he could create a 14-14-14 pattern that repeated Jesus's connection to King David three times.[29]

Another possible link between Jesus and David occurred at the triumphal entry. Shortly before David's death, he directed his servants to have his son Solomon "ride upon [his] own mule, and bring him down to Gihon: And let Zadok the priest and Nathan the prophet anoint him there king over Israel" (1 Kings 1:33–34).

Jesus, as "the son of David," also rode on a mule in the Kidron Valley, past the Gihon Spring, before triumphantly entering into Jerusalem (Matthew 21:1–11). The significance of these various elements all coming together seemed to have a powerful effect on the gathering crowd. As Jesus rode, the multitudes shouted a significant refrain from Psalm 118:25–26: "Hosanna *to the Son of David*: Blessed is he that cometh in the name of the Lord; Hosanna in the highest" (Matthew 21:9; emphasis added). The crowds that day seemed to be caught up in the belief that Jesus was the long-awaited Son of David who had finally come to restore the Davidic throne, which led either them or Matthew to insert the title "Son of David," something that the other three Gospels do not note.

The connection with Psalm 118 is significant. Psalm 118 forms part of the Jewish *Hallel* (comprising Psalms 113–18 and 136). The *Hallel* was recited each year on special occasions, including Passover. This particular psalm was a triumphant passage anticipating the long-awaited coming of the Messiah. Jesus validated this particular interpretation when referring to his own second coming in Matthew 23:39: "Ye shall not see me henceforth, till ye shall say, Blessed is he that cometh in the name of the Lord." Ironically, these triumphant *Hallel* verses shouted by the crowd (Psalm 118:25–26) are bracketed by allusions to rejection in verse 22, "The stone which the builders refused is become the head stone of the corner," and verse 27, "God is the Lord, which hath shewed us light: bind the sacrifice with cords, even unto the horns of the altar." Jesus's entry into Jerusalem thus ironically sets the stage for him, as David's heir, to be rejected by the leaders of the people and then be slain as a lamb. By shifting from a royal Christology to a more atonement or redemption Christology, Matthew was thus able to prepare his readers for something that many at the time of Jesus did not expect: their king was in fact a sacrifice that would open the door for the future day when Jesus would once again return like a lion for a second triumphal entry to begin his eternal reign as King of kings.

A New Moses

Moses prophesied of a future great prophet when he wrote, "The LORD thy God will raise up unto thee a prophet from the midst of thee, of thy brethren, like unto me; unto him ye shall hearken" (Deuteronomy 18:15).[30] A few verses later, Moses informs us that God would "put [his] words in [this prophet's] mouth; and he shall speak unto them all that [God] shall command him" (18:18).[31] Matthew signals that he saw Jesus as this promised prophet in his infancy narrative by pointing out similarities in the birth stories of these two deliverers. Then, having established this motif, he presents Jesus as a New Moses throughout much of the rest of his Gospel, using this typology to illustrate important aspects of the Messiah's work by showing how Jesus was the great lawgiver, provider, and deliverer of the New Testament.

Both Jesus and Moses had unusual infancies and childhoods. Both were born into poor families who were part of a conquered people. Both were spared from infanticide while most around them were not. Both were raised by a stepfather. In an inverse connection, Moses was born as a slave and became a prince in the royal house of the king; Jesus was "born King of the Jews" (Matthew 2:2) but became the ultimate servant and, as a child, was visited by the kingly magi in his humble house. Neither Jesus nor Moses seemed to have a permanent, settled home in their own land. Hosea wrote, "When Israel was a child, then I loved him, and called my son out of Egypt" (Hosea 11:1). This statement could be interpreted by seeing Israel collectively as the *son* that was called out of Egypt, and thus a statement that spoke to Israel's past experiences. Moses could also be seen as this saving son, or this verse could refer to Israel as a whole. Matthew chooses to interpret the Hosea passage typologically, seeing Hosea's statement as being consummated in the story of Joseph's taking Jesus and Mary to (and later from) Egypt (see Matthew 2:13–15).[32]

There are also symbolic connections with Moses's miraculous crossing of the Red Sea on dry ground, which Jesus echoes by crossing the Sea of Galilee, not by dividing it but by walking on it (Exodus

14:13–31; Matthew 14:24–33). After leading the children of Israel out of Egypt, Moses fasted for forty days while on Mount Sinai (Exodus 34:28); Jesus also fasted for forty days in the wilderness (see Matthew 4:1–2). Divine interactions on mountaintops, under cover of thick clouds, resulted in transfiguration and shining faces for both (Exodus 19:9; 24:16; 34:29; Matthew 17:1–12). Heavenly bread and miraculous loaves were provided in abundance for both Moses's and Jesus's followers (see Exodus 16:16; Matthew 14:19–21; 15:32–39). Both were repeatedly questioned on points of the law and their authority for carrying out their missions (see Numbers 12:1–2; 16:1–3; Matthew 22–23). Likewise, Moses and Jesus both instituted a richly symbolic meal for their people to perpetually remember their deliverance from captivity and bondage (see Exodus 12; Matthew 26:26–30). Latter-day Saint readers may find further similarities between Moses and Jesus in two sets of incidents related in the Pearl of Great Price and Joseph Smith's New Translation. In the first set, both went into a place apart to spend time with God in preparation for their appointed missions (see Moses 1:1–11 and Joseph Smith—Matthew 4:1). In the other, immediately following their experiences with God, both were directly and personally confronted by Satan (see Moses 1:12–22 and Matthew 4:2–11). Jesus overcame all three temptations he faced, showing his power over the devil. Moses, the great prophet, tried three times to cast out Satan but failed until he called upon the name of the Only Begotten in his fourth attempt that finally succeeded.

The very organization of Matthew's Gospel might reflect the motif of Jesus as the New Moses. Between the infancy narrative, which introduces *who* Jesus is as the Son of God and of David, and the passion and resurrection narratives at the end, which illustrate *what* he came to do, the body of the Gospel can be divided into five sections. Many scholars have noted that each of these sections concludes with a major discourse, each of which ends with phrases such as, "When Jesus had ended these sayings" (see Matthew 7:28; 11:1; 13:53; 19:1; 26:1): the Sermon on the Mount (chapters 5–7); the Mission Sermon (chapter 10); the Sermon in Parables (chapter 13); the Sermon on the

Church (chapter 18); and his End of Times and Judgment Discourse (eschatological, or "last days," prophecies in chapters 24–25). Many see this organization as an intentional allusion to the five books of Moses and yet another attempt to directly appeal to a Jewish audience, the fivefold division of Matthew being analogous to the five books traditionally attributed to Moses. If Moses delivered the law in five books, Jesus, the New Moses, delivered his teachings in five sections, each culminating in a major sermon.[33]

Arguably the most important and direct tie between Jesus and Moses is the fact that both delivered life-altering commandments to their people. Matthew, unlike the other Gospel writers, was careful to point out that Jesus delivered his sermon, much like Moses, from a mountain (see Exodus 20; Matthew 5–7). Few things are more "Matthean" than this sermon with its beatitudes and requirements that stretch disciples beyond the outward elements of the law of Moses and give them the pattern for Christian behavior. By fulfilling every jot and tittle of the law of Moses (Matthew 5:18), a point that would have been especially important to Matthew's audience, he embodied every principle of the higher law he taught in all his sermons.

Jesus as the Son of God

Although Matthew's infancy narrative presents Jesus's conception as divine, it does not explicitly call Jesus the Son of God. Nevertheless, various witnesses, both otherworldly and human, attest that Jesus was in fact God's Son. Ironically, Satan along with his followers also declared Jesus's true identity. The devil opened his first two direct temptations by attacking that identity: "If thou be the Son of God . . ." (Matthew 4:3, 6). The demoniacs of Gergesenes cried out, "What have we to do with thee, Jesus, thou Son of God?" (8:29). Only in Matthew's account do we see Jesus's disciples so dramatically affected by his walking on the water that they "worshipped him, saying, Of a truth thou art the Son of God" (14:33). Additionally, when the centurion at Golgotha "and they that were with him, watching Jesus, saw the earthquake, and those things that were done, they feared greatly, saying, Truly this was the Son of God" (27:54; compare Mark 15:39).[34] The question of Jesus's relation to God became the defining feature of his trial before the leaders of the Jews. "And the high priest answered and said unto him, I adjure thee by the living God, that thou tell us whether thou be the Christ, the Son of God" (Matthew 26:63). Jesus's response was confirming enough that the high priest rent his clothes in rage, condemning Jesus for blasphemy (see 26:64–66).[35]

The most striking, and powerful, human testimony of Jesus's divine sonship comes with Peter's confession at Caesarea Philippi in Matthew 16:15–19. Mark's version of this story records Peter saying, "Thou art the Christ" (Mark 8:29), and in Luke 9:20, Peter responded to the question of identity by saying, "the Christ of God." In Matthew's Gospel, however, Peter said, "Thou art the Christ, *the Son of the living God*" (Matthew 16:16; emphasis added). The Matthean Peter does not just know that Jesus is the chosen, anointed servant of God but also that he is actually God's own Son. Mark and Luke both finished this part of the dialogue with Jesus charging them to tell no man (Mark 8:30; Luke 9:21), but Matthew instead has Jesus follow up Peter's confession with a declaration on the nature and origins of Peter's testimony, with the implication that he is expected to share it: "Blessed art thou, Simon Bar-jona: for flesh and blood hath not revealed it unto thee, but *my Father* which is in heaven" (Matthew 16:17; emphasis added). The apostolic revelation to Peter that Jesus was the Son of God is particularly meaningful to Latter-day Saints. Not only do we have apostles who are special witnesses of Jesus Christ, but many others of our number can receive such spiritual surety: "To some it is given by the Holy Ghost to know *that Jesus Christ is the Son of God*, and that he was crucified for the sins of the world. To others is given *to believe on their words*, that they also might have eternal life if they continue faithful" (D&C 46:13–14; emphasis added).

Perhaps most importantly, Jesus's own actions, teachings, and the way he addressed God signaled his divine paternity. While all the

Gospels reveal that Jesus regularly called upon God as his Father, the title "Heavenly Father" (Greek, *ho patēr ho ouranios*), perhaps the most common title for God used by Latter-day Saints, is almost unique to Matthew. It never appears in Mark or John and only shows up once in Luke (Luke 11:13). By contrast, Matthew's Gospel uses the phrase five times (Matthew 6:14, 26, 32; 15:13; and 18:35). The three instances used in chapter 6 all consist of Jesus referring to "your heavenly Father" while the two passages in chapters 15 and 18 refer to "my heavenly Father." While there are dozens of other passages where Matthew refers to God as a Father or uses variations such as "your Father which is in heaven" (e.g., Matthew 5:16, 45, 48), "Father, Lord of heaven and earth" (Matthew 11:25), or simply "your Father," it is those passages where he refers to God as "his" Father that reflect a special, more personal relationship (e.g., Matthew 7:21; 10:29; 11:27; 12:50; 15:13; 16:17; 18:10, 19, 35; 24:36; 25:34; 26:39, 42, 53).

Matthew, like the other two synoptic writers, included Heavenly Father's own witness of the divinity of Jesus Christ at his baptism (see Matthew 3:17; Mark 1:11; and Luke 3:22) and at the Mount of Transfiguration (see Matthew 17:5; Mark 9:7; and Luke 9:35). In the baptism witness, Mark and Luke both record the voice as speaking directly to Jesus: "Thou art my beloved Son."[36] Matthew's version records the voice of the Father bearing testimony to the crowd: "*This is my beloved Son.*" In our dispensation, Heavenly Father personally introduced his Son in a grove we now call sacred, to a kneeling and pleading farm boy who would become the great Prophet of the Restoration. That introduction consisted of eight simple words: "Joseph, This is My Beloved Son, Hear Him!" (Joseph Smith—History 1:17). President Gordon B. Hinckley said, "Do you realize the import of that declaration? Here was God the Eternal Father, the Almighty, bearing testimony in words plainly spoken. No more important or compelling testimony has been given of the risen Lord than this testimony of his own Father."[37] Following President Hinckley's pattern, the inclusion of the baptism and transfiguration testimonies from God himself constitute the most important and compelling witness of Jesus's divinity compared to all others presented in the biblical records.

Jesus as Son of Man

In all four Gospels, one of Jesus's most common ways of referring to himself was the title "Son of man." This term appears eighty-five times in the Gospels and four other times elsewhere in the New Testament. It is a particularly important title in Matthew, appearing thirty-two times in this Gospel as opposed to fifteen times in Mark, twenty-six in Luke, and twelve times in John.[38] Latter-day Saint readers have often been prepared in advance to see this title as a testimony of Jesus's divinity, particularly because James E. Talmage (1862–1933), a noted LDS author and long-time member of the Twelve, connected the expression "the Son of Man" with passages of Restoration scripture that identify God the Father as "Man of Holiness" (see Moses 6:57 and 7:35; compare D&C 78:20 and 95:17).[39] For us, the fact that Jesus was the actual Son of God with divine authority to teach, act, and eventually conquer sin and death is a given, and certain instances of Jesus's use of this phrase that seem to center on his authority may be particularly good examples of this. For example, at the healing of the man with palsy, Jesus proclaims, "But that ye may know that the Son of man hath power on earth to forgive sins, (then saith he to the sick of the palsy,) Arise, take up thy bed, and go unto thine house" (Matthew 9:6). Similarly, Jesus's teaching that he was lord of the Sabbath day or had come to save that which was lost (Matthew 12:8; 18:11) might be further instances of this usage.

Nevertheless, without the benefit of Restoration insights, Jesus's listeners and perhaps even Matthew's readers might not have been prepared to understand Son of Man as the equivalent of Son of God. In fact, when the equivalent of this phrase was used in the Old Testament, it had two different possible meanings, and scholars have struggled to understand the title's history and New Testament usage.[40] From this perspective, the title itself is notoriously ambiguous. On the one hand, in the Old Testament it generally refers to someone who is mortal (e.g., Psalm 8:4; Isaiah 51:12; and throughout the book of Ezekiel). On the other hand, the eschatological, or "last days," figure described in Daniel 7:13 and 8:17 as "one like the son of man" who would come "with the clouds of heaven" led many Jews in the intertestamental period to expect a glorious, heavenly figure to return at the end of the world.[41] Both of these meanings seem to have been important for Matthew.

During his ministry, some instances of this title seem to have portrayed Jesus as having a typical, and sometimes more humble than usual, mortal experience: for example, he is portrayed as being homeless (Matthew 8:20) or somehow scandalizing the religious establishment for enjoying normal human comforts such as food and drink more than did the ascetic disciples of John the Baptist (11:19). The frequency of Son of Man references increased as Jesus traveled to Jerusalem for his final week when his so-called passion predictions increasingly stressed his imminent suffering and death. An example of this is found in Matthew 17:22–23: "And while they abode in Galilee, Jesus said unto them, The Son of man shall be betrayed into the hands of men: And they shall kill him, and the third day he shall be raised again. And they were exceeding sorry" (see also Matthew 16:13, 21–23; 20:17–19). Other allusions to Jesus's betrayal and death (e.g., 12:40; 20:18, 28), together with these passion predictions, prepare the readers for the conclusion of Matthew's Gospel, which consists of his passion and resurrection narratives (26:1–28:20). Just as Matthew's infancy narrative answers christological questions of *who* Jesus was, Matthew's concluding sections answer the major question of what he came to *do*, and several of the remaining Son of Man references in this section center on Jesus's betrayal, suffering, and crucifixion (see 26:2, 24, 45).

Immediately after Jesus gave up the ghost on the cross, "the veil of the temple was rent in twain from the top to the bottom; and the earth did quake, and the rocks rent" (Matthew 27:51; parallels Mark 15:38; Luke 23:45). Much has been written regarding the practical and symbolic significance of this veil rending. R. T. France noted "the fact that such a tall curtain is torn from the top rather than from below indicates that this is God's work." He continued, "The tearing of the curtain suggests that as Jesus dies the transfer of authority from the old temple-focused regime (which has been responsible for his death) to the shortly-to-be-vindicated Son of Man is already taking place." Ultimately, this would mean that "access to God will no longer be through the old, discredited cultic system but through Jesus himself, and more specifically through his death as a ransom for many."[42] T. J. Geddert listed thirty-five possible interpretive suggestions[43] for this event, including one that would have possibly held more meaning for Matthew's audience than those in Mark's or Luke's communities. The groaning of the earth and rending of the covering veil could be interpreted as heavenly responses from a heartbroken Father since the Jewish people were familiar with the practice of rending garments and deep lamenting at the suffering or death of a loved one.

The most common uses of Son of Man in Matthew, however, seem to be eschatological. An example of this is found in Matthew 16:27–28: "For the Son of man shall come in the glory of his Father with his angels; and then he shall reward every man according to his works. Verily I say unto you, There be some standing here, which shall not taste of death, till they see the Son of man coming in his kingdom" (see also Matthew 10:23; 13:41; 16:27, 28; 19:28; 24:27, 30, 37, 39, 44; 25:13, 31; 26:64). Occurring throughout Jesus's ministry, such passages function to remind readers that despite Jesus's suffering and death, he will not only rise from the grave but also one day return in glory. As with other uses of the Son of Man title, Matthew has more eschatological uses than the other Gospels. In line with this, he presents a significantly longer version of Jesus's Mount of Olives discourse, in which he prophesied of the coming destruction of Jerusalem and the eventual destruction of the wicked at the end of days. While Mark's version consists of one tightly written chapter (Mark 13:1–37), Matthew's consists of two that include more detail and additional parables of preparation and judgment (Matthew 24:1–25:46).

"I Am with You Alway"

By looking closely at Matthew's presentation of Jesus in view of his intended audience and his Gospel's focus, we are able to better understand his unique testimony of Jesus Christ. Through his infancy narrative, he stressed that Jesus was the actual Son of God, something that various witnesses and Jesus himself attest throughout the Gospel. His use of the Old Testament and his connection of Jesus to the respected figures of David and Moses helped form a foundation for building faith among his Jewish followers to accept Jesus as the Son of Man and the Son of God, sent here to save us. While it is helpful to use a historical perspective to interpret and understand a book of scripture, we can easily get so caught up in the ancient world that we forget to bridge the gaps of time, space, and culture between our world and theirs. A powerful part of Matthew's testimony of Christ is not reserved for history; it is found in *our* story. Matthew and other writers of scripture provide us with a set of lenses through which we can see Jesus in a particular culture and time, interacting with real people with real problems who desperately need divine help in fulfilling their earthly missions. But we can each find ourselves and lasting solutions in these accounts by applying these texts to ourselves and looking for the Lord's hand in our own lives. Even though Matthew's original words and primary audience are two thousand years removed from us, when we understand his intended meanings, overarching purposes, and literary techniques, we see that Jesus's promises are not bound by space or limited by time. "Where two or three are gathered together in my name, there am I in the midst of them" (Matthew 18:20) is just as true for us today as it was for Matthew's original audience.

One of many examples of this principle can be found in Jesus's judgment before Pilate. On that occasion, the leaders of the Jews had to decide whether they wanted Jesus or a "notable prisoner" named Barabbas released and freely forgiven (Matthew 27:16). Barabbas had been charged with sedition, murder, and robbery (see Luke 23:18–19).[44] The contrast was clear: the people were asked to choose between an insurrectionist and a peacemaker, between one who took life and one who gave it, between one who stole (see John 18:40) and one who freely gave to others. The crowd demanded that Barabbas be released and Jesus be crucified. It is easy to feel unkind feelings toward Barabbas. He was guilty but got released while an innocent Jesus was punished. Symbolically speaking, however, this is *our* story! In a sense, *we* are Barabbas. We are guilty and deserve punishment, yet we can be released because Jesus suffered in our place. When seen in this light, Jesus is no longer defined impersonally as the son of David, or son of Abraham, or as the New Moses. He becomes the personable Son of God who says, "Come unto me, all ye that labour and are heavy laden, and I will give you rest" (Matthew 11:28).

Like John, Matthew ends his Gospel by saying nothing about the ascension. He goes one step further than John, however, by showing that "for those of us who believe in him, keep his commandments, and trust in his promises, he is ever with us."[45] Matthew's ending is a fitting conclusion to his monumental witness of Jesus Christ as Emmanuel, or God with us. "Go ye therefore, and teach *all nations,* . . . teaching them to observe all things whatsoever I have commanded you: and, lo *I am with you alway, even unto the end of the world.* Amen" (Matthew 28:19–20; emphasis added).

TYLER J. GRIFFIN *is an associate teaching professor of ancient scripture at Brigham Young University.*

Notes

1. This paper would not have been possible without Eric Huntsman's many hours of mentoring, encouraging, and editing during the research, writing, and revisions of this chapter. Thanks also to Nicholas Frederick for his suggestions and support at critical points along the way.

    To see how the Gospels were ordered in various collections, see Edgar J. Goodspeed, *The Formation of the New Testament* (Chicago: University of Chicago Press, 1926), 187–203; Bruce M. Metzger, *The Canon of the New Testament* (Oxford: Clarendon, 1987), 296–97. See also Amy Easton-Flake, "Marcan Christology: Narrating the Christ," in this volume.

2. See Richard Neitzel Holzapfel, Eric D. Huntsman, and Thomas A. Wayment, *Jesus Christ and the World of the New Testament* (Salt Lake City: Deseret Book, 2006), 62–63.

3. The overwhelming consensus up through the middle of the nineteenth century was that Matthew was written first. "For more than a century after that it became the almost unquestioned scholarly consensus that Mark came first and that Matthew and Luke drew on Mark and on . . . a single lost document to which they both had access." R. T. France, *The Gospel of Matthew* (Grand Rapids, MI: Eerdmans, 2007), 20. More recent scholarship has shown the data to be too multifaceted and complex for a clean-cut, two-document hypothesis. Many scholars still believe in the priority of Mark, but they leave room for all the Gospel writers to be influenced by each other over time. For a useful introduction to the nuanced issues involved, see Mark Goodacre, *The Synoptic Problem: A Way through the Maze* (London: T&T Clark, 2001).

4. This is owing to the attribution of authorship to Matthew in key early Christian manuscripts (א, B, D, L, W, f^1, f^{13}, *Byz*, L) as well as to information provided by important early Christian writers such as Irenaeus (*Adv. Haer.* 3.1.1) and Eusebius (*Eccl. Hist.* 3.39.16, 6.14.6, 6.25.4).

5. R. T. France, *Matthew: Evangelist and Teacher* (Downers Grove, IL: InterVarsity Press, 1989), 71.

6. John Nolland, *The Gospel of Matthew*, The New International Greek Testament Commentary (Grand Rapids, MI: Eerdmans, 2005), 29–33.

In these pages, Nolland also noted that "there is an obvious likelihood that [Matthew] knows the OT in Greek." Matthew's usage of Old Testament passages is difficult to categorize, however, because he uses at least "fourteen different approaches to the generation of the wording of the quotations, . . . the overall impression is of a man who freshly scrutinizes [OT texts] . . . in Greek, Hebrew (not always the Hebrew of the preserved MT), and occasionally in Aramaic." For further verification of this, France observed that the Gospel of Matthew "as a whole does not read like translation Greek. The clearly Semitic turns of phrase and other features suggesting an Aramaic origin are largely confined to the sayings-material rather than to the narrative." France, *Matthew: Evangelist and Teacher*, 63–64. This conclusion was first introduced by Matthew Black, *An Aramaic Approach to the Gospels and Acts* (Oxford: Clarendon, 1967), 271–74. Matthew's writing clearly reflects familiarity with multiple language traditions and an ability to draw conclusions and applications from a wide variety of linguistic forms.

7.   Mark only did this once (Mark 15:28), and Luke did it twice (Luke 4:21; 24:44). John included seven such statements, all situated within the last twenty-four hours of Jesus's mortal life (John 12:38; 13:18; 15:25; 17:12; 19:24, 28, 36), with Jesus himself making the first four connections. See F. P. Viljoen, "Fulfilment in Matthew," *Verbum et Ecclesia* 28, no. 1 (2007): 301–24.

8.   No other New Testament author used the title Emmanuel. For a useful study of how Matthew's Gospel interprets Hebrew Bible prophecy, see David L. Turner, *Matthew* (Grand Rapids, MI: Baker Academic Books, 2008), 68–73. For this specific prophecy, see Jason R. Combs, "From King Ahaz's Sign to Christ Jesus: The 'Fulfillment' of Isaiah 7:14," in *Prophets and Prophecies of the Old Testament*, ed. Aaron P. Schade, Brian M. Hauglid, and Kerry Muhlestein (Provo, UT: Religious Studies Center; Salt Lake City: Deseret Book, 2017), 95–122.

9.   See LDS Bible Dictionary, "Gospels," 653.

10. Holzapfel, Huntsman, and Wayment, *Jesus Christ and the World of the New Testament*, 67–69.

11. There is some debate that adoptionist ideals did not emerge until late in the second century. For more evidence on this, see Michael F. Bird, *Jesus the Eternal Son: Answering Adoptionist Christology* (Grand Rapids, MI: Eerdmans, 2017).

12. For example, there are many similarities between the baby Jesus and a young Moses that will be discussed later. Matthew's account shows the new star prophecy in Numbers 24:15–19 being fulfilled. The visit of the magi fulfills elements of prophecy found in Psalm 72:10–11, 15; Isaiah 60:3–6; and Micah 5:2. Joseph saving the young child from death by fleeing to Egypt is one way to apply Exodus 4:19 to Jesus's story.

13. Raymond E. Brown, *Birth of the Messiah* (New York: Doubleday, 1999), 53.

14. John's Gospel also uses a genesis prologue but does so to identify Jesus as an incarnate God.

15. Brown, *Birth of the Messiah*, 67.

16. John the Baptist noted that some of the Pharisees were probably relying too much on their pedigree relation to Abraham for salvation when he said, "Think not to say within yourselves, We have Abraham to our father: for I say unto you, that God is able of these stones to raise up children unto Abraham" (Matthew 3:9).

17. Even though symbolic connections between the Father and Son in the New Testament and Abraham and Isaac in the Old Testament are not unique to Matthew's Gospel, his audience would have been the most likely to recognize such associations. Both sons were born through miraculous and divine intervention; neither birth should have been possible. Both pregnancies were heralded by heavenly messengers. Both sons were beloved by their fathers. The ultimate promises of future increase in posterity, possessions, and power could only be realized for each of the fathers through their sons' willingness to fulfill their purposes and foreordained roles. Both sons would carry the wood for their offering and be offered on or near Mount Moriah. Both sons questioned their fathers regarding the requirements for the sacrifice at critical points in both stories. Even if Matthew's original audience missed these symbolic connections between Jesus and Abraham, Jacob 4:4–5 makes a direct tie between them.

18. Eric D. Huntsman, *Good Tidings of Great Joy* (Salt Lake City: Deseret Book, 2011), 22.

19. Huntsman, *Good Tidings of Great Joy*, 20.

20. For a discussion on the differences between the Matthean and Lucan genealogies, see Brown, *Birth of the Messiah*, 84–94.

21. John Nolland said, "There has been an extended but inconclusive debate about the precise reason for the inclusion of these women. Is there a single perspective from which each is included, and, if so, is Mary to be included under the same perspective?" Nolland, *Gospel of Matthew*, 73.

22. Another possibility is connected with the fact that all five women mentioned had unique or unusual relationships with their partners. For expansion of these and other possibilities, see Brown, *Birth of the Messiah*, 73–74.

23. France, *Matthew: Evangelist and Teacher*, 53, notes that this interpretation of saving from sin would make sense to Joseph as well as Matthew's readers only if they understood the underlying meaning of the Hebrew name. Furthermore, *Yehôshua* is translated as "Joshua" in English. It was the Old Testament Joshua who took Moses's place and led the tribes of Israel into the promised land. A first-century Jewish-Christian audience would have likely recognized the angel's christological connections between *Yehôshua*, the adopted son of Joseph, and Joshua as Moses's successor. An understanding of Jewish scripture would also have allowed Matthew's audience to make connections between Jesus's saving work and that of YHWH in the Old Testament.

24. By contrast, the name "Jesus" appears 983 times, and the title "Christ" appears 555 times. King Saul's name appears 394 times, and Solomon is mentioned only 281 times. Moses's name appears 848 times, and Abraham/Abram is listed 285 times.

25. See the survey of Old Testament and intertestamental messianic scholarship by Stanley E. Porter, *The Messiah in the Old and New Testaments* (Grand Rapids, MI: Eerdmans, 2007), 4–6.

26. See "Son of David" in the appendix.

27. Brown, *Birth of the Messiah*, 132, 139; Huntsman, *Good Tidings of Great Joy*, 32–33.

28. *Dalet* is the fourth letter of the Hebrew alphabet, and *vav* is the sixth letter; 4 + 6 + 4 = 14.

29. For other possible explanations for the 3 x 14 pattern, see Brown, *Birth of the Messiah*, 74–80.

30. Jesus validated this direct tie to Moses when he told the Nephites and Lamanites, "Behold, I am he of whom Moses spake, saying: A prophet shall the Lord your God raise up unto you of your brethren, like unto me; him shall ye hear in all things whatsoever he shall say unto you" (3 Nephi 20:23).

31. For more details concerning the Book of Mormon statements connecting Jesus with Moses, see S. Kent Brown, "Moses and Jesus: The Old Adorns the New," in *From Jerusalem to Zarahemla: Literary and Historical Studies of the Book of Mormon* (Provo, UT: Religious Studies Center, 1998), 157–68, https://rsc.byu.edu/archived/jerusalem-zarahemla -literary-and-historical-studies-book-mormon/moses-and-jesus -old-adorns.

32. For discussions of how Hebrew Bible prophecies were used by New Testament authors (and how we as modern readers often continue to interpret them), see Nicholas J. Frederick, "The Use of the Old Testament in the New Testament Gospels," in *Prophets and Prophecies of the Old Testament*, 123–60.

33. See France, *Matthew: Evangelist and Teacher*, 143, and Holzapfel, Huntsman, and Wayment, *Jesus Christ and the World of the New Testament*, 63–65.

34. This declaration of Jesus as Son of God is not unique to Matthew (see also Mark 15:39). Luke 23:47 records it differently: "Certainly this was a righteous man."

35. For a sample list of potential sources the Sanhedrin might have used to condemn Jesus on legal grounds, see Leviticus 24:15–16; Deuteronomy 13:1–5; 17:2–7; 18:20–22.

36. Mark's and Luke's accounts reflect the wording from Psalms 2:7.

37. Russell Holt, *Special Witnesses of Christ* (Salt Lake City: The Church of Jesus Christ of Latter-day Saints, 2000), DVD.

38. See "Son of Man" in the appendix.

39. James E. Talmage, *Jesus the Christ* (1915; repr. Salt Lake City: Deseret Book, 1982), 143–44, 151.

40. See, for example, the sometimes differing discussions of Larry Hurtado, *Lord Jesus Christ: Devotion to Jesus in Earlier Christianity* (Grand Rapids, MI: Eerdmans, 2003), 290–306; Simon J. Gathercole, *The Preexistent Son: Recovering the Christologies of Matthew, Mark, and Luke* (Grand Rapids, MI: Eerdmans, 2006), 253–71; and Adela Yarbro Collins and John J. Collins, *King and Messiah as Son of God: Divine, Human, and Angelic Messianic Figures in Biblical and Related Literatures* (Grand Rapids, MI: Eerdmans, 2008), 75–100.

41. See Collins and Collins, *King and Messiah as Son of God*, 78–97.

42. France, *Matthew: Evangelist and Teacher*, 1080–81.

43. T. J. Geddert, *Watchwords: Mark 13 in Markan Eschatology*, Journal for the Study of the New Testament Supplement 26 (Sheffield: Sheffield Academic Press, 1989), 140–45.

44. Luke and John both mentioned this man's name once. Mark mentioned him three times. In comparison, Matthew prolonged this story and specifically referred to Barabbas five times, perhaps emphasizing Pilate's hesitancy to kill an innocent man.

45. Eric D. Huntsman, *God So Loved the World* (Salt Lake City: Deseret Book, 2011), 118–19.

6

Marcan Christology
Narrating the Christ

Amy Easton-Flake

Halfway through the Gospel of Mark, Jesus asks his disciples, "Whom do men say that I am?" (Mark 8:27) and then more piercingly, "But whom say ye that I am?" (8:29). Perhaps the earliest of the Gospels to have been written and likely a major source for both Matthew and Luke, the narrative of Mark presents a powerful christological understanding of Jesus's identity and salvific work. It loosely fits the genre of a first-century Roman biography, which has been defined as a "prose narration about a person's life, presenting supposedly historical facts which are selected to reveal the character or essence of the individual, often with the purpose of affecting the behavior of the reader."[1] Its fast-moving, vivid, action-packed story invites the reader into the narrative world to experience Jesus's mortal ministry and crucifixion through the perspective of his disciples. Mark's presentation of Jesus is also generally considered to be the most human and relatable portrait of Jesus because of the range of strong emotions Jesus displays.[2] At the same time, however, Mark's portrait of Jesus invites awe and wonder at Jesus's divinity, thus making Jesus's dualism as both human and divine a central aspect of the Marcan Jesus.[3]

While there are many ways to explore Mark's presentation of Jesus, the compelling story aspect of Mark's Gospel makes the use of a narrative lens particularly apt. By considering the work of scholars who take seriously Mark's narrative Christology—what Jesus says and does in the context of the narrative and actions of others—Latter-day Saints can gain new insights into Mark's presentation of Jesus. Through a focused, close reading of the scriptures, we can come to see a Savior who is fully human and fully divine; who experiences and portrays strong human emotions as he teaches, provides miracles, and challenges perceptions; and who acts as the model disciple, showing us all the necessity of service, suffering, and sacrifice.

Background of the Gospel of Mark

Though formally anonymous, early Christian tradition attributed this Gospel to John Mark and suggested that it was written in Rome (AD 60–75) as a record of Peter's teachings.[4] In the early centuries of Christianity, the Gospel of Mark was often overshadowed by the other Gospels because it was seen as an abbreviated version of Matthew. Its increase in popularity and scholarly attention in the nineteenth and twentieth centuries is largely due to the reversal of the traditional view that Matthew was the earliest Gospel.[5] Most New Testament scholars today favor Marcan priority because of the way the Gospels of Matthew and Luke follow the Marcan wording and ordering of events.[6] In recent years, scholars have also come to appreciate the Gospel of Mark as a carefully crafted story—most likely shared orally—that presents its own theological themes and understanding of Jesus.[7] Close analysis of the text reveals that Mark's Gospel is a highly structured literary work with a three-stage geographical progression, topical ordering of events, intercalation or sandwiching (placing one story within another), triads or sets of three, repetition, parallel scenes, foreshadows and echoes, and vivid details.[8] Each of these elements makes the text more memorable and performable, and collectively they indicate that Mark's Gospel was likely constructed as an oral text and performed multiple times before being written down.[9]

The Gospel of Mark had its beginning in an oral culture.[10] In first-century Mesopotamia, storytelling was ubiquitous, writing was largely seen as a representation of speech, oral communication was considered true communication, and people wrote to transfer oral stories rather than to replace oral performances.[11] Scholars estimate that in the ancient Roman Empire only between 5 and 10 percent of the people—mostly wealthy elites—were able to read or write in the first century; consequently, the vast majority of people experienced everything they learned aurally.[12] As Whitney Shriner reports, "Good speakers were admired and attracted the sorts of large crowds that we would associate with rock stars. Crowds would fill up theaters to hear a famous rhetorician from out of town."[13] Performance of sacred stories was also an important part of worship services, and letters such as those written by Paul would have been performed for their intended recipients.[14] Most people would have experienced the Gospel of Mark as an engaging two-hour performance because they had neither access to the text nor the ability to read it.[15]

From Titles to Narrative Christology

Recognizing that the Gospel of Mark most likely originally functioned as an oral story has important implications for our understanding and study of Mark's Gospel and its portrait of Jesus. First, this recognition invites a perceptual shift to consider the many aspects that make up a performative event: the storyteller, audience, location, sociohistorical circumstances, and rhetorical impact. The interpretive process largely shifts from the reader to the performer as the presentation of Jesus depends a great deal on who is telling the story. How does Jesus sound? What is his tone? What clues or suggestions does the text offer as a script for storytelling performances?[16] Second, it reinforces the importance of studying Mark's portrayal of Jesus from a narrative vantage point since the Gospel of Mark was intended to be experienced as a single story in a single sitting.

Earlier discussions on New Testament Christology focused almost exclusively on the titles for Christ found within the Gospels—namely, Son of God, Son of Man, Christ, and Lord—and what these titles revealed when placed within a historical or theological context.[17] While there is still value to such christological approaches, innovative approaches to the Gospels help us to see and understand the person and work of Jesus in new ways. Since Robert Tannehill introduced the term *narrative Christology* in 1979,[18] many scholars have begun looking at Mark's narrative holistically, arguing that Jesus can be grasped only within the narrative.[19] As M. Eugene Boring states simply, "Mark's narrative is already a Christology."[20] In essence, advocates of narrative Christology believe that "we learn who Jesus is through what he says and does in the context of the actions of others."[21] In other words, the narrator of Mark's Gospel does not offer many evaluative words or judgments of Jesus, preferring instead to show who Jesus is through his actions and dialogue and others' actions and dialogue in relation to him. Other aspects to consider when analyzing Mark's portrayal of Jesus are what drives and motivates Jesus, what his traits are, how they are illuminated by comparison or contrast with other characters, and what Jesus seeks and works for.[22] Narrative structure and plot must also be given due consideration as they too may reveal character.

A strength of narrative Christology, as pointed out by Boring, is its ability to hold ideas in tension and "allow paradox without synthesis."[23] Mark, for instance, composes a narrative in which Jesus is presented as both divine and human without qualification or dilution.[24] As Jacob Naluparayil writes, "The use of the narrative method produces an overall tendency to incorporate the different aspects of the Marcan presentation of Jesus instead of stressing one aspect at the expense of others."[25] This in turn allows us to see Jesus in his full complexity. Another strength of the narrative approach is the recognition that this is someone's depiction of Christ. Even though Jesus was a real, historical figure, any story that one hears of him is necessarily mediated through the teller.[26] This recognition encourages us to seek out and learn from the different portraits of Jesus offered by a myriad of individuals in the Bible, the Book of Mormon, and other Restoration scripture. Each of us—including the Gospel writers—has experienced Christ differently in our lives, and the narrative approach allows us to celebrate and learn from these differences rather than dismiss them. I begin with an analysis of Mark's narrative Christology in Mark 1 to illustrate how a close, careful reading of the text illuminates Mark's portrait of Jesus.

God's Beloved, Obedient Son

The prologue to Mark's Gospel (Mark 1:1–15) establishes Jesus's significance and prepares the audience to trust Jesus through statements made by the narrator, by John the Baptist, and by God. With the opening line, "The beginning of the gospel of Jesus Christ, the Son of God" (1:1), the narrator establishes Jesus as the central figure of his story. The opening line acts as a title for the work[27] and is highly distinctive as the only place where the narrator pronounces a direct, generalized assessment of Jesus—elsewhere, the narrator prefers to show who Jesus is through actions and dialogues and to place assessments of Jesus in the mouths of the characters.[28] At the outset of the story, however, the narrator wants to make it known that Jesus is "Christ or the anointed one"[29] and "the Son of God," but what these titles mean in the first century is highly debatable and becomes clear only as we explore the narrative as a whole.[30] The next assessment of Jesus is uttered by John the Baptist: "There cometh one mightier than I after me, the latchet of whose shoes I am not worthy to stoop down and unloose. I indeed have baptized you with water: but he shall baptize you with the Holy Ghost" (1:7–8). John's statement establishes Jesus's importance and authority as greater than that of a prophet and prepares us for what God will say about Jesus after his baptism: "Thou art my beloved Son, in whom I am well pleased" (1:11). God's proclamation of Jesus as his Son confirms the narrator's assessment of Jesus and is crucial to establishing Jesus's authority and the narrator's credibility.[31] Both can now be trusted because God, the highest authority in Mark's narrative world, has ratified Jesus's status as his Son. Thus, by the time Jesus speaks his first words, "The time is fulfilled, and the kingdom of God is at hand: repent ye, and believe the gospel" (1:15), the audience is prepared to listen to him and trust whatever he may say or do.

Looking closely at what Jesus says and does in chapter 1 of Mark's Gospel reveals Jesus's basic character. First, Jesus is obedient to God. His first act, baptism (Mark 1:9), signals his submission to God; and his second act, being "driven" by the Spirit into the wilderness (1:12), confirms his willingness to be obedient to God even when it is difficult. Significantly, God's pronouncement of Jesus as the one he loves and with whom he is "well pleased" (1:11) comes after Jesus has displayed his obedience by being baptized. Mark's concise version of Jesus's forty days in the wilderness—mentioning only that "angels ministered unto him" and Satan "tempted" him (1:13)—helps the audience see Jesus on a cosmic scale as he associates with immortal beings. It also announces a major theme of Mark's Gospel: Jesus is at battle with Satan and Satan's dominion.[32] After the trial in the wilderness, we have Jesus's first spoken utterance: "The time is fulfilled, and the kingdom of God is at hand: repent ye, and believe the gospel" (1:15). This is a significant line because it encapsulates what Jesus cares about: teaching the gospel and preparing people for "the kingdom of God." As David Rhoads, Joanna Dewey, and Donald Michie write, it also "discloses his understanding of himself as an agent of God and his purposes."[33] His next spoken line, uttered as he calls his first disciples, Simon and Andrew, propels this motif of repentance and preparation for God's kingdom forward as it indicates Jesus's role in the process. It is by following Jesus as the enabler—"Come ye after me, and I will make you to become fishers of men" (1:17)—that we may become something more than we are, that we may become whom he sees us as. Simon, Andrew, James, and John were fishermen until Jesus gave them a vision of what more they could be and suggested a path forward. Other foundational aspects of Jesus's character as a teacher, healer, and exorcist are set forth in rapid succession, as Mark moves quickly from one act of Jesus's to the next. Jesus teaches (1:21–22), casts out an unclean spirit (1:23–27), heals Simon's mother-in-law (1:30–31), heals the sick and casts out devils (1:32–34), departs to a solitary place to pray (1:35), preaches (1:39), casts out devils again (1:39), and heals a leper (1:40–45). Throughout all these actions, Mark emphasizes Jesus's authority and the crowd's astonishment.

By the end of chapter 1, Mark has established the image of Jesus's identity and salvific work that informs the first half of the story. Jesus is God's beloved, obedient Son, who acts to further God's kingdom through preaching and healing. Significantly, this image of Jesus will likely resonate with most believers' understanding of Christ because the similarities among the Gospel writers' Christologies are greater than their dissimilarities.

Mark's More Human Jesus

However, as we continue to pay close attention to what Jesus says and does and what others say about him, we will find in Mark a more human Jesus—a more emotional and harder-to-define Jesus—than that found in the other canonical Gospels, which will enrich our understanding of the Savior of the world. Mark's understanding of Jesus as one who felt and portrayed strong emotions may come as a surprise to the many individuals who picture an always composed and never ruffled Jesus—such as that presented in *The Life of Jesus Christ Bible Videos* made by The Church of Jesus Christ of Latter-day Saints. Notably, these moments of human realism in Mark are often omitted or toned down in the Gospels of Matthew and Luke.[34] For instance, Matthew and Luke omit the compassion that Jesus feels toward a leper that he heals—"And Jesus, moved with *compassion* [or *pity* in the New International Version],[35] put forth his hand, and touched him" (Mark 1:40–41; emphasis added; cf. Matthew 8:1–2; Luke 5:12–13)—as well as the love that Jesus feels for the rich young man—"Then Jesus beholding him *loved* him" (Mark 10:21; emphasis added; cf. Matthew 19:16–22; Luke 18:18–22). Matthew and Luke also do not mention Jesus's anger, such as the anger he feels toward the Pharisees for questioning the lawfulness of healing a man with a withered hand on the Sabbath—"And when he had looked round about on them with *anger*, being *grieved* [or *deeply distressed* in the NIV] for the hardness of their hearts" (Mark 3:5; emphasis added; cf. Matthew 12:9–14; Luke 6:6–11)—and the displeasure Jesus feels when the disciples forbid the little children to come unto him—"But when Jesus saw it, he was much *displeased* [*indignant* in the NIV and the New Revised Standard Version or *angry* in the Common English Bible and the Good News Translation]" (Mark 10:14; emphasis added; cf. Matthew 19:13–15; Luke 18:15–17). The moment when Jesus expresses surprise at the Nazarenes' unbelief is also omitted in the Gospels of Matthew and Luke—"And he *marveled* [*was appalled* in the CEB, *greatly surprised* in the GNT, *was amazed* in the NIV] because of their unbelief" (Mark 6:6; emphasis added; cf. Matthew 13:53–58; Luke 4:16–30). Jesus's desire for solitude and need to commune with God for strength and direction is also more apparent in Mark's narrative (Mark 1:35; 6:45–46).

As illustrated above, reading other translations may help us gain a better sense of the strong emotions that Jesus displays because the early modern English of the King James Version may in some instances mask Jesus's emotions to readers' contemporary ears. One example of this is when Jesus expresses his frustration at his apostles' inability to cast a spirit out of a young boy or, more likely, his frustration at the general lack of faith he perceives in all of Israel—"O faithless generation, how long shall I be with you? How long shall I suffer you?" (Mark 9:19). The much more prevalent translation of this statement—"You faithless generation, how much longer must I be among you? How much longer must I put up with you?" (Mark

9:19 NRSV)—changes the tone of Jesus's statement and makes his frustration much more palpable, as it seems he is being compelled to be with them—"how much longer must I"—rather than choosing to be with them. These differences in tone may be simply the result of our disconnect from early modern English or they may reflect a desire on the part of the King James translators, similar to that of the authors of Matthew and Luke, to soften Mark's portrayal of Jesus. Mark's portrayal of a more expressive Jesus, however, should be appreciated and studied because it provides a more relatable Jesus who has felt the emotions that we all commonly experience.

Both Human and Divine

One of the most notable aspects of Mark's Christology, however, is how he depicts a Christ that is both divine and human without qualification or dilution. In a narrative these oppositional aspects may exist together uncontested in a way that they could not in a theological treatise because the story may simply highlight different aspects at different moments.

Jesus's divinity may be seen most clearly in his actions and others' reactions to him. Jesus's power to heal and cast out spirits is a tangible manifestation of his divinity and authority from God. The other miracles he performs, such as calming the seas (Mark 4:38–41), walking on water (6:47–51), feeding the five thousand and four thousand (6:34–44; 8:1–9), raising Jarius's daughter from the dead (5:35–43), and—perhaps most significant—forgiving sins (2:5), are also manifestations of his divinity and authority. The most common reaction to Jesus, his teachings, and his works is astonishment and, for many, a desire to follow him.[36] Repeatedly throughout the Gospel, the narrator reports that all were astonished (1:22; 7:37; 10:24, 26; 11:18) or amazed (1:27; 2:12; 6:51; 9:15; 10:32) or that they marveled (5:20; 12:17; 15:5) because his teachings and works set him apart from any mortal being. Jesus also commonly evokes fear in his apostles as he shatters their understanding of what is possible when he calms the sea (4:41), walks on water (6:50), transfigures before them (9:2–6), and tells them of his life path to be killed and then rise the third day (9:31–32). In Mark's Christology, Jesus shares the human situation as a fellow human being even as he is the Son of God exercising divine power, evoking awe in all, and challenging mortal understanding. Such a display of seemingly contradictory elements shows how narrative Christology may incorporate the different aspects of the Marcan Jesus rather than flatten the multidimensional Jesus apparent within the text. For us readers, such a portrait is beneficial because it not only brings us much closer to the reality of Christ, which is of course complex, but it also helps us accept the complexity and paradoxes that invariably arise when we seek to more fully understand almost any aspect of theology.

Jesus's Understanding of Himself

Another important layer of Mark's Christology is ascertaining how Jesus sees himself. That Jesus sees himself as the agent through whom the kingdom of God is proclaimed and effected is clearly evident from the first line Jesus speaks—"The time is fulfilled, and the kingdom of God is at hand: repent ye, and believe the gospel" (Mark 1:15)—until his crucifixion on the cross.

While the Marcan Jesus is a Jesus of deeds, with Mark reporting the miracles of Jesus in the most fulsome and descriptive way of any of the Gospels and sharing Jesus teaching in parables and short, pithy statements rather the longer sermons and discourses reported in the other Gospels, Jesus emphasizes that he came primarily to teach. At the beginning of his ministry, Jesus tells Simon explicitly, "Let us go into the next towns, that I may preach there also: *for therefore came I forth*" (Mark 1:38; emphasis added); Mark portrays Jesus teaching or preaching more than any other act; and Jesus prioritizes his teaching over his healing. For instance, Jesus's desire for individuals not to share the miracles he performs seems to be motivated out of his desire to preach (see 1:43–45; 7:36–8:1). While news of his healings and miracles draws many people to him, it also seems to make it difficult at times for him to preach (1:45). On occasion, Mark depicts Jesus leaving the miracle-seeking crowds so that he may find other communities and individuals to share his message with (see 3:7–10; 6:31–34). Jesus also turns every situation into a teaching moment. For example, when his mother and brethren come seeking him, he uses it as a moment to explain a new conception of family—that all who do the will of God are Christ's family (3:31–35); when his disciples are disputing over who will be the greatest, he uses their concern to teach them what it actually means to be the greatest (9:33–35; 10:35–45); and when he sees the poor widow casting in her two mites, he uses her example to explain how God judges our actions and sacrifices (12:41–44).

Jesus Challenging Perceptions

Teaching is central to Jesus's mission because preparing people for the kingdom of God entails teaching them to see and judge as God does rather than as man does; consequently, the Jesus of Mark constantly challenges one perception after the other. One of the first religious practices that Jesus challenges is appropriate Sabbath-day observance. He does this first through his actions, as he performs his first two miracles (casting out a spirit and healing a disease) on the Sabbath (Mark 1:21–31). He later challenges the Pharisees' views of the Sabbath explicitly through dialogue after they condemn his disciples plucking ears of corn on the Sabbath and his healing a withered man's hand on the Sabbath because they viewed both as a form of work (2:23–3:5). Jesus uses these moments to teach the Pharisees that they have failed to understand what the Sabbath is for: "The sabbath was made for man, and not man for the sabbath" (2:27). Or in other words, the Sabbath is to give individuals rest from their troubles and worries; consequently, there could not be a more fitting time to heal someone.

Jesus also challenges Jewish purity laws (what makes a person clean or unclean). The catalyst for this discussion is when the Pharisees find fault with the disciples eating with unwashed hands

(Mark 7:1–5). Jesus uses their critique to first point out that they place the traditions of men above the commandments of God because the requirement to wash pots and cups before eating came from man, not God (7:6–9). He then goes on to redefine their understanding of what makes one clean or unclean when he proclaims, "There is nothing from without a man, that entering into him can defile him: but the things which come out of him, those are they that defile the man" (7:15). This statement shows Jesus to be revolutionary because if taken literally it essentially means that Jesus was nullifying a significant portion of the Levitical law code.[37] Cleanliness and purity were now to be determined by one's moral actions and attitude, not by one's eating or washing practices or those people one comes into contact with. Jesus taught this principle through his actions as well, as he regularly interacted with those who were considered unclean, such as sinners and those with various diseases (see 2:15–17). In this way, he also challenged the treatment of the marginalized and outcast. All were to be treated with kindness and invited to be part of the kingdom of God (2:17).

The most important perception Jesus alters is what it means for him to be the Christ and by extension what it means to be his disciple. Peter is correct when he answers Jesus's question "But whom say ye that I am?" with "Thou art the Christ" (Mark 8:29). But it is also clear from the text that Peter does not understand what it means for Jesus to be the Christ. This verse has often been seen as the turning point in Mark's Gospel because the rest of the Gospel may be seen as Mark's attempt to help his audience understand what it means for Jesus to be the Christ.[38] In many ways, being the Christ is not the glorious calling one would expect; instead, it is about suffering, sacrifice, and resurrection. Or as Jesus explains to his disciples, "the Son of man must suffer many things, and be rejected of the elders, and of the chief priests, and scribes, and be killed, and after three days rise again" (8:31). Here, Jesus radically redefines the role of the Messiah and then proceeds to radically redefine what it means to be his follower: "Whosoever will come after me, let him deny himself, and take up his cross, and follow me" (8:34). Clearly, this description of discipleship does not suggest ease and worldly accolades; instead, it asks disciples to forgo this world for the next and to follow his example of servant leadership. As Jesus will later explain to his disciples, "And whosoever of you will be the chiefest, shall be servant of all. For even the Son of man came not to be ministered unto, but to minister, and to give his life a ransom for many" (10:44–45).

Mark makes it clear that Jesus's disciples do not understand this message by juxtaposing Jesus's statements about his suffering and sacrifice with his disciples' continual desire for honor and prestige. The irony is palpable when Jesus's statement "The Son of man is delivered into the hands of men, and they shall kill him; and after that he is killed, he shall rise the third day" (Mark 9:31) is immediately followed by the disciples disputing among themselves who is the greatest (9:33–34). And then again a chapter later, when Jesus's statement "Behold, we go up to Jerusalem; and the Son of man shall be delivered unto the chief priests, and unto the scribes; and they shall condemn him to death, and shall deliver him to the Gentiles: And they shall mock him, and shall scourge him, and shall spit upon him, and shall kill him: and the third day he shall rise again" (10:33–34) is immediately followed by James and John asking to sit on his right hand and on his left hand in the next life (10:35–37). In both instances, Jesus uses their inappropriate question to reorient their understanding of what it means to be the greatest and what it means to have authority: "But whosoever will be great among you, shall be your minister: And whoever of you will be the chiefest, shall be servant of all" (10:43–44). Observant readers may note that these juxtaposed events are actually separate events that may not necessarily have taken place one after another. This observation should in turn highlight for readers that Mark has deliberately constructed his narrative to emphasize the disciples' inability to comprehend what Jesus was teaching them about his role as well as theirs. A possible reason for this is that Mark's Jesus teaches both in words and in actions that suffering, service, and sacrifice are essential aspects of being part of God's kingdom—"If any man desire to be first, the same shall be last of all, and servant of all" (9:35)—and his disciples' inability to comprehend Jesus's message about himself and his followers indicates just how radical, unexpected, and difficult his teachings were.

Jesus's Suffering

At the center of Mark's Christology is Jesus as the suffering servant who faithfully follows God's will and gives his life before rising three days later. He is the model disciple who shows us that service, suffering, and sacrifice are necessary qualifications for being part of God's kingdom. While this may be ascertained by looking at Jesus's words and actions, as we have discussed thus far, perhaps it is best emphasized by looking at Mark's basic narrative structure and plot. Mark's Gospel is generally divided into a prologue (Mark 1:1–1:13 [15]) followed by three major divisions: Jesus's authoritative ministry in and around Galilee (1:14 [16]–8:22 [26]), Jesus's journey to Jerusalem (8:27–10:52), and Jesus in Jerusalem (11:1–16:8).[39] Dividing Mark's Gospel in half is Jesus's crucial question to Peter, "But whom say ye that I am?" (8:29). In the first half of the narrative, Mark presents Jesus as the Messiah and Son of God, who teaches and acts with authority and power and grows in popularity. Miracle working, teaching, and challenging norms and perceptions are central to Mark's depiction of Jesus in the first half of the narrative and affirm that Jesus is indeed the Messiah. The second half of the narrative then shifts the focus to Jesus's suffering, death, and resurrection in order to reorient the meaning of being the Messiah.

That Mark wants the passion narrative—the account of Jesus's suffering, death, and resurrection—to be the center of his story is indicated by the fact that the narrative slows down significantly once Jesus enters Jerusalem. This fact has not been lost on readers, as Mark's Gospel has famously and repeatedly been described as "a passion narrative with an extended introduction" because Mark proportionally spends more time expounding on Jesus's suffering, death, and resurrection than any other Gospel writer.[40] As Donald H. Juel further explains, "One-third of Mark's Gospel is devoted to an account of Jesus's last few days [other scholars will more accurately list this as 40 percent].[41] One-sixth to his last twenty-four hours."[42] Up until this point, Mark's narrative has offered a fast-moving overview of the highlights of Jesus's ministry, but now the narrative moves slowly, offering a detailed look at the events leading to Jesus's death and resurrection. We see Jesus's escalating confrontations with the scribes and Pharisees as he continues to perform miracles, teach, and challenge accepted norms. Most moving is Mark's depiction of Jesus in Gethsemane, where we see a very human Jesus cry out to God his Father, "Abba, Father, all things are possible unto thee; take away this cup from me: nevertheless not what I will, but what thou wilt" (Mark 14:36).

Though Mark does not share the significance of what occurs in the Garden of Gethsemane (that is disclosed only in Restoration scripture), he does share an image of Jesus that encapsulates much of what Mark wants his audience to understand about Jesus: his faith, humility, and absolute obedience to God (Mark 14:36); his common humanity that allows him to feel that his "soul is exceeding sorrowful unto death" and causes him to shrink from the suffering and death that awaits him (14:33–35); his compassion towards and understanding of his disciples' human frailties (14:38–41); and his divinity that enables him to see the future and to meet it resolutely (14:41–49). This portrait is reinforced through Jesus's trials and time on the cross. With his death as the critical act, his last words—"My God, my God, why hast thou forsaken me?"—indicate the depth to which Jesus has had to suffer in order to be God's saving agent (15:34). Mark's very brief depiction of events after the resurrection—ending, as most scholars agree, with the women finding his empty tomb and being told by a messenger that Jesus is risen and to go and "tell his disciples and Peter that he goeth before you into Galilee: there shall ye see him, as he said unto you" (16:7) and their subsequent fear, amazement, and silence (16:8)[43]—keeps the narrative focused on the crucial acts of Jesus's death and resurrection. And the open, rather than closed, nature of the ending invites Mark's audience into the narrative to take the place of the women at the empty sepulchre and to share the message of Christ's crucifixion and resurrection.[44] Through the precision with which he constructs his narrative, and in particular that final week of Jesus's life, Mark has created his Christology.

Coming to Know Jesus through Mark

Jesus's question to Mark "But whom say ye that I am?" (Mark 8:29) is the crucial question for each of us. There are many ways that we may come to know that Jesus is the Christ—prayer, scripture study, experience, following the counsel of the Spirit, and modeling our life after Jesus all help us answer that piercing question. For many, a critical aspect of knowing that Jesus is the Christ is seeking to learn about and understand the mortal Messiah who lived two thousand years ago. Because each of the Gospels provides unique insights into Jesus's life, ministry, and death, a close, careful narrative reading of the texts helps reveal aspects of the text and Jesus's life that may otherwise remain unnoticed. In Mark's Gospel, we find a Savior who is fully human and fully divine. The Son of Man experiences and portrays strong emotions as he teaches, heals, and acts with divine authority and power. He is God's Beloved Son and the agent through whom the kingdom of God is proclaimed and effected. He is the suffering servant who faithfully follows God's will and gives his life before rising three days later. He is the model disciple who shows us all that service, suffering, and sacrifice are necessary qualifications for being part of God's kingdom. He is as declared in the opening line of the Gospel of Mark, "Jesus Christ, the Son of God" (1:1), and it is by coming to know him and following his example that we may become his disciples.

AMY EASTON-FLAKE *is an assistant professor of ancient scripture at Brigham Young University.*

Notes

1. Charles H. Talbert, *What Is a Gospel? The Genre of the Canonical Gospels* (Philadelphia: Fortress, 1977), 17. For more information on how Mark fits within the genre of first-century Roman biographies, see Ben Witherington III, *The Gospel of Mark: A Socio-Rhetorical Commentary* (Grand Rapids, MI: Eerdmans, 2001), 5–7; R. T. France, *The Gospel of Mark*, The New International Greek Testament Commentary (Grand Rapids, MI: Eerdmans, 2002), 5–6, 10; John R. Donahue and Daniel J. Harrington, *The Gospel of Mark*, Sacra Pagina 2 (Collegeville, MN: Liturgical Press, 2002), 14–15. Written in the vernacular of popular spoken Greek, the Gospel of Mark belongs more in the category of popular literature than the elite literary works scholars typically analyze. For more information, see Mary Ann Tolbert, *Sowing the Gospel: Mark's World in Literary-Historical Perspective* (Minneapolis: Augsburg Fortress, 1996), 70–78.

2. Scholars who discuss this include Mark L. Strauss, *Four Portraits, One Jesus: A Survey of Jesus and the Gospels* (Grand Rapids, MI: Zondervan, 2007), 294; John R. Donahue, "Jesus as the Parable of God in the Gospel of Mark," in *Interpreting the Gospels*, ed. James Luther Mays (Philadelphia: Fortress Press, 1981), 159–60; Stephen H. Smith, *A Lion with Wings: A Narrative-Critical Approach to Mark's Gospel* (Sheffield: Sheffield Academic Press, 1996), 58.

3. M. Eugene Boring, "The Christology of Mark: Hermeneutical Issues for Systematic Theology," *Semeia* 30 (1984): 138–39.

4. For a brief discussion of this, see Strauss, *Four Portraits*, 201; Witherington, *Gospel of Mark*, 24–26; France, *Gospel of Mark*, 7–8, 38–40.

5. For more information, see Strauss, *Four Portraits*, 173; Donahue and Harrington, *Gospel of Mark*, 3–4; France, *Gospel of Mark*, 15–16.

6. For more information, see Donahue and Harrington, *Gospel of Mark*, 4–5; Witherington, *Gospel of Mark*, 18–19.

7. For an extended discussion, see David Rhoads, Joanna Dewey, and Donald Michie, *Mark as Story: An Introduction to the Narrative of a Gospel*, 3rd ed. (Minneapolis: Fortress Press, 2012). For a brief overview, see France, *Gospel of Mark*, 16–20.

8.   For more information, see Strauss, *Four Portraits*, 174–77; Donahue and Harrington, *Gospel of Mark*, 16–19; France, *Gospel of Mark*, 11–14.

9.   Scholars who discuss this include Philip Ruge-Jones, "The Word Heard: How Hearing a Text Differs from Reading One," in *The Bible in Ancient and Modern Media: Story and Performance*, ed. Holly E. Hearon and Philip Ruge-Jones (Eugene, OR: Cascade, 2009), 102; Richard A. Horsley, "Oral and Written Aspects of the Emergence of the Gospel of Mark as Scripture," *Oral Tradition* 25, no. 1 (2010): 95; Joanna Dewey, *The Oral Ethos of the Early Church: Speaking, Writing, and the Gospel of Mark* (Eugene, OR: Cascade, 2013), 158–60; France, *Gospel of Mark*, 9–10.

10. Some of the best works on this issue include Whitney Shriner, *Proclaiming the Gospel: First-Century Performance of Mark* (Harrisburg, PA: Trinity Press, 2003); Dewey, *Oral Ethos*; Hearon and Ruge-Jones, *Bible in Ancient and Modern Media*.

11. For more information, see Dewey, *Oral Ethos*, 160; David Rhoads, "What Is Performance Criticism?," in *Bible in Ancient and Modern Media*, 85–86; Whitney Shriner, "Oral Performance in the New Testament World," in *Bible in Ancient and Modern Media*, 49–51; Ruge-Jones, "Word Heard," 102.

12. Rhoads, "What Is Performance Criticism," 85; Shriner, "Oral Performance," 49; Horsley, "Oral and Written Aspects," 95, 104–8.

13. Shriner, "Oral Performance," 51.

14. Dewey, *Oral Ethos*, 160; Rhoads, "What Is Performance Criticism?," 86.

15. Shriner, "Oral Performance," 49; Christopher W. Skinner, "The Study of Character(s) in the Gospel of Mark: A Survey of Research from Wrede to the Performance Critics (1901 to 2014)," in *Character Studies and the Gospel of Mark*, ed. Christopher W. Skinner and Matthew Ryan Hauge (London: Bloomsbury, 2014), 32.

16. Holly E. Hearon, "The Storytelling World of the First Century and the Gospels," in *Bible in Ancient and Modern Media*, 22; For a fuller discussion of the implication of biblical performance, see Rhoads, "What Is Performance Criticism?," 88–99.

17. See France, *Gospel of Mark*, 23; Jacob Chacko Naluparayil, "Jesus of the Gospel of Mark: Present State of Research," *Currents in Research: Biblical Studies* 8 (2000): 192–93.

18. Robert C. Tannehill, "The Gospel of Mark as Narrative Christology," *Semeia* 16 (1979): 57–95.

19. Leading scholarship on narrative Christology includes Elizabeth Struthers Malbon, *Mark's Jesus: Characterization as Narrative Christology* (Waco, TX: Baylor University Press, 2009); Rhoads, Dewey, and Michie, *Mark as Story*; Ole Davidson, *The Narrative Jesus: A Semiotic Reading of Mark's Gospel* (Aarhus, DK: Aarhus University Press, 1993); Jacob Chacko Naluparayil, *The Identity of Jesus in Mark: An Essay on Narrative Christology*, Studium Biblicum Franciscanum Analecta, no. 49 (Jerusalem: Franciscan Printing Press, 2000); Paul L. Danove, *The Rhetoric of the Characterization of God, Jesus, and Jesus' Disciples in the Gospel of Mark* (New York: T&T Clark, 2005).

20. Boring, "Christology of Mark," 136–37.

21. Tannehill, "Narrative Christology," 58.

22. Rhoads, Dewey, and Michie, *Mark as Story*, 100.

23. Boring, "Christology of Mark," 138.

24. Boring, "Christology of Mark," 138–39.

25. Naluparayil, "Jesus of the Gospel of Mark," 217.

26. For more on this idea, see Smith, *Lion with Wings*, 16; James L. Resseguie, *Narrative Criticism of the New Testament: An Introduction* (Grand Rapids, MI: Baker Academic, 2005), 121; Scott S. Elliott, *Reconfiguring Mark's Jesus: Narrative Criticism after Poststructuralism* (Sheffield: Sheffield Phoenix Press, 2011), 8–9.

27. Donahue and Harrington, *Gospel of Mark*, 60; Malbon, *Mark's Jesus*, 59.

28. Malbon, *Mark's Jesus*, 60–61, 66.

29. The Greek word *christos* means anointed; the Hebrew word *māšîaḥ* means anointed one. Donahue and Harrington, *Gospel of Mark*, 25.

30. For an overview of some of the meaning of these terms in the first century, see Malbon, *Mark's Jesus*, 62–66. For instance, "son of God" in the Bible refers to "a person or people with a special relationship to God, often with a special role in salvation history" (65).

31. Rhoads, Dewey, and Michie, *Mark as Story*, 104; Malbon, *Mark's Jesus*, 77.

32. Witherington, *Gospel of Mark*, 59.

33. Rhoads, Dewey, and Michie, *Mark as Story*, 105.

34. Donahue and Harrington, *Gospel of Mark*, 17; Witherington, *Gospel of Mark*, 18–19.

35. There are, however, some textual problems with this passage, with some early manuscripts reading "stirred with anger" rather than compassion. See Bruce M. Metzger, *A Textual Commentary on the Greek New Testament*, 2nd ed. (Stuttgart: Deutsche Bibelgesellschaft, 1994), 65; Huntsman, *Miracles of Jesus*, 45 and 148n9.

36. Expressions of astonishment and a desire to follow Jesus are repeated fifteen times in the Gospel of Mark.

37. For more information and the debate surrounding Jesus's statement, see Witherington, *Gospel of Mark*, 227–29.

38. Among the many scholars who have made this observation are Strauss, *Four Portraits*, 183–85; Witherington, *Gospel of Mark*, 239; Donahue and Harrington, *Gospel of Mark*, 264–65; France, *Gospel of Mark*, 11.

39. France, *Gospel of Mark*, 11–14; Donahue and Harrington, *Gospel of Mark*, 46–50.

40. Martin Kahler, *The So-Called Historical Jesus and the Historic Biblical Christ* (Philadelphia: Fortress Press, 1964), 80.

41. Witherington, *Gospel of Mark*, 301.

42. Donald H. Juel, *The Gospel of Mark* (Nashville: Abingdon, 1999), 139.

43. Strauss, *Four Portraits*, 194; Rhoads, Dewey, and Michie, *Mark as Story*, 9; Donahue and Harrington, *Gospel of Mark*, 460; Witherington, *Gospel of Mark*, 412–13.

44. For a discussion of an open versus a closed story, see Wolfgang Iser, *The Implied Reader* (Baltimore: John Hopkins Press, 1974), especially chapter 11. For a look at how New Testament scholars have used the idea of an open ending to explain the unsettling conclusion of Mark's Gospel, see Thomas E. Boomershine and Gilbert L. Bartholomew, "The Narrative Technique of Mark 16:8," *Journal of Biblical Literature* 100 (1981): 213–23; David J. Hester, "Dramatic Inconclusion: Irony and the Narrative Rhetoric of the Ending of Mark," *Journal for the Study of the New Testament* 17, no. 57 (1995): 61–86; Norman R. Petersen, "When Is the End Not the End? Literary Reflections on the Ending of Mark's Narrative," *Interpretation* 34, no. 2 (1980): 151–66.

7

Luke's Jesus
The Compassionate and Saving Son of God

Eric D. Huntsman

The familiar, poetic lines by Anna Bartlett Warner (1824–1915) reflect a gentle, uncomplicated understanding of who Jesus is, what he is like, and what he has done for us:

> *Jesus loves me, this I know, for the Bible tells me so.*
> *Little ones to him belong; they are weak, but he is strong.*
>
> *Jesus loves me—he who died, heaven's gate to open wide.*
> *He will wash away my sin, let his little child come in.*[1]

Written in 1859 and appearing in many Christian hymnals and songbooks since,[2] this children's favorite assumes that the Bible presents a uniform, simple portrayal of Jesus. As the essays in this volume demonstrate, the New Testament texts actually present many different portraits of the figure whom Latter-day Saints and other Christians accept as the Son of God. Still, if one of these sources contributed disproportionately in shaping the depiction of Jesus as a kind, compassionate, but still divine Savior of the world, it might well be the image painted by the Gospel of Luke. Nevertheless, this Gospel's presentation of Jesus is anything but simple and unsophisticated. Rather it is a carefully crafted literary account that drew upon its sources and the cultural context from which it emerged. Perhaps above all, the Gospel of Luke is informed by its author's sensitivities and shaped by his own understanding of *who* Jesus was and *what* he had come to do.

Traditionally the evangelist who wrote this Gospel has been identified as Luke, the missionary companion and "beloved physician" of Paul (Colossians 4:14; 2 Timothy 4:11; and Philemon 1:24), who seems to have written it sometime in the seventies or eighties.[3] As the third of the Synoptic Gospels, Luke follows the basic order of the Marcan narrative, weaving into it many of the sayings of Jesus that are also found in Matthew. Nevertheless, Luke contains more unique material—such as the so-called Perean ministry, some unique sayings, and other episodes—than either of the other two Synoptics.[4] Although Luke's connection with the source of John's Gospel is unclear, similarities between some portions of the Lucan passion and resurrection narratives and the later Fourth Gospel also allow Luke to serve as a theological bridge between the Synoptics and the Gospel of John.[5] Generally assumed to have been written by a Greek for a largely gentile audience, this Gospel is characterized by both universalism—or the import of Jesus and his work for all peoples—and a patent concern for outsiders and the oppressed, such as gentiles, women, the poor, and others on the margins of society. Nevertheless, the author was very familiar with the Judaism of his time and drew freely from the Septuagint, or Greek translation of the Hebrew scriptures.[6]

The result is not only a higher Christology than that of Mark or even Matthew but also one that has several unique aspects. This Lucan presentation of Jesus is particularly evident in the christological titles he uses or the roles that he describes, designations which, while largely drawn from Jewish scripture, often had resonance with similar titles in the Roman world. While these titles are often common to the other Gospels, their frequency in Luke or his particular use of them often differentiates his portrait of Jesus from theirs. These include identifying Jesus as Savior, the anointed Servant of God, Redeemer, the Lord, and Son of God. Luke's depiction is also influenced by its author's own sensitivities, resulting in the Lucan emphasis on Jesus's obedience and suffering, his healing ministry, and his compassion and mercy. Above all, Luke's tendency to retroject later Christian terminology and perspectives onto the identity and work of the mortal Jesus arose out of his conviction that the earthly and heavenly Jesus were the same Risen Lord that the evangelist worshipped.[7] Because Luke's understanding of this Risen Lord so informed his Christology, his reverence for Jesus restrained him from portraying any of Jesus's human limitations and kept him from preserving instances where the disciples might have displayed any irreverence for the Lord.[8] The result was a divine yet gentle, lordly but loving Jesus that in many ways reflects the Jesus assumed by Anna Bartlett Warner and countless others.

Promised Savior

Like Matthew, the Gospel of Luke begins with an infancy narrative. Whereas Mark begins his Gospel account with Jesus's baptism and ministry (Mark 1:2–15) and John starts his with an account of the Word "in the beginning" (John 1:1–3), these infancy narratives present what can be called a "conception Christology" that stresses that Jesus was divinely conceived and miraculously born.[9] Set as the introductions of their respective Gospels, when taken with the passion and resurrection narratives that conclude Matthew and Luke, these infancy narratives serve as christological frames, demonstrating both who Jesus was and what he came to do. While serving similar functions, the Matthean and Lucan infancy narratives are nonetheless distinctive and not easily harmonized because they draw upon different sources, focus on different episodes and themes, and emphasize different aspects of the identity of the newborn Jesus.[10]

The Lucan infancy narrative provides a bridge with the Septuagint, connecting its characters with the history of Israel and showing how God continued his salvific work in the person of his Son.[11] Much of it consists of two interwoven stories, those of John the Baptist and Jesus, resulting in what is sometimes called the Lucan diptych, a description that comes from the term used for a double-paneled painting or carving. This literary structure emphasizes the uniqueness of Jesus by comparing and contrasting the two stories. The births of both promised children were preceded by angelic annunciations, the children were miraculously conceived, and their births took place under unusual circumstances; however, Mary responded differently than Zacharias, Jesus was divinely rather than just miraculously conceived, and Jesus was born in unusually humble circumstances while John was born at home surrounded by family and friends. Finally, while Zacharias prophesied at his son's birth, angels sang at Jesus's birth.[12]

While there is some question whether Matthew and Luke wrote their infancy narratives first or, more likely, after the bodies of their Gospels were completed,[13] these opening chapters nonetheless serve as "Gospel overtures," setting forth the major themes and motifs, including christological titles and propositions, that recur throughout the rest of Matthew and Luke.[14] Thus while the major purpose of Luke's infancy narrative is to stress that Jesus was actually the Son of God from the moment of his conception, other aspects of Luke's Christology are also introduced in these opening chapters. One aspect that is quite distinctive to Luke is the image of Jesus as the promised Savior. This title first occurs in the opening of the canticle, or poetic song, known as the *Magnificat*, in which Mary, during her visit to Elisabeth, sings,

> My soul doth magnify the Lord,
>> And my spirit hath rejoiced in God my *Saviour*.
>>> (Luke 1:46–47; emphasis added)

The title "Savior," or deliverer (Hebrew, *môšîā‘*; Greek, *sōtēr*), was one frequently used of God in the Old Testament,[15] but it is surprisingly rare in the New, especially in the Gospels, where it appears twice in Luke and only once in John.[16] Given the context and the Old Testament models—such as the song of Hannah—for the *Magnificat*, the meaning here is no doubt consonant with Jewish thought and expectation, namely of a national and perhaps, by extension, spiritual deliverer.

The meaning of the term broadens, however, the second time it is used in Luke, this time in the mouth of a heavenly witness when the angel announces to the shepherds, "Fear not: for, behold, I bring you *good tidings* of great joy, which shall be to all people. For unto you is born this day in the city of David *a Saviour*, which is Christ the Lord" (Luke 2:10–11; emphasis added). While Luke's use here would clearly have been influenced by Old Testament precedent,[17] it was also a term that his audience would have known well from Hellenistic and imperial Roman propaganda, where it was frequently used of rulers who were benefactors to their subjects, bringing peace, security, and prosperity.[18] Indeed, Luke's account compares interestingly to the proclamation of Priene, a Greek city in Asia Minor, regarding the emperor Augustus that dates to 9 BC, just shortly before the birth of Jesus: "Providence, which has ordered all things and is deeply interested in our life, has set in most perfect order by giving us Augustus, whom she filled with virtue that he might benefit humankind, sending him as *a savior*, both for us and for our descendants; . . . the birthday of the god Augustus was the beginning of the *good tidings* for the world."[19]

While the title Savior does not appear again in the Lucan text, forms of the verb save (*sōzō*) appear eleven more times,[20] and it is implied in the infancy narrative and elsewhere in the Gospel by the depiction of Jesus as the bringer of salvation and redemption. In the *Benedictus*, for instance, Zacharias prophesies,

> Blessed be the Lord God of Israel;
>> for he hath visited and *redeemed* his people,

> And hath raised up an horn of *salvation* for us
> > in the house of his servant David.
> > > (Luke 1:68–69; emphasis added)

At the end of this canticle, he concludes by stating that his son, John, would "give knowledge of *salvation* unto his people" (1:77) and "give *light* to them that sit in darkness" (1:79), light being a symbol here of salvation.[21] Similarly, at the Presentation of Jesus in the temple, in the *Nunc dimittis* Simeon sings,

> For mine eyes have seen thy *salvation*,
> > Which thou hast prepared before the face of all people;
> A *light* to lighten the Gentiles,
> > and the glory of thy people Israel.
> > > (Luke 2:30–32; emphasis added)

Picking up the imagery of Isaiah 60:1–3, this canticle explicitly extends salvation to the gentiles as well as to Israel, even as the title *sōtēr*, or Savior, applied in both a Jewish and a Greco-Roman context. Finally, Anna, in her prophetic parallel to Simeon's proclamation, "gave thanks likewise unto the Lord, and spake of him to all them that looked for *redemption* in Jerusalem" (2:38).

Salvation appears again as an important term in Luke,[22] and, as we will see, Luke expands the idea of redemption in his portrayal of Jesus as a healing redeemer. Yet even though the title "Savior" only appears twice in this Gospel, its impact on our understanding of Jesus far outweighs its frequency. Further, because Savior is such a common term in Restoration scripture—appearing twelve times in the Book of Mormon, nineteen times in the Doctrine and Covenants, and four times in the Pearl of Great Price—it is a christological title and concept that Latter-day Saint readers find particularly familiar and beloved in Luke.

Anointed Servant of God

The pattern of Jesus always doing the will of his Father is established in the story of the boy Jesus in the temple (Luke 2:49), and once established at the end of the "overture," it is a theme throughout the Gospel.[23] Although we generally see being about his "Father's business" as a testimony that Jesus was God's Son, it is also part of the larger theme of Jesus, like the prophets before him, being God's obedient servant. As does Matthew, Luke compares Jesus to the prophet Moses by including the forty-day period in the wilderness that precedes the temptation narrative (Luke 4:1–2; compare Matthew 4:1–2). While prophecy had lapsed among the Jews by this period, Luke then presents John the Baptist and especially Jesus as the "Prophet" promised by Moses in Deuteronomy 18:15.[24] When Jesus returns from the wilderness to his hometown of Nazareth,[25] however, Luke takes the image of the promised prophet and weds it to the anointed servant foretold in the later prophecies of Isaiah. In what is in many ways the programmatic passage of the entire Gospel,[26] Jesus takes up the scroll in the synagogue in Nazareth and reads a version of Isaiah 61:1–2:

> The Spirit of the Lord is upon me,
>> because *he hath anointed me* to preach the gospel to the
>> poor;
> he hath sent me to heal the brokenhearted,
>> to preach deliverance to the captives,
> and recovering of sight to the blind,
>> to set at liberty them that are bruised,
>> To preach the acceptable year of the Lord.
>>> (Luke 4:18–19; emphasis added)[27]

When Luke has Jesus say "This day is this scripture fulfilled in your ears" (4:21), he presents Jesus as the one especially chosen, authorized, and sent to preach the good news of the kingdom through a ministry to the poor, sick, and marginalized.

Not limiting himself to words related to *save* (Greek, *sōzō*), in this passage Luke expands Jesus's work of redemption to healing, deliverance, and recovery.[28] These activities are then seen by the people as the work of God's chosen prophet. For instance, after the raising of the son of the widow of Nain, the people proclaim, "A great prophet is risen up among us; and, That God hath visited his people" (Luke 7:16). The people subsequently have different opinions of Jesus, comparing him with this or that prophet (Luke 9:7–8, 18–19), and as late as the day of the resurrection, some of his own followers are still considering him "a prophet mighty in deed and word before God and all the people" (Luke 24:19).

More significantly, the reference to anointing in the Isaiah 61 passage that Jesus reads identifies him as Messiah or Christ, since the Hebrew *māšîaḥ* and the Greek *christos* both mean "anointed one."[29] While many Jews in Jesus's time would have expected Messiah to have been an anointed Davidic king or other deliverer figure,[30] after the resurrection and by the time Luke wrote, "Christ" had become preeminent title among Christians for the Risen Lord. Because of Luke's tendency to read contemporary terminology back into Jesus's ministry, it is not surprising that Luke favors this title, using it sixteen times in the Gospel and an additional thirty-one times in Acts.[31] While the title is used by the angels and Simeon in the infancy narrative (Luke 2:11, 26), the number of times that Christ is used directly of Jesus in his ministry is small until the passion narrative. Other than the testimony of devils (4:41), as in the other Synoptics, only Peter at Caesarea Philippi confesses that Jesus is "Christ" (9:20). Rather, Luke reserves this title for discussions of who Jesus is, or is not, during his final days and hours (20:41; 21:8; 22:67; 23:2, 35, 39). Only in his resurrection appearances to the two disciples on the road to Emmaus and to the gathered eleven does Jesus use the title of himself (24:26, 46), in both cases connecting it with the necessity of his suffering.

The necessity of Jesus's suffering also connects him with the suffering servant of the LORD (*eḇed YHWH*) of Isaiah (e.g., Isaiah

42:1–9; 49:1–7; 50:4–9; 52:13–53:12), a figure that personified vicarious suffering for the purpose of restoring the covenant relationship between God and his people.[32] While the other evangelists, especially Matthew, knew this concept, Luke develops it thematically throughout his Gospel. Beginning with examples of his rejection, starting with his expulsion from Nazareth, it focuses with Jesus's steadfast decision to go to Jerusalem, since "it cannot be that a prophet perish out of Jerusalem" (Luke 13:33–35). It culminates in Jesus's willing and passive deportment in the Lucan passion narrative,[33] especially seen in his refusal to speak to Herod Antipas or answer other charges against him, fulfilling Isaiah 53:7, which prophesied,

> He was oppressed, and he was afflicted,
>> yet he opened not his mouth:
> he is brought as a lamb to the slaughter,
>> and as a sheep before her shearers is dumb,
> so he openeth not his mouth.

Also frequently associated with the theme of a willing, suffering servant are some of Luke's uses of the expression "Son of Man." A much discussed but elusive title, it appears eighty-five times in the Gospels, all but once in the mouth of Jesus, and only four times elsewhere in the New Testament.[34] Although in Restoration scripture it means "Son of Man of Holiness" (see Moses 6:57; 7:53; D&C 78:20; 95:17), in the New Testament it seems to arise from its common Old Testament usage, where it means "a mortal," and from its particular use in Daniel 7:13–14 and intertestamental literature, where it refers to an eschatological figure coming from God in the last days with power and authority.[35] As with the other Synoptics, Lucan usage seems to fall into four categories, reflecting Jesus's mortality, divine authority, suffering in his coming passion, and future role of returning with glory.[36] In each of these instances, Jesus is the unique servant of God.

Healing Redeemer

Healing miracles are a prominent part of Jesus's ministry in all four of the Gospels, and Jesus's rescuing people from physical infirmities can be seen as symbolic of his larger redeeming work. Perhaps because of Luke's conventional identification as a physician, they receive particular attention in his Gospel, as he often adds details to healings common to the other Synoptics or preserves miracles not mentioned in the others.[37] In particular, in harmony with Luke's wider interest in women, he records instances of healing women not preserved elsewhere, including Mary Magdalene and the female followers from Galilee (Luke 8:1–3) as well as the woman bent over with a debilitating infirmity (13:10–17). As with the accounts in Mark and Matthew, frequently when Jesus heals someone, Luke uses the same Greek phrase, *pistis sou sesōken se*, which the King James translation usually renders as "thy faith hath made thee whole" (see Mark 5:34; 10:52; Matthew 9:22; Luke 8:48; 17:19; 18:42). In fact, the therapeutic context of these miracles has led LDS scholars Fiona and Terryl Givens to suggest that perhaps the verb *sōzō* here should be interpreted "heal."[38] Literally, however, *sōzō*, means "save," and is translated that way in the King James Bible in one of the Lucan passages under consideration, when Jesus heals blind Bartimaeus and announces, "Receive thy sight: thy faith hath *saved* thee" (Luke 18:42). Clearly, Jesus saw his healing ministry as part of his larger saving work as he freed people from their infirmities.[39]

Another instance in Luke where Jesus used the expression *pistis sou sesōken se* extends the concept to the idea of spiritual healing. In the story of the woman who washed Jesus's feet with her tears, dried them with her hair, and then anointed them, Jesus forgave her because of her great love for him, saying, "Thy faith hath saved thee; go in peace" (Luke 7:50). In the earlier miracle of healing the man with palsy, Jesus had combined physical healing with forgiveness of sins (Mark 2:1–12; Matthew 9:1–8; Luke 5:17–26), suggesting that salvation includes both the body and the spirit. Physical healing and forgiveness are both acts of redemption whereby Jesus ransoms, or redeems, men and women from the effects of the fall that separates us from God and makes us prone to sickness and sin.

Deliverance from the power of the devil can serve as a type of how Jesus redeems us from the power of the fall. As do the other Synoptics, Luke records instances of Jesus's freeing people from demonic possession (Luke 4:33–37; 8:26–39; 9:37–42; 11:14), but he also uses exorcism terminology in what are clearly physical healings.[40] For instance, Jesus "rebukes" (Greek, *epetimēsen*) the fever of Simon Peter's mother-in-law using the same term that is used elsewhere for rebuking and casting out devils (4:39). Similarly, when healing the woman who was bent over from some disability, he describes her as suffering from "a spirit of infirmity" and indicates that Jesus "loosed" (Greek, *apolelusai*) her from her disability (13:11–12). In both cases, Luke treats a physical ailment as an enemy to be subdued or a bondage from which the victims must be freed.[41]

While "Redeemer" is not a title that appears in the New Testament,[42] the concept of God or his servant as being a personal and national redeemer was an important promise in the Old Testament, especially in the later writings of Isaiah.[43] Redemption, however, does continue to figure in the Lucan narrative, both in Jesus's prophecy of his return in the Olivet Discourse (Luke 21:28) and in the hopes of the two disciples on the road to Emmaus (24:21). The revelation of the Risen Lord to these two disciples resonates, in fact, with the testimony of Job. Just as they "trusted that it had been he which should have redeemed Israel" (24:21), so Job is described as proclaiming, "For I know that my redeemer liveth, and that he shall stand at the latter day upon the earth" (Job 19:25). Beyond these explicit references to redemption, however, the healing and spiritually liberating ministry of Jesus is a constant reminder of his redeeming work. As with Savior, Redeemer is a term much used in the Church today, appearing forty-one times in the Book of Mormon, twenty-two times in the Doctrine and Covenants, once in the Pearl of Great Price, and in the beloved hymn "I Know That My Redeemer Lives," which appeared in the first Latter-day Saint hymnbook and has been frequently sung ever since.

Compassionate, Merciful Lord

The title "Lord" (Greek, *kyrios*) appears eighty-three times in Luke, more frequently than in any of the other Gospels.[44] The term's usage, however, is broad, having as many as four possible meanings. These include its simple use for "master" or "owner"; as a form of polite address, meaning simply "sir"; in a courtly sense when used of a social superior; and, significantly, as a Greek translation of the Hebrew term *'adōnay*, which was regularly used to substitute for the divine name YHWH, or "Jehovah."[45] As a result, only the context of each occurrence can determine which meaning best applies. For instance, in stories such as the parable of the barren fig tree (Luke 13:1–9) or the parable of the pounds (19:11–27), the "lord" is either the owner or master, and when individuals who do not know Jesus come and address him, they likely mean the polite "sir" (see, for example, the centurion in 7:6). On the other hand, in the Hellenistic and Roman context, *kyrios* was used for the gods of mystery religions as well as for the political rule of Hellenistic kings and Roman emperors,[46] which may have predisposed many of Luke's readers to see one of the latter two uses in the title, and many of Luke's references have one of these elevated meanings.

In fact, among the evangelists Luke alone regularly refers to Jesus as Lord in the narrative, probably reflecting the elevated usage among Christians in his own day.[47] However, the fact that Luke at times interweaves his own use of *kyrios* to refer to Jesus with his characters' use of it in dialogue, as in the case of the Martha story of Luke 10:39–41, might suggest that original disciples used the term for Jesus in an elevated sense as well.[48] Significant are the instances where *kyrios* seems to reflect the Hebrew use of *'adōnay*. Particularly in the infancy narrative, Luke uses Lord to refer to YHWH, the God of Israel,[49] and many of his later uses of the title may also suggest the

divinity of Jesus. Contemporary Latter-day Saints are perhaps particularly receptive to this identification because of our understanding
that the Jehovah of the Old Testament was, in most instances, the premortal Jesus Christ.[50] Despite the frequent assumption that God in
the Old Testament is associated with judgment, one of the most common descriptions of Jehovah in the Old Testament is ḥesed, or "loving
kindness."[51] This is the aspect of "the Lord" that regularly character-
izes Jesus in the New Testament, especially in the Gospel of Luke.

Most commonly the Septuagint translates ḥesed with the Greek
term eleos, which means "mercy," "compassion," or "pity." Especially
in Luke, these very terms are common, helping paint the Lucan portrait of a compassionate, loving Jesus.[52] Of course, descriptions of
Jesus's compassion are not unique to Luke. For instance, early in the
Marcan narrative, most manuscripts describe Jesus as having been
moved with compassion when he encounters and then heals the first
leper (Mark 1:41).[53] Likewise, before the feeding of the five thousand,
Jesus had compassion on the hungry multitude (Mark 6:34; parallel Matthew 15:32). To these common Synoptic examples, however,
Luke adds several others, such as Jesus's having compassion at the
plight of the widow of Nain (Luke 7:13–15) and the ten lepers (17:11–
19). Additionally, while Jesus is always willing to heal those who
needed it (9:11), he will not call down fire upon the Samaritan village
that would not receive him, pronouncing, "For the Son of man is not
come to destroy men's lives, but to save them" (9:56). Further, only
Luke adds that Jesus not only laments over Jerusalem (see Matthew
23:37–39) but actually weeps over it (Luke 19:41–44).[54]

Jesus is gentle with other characters in Luke, and the evangelist
consciously downplays the failings of others, particularly his disciples,
so that he does not need to portray Jesus as being harsh with them,
as happens in the other Synoptics. For example, after Jesus's first
passion prediction in the other accounts, Peter impulsively rebukes
Jesus, leading Jesus to scold him, calling him Satan (Mark 8:31–33;
parallel Matthew 16:21–23). Luke, however, completely omits both
Peter's rebuke and Jesus's harsh response, moving directly to other

teachings (see Luke 9:22–27). Similarly, while Luke acknowledges that Peter, James, and John failed to stay awake and watch with him in Gethsemane, he only mentions their falling asleep once as opposed to three times as in the other Synoptics and only refers to "disciples" rather than singling these three out (Luke 22:45; cf. Mark 14:32, 37–41; Matthew 26:36, 40–45). Further, in Luke Jesus considers others before himself, even in times of great duress, such as when he heals the ear of the servant of the high priest (Luke 22:50–51), comforts the weeping women of Jerusalem on the way to Calvary (23:27–31), and forgives his crucifiers and those who mock and mistreat him (23:34). He even takes time to teach and comfort the penitent malefactor even as he himself hangs on the cross (23:40–43).[55]

Suffering Son of God

A distinctively Lucan characteristic is his clear identification of Jesus as God's Son in the annunciation (Luke 1:32–33, 35), which contrasts with the more vague "that which is conceived in her is of the Holy Ghost" of Matthew 1:20.[56] As representatives of YHWH, the kings of ancient Judah had been viewed as the Lord's adoptive sons, which can be seen in the various royal psalms, in particular Psalm 2, which declared, "The LORD hath said unto me, Thou art my Son; this day have I begotten thee" (Psalm 2:7).[57] Perhaps the prime example of such a divinely adopted and approved king, after David himself, was the ideal figure in an early prophecy of Isaiah:

> For unto us a child is born, unto us a son is given:
> > and the government shall be upon his shoulder:
> and his name shall be called
> > Wonderful Counsellor,
> > The mighty God,
> > The everlasting Father,
> > *The Prince of Peace.* (Isaiah 9:6; emphasis added and punctuation corrected)[58]

The royal title "Prince of Peace" finds an echo in the acclamation of the heavenly hosts in the canticle *Gloria in excelsis*:

> Glory to God in the highest,
>> and *on earth peace*, good will to men.
>>> (Luke 2:14; emphasis added)[59]

While Luke's gentile audience would have been well familiar with Greek and Roman myths in which heroes were frequently semi-divine children of godly and mortal parents, more pertinent would have been the titular style of Roman emperors. Augustus had begun using the element *Divi filius*, or "son of the God," when his adoptive father Julius Caesar was decreed a god in 42 BC.[60] Given the role of Augustus in establishing the *Pax Romana*, or "Roman Peace," the *Gloria in excelsis* would have had resonance to gentile readers of Luke as well.

Luke's usage in his infancy narrative exceeded the idea of royal adoption or imperial acclamation: it presents Jesus as the divinely conceived Son of God who would come to establish peace on the earth. Nevertheless, Luke is restrained in how this truth is conveyed throughout the course of his Gospel. As in the other Synoptics, the surest source of this knowledge is from God himself, who proclaims Jesus his beloved Son at the baptism (Luke 3:22), a point which Luke reinforces with the final entry in Jesus's genealogy (3:38). This happens again at the transfiguration (9:35). Likewise, Jesus himself implies that he is God's Son by referring to God as his Father both as a boy in the temple and in a later Galilean prayer that is almost Johannine in its understanding of the unity of the Father and the Son (Luke 10:21–22; cf. Matthew 11:25–27).[61]

Otherwise, during Jesus's ministry the only testimony of his divine Sonship comes from Satan or his devils (4:3, 9, 41; 8:21). While this follows the basic pattern of Mark and Matthew, a confession that Jesus is God's Son never appears in the mouth of a human witness in Luke.[62] He omits the scene of Jesus walking on the water, which leads the disciples to say, "Of a truth thou art the Son of God"

(Matthew 14:33), and like Mark, Luke does not expand Peter's confession at Caesarea Philippi that Jesus is the Christ to include "the Son of the living God" as does Matthew (Mark 8:29; Luke 9:20; Matthew 16:16). He even alters the powerful christological declaration of the centurion at the foot of the cross, changing it from "Truly this man was the Son of God" (Mark 15:39; parallel Matthew 27:54) to "Certainly this was a righteous man" (Luke 23:47).

Not using this title for the adult Jesus as a miracle worker or a teacher, Luke largely reserves it for his depiction of Jesus as the obedient son who suffers to fulfill his saving task.[63] As a result, most Lucan references or allusions to the title "Son of God" appear in the passion and resurrection narratives, where Jesus continues as the Suffering Servant who, although the Son of God, paradoxically goes to the cross to die.[64] This paradox tightly connects Luke's presentation of Jesus to an atonement or sacrificial Christology, underscoring that the work of this chosen Son of God was to suffer and die for his people.

During his hearing before the Jewish authorities, Mark, the earliest account, has Caiaphas ask Jesus, "Art thou the Christ, the Son of the Blessed?" (Mark 14:61), using a respectful circumlocution for the divine name. Like Matthew, Luke has Caiaphas ask whether he was the Son of God, but unlike Matthew, who combines it with a question about whether he was the Christ, or the Messiah (Matthew 26:63), Luke makes it a separate question, "Art thou then the Son of God?" (Luke 22:70). Yet Jesus's status as God's beloved Son in Luke is most patent in the close relationship between the two that the narrative portrays. In a unique Lucan passage at the Last Supper, Jesus speaks of the kingdom that "my Father hath appointed unto me" (22:29). While all four Gospels have Jesus pray intimately with God as his Father either right before or in the garden (Mark 14:35–36; Matthew 26:39; Luke 22:41–42; John 17:1–26), the received version of Luke is the only one that recounts how God sent an angel to strengthen him during agony that made his sweat "as it were great drops of blood falling down to the ground" (Luke 22:43–44). While there are textual problems with these passages,[65] Restoration scripture confirms that

Jesus did indeed suffer to fulfill his mission, bringing glory to the Father (see Mosiah 3:7; D&C 19:16–19).

Luke continues to have Jesus speak directly with God as his Father on the cross. Only in Luke does Jesus plead, "Father, forgive them; for they know not what they do" (Luke 23:34), and Luke paints a much more intimate, uninterrupted Father-Son relationship in his final moments. First, he omits any sense that he was abandoned by God (Mark 15:34; parallel Matthew 27:46). Second, by focusing on Jesus's completing his mission (John 19:30) rather than ending with an anguished cry (Mark 15:37; parallel Matthew 27:50), in Luke Jesus's final words are, "Father, into thy hands I commend my spirit" (Luke 23:46). With his death, Jesus's mission as obedient Son and suffering servant is complete.

"Who died, heaven's gate to open wide . . ."

As in the other Gospels, Jesus completes his saving work by overcoming the grave, but Luke's account of the resurrection is much richer in detail than the other Synoptics and is more effective in demonstrating the reality of an actual, bodily resurrection.[66] Although his resurrection narrative begins with the women at the empty tomb as do the other Synoptics, he universalizes the good news of Jesus's rising by appearing first not to the gathered eleven but to two "average" disciples on their way to Emmaus (Luke 24:13–32). As has been noted, it is here that Jesus uses the title "Christ" of himself for the first time, identifying his sufferings as God's anointed servant as the source of his glory (24:26). Appearing to the eleven, he gives evidence of the reality of his rising, letting them handle him and see him eat. Helping them understand the scriptures, he then proclaims, "Thus it is written, and thus it behoved Christ to suffer, and to rise from the dead the third day" (24:46), emphasizing that it was not just his death but also his resurrection that fulfilled his messianic mission. Indeed, though Luke affirmed Jesus's divine Sonship through the Savior's earthly ministry, both in his Gospel and in Acts, Luke's emphasis on the resurrection, his presence in heaven, and the promise of the Risen Lord's return represents an important exaltation Christology.[67]

Luke alone gives a secure account of Jesus's ascension into heaven (Luke 24:51), an account that he repeats in more detail in Acts 1:9.[68] The longer ending of Mark—probably composed later to complete the original ending or to replace one that was lost—likely draws upon Luke for its version of Jesus's ascension (Mark 16:19).[69] In Matthew, after Jesus appears to his disciples at a mountain in Galilee and gives them their apostolic commission, the Gospel ends with the words "and, lo, I am with you alway, even unto the end of the world" (Matthew 28:20). The Gospel of John, likely written after Luke, ends with Peter and the Beloved Disciple still with Jesus. Thus while these two Gospels leave us with the image of Jesus still present with his followers, only Luke presents him as the Risen Lord ascended into heaven, where he awaits those who will follow him. Luke then concludes his Gospel by writing, "And they *worshipped* him, and returned to Jerusalem *with great joy*: And were continually in the temple, praising and blessing God. Amen" (Luke 24:52–53; emphasis added). The image of people worshipping Jesus is unprecedented in the Gospel of Luke,[70] but the homage and great joy of the disciples here parallel the angelic praise of the promised Savior in the opening infancy narrative (Luke 2:10–14). Just as the windows of heaven were opened to welcome the birth of the newborn Son of God, they have opened again to receive him. Having opened those windows with his suffering and death, as Anna Bartlett Warner penned, they have remained open wide for all believers since.

ERIC D. HUNTSMAN *is a professor of ancient scripture and coordinator of the Ancient Near Eastern Studies Program at Brigham Young University.*

Notes

1. I appreciate the research and proofing help of my long-time assistants Stephen Betts and Julia Min-tsu Chiou, which, as always, was invaluable.

2. Anna Bartlett Warner, "Jesus Loves Me," no. 68, in *Bradbury's Golden Shower of S.S. Melodies: A New Collection of Hymns and Tunes for the Sabbath School*, ed. Wm. B. Bradbury (New York: Ivison, Phinney, 1862), 67–98. See https://hymnary.org/person/Warner_Anna.

3. Patristic sources that identify "Luke" as the author of the Third Gospel include the Muratorian Canon (c. AD 170), Irenaeus (c. AD 130–c. 200; *Adversus Haereses* 3.1.1; 14.1–3); Clement of Alexandria (AD 150–215; *Stromata* 5:12); and Tertullian (c. AD 155–c. 240; *Adversus Marcionem* 4.2.1–5). See the discussion of Joseph A. Fitzmyer, *The Gospel according to Luke*, Anchor Bible 28 (New York: Doubleday, 1970), 35–41; I. Howard Marshall, *The Gospel of Luke*, New International Greek Testament Commentary (Grand Rapids, MI: Eerdmans, 1978), 33–35; S. Kent Brown, *The Testimony of Luke* (Provo, UT: BYU Studies, 2015), 72–76.

4. Fitzmyer, *Gospel according to Luke*, 63–87; Marshall, *Gospel of Luke*, 30–31. For other approaches to the sayings source, including the possible priority of Luke over Matthew, see Martin Hengel, *The Four Gospels and the One Gospel of Jesus Christ*, trans. John Bowden (Harrisburg: Trinity Press, 2000), 169–207; and Brown, *Testimony of Luke*, 52–61.

5. Raymond E. Brown, *The Gospel according to John*, Anchor Bible 29 (New York: Doubleday, 1966), xlvi–xlvii; Fitzmyer, *Gospel according to Luke*, 87–89; Mark A. Matson, *In Dialogue with Another Gospel? The Influence of the Fourth Gospel on the Passion Narrative of the Gospel of Luke* (Atlanta: Society of Biblical Literature, 2001), 6–10, 155–63, 263–438.

6. Fitzmyer, *Gospel according to Luke*, 41–47, 57–59, 113–25; Joel B. Green, *The Gospel of Luke*, The New International Commentary of the New Testament (Grand Rapids, MI: Eerdmans, 1997), 13–14, 51–58, and passim; Brown, *Testimony of Luke*, 3–7, 32–34.

7. Robert F. O'Toole, *Luke's Presentation of Jesus: A Christology*, Studia Biblica 25 (Rome: Editrice Pontificio Istituto Biblico, 2008), 1–2.

8. Raymond E. Brown, *An Introduction to New Testament Christology* (New York: Paulist Press, 1994), 120–21.

9. Brown, *Introduction to New Testament Christology*, 129–33; H. Douglas Buckwalter, *The Character and Purpose of Luke's Christology* (Cambridge: Cambridge University Press, 1996), 23–24.

10. Raymond A. Brown, *The Birth of the Messiah* (1977; repr., New York: Doubleday, 1993), 33–37.

11. Brown, *Birth of the Messiah*, 242–43; Eric D. Huntsman, *Good Tidings of Great Joy* (Salt Lake City: Deseret Book, 2011), 41, 142.

12. Brown, *Birth of the Messiah*, 250–52; Huntsman, *Good Tidings of Great Joy*, 41.

13. Brown, *Birth of the Messiah*, 31–32, 48–49, 239–40.

14. Marcus J. Borg and John Dominic Crossan, *The First Christmas* (New York: HarperOne, 2007), 38–39.

15. See 2 Samuel 22:3; Psalm 106:21; Isaiah 19:20; 43:3, 11; 45:15, 21; 49:26; 60:16; 63:8; Jeremiah 14:8; Hosea 13:4; see Oscar Cullmann, *The Christology of the New Testament*, trans. Shirley C. Guthrie and Charles A. M. Hall (Philadelphia: Westminster, 1959), 239–40.

16. Luke 1:47; 2:11; John 4:42; Acts 5:31; 13:23; Ephesians 5:23; Philippians 3:20; 2 Timothy 1:1; 2:3; 4:10; 2 Timothy 1:10; Titus 1:4; 2:13; 3:6; 2 Peter 1:1, 11; 2:20; 3:2, 18; 1 John 4;14; Jude 1:25. In 1 Timothy, Titus, and Jude, however, the title is used of God, not Jesus Christ.

17. Cullmann, *Christology of the New Testament*, 242–43.

18. K. H. Schelke, "sōtēr," in *Exegetical Dictionary of the New Testament*, ed. Horst Balz and Gerhard Schneider (Grand Rapids, MI: Eerdmans, 1990), 3:325–27. See Dominique Cuss, *Imperial Cult and Honorary Terms in the New Testament*, Paradosis 23 (Fribourg, Switzerland: University Press, 1974), 63–69; Stanley Porter, *Empire in the New Testament* (Eugene, OT: Wipf & Stock, 2011), 172; Pyung-Soo Seo, *Luke's Jesus in the Roman Empire and the Emperor in the Gospel of Luke* (Cambridge: James Clarke, 2015), 116–18.

19. Priene Calendar Inscription, *Orientis Graeci Inscriptiones Selectae* 458; emphasis added; see Craig A. Evans, "Mark's Incipit and the Priene

Calendar Inscription: From Jewish Gospel to Greco-Roman Gospel," *Journal of Greco-Roman Christianity and Judaism* 1 (2000): 67–81.

20. Luke 6:9; 7:50; 8:12, 48; 9:24, 56; 23:23; 17:19; 18:26, 42; 19:10; 23:35, 37, 39.

21. O'Toole, *Luke's Presentation of Jesus*, 58, 66–69.

22. Luke 3:6; 19:9.

23. O'Toole, *Luke's Presentation of Jesus*, 11–12.

24. Cullmann, *Christology of the New Testament*, 13–16, 23–38.

25. Luke mentions that Jesus is from Nazareth more than any other Gospel, emphasizing his humanity and the reality of his upbringing (Luke 1:26; 2:4, 39, 51; 4:16, 34; 24:19); see O'Toole, *Luke's Presentation of Jesus*, 8–9.

26. Stanley E. Porter, "The Messiah in Luke and Acts: Forgiveness of the Captives," in *The Messiah in the Old and New Testaments*, ed. Stanley E. Porter (Grand Rapids, MI: Eerdmans, 2007), 150–51; O'Toole, *Luke's Presentation of Jesus*, 29–33, 42–44, 118–19.

27. While the Masoretic Hebrew text of Isaiah 61:1, which was the basis of the King James Version translation, makes no reference to giving sight to the blind, the Greek Septuagint version of this Isaiah passage explicitly reads *kai typhlois anablepsin*, which is translated as "recovery of sight to the blind."

28. Simon J. Gathercole, *The Preexistent Son: Recovering the Christologies of Matthew, Mark, and Luke* (Grand Rapids, MI: Eerdmans, 2006), 181; O'Toole, *Luke's Presentation of Jesus*, 56.

29. F. Hahn, "christos," in *Exegetical Dictionary of the New Testament*, 478–82; see Porter, "The Messiah in Luke and Acts," 151–53; O'Toole, *Luke's Presentation of Jesus*, 118–20.

30. *The Messiah in the Old and New Testaments*, ed. Stanley E. Porter (Grand Rapids, MI: Eerdmans, 2007), 1–12.

31. Fitzmyer, *Gospel according to Luke*, 197–99; for the count used here, see Appendix, pp. 392, 395–97.

32. O'Toole, *Luke's Presentation of Jesus*, 95, 110–12.

33. O'Toole, *Luke's Presentation of Jesus*, 111.

34. Brown, *Introduction to New Testament Christology*, 89–91; Fitzmyer, *Gospel according to Luke*, 210, argues that it is actually a narrative insertion by the evangelists in Matthew 9:6 and Luke 5:24. For my count, see "Son of

Man" in the appendix. Outside of the Gospels, it occurs in the martyrdom speech of Stephen in Acts 7:56, in a quotation of Psalm 8:4 in Hebrews 2:6, and in visions of the apocalyptic Jesus in Revelation 1:13 and 14:14.

35. Brown, *Introduction to New Testament Christology*, 91–100; Gathercole, *Preexistent Son*, 268–71.

36. Gathercole, *Preexistent Son*, 266–68; O'Toole, *Luke's Presentation of Jesus*, 141–53.

37. Eric D. Huntsman, *The Miracles of Jesus* (Salt Lake City: Deseret Book, 2014), 41–63.

38. Fiona Givens and Terryl Givens, *The Christ Who Heals: How God Restored the Truth That Saves Us* (Salt Lake City: Deseret Book, 2017), 64–65.

39. Cullmann, *Christology of the New Testament*, 24.

40. Huntsman, *Miracles of Jesus*, 66.

41. Graham H. Twelftree, *Jesus the Miracle Worker* (Downers Grove, IL: InterVarsity Press, 1999), 175–77.

42. K. Kertelge, "lytron/6. lytrōtēs," in *Exegetical Dictionary of the New Testament*, 2:366.

43. Job 19:25; Psalms 19:14; 78:35; Proverbs 23:11; Isaiah 41:14; 43:14; 44:6, 24; 47:4; 48:17; 49:7, 26; 54:5, 8; 59:20; 60:16; 63:16; Jeremiah 50:34.

44. For my figures, see "Lord" in the appendix, where the Lucan figures compare strikingly to the forty-eight occurrences in Matthew, nineteen in Mark, and forty-three in John. In addition to eighty-three clear uses in regard to Jesus in Luke, *kyrios* appears an additional twenty times in a more mundane sense not in relation to Jesus. For a discussion of the significance of the Lucan usage, see J. A. Fitzmyer, "kyrios," in *Exegetical Dictionary of the New Testament*, 328–31; see Fitzmyer, *Gospel according to Luke*, 200–201; Thomas P. Rausch, *Who Is Jesus? An Introduction to Christology* (Collegeville, MN: Michael Glazier Books, 2003), 136; C. Kavin Rowe, *Early Narrative Christology: The Lord in the Gospel of Luke* (New York: Walter de Gruyter, 2006), 232–33.

45. Gathercole, *Preexistent Son*, 243–44; Rowe, *Early Narrative Christology*, 210–16.

46. Cullmann, *Christology of the New Testament*, 197–98.

47. Fitzmyer, *Gospel according to Luke*, 202–4; Rowe, *Early Narrative Christology*, 10. See the appendix, where I have identified thirteen instances of Luke as a post-Easter narrator referring to Jesus as "Lord." Contra Fitzmyer and Rowe, there are also four instances where John does likewise.

48. Gathercole, *Preexistent Son*, 247–48.

49. Luke 1:6, 9, 11, 15, 16, 17, 25, 28, 32, 38, 43, 45, 46, 58, 66, 68, 76; 2:9 (2x), 15, 22, 23 (2x), 24, 26, 29, 38, 39; 3:4; 4:8, 12, 18, 19; 5:17; 10:2, 27, 41; 12:37; 13:35; 19:38; 20:37, 42.

50. Talmage, *Jesus the Christ*, 4, 34–39, 382–83. For earlier LDS uses of the title, however, see Boyd Kirkland, "Elohim and Jehovah in Mormonism and the Bible," *Dialogue* 19 (1986): 77–93; and Ryan Conrad Davis and Paul Y. Hoskisson, "Usage of the Title *Elohim*," *Religious Educator* 14, no. 1 (2013): 109–27.

51. F. Brown, S. Driver, and C. Briggs, *The Brown-Driver-Briggs Hebrew and English Lexicon* (Peabody, MA: Hendrickson, 1996), 338–39.

52. Most commonly *ḥesed* in the Old Testament is translated as "mercy," "compassion," or "pity" in the Septuagint, all with the Greek term *eleos*; see Johan Lust, Erik Eynikel, and Katrin Hauspie, *Greek-English Lexicon of the Septuagint* (Peabody, MA: Hendrickson, 2008), 193; F. Staudinger, "eleeō," *Exegetical Dictionary of the New Testament*, 1:429–31.

53. Bruce M. Metzger, *A Textual Commentary on the Greek New Testament*, 2nd ed. (Stuttgart: Deutsche Bibelgesellschaft, 1994), 65; Huntsman, *Miracles of Jesus*, 45 and 148n9.

54. O'Toole, *Luke's Presentation of Jesus*, 25–26.

55. O'Toole, *Luke's Presentation of Jesus*, 26–27.

56. See Gathercole, *Preexistent Son*, 281.

57. Nancy deClaissé-Walford, Rolf A. Jacobson, and Beth LaNeel Tanner, *The Book of Psalms*, The New International Commentary on the Old Testament (Grand Rapids, MI: Eerdmans, 2014), 65, 68–69.

58. Often this figure is thought to be good king Hezekiah, though this suggestion presents certain chronological difficulties. See John N. Oswalt, *The Book of Isaiah: Chapters 1–39*, The International Commentary on the Old Testament (Grand Rapids, MI: Eerdmans, 1986), 244–48.

59. The later Byzantine texts, upon which the KJV was based, read Son. Earlier manuscripts, however, had *eudokias* rather than *eudokia*, yielding "and on earth peace to men of good will." See Metzger, *Textual Commentary on the Greek New Testament*, 111, and Huntsman, *Good Tidings of Great Joy*, 83.

60. Cuss, *Imperial Cult*, 71–74.

61. O'Toole, *Luke's Presentation of Jesus*, 178.

62. Rausch, *Who Is Jesus?*, 135; Gathercole, *Preexistent Son*, 281; O'Toole, *Luke's Presentation of Jesus*, 155–56.

63. Cullmann, *Christology of the New Testament*, 277–78.

64. Gathercole, *Preexistent Son*, 281–82.

65. Metzger, *Textual Commentary on the Greek New Testament*, 151. See Lincoln M. Blumell, "Luke 22:43–44: An Anti-Docetic Interpolation or an Apologetic Omission?," *Journal of Biblical Textual Criticism* 19 (2014): 1–35.

66. Buckwalter, *Character and Purpose of Luke's Christology*, 101, 113–14, 118.

67. Rausch, *Who Is Jesus?*, 129–30, 137.

68. For a discussion of whether this is a doublet of the ascent in Acts or an "interim ascent," see Brown, *Testimony of Luke*, 1141.

69. Metzger, *Textual Commentary on the Greek New Testament*, 102–6.

70. Marshall, *Gospel according to Luke*, 910.

8

God Incarnate
The Word Made Flesh

Jennifer C. Lane and Keith H. Lane

The Gospel of John presents perhaps the highest Christology in the New Testament, providing us with resources to think more deeply about what it means to say that Jesus Christ is God. Although the authorship of the Gospel according to John and its compositional history have been much debated by biblical scholars, the text as we have received it provides a powerful, scriptural witness of Jesus's divinity and his pivotal role in helping us fully realize our potential as sons and daughters of God.[1]

John clearly distinguishes Christ from the Father by emphasizing that he was sent from God and always does the will of the Father. But at the same time, John does not shy away from presenting Jesus as God. This became a source of tremendous theological speculation in the early Christian period as people sought to make sense of how to understand the oneness of God in light of the definite New Testament witness of Christ's divinity. The Gospel of John gives a witness of two equally true points of Christ's nature: his divinity and his obedience to the Father. It was written so that "ye might believe that Jesus is the Christ, the Son of God; and that believing ye might have life through his name" (John 20:31). In the same spirit, it can be of very practical personal benefit to deepen our understanding and faith in Christ's divinity.[2]

As Latter-day Saints, we often put our theological emphasis on our status as the children of God and thus are sometimes misunderstood as either putting ourselves on the same level as Christ or denying his divinity. The Latter-day Saint doctrine of a premortal existence for human beings and of Heavenly Father as the literal Father of our spirits represents a radically different way of understanding our relationship with God. While we do want to preserve the power of this Restoration doctrine of our being spirit children of God, it must be combined with an appreciation and reverence for the unique status of Christ as the Only Begotten and the one through whom we become "the sons [and daughters] of God" (John 1:12). The Gospel of John offers a powerful vision of the divinity of Christ, that he "was with God" and "was God." Many Latter-day Saints may be hesitant to take seriously the claim that Christ is God because of fear of slipping into Trinitarian thinking. Nevertheless, the Gospel of John's high Christology can help us more fully appreciate our need to *become* the sons and daughters of God through Christ's divine person and power.

In the Gospel of John, Jesus regularly testifies of his Father and how he gets his power and authority from him, but the same Gospel presents Jesus as God. John does not work out all the philosophical or theological nuances in the relationship of the Father and the Son as members of the Godhead, but John does present Jesus as God as well as the Son of God, using biblical imagery and language to clearly emphasize both Christ's divinity and the need for his divinity to take on mortality. The biblical images and language that John uses would have been meaningful for his audience to testify of Christ's divinity and to show how that divinity is manifest in his incarnation. We will explore John's presentation by looking at Jesus as the Word, Christ as the Creator, and Jesus as the Lamb of God, as well as by examining overarching patterns that link Jesus to Jehovah, such as the I Am statements. Given the depth of this topic, these examinations provide tools for meditation and closer reading but do not presume to exhaust John's presentation of Jesus Christ as divine.

The Word Was Made Flesh and Dwelt among Us

The Gospel of John sets out a clear preexistence Christology, beginning by referencing Genesis 1 and the Creation: "*In the beginning* God created the heaven and the earth" (Genesis 1:1; emphasis added). "*In the beginning* was the Word, and the Word was with God, and the Word was God" (John 1:1; emphasis added). In this way the Gospel not only proposes a powerful preexistence Christology, it also establishes that the Word, or Logos, is the means by which God creates.[3] The Logos is the equivalent of the Old Testament Hebrew term *dabar*. In addition to the repetition of "God said" in the creation account of Genesis, in Psalm 147:18 God's creative power is connected to his word: "He sendeth out his word, and melteth them: he causeth his wind to blow, and the waters flow." Here his word is "the proclamation of the creating power and loving will of God . . . which acts as a power of creation and proclaims God's will."[4] John is using language that recalls the creation and Old Testament language for God's creative power.

While there were contemporary philosophical issues related to the concept of the Logos, the Gospel of John is distinct from the philosophical or theological efforts of contemporary Jews or later Christians. As T. E. Pollard argues, "this conjunction of divine and human, Logos and flesh, God and a man, is nowhere defined or analysed by St. John; it is simply part of his witness that this Jesus is the God-man through faith in whom men may have eternal life."[5] John seems to simply use biblical language that his audience would have understood to give his witness of the paradoxical truth of Jesus's humanity and divinity.

A critical part of John's incarnation Christology is not just that the Word was in the beginning with God and was God, but that the Word was made flesh. The term for "flesh" here in John is the same found in the Septuagint of Isaiah that emphasizes the "transient nature of what is created."[6]

> The voice said, Cry. And he said, What shall I cry? All flesh is grass, and all the goodliness thereof is as the flower of the field: The grass withereth, the flower fadeth: because the spirit of the Lord bloweth upon it: surely the people is grass. The grass withereth, the flower fadeth: but the word of our God shall stand for ever. (Isaiah 40:6–8)

The Word is eternal, but flesh is as the grass. This verse contains the paradox of the incarnation and some of the likely tension for those who were taught it. John is emphasizing that the Word was made flesh, meaning that the eternal took on a temporary body, a paradoxical contrast difficult for many of this era.[7]

In addition to the biblical allusions with the term *flesh*, John uses another Old Testament term that can help us understand the condescension of God. He declares that "the Word was made flesh, and dwelt among us" (John 1:14), but this could literally be translated "tabernacled [*eskēnōsen*] among us" from *skeneoō*, to dwell in a tent. In the Septuagint the noun form of that verb, *skēnē*, is used to translate the Hebrew term for tabernacle (*miškān*). John is the only New Testament Gospel to use this verb. In Exodus 25:8 the Lord explains why they are being commanded to build the tabernacle: "And let them make me a sanctuary; that I may dwell among them." God was able to dwell among his people by having a tabernacle or temple as his dwelling place.[8]

In the Old Testament the tabernacle or temple was a place where the glory of the Lord could be manifest. In Exodus 40:34–35 we read: "Then a cloud covered the tent of the congregation, and the glory of the Lord filled the tabernacle. And Moses was not able to enter into the tent of the congregation, because the cloud abode thereon, and the glory of the Lord filled the tabernacle." John continues this connection to the Old Testament tabernacle by emphasizing the "glory" that was made manifest in the incarnation. "And the Word was made flesh, and dwelt among us, (and we beheld his glory, the glory as of the only begotten of the Father,) full of grace and truth" (John 1:14). In the Hebrew Old Testament and the Greek Septuagint, "glory" "denotes the visible manifestation accompanying a theophany, which, in the Fourth Gospel was manifest in the signs of Jesus."[9] God's glory is manifest when he reveals himself. Jesus's miracles, called "signs" by John, are an important way in which Jesus reveals his divinity.

Another way that, paradoxically, the incarnate Lord reveals his glory is in his death. In the Gospel of John, the verb *glorify* "is used distinctively to signify the dying of Jesus. . . . It was a dying which revealed a life of *ḥesed we-emet* [grace and truth] faithfulness to the Father, who sent him, in compassion and faithfulness, to his own."[10] "The incarnate life of Jesus revealed God's glory as *ḥesed we-emet* [grace and truth], and this was sharply focused in the moment of his dying."[11] During Jesus's suffering, he was manifesting God's glory. At the end of the Last Supper, as he went to the Garden of Gethsemane, Jesus explained: "Now is the Son of man glorified, and God is glorified in him. If God be glorified in him, God shall also glorify him in himself, and shall straightway glorify him" (John 13:31–32). Then in the Intercessory Prayer Jesus exclaimed, "Father, the hour is come; glorify thy Son, that thy Son also may glorify thee: . . . I have glorified thee on the earth: I have finished the work which thou gavest me to do. And now, O Father, glorify thou me with thine own self with the glory which I had with thee before the world was" (John 17:1, 4–5). Unlike some who might not be able reconcile the incarnation and the glory of God, John testifies of the paradox that only by being in a mortal tabernacle, and therefore being subject to suffering and death, could the glory of Jesus's submission to the Father and his perfect love be manifest.

John's use of the expression "tabernacled among us" gives deeper insight to the angel's teaching to King Benjamin in Mosiah 3: "The

Lord Omnipotent who reigneth, who was, and is from all eternity to all eternity, shall come down from heaven among the children of men, and shall dwell in a tabernacle of clay" (Mosiah 3:5). Just as John testifies, we can see the incarnation as God (the Word made flesh) coming to dwell in an impermanent tabernacle of clay, just as previously God had come down to dwell in the temporary tabernacle in the wilderness.

All Things Were Made by Him

Another way we see John's witness of Jesus as God is his identification of Christ as the Creator. This identification is designed not only as a witness of his previous divine acts from the foundation of the world, but as a framework to understand the new life that Jesus comes to give. Having confidence that Jesus created the world gives confidence that he can re-create us in his image, as his sons and daughters. "But as many as received him, to them gave he power to become the sons of God, even to them that believe on his name: Which were born, not of blood, nor of the will of the flesh, nor of the will of man, but of God" (John 1:12–13). John frames "the work of Jesus [as] the work of creation,"[12] but broadly conceived so that "it refers not only to what is established at the beginning, but also to what is brought to fulfillment at the end. Creation includes consummation and embraces therefore what can also be called redemption."[13] It has been argued that John's introductory phrase in chapter 1, "in the beginning," was designed not only to identify the Word as the means of creation, but to point out that it was John's purpose "for the *whole* of the gospel to be read in light of Genesis, that it is in itself a new 'first book.'"[14]

John seems to echo the biblical account of creation in a spiritual parallel between the giving of life to Adam through breath in Genesis 2:7 ("And the Lord God formed man of the dust of the ground, and breathed into his nostrils the breath of life; and man became a living soul") and John 20:22 when the risen Lord breathed on the apostles "and saith unto them, Receive ye the Holy Ghost." As Murray Rae notes, "Like the Creator in Genesis 2—indeed, precisely because he

is the same one through whom all things came to be (John 1:3, 10)—
Jesus has the power to give life. Again, this is not mere existence, but
life in its fullness—that life which is God's purpose from the beginning."[15] The connection between the reception of the gift of the Holy
Ghost and a new life in Christ is a critical gospel insight that can help
to explain the concept of being "born of God."

After Jesus tells Nicodemus about the need to be "born again,"
he uses the concept of breath in association with life in the Spirit.
Jesus tells him: "The wind [*pneuma*, breath, spirit] bloweth where it
listeth, and thou hearest the sound thereof, but canst not tell whence
it cometh, and whither it goeth: so is every one that is born of the
Spirit" (John 3:8). This discussion with Nicodemus follows the connection of Spirit and breath in Genesis 2. "Just as the spirit of God
blows mysteriously at the dawn of creation, so too here, the blowing
of the Spirit is a portent of new creation."[16] Jesus's use of the term
breath here might also be an allusion to Psalm 104:29–30: "Thou tak-
est away their breath, they die, and return to their dust. Thou sendest
forth thy spirit, they are created." Connecting Jesus as the creator of
the world with the re-creation that he offers to those who believe and
follow him is a central point of the Fourth Gospel.

Jesus's works bear testimony of him and point to spiritual realities: "one discerns in the work that Jesus performs the fulfillment of
God's purposes in creation."[17] In each of his healings we learn that
we were created to be whole. In each of his miraculous interven-
tions with water and food we learn that we were created to be nour-
ished with his abundance. Marianne Meye Thompson observes that
"John interprets the miracles by labeling them 'signs.' That is, they
are tokens of Jesus' own identity as the agent of God's salvation . . .
the Johannine miracles acclaim him as the agent through whom God
brings life to the world."[18] John uses the Greek term translated "sign"
seventeen times in his Gospel, compared to nine in Matthew, six in
Mark, and nine in Luke.[19] In the Synoptic Gospels the writers more
often use other words such as *dynamis*, or "powerful deed or work,"
to describe the miracles of Jesus.[20] Out of the seventeen uses of the

term *sēmeion*, or "sign," sixteen of those usages are in the first half of the Gospel of John, known as the "Book of Signs."[21] "The signs of the Fourth Gospel are essential manifestations of the creative power of the incarnate Word (John 1:14) and are the very means by which the identity of Jesus, who was with and who was God (John 1:1), is revealed."[22] Through the carefully organized presentation of these "signs" to echo the days of creation, the Gospel of John allows the accounts of these miracles to function as tokens of the divine identity of Jesus.[23]

In the Gospel of John, Jesus declares: "I am come that they might have life, and that they might have it more abundantly" (John 10:10). From a Restoration point of view, we can appreciate how, through the gift of the Holy Ghost, the new life that is in Christ is made available to those who believe and covenant to follow him. While Paul, not John, uses the language of believers becoming a "new creature" "in Christ" (see 2 Corinthians 5:17), "John does speak of 'new life,' and it is clear that by virtue of the transforming work of Christ the things of creation are made new."[24] The book of Revelation likewise gives us a vision of Jesus's work of re-creation, picking up the same when it relates, "And he that sat upon the throne said, Behold, I make all things new. . . . He that overcometh shall inherit all things; and I will be his God, and he shall be my son" (Revelation 21:5, 7). All the miracles or "signs" that Jesus performed point to his creative power and ability to give life and can build our confidence in this ultimate creation of giving us eternal life and being re-created as sons and daughters in his image in celestial glory.

Behold the Lamb of God, Which Taketh Away the Sin of the World

Once we appreciate the extent to which "John's very concept of glory is 'anchored . . . to the paradox of the crucifixion,'"[25] we are better prepared to see the subtle ways in which he points to Jesus's mission of salvation throughout his Gospel.[26] Some have discounted John's use of terms that show up only in the first chapter, but a strong case can be made that "though 'Lamb,' like 'Logos,' appears only at the head of the Gospel, its placement there is programmatic. The Evangelist wants us to read the entire book as the story of the Logos-become-flesh who laid down his life as God's Lamb."[27] In chapter 2, at the wedding at Cana, the shift from water to wine and Jesus's comment that "mine hour is not yet come" (John 2:4) point toward his final sacrifice because at the cross blood and water come out of his side. "Blood and water, water and wine. John is telling us of the transformation from old life to new, from the blandness of water to the richness of wine. Is it new life we want? In linking the first sign to the seventh, John is telling us how we may have it. The new creation comes about because of the work of Jesus, brought to its climax on the cross."[28] John's entire Gospel narrative builds up to his "hour," "the hour when he is lifted up on the cross and his glory is made known."[29] In the incarnation Christology of the Gospel of John, Jesus's humanity made his death possible and his divinity made his death glorious and redemptive.

Thompson observes that "one of the striking features of John's account is the way in which he presents Jesus as deliberately advancing towards his death with the full knowledge that it accomplished God's salvation of the world."[30] John's use of the sacrificial language of Lamb of God in chapter 1 ties to the hour of his sacrifice: "Jesus' hour, the lifting up of the Son of Man, is the moment toward which, according to John, the whole of Jesus' ministry is directed. The signs of the Gospel are to be understood in this context as a foreshadowing of this glory and a participation ahead of time in the new life that is to come."[31] Again, the structure of the Gospel of John has the first six "signs" of his divinity in the first half, and then presents the account of his crucifixion in the second half as the seventh sign, helping the readers to make sense of the glory of his sacrifice rather than to see it simply as a defeat.

So, while there is not extensive explicit elaboration on this Lamb of God imagery in the Gospel of John, it is clearly central to John's vision of Jesus's identity and the meaning of Christ's incarnation—to become mortal to give his life as "the Lamb of God, which taketh away the sin of the world" (John 1:29). John's witness mirrors that of Abinadi who testified that "God himself shall come down among the children of men, and shall redeem his people" and "after working many mighty miracles among the children of men, he shall be led, yea, even as Isaiah said, as a sheep before the shearer is dumb, so he opened not his mouth" (Mosiah 15:1, 6).

I Am

Just as the use of Logos and the Lamb in the first chapter create a framework for thinking about Jesus's divinity and the purpose of his incarnation, the biblical "I Am" (or in Greek, *egō eimi*) statements in John can also be seen as a structuring device "for invoking [a] christological framework and thought about Jesus."[32] In passages unique to the Gospel of John, Jesus gives the Greek equivalent of the divine name that Moses was given by Jehovah and is then subsequently threatened with stoning for blasphemy. At the burning bush, Moses asks what name to give the children of Israel when they ask who sent him. We read that "God said unto Moses, I Am That I Am: and he said, Thus shalt thou say unto the children of Israel, I Am hath sent me unto you" (Exodus 3:14). While scholars discuss both linguistic and theological issues with these I Am statements, a compelling argument can be made that these passages should be understood as Christ's self-revelation of his divinity.[33]

There are two sets of I Am statements in the Gospel of John, and they can be categorized as either absolute I Am statements or I Am statements with predicates, that is, where Jesus is equating himself with something. Significantly, in both Hebrew- and Greek-language Old Testaments, one can likewise identify seven I Am statements made by Jehovah.[34] By having Jesus echo these seven biblical pronouncements of YHWH's unique divinity, the Gospel of John powerfully asserts his divinity.[35] The statements with predicates are easier to distinguish in English:

+ "I am the bread of life" (John 6:35, 41, 48)
+ "I am the light of the world" (John 8:12; 9:5)
+ "I am the door [gate] of the sheep" (John 10:7, 9)
+ "I am the good shepherd" (John 10:11, 14)
+ "I am the resurrection and the life" (John 11:25)
+ "I am the way, the truth, and the life" (John 14:6)
+ "I am the true vine" (John 15:1)[36]

The absolute I Am *egō eimi* statements, however, are more easily buried in the translation, and while they are more fiercely debated, they provide stronger identification of Jesus with the God of the Old Testament.[37]

+ To the Samaritan woman: "Jesus saith unto her, I that speak unto thee am he" (John 4:26 KJV) or "Jesus said to her, 'I am he, the one who is speaking to you'" (John 4:26 New Revised Standard Version)
+ To the disciples on the boat: "But he saith unto them, It is I; be not afraid" (John 6:20)
+ At the temple: "I said therefore unto you, that ye shall die in your sins: for if ye believe not that I am he" (John 8:24)
+ and "When ye have lifted up the Son of man, then shall ye know that I am he" (John 8:28)
+ and "Verily, verily, I say unto you, Before Abraham was, I am" (John 8:58)
+ At the Last Supper: "Now I tell you before it come, that, when it is come to pass, ye may believe that I am he" (John 13:19)
+ At the arrest: "Jesus saith unto them, I am he" (John 18:5, 6, 8)[38]

These absolute I Am statements seem to function as places where the Gospel of John has Jesus directly identifying himself as Jehovah.

One theological issue that gives some scholars pause when Jesus seems to use these statements as a simple way to identify himself with

YHWH, or Jehovah, relates to the passage in John 8:28 where Jesus says: "When ye have lifted up the Son of man, then shall ye know that I am he, and that I do nothing of myself; but as my Father hath taught me, I speak these things." The concern some have with this passage has been articulated in this way: "It is simply intolerable that Jesus should be made to say, 'I am God, the supreme God of the Old Testament, and being God I do as I am told.'"[39] In some ways this reflects an effort to preserve the sovereignty and perfection of God by bringing into question the idea that Jesus is really claiming to be God with this I Am language. For some the idea of an obedient God can seem untenable. If he is actually God, what would be greater than him that he would he need to obey? For many Christians, however, and certainly for us as Latter-day Saints, John's statement seems perfectly reasonable. John shows us Christ with his divinity manifest in his submission to his Father, just as it was manifest in his incarnation in the flesh. The Gospel of John testifies of Jesus Christ as God, the Creator, the Great I Am, and also as the perfect Son of God who came to do the will of the Father.

The Divine Word

Through repeated connections to Old Testament imagery and language, the Fourth Gospel testifies that Jesus is God. It thereby witnesses that he has power to heal and change our very natures, to re-create us in his image and give us the kind of life that he experiences, if we believe and accept the gift he is offering. Only faith in a God who is mighty to save can allow us to be one with him as he is one with the Father (see John 17:11, 21–24). John testifies that Christ is the perfect Son, including being human with us and setting an example, but also that he is the Lord God Almighty, Creator of Heaven and Earth. He testifies that the Word who was with God and who was God came down into a frail, mortal tabernacle to be the Lamb of God who taketh away the sin of the world, "that whosoever believeth in him should not perish, but have everlasting life" (John 3:16).

JENNIFER C. LANE *is a professor of religious education and former dean of the College of Human Development at Brigham Young University—Hawaii.*

KEITH H. LANE *is an associate professor of religious education and former chair of the Department of Religious Education at Brigham Young University— Hawaii.*

Notes

1. For an overview of the consensus of most scholars on these questions, see Raymond E. Brown, *An Introduction to the Gospel of John*, ed. Francis J. Moloney (New York: Doubleday, 2003). For an argument for earlier authorship, see Craig L. Blomberg, *The Historical Reliability of John's Gospel: Issues and Commentary* (Downers Grove, IL: InterVarsity Press, 2011). We refer to John as the author for simplicity, but are not making claims about a particular theory of authorship or compositional history.

2. Significantly, the Book of Mormon also witnesses that Jesus Christ was God Incarnate. In the title page itself, Moroni explains that he is writing to convince "the Jew and Gentile that Jesus is the Christ, the Eternal God." Abinadi testifies that in the mortal life of Christ we have the fulfillment of the promise that "God himself shall come down among the children of men, and shall redeem his people" (Mosiah 15:1). Christ himself uses language very close to that in John 1 in 3 Nephi 9: "Behold, I am Jesus Christ the Son of God. I created the heavens and the earth, and all things that in them are. I was with the Father from the beginning. I am in the Father, and the Father in me; and in me hath the Father glorified his name. I came unto my own, and my own received me not. . . . And as many as have received me, to them have I given to become the sons of God" (3 Nephi 9:15–17). Here we find both the emphasis on Christ as God and as Creator that is articulated in John as well as his role in our becoming the "sons of God," that by having sufficient faith we can be re-created, reborn through him.

3. The idea that God's Word had almost a separate existence had previously been articulated by Philo, a Hellenized Jew living in Alexandria in the early first century. Pollard argues that the Logos-concept functioned for John as only a "point of contact" and that his use went beyond the Hellenistic worldview, having deep roots in Jewish and Old Testament meaning. T. E. Pollard, *Johannine Christology and the Early Church* (London: Cambridge University Press, 1970), 6, 13.

4. Martin Hengel, "The Prologue of the Gospel of John as the Gateway to Christological Truth," in *The Gospel of John and Christian Theology*, ed. Richard Bauckham and Carl Mosser (Grand Rapids, MI: Eerdmans, 2008), 273.

5. Pollard, *Johannine Christology*, 19.

6. John Painter, "The Prologue as an Hermeneutical Key to Reading the Fourth Gospel," in *Studies in the Gospel of John and Its Christology*, ed. Joseph Verhyden et al. (Leuven: Peeters, 2014), 56.

7. For an introduction to some of the concerns that some gentiles would have had about the message of the incarnation and resurrection, see Jennifer C. Lane, "Jews and Greeks: The Broader Context for Writing the New Testament," in *How the New Testament Came to Be*, ed. Kent P. Jackson and Frank F. Judd Jr. (Provo, UT: Religious Studies Center; Salt Lake City: Deseret Book, 2006), 62–77.

8. Paul A. Rainbow, *Johannine Theology: The Gospel, The Epistles and the Apocalypse* (Downers Grove, IL: InterVarsity Press, 2014), 174. Painter, "Incarnation of the Word," 56.

9. Painter, "Incarnation of the Word, 57.".

10. Painter, "Incarnation of the Word," 57.

11. Painter, "Incarnation of the Word," 57.

12. Murray Rae, "The Testimony of Works in the Christology of John's Gospel," in *The Gospel of John and Christian Theology*, ed. Richard Bauckham and Carl Mosser (Grand Rapids, MI: Eerdmans, 2008), 295.

13. Rae, "Testimony of Works," 296. See also Anthony M. Moore, *Signs of Salvation: The Theme of Creation in John's Gospel* (Cambridge: James Clarke, 2013), 49.

14. Moore, *Signs of Salvation*, 134.

15. Rae, "Testimony of Works," 299.

16. Rae, "Testimony of Works," 300.

17. Rae, "Testimony of Works," 298.

18. Marianne Meye Thompson, "The Historical Jesus and the Johannine Christ," in *Exploring the Gospel of John: In Honor of D. Moody Smith*, ed. R. Alan Culpepper and C. Clifton Black (Louisville, KY: Westminster John Knox, 1996), 24. This is in contrast to the role of miracles in the Synoptic Gospels: "whereas the Synoptic miracles are linked to the fulfillment of the messianic age (Matt. 11:4; Luke 7:22) and to the manifestation of God's kingdom" (p. 24).

19. Moore, *Signs of Salvation*, 133.

20. Eric D. Huntsman, *The Miracles of Jesus* (Salt Lake City: Deseret Book, 2014), 3.

21. Moore, *Signs of Salvation*, 133. John 12:37 is the last of the first group of usages of the term.

22. Moore, *Signs of Salvation*, 134.

23. Moore observes that "the seven miracles of Jesus described in the narrative of the gospel correspond closely to the 'seven days' of creation described in the opening chapter of Genesis, and so do make Jesus' divinity explicit. They reveal him to be at one with the Father (cf. John 10:30), manifesting the creativity of the Father and reaping the harvest (Jn 4:34–35; cf. 17:4) and, as the Resurrection and the Life, breathing the life of the Father, the one who sent him (Jn 4:34; 5:24; 5:30; 5:37; etc.) into the created order" (Moore, *Signs of Salvation*, 134).

24. Rae, "Testimony of Works," 296.

25. Rainbow, *Johannine Theology*, 179; citing Günther Bornkamm, "Towards the Interpretation of John's Gospel: A Discussion of *The Testament of Jesus*," in *The Interpretation of John*, ed. John Ashton, Issues in Religion and Theology 9 (Philadelphia: Fortress Press, 1986), 88.

26. Eric D. Huntsman provides an important discussion of how the Gospel of John consistently frames Jesus as the paschal lamb in the imagery of his being "lifted up" and having his flesh eaten by believers, as well as John's timing of the crucifixion to coincide with the slaying of the lambs by the

priests in "The Lamb of God: Unique Aspects of the Passion Narrative in John," in *Behold the Lamb of God: An Easter Celebration*, ed. Richard N. Holzapfel, Frank F. Judd Jr., and Thomas A. Wayment (Provo, UT: Religious Studies Center, 2008), 52–55.

27. Rainbow, *Johannine Theology*, 183.

28. Rae, "Testimony of Works," 308.

29. Rae, "Testimony of Works," 303.

30. Thompson, "Historical Jesus," 31.

31. Rae, "Testimony of Works," 303.

32. Stanley E. Porter, *John, His Gospel, and Jesus: In Pursuit of the Johannine Voice* (Grand Rapids, MI: Eerdmans, 2015), 148.

33. See Andreas J. Köstenberger and Scott R. Swain, *Father, Son, and Spirit: The Trinity and John's Gospel* New Studies in Biblical Theology 24 (Downers Grove, IL: InterVarsity Press, 2008), 37. "At times, the expression is used simply meaning 'I am' without indicating a claim to deity on Jesus' part. At other times, especially in the seven absolute 'I am' sayings, Jesus' deity is clearly implied" (p. 37). "These pronouncements constitute clear allusions to Yahweh's own sevenfold self-declaration of unique and unrivaled divinity that occurs in the OT. John's point is clear: Jesus is Yahweh" (p. 125).

34. See Richard Bauckham, *The Testimony of the Beloved Disciple: Narrative, History, and Theology in the Gospel of John* (Grand Rapids, MI: Baker Academic, 2007), 245–47.

35. Bauckham, *Testimony of the Beloved Disciple*, 247.

36. See Bauckham, *Testimony of the Beloved Disciple*, 243.

37. See Bauckham, *Testimony of the Beloved Disciple*, 246.

38. One issue that some scholars bring up about these references is that in some cases the "I am" might simply be part of the normal conversation rather than a reference to the divine name (see Bauckham, *Testimony of the Beloved Disciple*, 244). Another point of debate centers on the Old Testament reference. The Septuagint uses a slightly different phrase than *egō eimi* in Exodus 3:14, *egō eimi ho ōn* ("I am the one who is"). Bauckham, *Testimony of the Beloved Disciple*, 246. The Hebrew for I Am in Exodus 3:14 might, however, be the source of the reference. See Bauckham, *Testimony*

of the Beloved Disciple, 246. Another Greek language biblical reference point for *egō eimi* looks to Deuteronomy 32:39 and a number of places in Isaiah when Jehovah declares: "See now that I, even *I, am he*, and there is no god with me" (Deuteronomy 32:39; emphasis added) and "Who hath wrought and done it, calling the generations from the beginning? I the Lord, the first, and with the last; *I am he*" (Isaiah 41:4; emphasis added).

39. C. K. Barrett, "Christocentric or Theocentric? Observations on the Theological Method of the Fourth Gospel," in *Essays on John* (Philadelphia: Westminster Press, 1982), 12. There are a variety of views about the subordination of the Son to the Father in Christian thought. Some traditions, particularly Orthodox, are more comfortable with the idea of subordination while others see it as a heresy.

9

Johannine Christology through the Lens of Three of Its Dialogues

Gaye Strathearn

In comparison with the Synoptic Gospels of Matthew, Mark, and Luke, the Gospel of John has a very different interpretive lens through which it answers the age-old question "Who is Jesus?" The Gospel itself identifies its purpose: "These are written, that ye might believe that Jesus is the Christ, the Son of God; and that believing ye might have life through his name" (John 20:31). While many individuals in the Synoptic Gospels declare Jesus to be the Son of God, there are very few accounts of Jesus himself declaring so until the latter part of his ministry. In this respect, John's Gospel is very different because in it Jesus makes frequent declarations about his divine status throughout his entire ministry.[1] Thus John's Gospel is frequently described as having a high Christology, and Clement of Alexandria identified it as "a spiritual gospel."[2]

The Gospel's introductory prologue declares Jesus to be the eternal Word who, in the premortal realm, was not only with God but "was God" (John 1:1). This Divine Word was then the God who "was made flesh" (1:14). John the Baptist, recognizing that this unique combination of divinity and flesh separated Jesus from him and the rest of humanity, declared, "He that cometh from above [Greek, *anōthen*] is above all: he that is of the earth is earthly, and speaketh of the earth: he that cometh from heaven is above all" (3:31; see also 8:23).[3] John's statement was not meant to denigrate humanity, but it does highlight the "otherness" of Jesus and helps readers understand why so many people in the Gospel of John misunderstood Jesus's teachings. His audiences were "earthly" and spoke "of the earth," terms that become both synonyms of and symbols to describe those who lack the eternal perspective necessary to fully understand the implications of Jesus's status as God even though he "was made flesh."

One of the strategies John's Gospel employs to reinforce this high Christology is its repeated use of dialogues. It has been calculated that more than half of Jesus's direct speech in John's Gospel is found in these dialogues.[4] Whereas the Synoptic Gospels, with a few exceptions, concentrate on Jesus's "short, pithy sayings and parables," John's Gospel emphasizes Jesus's teachings through dialogues with those "whose misunderstandings further the conversation and enable Jesus to develop his theological teaching in more detail."[5] These dialogues function in two major ways. First, they serve to draw in and engage Jesus's dialogue partners so they can move beyond their "earthly" perspective and recognize that he "cometh from above." Second, the dialogues also provide an important forum for Jesus to declare his own divine status. Thus they function as a major platform for much of the Christology found in this Gospel.

In this paper we will examine these functions by reviewing three of the Johannine dialogues: Jesus's dialogues with Nicodemus (John 3:1–21), with the Samaritan woman at the well (4:5–29), and with the man born blind (9:1–38). Although these are not the only dialogues that function in these ways,[6] I have chosen them because they have points of continuity with each other that reinforce the overall christological emphasis of John's Gospel and because they each bring unique elements that enrich the overall christological tapestry. It is hoped that by recognizing the christological focus in these dialogues, modern readers will be better equipped to recognize the nuances of John's witness that Jesus is the Christ, the Son of God.

Jesus's Dialogue with Nicodemus (John 3:1–21)

Jesus's dialogue with Nicodemus "is the first extended discourse in the Fourth Gospel."[7] We know little about the man himself. He is mentioned only three times in the New Testament, all of which are in John's Gospel. In those three accounts, as we shall see, he is somewhat of an enigmatic figure.[8] Before the actual dialogue begins, the narrative alerts the reader to the tentative and seemingly fragile nature of Nicodemus's commitment to Jesus and lays the groundwork for his limited perspective and for why he struggles to understand both who Jesus is and what he is trying to teach.

First, John describes Nicodemus as a "man of the Pharisees" and a "ruler of the Jews" (John 3:1). Clearly he is someone of stature in the Jewish community, a representative of the leadership, though John's use of the term "the Jews" (Greek, *hoi Ioudaioi*) is often problematic. However, as Jouette M. Bassler has noted, even this early in John's Gospel, the term "Jews" has more to do with a lack of receptivity to Jesus than it does with national or religious identity (see, for example, John 1:19, 24, 26; 2:18).[9]

Second, although we know little about why he came looking for Jesus, Nicodemus appears to have been among those who had "believed" (Greek, *episteusan*) when they saw the miracles Jesus performed during the first Passover of his ministry (John 2:23; compare 3:2). At first glance a reader could reasonably consider this belief to be a positive attribute. This seems to have been the case for the disciples who "believed on him" (again, Greek, *episteusan*) after witnessing the miracle of turning water into wine (2:11). In this instance, there is no indication that Jesus questioned their faith. But John quickly distances the two groups. He records that Jesus did not reciprocate the trust (Greek, *episteusan*) of the believers who were at the Passover "because he knew all men" (2:24). The sense of this statement seems clear: Jesus had reservations about the motives behind their belief. In his encounter with Nathaniel, Jesus had already shown that he could read people's hearts. Even before he met Nathaniel, Jesus declared that he was "an Israelite [note, he does not call him a Jew] indeed, in whom is no guile" (1:47). Whatever Jesus saw in the hearts of this group of believers, he knew that their level of belief was not equivalent to that of the disciples in John 2:11, nor was it developed sufficiently for them to receive "power to become the sons of God, even to them that believe [Greek, *tois pisteuousin*] on his name" (1:12).[10]

A third clue that suggests Nicodemus's limited perspective is the seemingly innocuous statement that he came to Jesus "by night." This phrase is more important than just indicating time. The contrast between light and darkness is an important theme frequently woven throughout John's narrative. It is introduced in the Gospel's prologue: "In him [i.e., the Word] was life; and the life was the light of men. And the light shineth in darkness; and the darkness comprehended it not" (John 1:4–5). The Greek word which the King James Bible renders as "comprehended" is *katalambanō*, which frequently has the sense of pursuing something in order to gain control of it.[11] The word can thus be translated as "seize," and hence the phrase could also be translated like this: "and the darkness could not seize the light." John's Gospel repeatedly describes Jesus as the "light of the world" (John 8:12; 1:8–9; 9:5; 12:35–36, 46). Latter-day Saints understand that in the premortal world there was a war in heaven whereby Satan (as represented by darkness) could not seize or overcome the light. Darkness, therefore, is frequently used as a symbol in John's Gospel for those who, in mortality, continue the attempt to overcome the light. Thus, while Nicodemus seems to have been genuinely intrigued by Jesus's miracles, the narrative indicates that he was not yet ready to openly confess and give his loyalty to Jesus. He still valued the things of the world and probably did not wish to incur the condemnation of his peers by seeking out Jesus during the day. Such an assessment of Nicodemus's actions seems warranted by Jesus's condemnation of those who seek darkness later in the chapter: "And this is the condemnation, that light is come into the world, and men loved darkness rather than light, because their deeds were evil. For everyone that doeth evil hateth the light, neither cometh to the light, lest his deeds should be reproved. But he that doeth truth cometh to the light, that his deeds may be made manifest, that they are wrought in God" (3:19–21).[12] At the end of the Gospel, the fact that Nicodemus came to Jesus at night is how he is identified when he comes with Joseph of Arimathea to procure Jesus's body: "And there came also Nicodemus, which at the first came to Jesus by night" (19:39).

Fourth, having seen the miracles, Nicodemus declares to Jesus, "Rabbi, we know that thou art a teacher [Greek, *didaskalos*] come from God: for no man can do these miracles that thou doest, except God be with him" (John 3:2). In this one statement Nicodemus shows that he does not understand who Jesus is, at least in the Johannine context. His use of the title *rabbi* is certainly a title of respect, used by others in John's Gospel (see John 1:38, 49; 6:25). But it is "a partial confession of faith."[13] Nicodemus's lack of understanding is highlighted in the contrast between his definition and that of Philip. Whereas Nicodemus uses *rabbi* as a title for "a teacher who comes from God," Philip uses it as a title for the "Son of God" (1:49). While it is clearly evident in John's Gospel that Jesus *is* indeed a teacher, what Nicodemus fails to realize as he approaches Jesus is that he is much more than that. As we have learned in the introductory prologue, Jesus is not just sent from God—he is the Word who was not only with God in the premortal realm but who was in fact God.

Understanding all of Nicodemus's limitations, Jesus nevertheless chose to engage him in a dialogue in an effort to help him raise his limited "earthly" perspective and begin to see Jesus from an eternal perspective. Jesus begins this dialogue with a discussion about entrance into the kingdom of God. "Jesus answered and said unto him, Verily, verily, I say unto thee, Except a man be born again, he cannot see the kingdom of God" (John 3:3). The Greek word translated as "again" is *anōthen*. While it can refer to a repeated action, it is the same word used later in chapter 3 to describe Jesus as being "from above" (3:31; 19:11), as we have noted. As one who is "of the earth . . . and speaketh of the earth," Nicodemus misunderstands the spiritual intent of Jesus's statement and interprets *anōthen* according to the first definition: "How can a man be born when he is old? can he enter the second time into his mother's womb, and be born?" (John 3:4). So Jesus clarifies the spiritual intent of his teaching: "Verily, verily, I say unto thee, Except a man be born of water and of the Spirit, he cannot enter into the kingdom of God. That which is born of the flesh is flesh; and that which is born of the Spirit is spirit" (3:5–6).

Thus Jesus teaches Nicodemus that to be born "from above" is to be born of both water and the spirit. Seeing miracles was an important experience that led Nicodemus to seek out Jesus, but Jesus wants more for him. He wants Nicodemus to transition from being a spectator watching Jesus's miracles to one who enters and becomes a part of the kingdom of God. This type of transition is facilitated not just by the ordinance of baptism—that only enables a person to "see the kingdom of God" (John 3:3). Rather, to be fully engaged in the kingdom, one needs a baptism that is sanctified by the outpouring of the Spirit. The Prophet Joseph Smith taught that principle this way: you "might as well baptise a bag of sand as a man if not done in view of the getting of the Holy ghost.— baptism by water is but 1/2 a baptism.— & is good for nothi[n]g with[out] the other.—the Holy Gho[s]t."[14]

This process is not something immediately tangible, but its effects are nevertheless apparent. Using a play on words that is not discernible in the English translation, Jesus continues: "Marvel not that I said unto thee, Ye must be born again [Greek, *anōthen*]. The wind [Greek, *pneuma*] bloweth where it listeth, and thou hearest the sound thereof, but canst not tell whence it cometh, and whither it goeth: so is every one that is born of the Spirit [Greek, *pneuma*]" (John 3:7–8). Thus, as one scholar has noted, "The effects of the Spirit's work can be discerned in creating the children of God, those who 'believe in his name,'" mentioned in John's prologue (1:12–13).[15]

Unfortunately, Nicodemus still struggles to understand Jesus's teaching. "How can these things be?" (John 3:9). He is so mired in his earthly experience that he is "incapable of grasping Jesus's words about rebirth."[16] Jesus responds to Nicodemus, "Art thou the teacher [Greek, *ho didaskalos*] of Israel, and knowest not these things?" (3:10; my translation). The definite article suggests that Nicodemus represents all the teachers of Israel who "speaketh of the earth." It is not just he who fails to understand. Jesus continues, "Verily, verily, I say unto thee, We speak that we do know, and testify that we have seen; and ye receive not our witness. If I have told you earthly things, and ye believe not, how shall ye believe, if I tell you of heavenly things? And no man hath ascended up to heaven, but he that came down from heaven, even the Son of man which is in heaven" (3:11–13). Neither Nicodemus nor any other teacher can understand the things of heaven, including understanding who Jesus is, through their earthly study. As the Lord taught Isaiah, "For my thoughts are not your thoughts, neither are your ways my ways, saith the Lord. For as the heavens are higher than the earth, so are my ways higher than your ways, and my thoughts than your thoughts" (Isaiah 55:8–9). Nevertheless Jesus, as the Son of Man, came down from heaven to teach them.

What is it that Jesus wants Nicodemus and all Israel to understand about heaven? "And as Moses lifted up the serpent in the wilderness, even so must the Son of man be lifted up: That whosoever believeth in him should not perish, but have eternal life. For God so loved the world, that he gave his only begotten Son, that whosoever believeth in him should not perish, but have everlasting life. For God sent not his Son into the world to condemn the world; but that the world through him might be saved" (John 3:14–17).[17]

Unfortunately, John's narrative does not include Nicodemus's immediate response to Jesus's teachings. Perhaps Nicodemus, like those who experienced day one of Jesus's ministry at the Bountiful temple (see 3 Nephi 17:2–3), needed time to ponder, pray, and receive the outpouring of the Spirit so as to comprehend what he had been taught and recognize the implications for his life. Certainly in John 7 he was willing to stand up to his peers on Jesus's behalf, even though they ridiculed him for it (John 7:45–52). He also came with Joseph of Arimathea, bringing spices for Jesus's burial when they procured Jesus's body from Pilate (19:38–42). Both of these acts suggest that Nicodemus did indeed begin to understand the heavenly perspective of who Jesus really is. The dialogue with Nicodemus reminds all readers that only through being born from above is one able to fully comprehend how the crucified Jesus could bring eternal life to the inhabitants of this world and also provide evidence of God's great love for his people.

The Samaritan Woman at the Well (John 4:5–29)

In the story of Nicodemus, his earthly qualities were highlighted, at least in part, by his designation as a "man of the Pharisees" and "a ruler of the Jews," a communal leader who came to Jesus "by night." In John's second extended dialogue, the qualities of his dialogue partner are "a mirror image" of Nicodemus.[18] This time Jesus engages a woman, a Samaritan, and does so in broad daylight (John 4:6). Unlike Nicodemus who came in search of Jesus, in this instance Jesus initiates the dialogue. As part of his journey between Judea and Galilee, Jesus stopped at Jacob's well in Sychar (4:3–5). The imperfect tense of the verb in verse 6 "was sitting" (Greek, *kathezomai*) indicates that he was specifically waiting for the woman to come and draw water[19] so that he could ask her for a drink.

Collecting water for drinking and household chores was a laborious part of a woman's daily responsibilities. In both Judea and Samaria, the people relied on wells and cisterns to collect water during the brief rainy season to ensure their survival during the hot, dry summers. When the Samaritan woman arrived at the well in the middle of the day, her mind was undoubtedly focused on the grind of her daily chore, which the narrative suggests she was anxious to eliminate (John 4:15).

Jesus's request for a drink seems to have startled the woman: "How is it that thou, being a Jew, askest drink of me, which am a woman of Samaria? for the Jews are not on friendly terms [Greek, *synchraomai*] with the Samaritans" (John 4:9).[20] Relations between Jews and Samaritans were at a low point during New Testament times.[21] Her questions highlight that at the beginning of this dialogue, from her earthly perspective, the woman saw Jesus simply as "a Jew," which in her mind would have been the equivalent of an enemy. The narrative uses two literary techniques to indicate that the woman acted as a spokesperson for the Samaritan people as Nicodemus was for the teachers of Israel. First, unlike Nicodemus, she remains nameless throughout the narrative, known only by her ethnic status as a "woman of Samaria." Second, by verse 12, the dialogue shifts from the single forms of speech into plural forms:[22] "Art thou greater than *our* father Jacob, which gave *us* the well, and drank thereof himself, and his children, and his cattle?" (emphasis added; see also John 4:20).

Jesus uses the dialogue to engage the woman and capture her attention by teaching of the living water that he promised to provide for her. Like Nicodemus before her, the Samaritan woman misunderstood the intent of Jesus's teachings, understanding them only from an earthly perspective: "Sir, thou hast nothing to draw with, and the well is deep: from whence then hast thou that living water? Art thou greater than our father Jacob, which gave us the well, and drank thereof himself, and his children, and his cattle?" (John 4:11–12). Jesus's response further accentuated the woman's misunderstanding. "Whosoever drinketh of this water shall thirst again: But whosoever drinketh of the water that I shall give him shall never thirst; but the water that I shall give him shall be in him a well of water springing up into everlasting life" (4:13–14). Given the laborious chore of collecting the water each day, the woman's response is understandable, even if misguided. "Sir, give me this water, that I thirst not, neither come hither to draw" (4:15).

Only after Jesus had gained her attention with the hope of living water did he move to help her raise her sights. To do so he had to accomplish two things. First, he had to bring her to a point where she felt a sense of sin and therefore a need for help. Second, he had to establish his authority as God. He accomplished both of these as he shifted the dialogue away from living water and focused on her marital status. He simultaneously raised a mirror of spiritual introspection and opened the door for her to see him from a higher spiritual perspective. He revealed to her that even though they had just met, he knew who she was: more than the fact that she was a Samaritan, she was a woman who had had five husbands but was then living in an adulterous relationship (John 4:16–18).

The revelation clearly affected the woman. Later, she told the men in her village that Jesus "told me all things that ever I did" (John 4:29). In light of the details recorded in John, this statement appears to be a hyperbole, but it illustrates how profound the revelation of her life was to the woman. She now saw this man at the well in a different light. She knew that Jesus was much more than a Jew: "Sir, I perceive that thou art a prophet" (4:19).

This was a significant realization for her. The Samaritans anticipated the coming of a prophet like unto Moses (Deuteronomy 18:15–18), which they identified as a *Taheb*, or a revealer.[23] But with this realization, the woman was faced with an internal quandary. On the one hand, she recognized Jesus as a prophet; on the other, she was torn by the reality that "*our* fathers worshipped in this mountain; and ye say, that in Jerusalem is the place where men ought to worship" (John 4:20; emphasis added). Note how she again uses the plural form of speech to reinforce her status as spokesperson. The mountain that the Samaritans worshipped on was Mount Gerizim, located just to the south of Sychar, and would have been clearly visible to both Jesus and the woman. The Samaritans had built a temple there that had been destroyed by the Jewish leader John Hyrcanus in 109 BC. The past tense of the woman's statement that her ancestors worshipped on Mount Gerizim reflects the historical reality of Hyrcanus's actions. Even though the temple was never rebuilt, Samaritans continued to worship and offer sacrifices there in New Testament times, a practice that has continued into the present day.

Jesus's response to the question of where to worship was again calculated to move the Samaritan woman's perspective to an even higher level: "Woman, believe me, the hour cometh, when ye [plural] shall neither in this mountain, nor yet at Jerusalem, worship the Father" (John 4:21). Here Jesus acknowledged the woman's status as spokesperson by also using the plural form of speech. The physical temple on Mount Gerizim had been destroyed. The physical temple in Jerusalem would be destroyed within a few years. But the purpose of temples had always been to provide a way for individuals to enter the presence of God. The Samaritan woman was so concerned about the Jewish-Samaritan debate over the correct location for the temple that she had not recognized that she was then standing in the presence of God: he was the Word, who was God. At this point, the woman did not know what she worshipped (4:22). Salvation was "of the Jews" because the prophet standing before her was the source of salvation and because he, as she had quickly recognized at the beginning of their interaction, was a Jew.

Jesus taught her that the elements of "true worship" are not always a function of location or of having a physical building in which to worship. Just as Jesus taught Nicodemus the importance of the Spirit in helping earthly people to understand spiritual things, so Jesus taught the Samaritan woman that those who worship him "must worship him in spirit and in truth" (John 4:24). Again, with this added teaching the woman was confused. As we have noted, the Samaritans anticipated the coming of a *Taheb*, to whom she is probably referring when she declared, "I know that Messias cometh, which is called Christ: when he is come, he will tell us all things" (4:25). The Samaritans did not anticipate a messianic Davidic king. Having used the dialogue to create a teaching moment, Jesus was then ready to reveal fully his identity to the Samaritan woman. He was the fulfillment of this Samaritan hope; he was the prophet "like unto [Moses]" (compare 3 Nephi 20:23). But, in making that identification, he went further. He applied the divine title to himself. Literally, he says, "The one who speaks to you [is] I Am [Greek, *egō eimi*]" (4:26; author's translation; compare John 8:58; Exodus 3:11–14). Jesus was indeed the prophet like unto Moses, but he was also the God who directed Moses. In both of these roles, he had indeed come to tell her "all things" (John 4:25).

In this instance, unlike the Nicodemus narrative, we are not left to wonder about how the Samaritan woman responded to her dialogue with Jesus. John tells us that she "then left her waterpot" (John 4:28). At the beginning of the narrative she had come to the well with her waterpot in search of water, and she did indeed leave with water, but it was not the kind that she could carry in a pot. She had found the living water that Jesus had promised her. She then returned to Sychar and invited the villagers to "Come, see a man, which told me all things that ever I did: is not this the Christ?" (4:29).

In this dialogue Jesus helped the nameless woman of Samaria come to know that he was not just a Jew. He was the promised prophet, like unto Moses, who would speak the words of God; he was the Messiah; and he was the I Am. As such he was willing to cross social, religious, and political boundaries to seek out even those who lived in the periphery of society.

Jesus and the Man Born Blind (John 9:1–38)

Jesus's dialogue with the man born blind has points of both continuity and discontinuity with those of Nicodemus and the Samaritan woman at the well. With both Nicodemus and the Samaritan woman the dialogue was with *only* Jesus, but in this example of the man born blind, his interactions with Jesus act as bookends for a narrative that is interrupted by an ongoing dialogue, first with the man's neighbors and then with the Pharisees, both of whom question him extensively about how he received his sight. Even with this difference, however, there is also a continuation of themes that are important for John's Gospel as a whole and are also found in Nicodemus's experience.

The theme of darkness that we saw in the Nicodemus narrative returns. This man had been blind since birth, so the only thing that he had ever known was darkness. Unlike Nicodemus, however, the darkness is not a choice but something that happened "that the works of God should be made manifest in him" (John 9:3). His visual limitation was not only a physical reality but a symbol for his spiritual blindness. While receiving his physical sight from Jesus is an important miracle—one of the seven "signs" in the first half of John's Gospel[24]—the major focus in John's narrative is the spiritual aspect of helping him to see and recognize the eternal nature of Jesus's identity. His story reiterates that the process of coming to "see" Jesus is a progressive one.

Like the Samaritan woman, the blind man is also unnamed in the narrative, and his handicap means that he also exists in the marginal shadows of his religious and social community. He also functions as a representative of disciples. His story shows that even with an incomplete knowledge one can remain loyal to Jesus in his absence.

The narrative begins after Jesus had left the temple (John 8:59). When he and his disciples encountered the blind man, Jesus used the opportunity to reveal the works of God, and by so doing, he taught about his own mission. He declared to his disciples, "I must work the works of him that sent me, while it is day: the night cometh, when no man can work. As long as I am in the world, I am the light of the world" (9:4–5). At the beginning of this narrative, the dialogue is confined to Jesus and his disciples with the blind man lingering in the background, although it is probable that he could hear the interchange.

Jesus's first direct interaction with the man was when he made clay by mixing his saliva with some of the dirt on the ground and then anointed the man's eyes with it.[25] The first words that he speaks do not initiate a dialogue; he simply directs him to go and wash in the pool of Siloam, which he does.[26] One can only imagine the experience he must have had as he washed the clay from his eyes, opened them and, for the first time in his life, was able to see. The sensory overload must have been overwhelming as he was able to connect the vibrant colors with the sounds of Jerusalem with which he was accustomed.

As he then left the pool, those neighbors who knew him recognized that a miracle had taken place and questioned whether he was the same person that they knew. When he affirmed his identity, they naturally asked, "How were thine eyes opened?" (John 9:10). I'm not sure that with everything he had experienced up to that point he had given much thought to answering this question. So he almost mechanically rehearsed the events, "A man that is called Jesus made clay, and anointed mine eyes, and said unto me, Go to the pool of Siloam, and wash: and I went and washed, and I received sight" (9:11). When they asked him where this Jesus was, he simply replied, "I know not" (9:12).

Because the event took place on the Sabbath day, the Pharisees were very interested in what had transpired. They also wanted to know how the man had received his sight. His response to them was just a shortened version of what he had told his neighbors, "He put clay upon mine eyes, and I washed, and do see" (John 9:15). This answer divided the Pharisees. Some of them said, "This man is not of God, because he keepeth not the sabbath." But others asked, "How can a man that is a sinner do such miracles?" (9:16). So they again questioned him about Jesus. But by now the repeated questioning seems to have forced the man to consider more deeply the events of the day. Who was this Jesus who had enabled him to see? Initially he had simply considered him to be some man. But was he? In all his years of blindness many "men" must have passed by without performing such a miracle. Surely this Jesus must be more than a man, and so, like the Samaritan woman, he answered, "He is a prophet" (9:17).

The Pharisees clearly did not like that answer. At this point, they were not convinced that the man they were in conversation with had ever been blind. So they questioned his parents, who confirmed the fact but who, fearing possible retribution, refused to be drawn into the debate about how the miracle had occurred. So the Pharisees tried again, refocusing their inquisition on the miracle recipient. More and more they were convinced that Jesus must have been a sinner because, in their minds, he had broken the Sabbath day. They therefore confronted the man again: "Give God the praise," they declared, "we know that this man is a sinner." But his response was simply, "Whether he be a sinner or no, I know not: one thing I know, that, whereas I was blind, now I see" (John 9:24–25). So they continued to push him, "What did he to thee? how opened he thine eyes?" (9:26). It seems to me as I read this account that by this point the man was getting frustrated by the barrage of questions. Let me paraphrase his response: "I have repeatedly answered your questions, but you're not listening to me! If I give you the same answer again, is it going to make any difference? Will you then become one of Jesus's disciples?" (9:27). Again, that was certainly not what they wanted to hear.

As annoying as all these questions must have been, they served a purpose because they apparently caused the man to move beyond the sensory overload that the miracle must have stimulated and forced him to reflect more deeply on what had happened to him. Their unrelenting questioning had, I think, triggered an unintended consequence. Not only had the man now acknowledged that Jesus was a prophet, their questioning had enabled him to recognize that Jesus could not be the sinner that the Pharisees had categorized him as. He was beginning to raise his sights and see differently from the other "earthly" people who peppered him with questions. He was now using the light that only Jesus could provide to illuminate his path, and so he said, "Why herein is a marvellous thing, that ye know not from whence he is, and yet he hath opened mine eyes. Now we know that God heareth not sinners: but if any man be a worshipper [Greek, theosebēs] of God, and doeth his will, him he heareth. Since the world began was it not heard that any man opened the eyes of one that was born blind? If this man were not of God, he could do nothing" (John 9:30–33). This increasing spiritual sight that he was gaining resulted in the Pharisees casting him out (John 9:34), but it also opened a door.

When Jesus heard that the man had been cast out, he sought him out for the second time and now engaged him in a dialogue, albeit a brief one. "Dost thou believe on the Son of God?"[27] (John 9:35). Remember that this man had never seen Jesus, and so he asked, "Who is he, Lord, that I might believe on him?" (9:36). In Greek the word translated here as "Lord" is *kyrios*. It is often used to identify someone who is the master of a house or the owner of a vineyard. In this sense it is a title of respect. "And Jesus said unto him, Thou hast both seen him, and it is he that talketh with thee" (9:37). Now the man understood with whom he was talking, and he again addressed him as Lord, but this time he used it in a different context. *Kyrios* is also used as a title for deity. It is frequently used to translate YHWH, or Jehovah, in the Greek version of the Hebrew Bible. This now seems to be the sense in which he then used it when he said, "Lord, I believe" because he then worshipped Jesus (9:38). Here the Greek word for worship is *proskyneō*, which means that he fell down and prostrated himself before Jesus. It is a form of worship reserved for kings and gods. It is the same word used to describe what the wise men did when they found the child Jesus (Matthew 2:11) and what the disciples did when Jesus and Peter returned to the boat after Peter's attempt to walk on the water. "Then they that were in the ship came and worshipped him, saying, Of a truth thou art the Son of God" (Matthew 14:33). The man's act of *proskyneō* is evidence that he now recognized who Jesus really was: he was not of this world; he was "from above" and was God.

His ability to recognize Jesus from this christological perspective was now in stark contrast to the Pharisees. They had always had their physical sight, but they lacked the spiritual sight that this man had now gained. For them Jesus was a sinner. If they did not see him as a prophet, they certainly did not see him as God. Jesus said to them, "For judgment I am come into this world, that they which see not might see; and that they which see might be made blind." The Pharisees recognized that this statement was a direct condemnation of them. "And some of the Pharisees which were with him heard these words, and said unto him, Are we blind also? Jesus said unto them, If ye were blind, ye should have no sin: but now ye say, We see; therefore your sin remaineth" (John 9:39–41).

The miracle that John wants his readers to understand in this story is not limited to the man receiving his physical sight, as impressive as that miracle was. The Pharisees had always had their physical sight, yet they could not "see" who Jesus was. The real miracle was that the man received his spiritual sight, which enabled him to break free from his earthly shackles and "see" who Jesus really was: not just a man, or even a prophet, but his God.

Knowing the One "Come from Above"

In all three of these dialogues Jesus reached out to individuals who in their own way were stymied by their environmental limitations of being "of the earth." As a result, they struggled to understand that Jesus was not just another man or miracle worker or even a prophet. He was, and is, all of those things, but he was also far more. As the one "come from above," he was and is God who came to earth to help each of us realize that there is so much more to life—eternal life—than just our mortal reality. Each of his dialogue partners was, to some extent, in darkness. For both Nicodemus and the blind man, that darkness was both physical and spiritual; for the Samaritan woman, it was the latter. Nicodemus chose the darkness, but for the blind man it was out of his control. The message of John's Gospel is that as the creator God, Jesus brings both physical and spiritual light to the world and its inhabitants.

That fact is as true today as it was in the first century. Jesus wants to engage all of us in dialogues so that he can personally bring his light to illuminate both our minds and the spiritual path that lays ahead of us. It does not matter to him whether we are a person of stature in the community or someone who is marginalized by his or her community. He wants each of us, wherever we are in our personal journeys, to understand more fully who he is eternally and why that matters for us. Sometimes Jesus, as in the instance of Nicodemus, waits for us to approach him and initiate the dialogue. Sometimes, as was the case with both the Samaritan woman and the blind man, he will be the one to seek us out and initiate the dialogue. Sometimes, as with the blind man, he will allow other dialogues to help us recognize the great things he has done for us so that we are better prepared to be taught when he does seek us out. On some occasions, during these dialogues we will need time to absorb the magnitude of what Jesus is trying to teach us and the implications for our personal lives. For all of us the learning curve will be incremental, as it was for the Samaritan woman and the blind man. Whatever our individual case may be, the important question that we all must consider is this: How will we respond to the dialogues that Jesus seeks to have with us? Will we allow him to stretch our minds, and perhaps take us out of our comfort zones, so that we can at least begin to see and understand heavenly things?

The dialogues are an important tool to help readers better understand the Gospel of John's premise that "in the beginning was the Word . . . and the Word was God." They provide the forum for Jesus to give his own christological witness and help individuals in his day, along with modern readers, to believe that "Jesus is the Christ, the Son of God; and that believing [we] might have life through his name" (John 20:31).

GAYE STRATHEARN *is an associate professor of ancient scripture at Brigham Young University.*

Notes

1.   For a discussion, see Eric D. Huntsman, "Jesus on Jesus: John 5 and 7," in *Perspectives on Mormon Theology: Scriptural Theology,* ed. James E. Faulconer and Joseph M. Spencer (Salt Lake City: Greg Kofford Books, 2015), 69–80.

2. Clement of Alexandria seems to be the first to call John's Gospel a "spiritual gospel" (as quoted by Eusebius, *History of the Church* 6.14.5).

3. In Johannine theology, coming from above is associated with coming from the Father, a theme that is repeated throughout the Gospel (see John 5:43–44; 8:42; 13:3; 16:27–30).

4. Philipp F. Bartholomä, *The Johannine Discourses and the Teaching of Jesus in the Synoptics: A Contribution to the Discussion concerning the Authenticity of Jesus's Words in the Fourth Gospel*, Texte und Arbeiten zum neutestamentlichen Zeitalter 57 (Tübingen: Francke, 2012), 1.

5. Bartholomä, *Johannine Discourses*, 3–4.

6. Other examples of dialogues that function in similar ways to these three include the discourses on the bread of life (John 6), on slave and son (John 8:31–58), and during the washing of the feet (John 13).

7. Bartholomä, *Johannine Discourses*, 107.

8. Jouette M. Bassler, "Mixed Signals: Nicodemus in the Fourth Gospel," *Journal of Biblical Literature* 108, no. 4 (1989): 635–46.

9. Bassler, "Mixed Signals," 636–37.

10. J. Ramsey Michaels, *The Gospel of John*, The New International Commentary on the New Testament (Grand Rapids, MI: Eerdmans, 2010), 174–75.

11. Walter Bauer, *A Greek-English Lexicon of the New Testament and Other Early Christian Literature*, 2nd ed., rev. Frederick William Danker (Chicago: University of Chicago Press, 1958), s.v. καταλαμβάνω.

12. Likewise, John's Gospel records that "it was night" when Judas left to betray Jesus (John 13:30). In addition to providing a temporal marker, it also served as a commentary on Judas's actions. He was about to engage in the work initiated in the premortal world that attempted to overcome the light.

13. Laurence Cantwell, "The Quest for the Historical Nicodemus," *Religious Studies* 16, no. 4 (1980): 484.

14. "Discourse, 9 July 1843, as Reported by Willard Richards," p. [304], *The Joseph Smith Papers*, accessed March 28, 2018, http://www.joseph smithpapers.org/paper-summary/discourse-9-july-1843-as-reported -by-willard-richards/5.

15. Marianne Meye Thompson, *John: A Commentary*, The New Testament Library (Louisville: Westminster John Knox, 2015), 83.

16. Johannes Beutler, SJ, *A Commentary on the Gospel of John*, trans. Michael Tait (Grand Rapids, MI: Eerdmans, 2017), 95.

17. Scholars have debated where the dialogue with Nicodemus closes and where John's comments begin. Some argue that it closes with verse 12 because in verse 13 Jesus is spoken of in the third person. George R. Beasley-Murray, *John*, Word Biblical Commentary 36 (Waco, TX: Word Books, 1987), 50. Still others view all of verses 13–21 "as the continuation of Jesus's answer to Nicodemus's last question in v. 9." Beutler, *Commentary on the Gospel of John*, 91; see also Michaels, *Gospel of John*, 200. I favor the latter position.

18. Craig R. Koester, *Symbolism in the Fourth Gospel: Meaning, Mystery, Community*, 2nd ed. (Minneapolis: Fortress Press, 2003), 47.

19. Michaels, *Gospel of John*, 237.

20. I have chosen to translate *synchraomai* as "are not on friendly terms with" instead of the KJV's "have no dealings with" because in verse 2 clearly the disciples are having dealings with the Samaritans as they go into the city to buy food.

21. In 109 BC the Jewish leader John Hyrcanus had destroyed the Samaritan temple on Mount Gerizim (Josephus, *Antiquities of the Jews* 13.255). Josephus describes Samaritans as "apostates of the Jewish nation" (*Antiquities of the Jews* 11:340). See also Ben Sira 50:25–26: "Two nations I detest, and a third is no nation at all: the inhabitants of Mount Seir, the Philistines, and the senseless folk that live at Shechem" (RSV). This antipathy is supported in John's Gospel when Jesus's opponents seek to ostracize him by saying, "Say we not well that thou art a Samaritan, and hast a devil?" (John 8:48). However, while Jesus vigorously objects to the claim that he has a devil (John 8:49), he seems to have no problems with being called a Samaritan. In Luke's Gospel, Samaritans are portrayed in a very positive light in the stories of the good Samaritan (Luke 10:30–35) and the ten lepers (Luke 17:11–19).

22. Koester, *Symbolism in the Fourth Gospel*, 47–48.

23. Samaritans believe that Eli's decision to move the ark from Shechem to Shilo initiated a transition from *Rhwth*, the age of Divine Favor, to the *Fanūta*, the age of Divine Wrath. They believe that the *Fanūta* will continue until the coming of the *Taheb*, an eschatological prophet who will restore the *Rhwth*. Secondary developments variously describe this prophet as being part of the eschatological scene, coming from the east, possessing the staff of Aaron and the manna, bringing the holy tabernacle, and revealing truth. Ferdinand Dexinger, "*Rhwth*," in *A Companion to Samaritan Studies*, ed. Alan D. Crown, Reinhard Pummer, and Abraham Tal (Tübingen: Mohr [Paul Siebeck], 1993), 202–4.

24. Scholars have long noted two major sections in John's Gospel with chapter 11 acting as a bridge between them: the Book of Signs (John 2–11) and the Book of Glory (John 11–17). The Book of Signs consists of seven miracles or signs (Greek, *sēmeiōn*): turning water into wine, which John describes as the "beginning of the miracles" (John 2:1–11; Greek, *archēn tōn sēmeiōn*); healing the nobleman's son, which "is again the second miracle that Jesus did" (John 4:46–54); healing the paralytic at Bethesda (John 5:1–18); feeding the five thousand (John 6:5–14); walking on the water (John 6:16–24); healing the man born blind (John 9:1–7); and raising Lazarus from the dead (John 11:1–46). These signs may have been based on a separate written source that John used when compiling his Gospel. For some discussions, see C. H. Dodd, *The Interpretation of the Fourth Gospel* (Cambridge: Cambridge University Press, 1965), 287–389, especially 290; Raymond E. Brown, *The Gospel according to John I–XII; A New Translation with Introduction and Commentary*, The Anchor Bible 29 (New York: Doubleday, 1966), cxxxix–cxliv. However, it is clear that Jesus performed more than seven signs, "And many other signs [Greek, *sēmeiōn*] truly did Jesus in the presence of his disciples" (John 20:30). John H. Bernard has argued that it is pointless to try and identify the number of them. *A Critical and Exegetical Commentary on the Gospel according to St. John*, The International Critical Commentary (Edinburgh: T&T Clark, 1928), 1:lxxxix–xc.

25. Jesus also used spittle in other healings (Mark 7:33; 8:23). Pliny the Elder discusses the therapeutic value of spittle in general, and a number of

ancient sources record that Vespasian specifically cured a blind man by spitting in his eye (Tacitus, *History* 4.81; Suetonius, *Life of Vespasian* 7.2–3; Dio Cassius, *Roman History* 65.8). See Thompson, *John: A Commentary,* 207. The second-century Christian theologian Irenaeus understood Jesus's actions as an allusion to the creation of Adam in Genesis 2:7 (*Against Heresies* 5.15.2). See Daniel Frayer-Griggs, "Spittle, Clay, and Creation in John 9:6 and Some Dead Sea Scrolls," *Journal of Biblical Literature* 132, no. 3 (2013): 659–70; Michaels, *Gospel of John,* 545–46.

26. The Roman pool of Siloam must be distinguished from the Byzantine one that was for centuries frequented by pilgrims, including Orson Hyde. *A Sketch of the Travels and Ministry of Elder Orson Hyde* (Salt Lake City: Deseret News, 1869), 13. The pool was located about a third of a mile south of the Temple Mount. In 2004 the northeast corner of the pool was located and excavated so that it is visible today. See Ronny Reich, Eli Shukron, and Omri Lernau, "Recent Discoveries in the City of David, Jerusalem," *Israel Exploration Journal* 57, no. 2 (2007): 163–69.

27. Our earliest texts of John have the phrase "Son of Man" instead of "Son of God": P[66], P[75], ℵ, B, D, W. The title "Son of Man," in this context, comes from Daniel 7:13–14 and describes an eschatological figure who would come "with the clouds" and would be given dominion, glory, and a kingdom, that all people, nations, and languages should serve him. This "dominion is an everlasting dominion, which shall not pass away, and his kingdom that which shall not be destroyed." It is a title that Jesus uses for himself and that, at times, he prefers over the title Messiah (Mark 8:27–31).

10

The Fourth Gospel and Expectations of the Jewish Messiah

Joshua M. Matson

The author of the Gospel of John emphatically stated that the Fourth Gospel was "written, that ye might believe that Jesus is the Christ, the Son of God" (John 20:31).[1] This gospel actively seeks to present an elevated portrait of the attributes, nature, and character of Jesus through a high Christology that connects him with messianic prophecies. Indeed, John seems to share an objective with the Latter-day Saints' *Lectures on Faith*, which emphasizes the importance of having "a correct idea of [God's] character, perfections, and attributes."[2] Only recently have scholars and students of the Bible begun to move from earlier assumptions that Jews in the Second Temple period had monolithic and rigid prophecies regarding a promised messiah.[3] Instead, the Gospel of John presents a more nuanced messianic view through the conversations that different individuals had with Jesus during his mortal ministry. These characters articulate different opinions concerning the prophesied messiah and then reach conclusions about Jesus based on their beliefs and assumptions. As a result, the Fourth Gospel presents a disparate picture of contemporary expectations of the coming of the Jewish messiah. While a recognition of the Gospel of John's more nuanced view of the Jewish messiah is not new from a historical perspective,[4] the purposes behind this literary presentation are less certain. Nevertheless, the Fourth Gospel attempts to pave the way for its readers to gain an accurate understanding of Jewish messianic expectations within the historical context of Second Temple Judaism.

Above all, the Fourth Gospel presents an understanding of the Messiah intended to dispel wrong beliefs about the Anointed One who should come. In the process, it provides "a correct idea of the character and attributes" of the Messiah, allowing its readers "to exercise belief in Jesus Christ unto life and salvation."[5] After reviewing some of the texts that established the Jewish messianic expectations presented in the Gospel of John, we will examine the literary and historical context of seventeen occurrences of the term *christos* ("Christ" or "Anointed One") in the Fourth Gospel.[6] By paying special attention to the characters who invoke the term and the literary context in which the term occurs, it becomes clear that the Gospel of John deliberately presents these contrasting interpretations of messianic prophecy to emphasize how misguided expectations were detrimental to belief in Jesus as the Christ. These expectations were the determining factors that led some to accept Jesus as the Messiah and others to reject him. While John's seemingly disparate presentation of messianic expectations appears to create tension in the text, it is intended to aid the readers, both ancient and modern, to "believe that Jesus is the Christ."

The Origins of the Jewish Messiah

For centuries, students of the Bible believed that Second Temple Judaism held a monolithic collection of messianic expectations and prophecies.[7] The discovery of ancient Jewish texts like the Dead Sea

Scrolls have increased our understanding of Jewish tradition and history and has resulted in a more nuanced and complete picture of ancient messianic expectations.[8] While scholars still struggle to reach a consensus concerning the extent to which messianism influenced the formation and beliefs of Jewish communities in the Second Temple period,[9] they widely recognize a body of ancient texts that appear to have served as the foundation for messianic expectations. This body includes texts in the Hebrew Bible (Genesis 49:8–12; Numbers 24:15–19; 2 Samuel 7:12–17; Isaiah 11:1–9; Psalm 89:36–38; Amos 9:11–15; and Jeremiah 23:5–8; 33:15–18) and expansions on biblical traditions in nonbiblical texts (Psalms of Solomon 17–18; 4 Ezra 13; 2 Baruch 72–74; and texts from the Dead Sea Scrolls like 1QM V and 4Q175). Central to these texts is the promised "sudden end of the present age, which they regarded as evil and corrupt, and the inauguration of a new age in which God's people would see the wicked punished and the world ruled in righteousness."[10] The sheer number of publications that have attempted to identify the number of messianic figures that were to fulfill the prophesied transformation manifests a current lack of consensus concerning these beliefs.[11] These secondary texts are instructive because they provide firm evidence that the controversy concerning the Messiah is not rooted in the Jewish authoritative texts of the age, but in the interpretations of those texts by various Jewish groups and individuals who adhere to them. When analyzed, these texts provide the basis for messianic expectations among Jews of the Second Temple period.

Biblical Expectations

A detailed commentary on each of the biblical and nonbiblical passages that provide insight into messianic expectations is not necessary to create a picture of the Jewish messiah.[12] However, an overview of these texts reveals three primary themes that, when interpreted, outline the expected mission of the Messiah in ancient Judaism. These themes of messianism include the lineage of the Messiah, peculiarities about the Messiah's life/mission, and the Messiah's ability to restore the kingdom of Israel.

The declaration of the Messiah's lineage is the most recognizable and utilized theme from the Hebrew Bible that draws attention to a promised messiah. For instance, 2 Samuel 7:12–16 is a comprehensive and influential declaration of the promised messiah's lineage. Here the Lord proclaims to David through the prophet Nathan, "And when thy days be fulfilled, and thou shalt sleep with thy fathers, *I will set up thy seed after thee, which shall proceed out of thy bowels, and I will establish his kingdom. . . .* I will stablish the throne of his kingdom for ever. I will be his father, and he shall be my son. . . . And thine house and thy kingdom shall be established for ever before thee: thy throne shall be established for ever" (emphasis added). Jews in this period often interpreted this passage as a messianic promise. In a commentary on this text found among the Dead Sea Scrolls, for example, the promise was interpreted and reiterated. The Qumran community declared their interpretation of this figure as "the branch of David who will stand with the Interpreter of the Law, who will sit on the throne in Zion at the end of days" (4Q174 I, 10–13). Biblical scholar Craig A. Evans synthesizes these texts by stating, "The expectation of this David is quite clear: he is to rule and save Israel."[13]

The lineage of the Messiah becomes a point of interest in many of the biblical messianic texts. As mentioned in 2 Samuel 7, David occupies the predominant position as the forefather of the Messiah. This predominance is reiterated in Jeremiah 23:5 and 33:15. Additional ancestors of the Messiah are also mentioned in biblical texts, including Judah (Genesis 49:10), Jacob/Israel (Numbers 24:17), and Jesse (Isaiah 11:1). However, among these, only David is mentioned in the messianic expectations of the Fourth Gospel (see John 7:42).

Specific events or deeds from the Messiah's life comprise the second notable theme found among messianic texts from antiquity. These peculiarities emphasize miscellaneous aspects of the Messiah's life and are interpreted as specific identifying markers of the Messiah to those who were actively looking for him. One such messianic expectation is found in Psalm 89. "His seed shall endure for ever, and his throne as the sun before me. It shall be established for ever as the moon, and as a faithful witness in heaven" (Psalm 89:36–37). Some groups concluded that the Messiah, the seed of David, is the one who would live forever.[14] Other ancient interpreters viewed the text of Micah 5 as equally specific. "But thou, Beth-lehem Ephratah, though thou be little among the thousands of Judah, yet out of thee shall he come forth unto me that is to be ruler in Israel" (Micah 5:2). Commenting on this text, noted linguist Bruce Waltke observes that the specificity of the verse "focuses on the Messiah's origins from David's roots."[15] A final attribute granted to the Messiah is the role of an eternal judge (Isaiah 11:3–4). These specific interpretations, derived from select biblical texts, attempt to identify the Messiah upon his arrival in Israel, prior to his fulfilling the primary purpose of liberating his people.

Recognizable themes from the messianic texts of the Old Testament center on conquest, restoration, and the reestablishment of the kingdom of Israel. The themes of lineage and restoration of the kingdom of Israel frequently are found together in many interpretations of messianism. In Genesis 49, the images of kingship are accompanied with those of gathering: "The sceptre shall not depart from Judah, nor a lawgiver from between his feet, until Shiloh come; and unto him shall the gathering of the people be" (Genesis 49:10). Furthermore, Balaam declares that among the Israelites, "there shall come a Star out of Jacob, and a Sceptre shall rise out of Israel, and shall smite the corners of Moab, and destroy all the children of Sheth. And Edom shall be a possession, Seir also shall be a possession for his enemies; and Israel shall do valiantly. Out of Jacob shall come he that shall have dominion, and shall destroy him that remaineth of the city" (Numbers 24:17–19). Other verses also incorporate these themes. However, a passage from Amos emphasizes the restoration responsibilities of the Messiah. "In that day will I raise up the tabernacle of David that is fallen . . . and I will build it as in the days of old" (Amos 9:11). The ability not only to lead the people of Israel but to overthrow their enemies in order to reestablish themselves in the land of their inheritance is reminiscent of the ancient stories of Joshua and David. Regaining political control of their land was most important among some Jewish groups, and their conceptualization of the Messiah hinged directly upon it.[16]

Nonbiblical Expectations

The foundations for messianic expectations are derived from the texts of the Hebrew Bible. The interpretation of those biblical texts arose from literature that scribes composed in the centuries before and after the meridian of time. The authors of these works of Jewish literature drew upon the same messianic themes as the biblical books did but often expanded their reach and intensity. Such is the case with the preservation of expectations in the Psalms of Solomon. Among other intended outcomes, the messianic figure of this first-century-BC text is expected to be raised up by the Lord, rule over Israel, shatter unjust rulers, "purge Jerusalem from nations that trample her," destroy lawless nations, gather together the holy people, "thrust out sinners from" the land of Jewish inheritance, and perform the will of God "for the generation that is to come," even under the rod of discipline (Psalms of Solomon 17:21–18:7). Noted biblical scholar David Levenson observes that this is "the future ideal Davidic king, the Lord's 'anointed one'. . . the figure who will conquer the nations and judge the world."[17] Further, this king is not noted for his military strength but for the mighty power of his words (Psalms of Solomon 17:26). Expanding upon the traditions of Davidic lineage and great physical strength, some Jewish communities eagerly awaited the arrival of their warrior deliverer.

In the apocalyptic work of 4 Ezra, the Messiah is given further power over the nations of the earth as he "reprove[s] the assembled nations for their ungodliness and will destroy them without effort by the law" (4 Ezra 13:37–38). The term *anointed* is again employed to discuss this promoted figure. Debra Ballentine observes, "The passage just described within 4 Ezra promote[s] a secondary divine figure who receives endorsement from the primary deity. The primary deity is portrayed as the creator who has made specific preparations for the eschaton, at which time various oppressive and wicked rulers will be rebuked and destroyed."[18] Ballantine continues, "These texts contain a significant commentary on their contemporary political setting, portraying disfavored governing bodies as oppressive, wicked, and destined for defeat."[19]

Further expansions concerning the messianic expectations of the Second Temple period are found in the numerous fragments of the Dead Sea Scrolls. In the War Scroll, the Messiah is an idealized priest of Aaron and described as carrying a shield with the names of Israel, Levi, and Aaron inscribed upon it. The children of light are expected to rally behind this divine leader into battle against the children of darkness (1QM V, 1–21; XV). The Community Rule similarly describes an important future prophet and warrior king (1QS IX) who will aid in ushering in the messianic age (1QS^a II). Noted Dead Sea Scrolls scholar Martin Abegg summarizes the messianic expectations at Qumran, stating, "Clear signs that the messianic picture was not so focused as to conclude that messianic hopes were only or always singular."[20] This lack of congruency among Jewish parties and groups created the disparate messianic climate in which the author of the Fourth Gospel was writing.

The Expected Jewish Messiah

In the Gospel of John, individuals appear to accept or reject Jesus based on their interpretations of messianic prophecy. When encountering Jesus, some individuals proclaim him to be the realization of Jewish messianic expectations, others question or oppose this fulfillment, and yet others question the messianic expectations themselves. Each of these encounters forces the questioning individuals or groups to search and wrestle for their own messianic conclusions about Jesus. The Fourth Gospel places these differing opinions at the center of the narrative's discourse between individuals in discrete situations as representations of various Jewish groups, including Jews, Samaritans, and followers of John the Baptist. The Gospel of John presents and highlights this pluralistic view of messianic expectations as a literary critique on the interpretation of messianic prophecies by those who do not believe in Jesus's messiahship. The Fourth Gospel attempts to dispel incorrect understandings about messianic expectations that can serve as a stumbling block for those who are presented with the message that Jesus is the Christ. The Fourth Gospel clearly emphasizes that those who open themselves to receiving the message that Jesus is the Messiah, adjusting their preconceived messianic expectations if necessary, will believe in him as the Anointed One. Conversely, those who maintain trendy beliefs and expectations about the Messiah will not believe. James Charlesworth's conclusion about messianic expectations provides an interesting observation about Judaism. "I am convinced that the ancient Jew was often intentionally ambiguous. He comprehended that only God knew who would be the Messiah, and what the Messiah would accomplish."[21] There is no other Gospel that allows such ambiguity to be on full display, and nowhere is a presentation of Jesus as the Messiah grander.

Jews of Jerusalem (Unyielding Misguided Messianic Expectation)

The Fourth Gospel makes no attempt to veil the fact that the Jews from Jerusalem, or at least their leaders, are the most unwilling to accept Jesus as the Christ and change their misguided expectations concerning the Messiah. The expression "the Jews" (Greek *hoi Ioudaioi*) occurs frequently in John, often negatively. In these instances, it appears to refer to either the Jewish leadership or a specific group of opponents to Jesus. In the Fourth Gospel, this collective group always engages with Jesus cynically and often from a distance (see John 2:18–20; 5:10–18; 10:24, 31–33). Elder Dieter F. Uchtdorf described such groups of inquirers, stating, "Instead of enjoying . . . spiritual gifts, the cynics content themselves with observing from a distance, sipping from their cups of skepticism, doubt, and disrespect."[22] Such a literary presentation shows that for one to know that Jesus is the Messiah, one must have an open mind, spend time with him, and not speak of him only with his opponents.

Early in the Gospel's narrative, this group confronts John the Baptist to interrogate him concerning his work and his understanding of the promised messiah. The Jerusalem Jews question John because he has attracted a following by teaching of the Messiah while not proclaiming their dogmatically held messianic beliefs. As Francis Moloney has concluded, "The representatives of the Jewish world are determined not to move from their criteria [concerning the Messiah]."[23] Exemplifying this determination, "the Jews" inquire of John, "Why baptizest thou then, if thou be not that Christ, nor Elias, neither that prophet?" (John 1:25). This inquiry, and those that preceded it in the text of John 1, asks if John is not only "that Christ," but "that prophet." This clear reference to the messianic prophet that should come (see 1QS IX above) is an attempt by the Jewish leaders to catch John in his own messianic expectations. John the Baptist responds to the Jewish leaders with humble recognition of his own activities and, as discussed further below, his pure belief that the Messiah is among them (John 1:26–27). The Fourth Gospel's presentation of these religious leaders of Jerusalem focuses on their interest to aggressively enforce their own understanding of messianic expectations on others, refusing to learn of "things as they really are" (Jacob 4:13).

The Gospel of John preserves two accounts of the Jewish leaders arrogantly confronting Jesus to question the validity of the claim that he is the Messiah. Their first confrontation occurs in the presence of patrons at the temple in Jerusalem and is centered on the belief that the Messiah would come from an unknown land (John 7:27), a claim that is not in any preserved Jewish texts from antiquity but must have resonated with some of those in the temple since they then sought to take him away (John 7:30). The second confrontation occurs in the presence of both Jews and Greeks as Jesus triumphantly enters Jerusalem. The confrontation revolves around their interpretation of Psalm 89:36–37 that the Messiah cannot die (John 12:20–36). To these contenders, Jesus's responses are instructive.

The Fourth Gospel records Jesus's response to the first confrontation in an interesting way. John records, "Then cried Jesus in the temple as he taught," a suggestion that Jesus is attempting through an elevated voice to garner the attention not only of those mocking him but all present. "Ye both know me, and ye know whence I am: and I am not come of myself, but he that sent me is true, whom ye know not. But I know him: for I am *from* him, and he hath sent me" (John 7:28–29; emphasis added). Although this response proves fruitless in persuading the Jerusalem leaders, Jesus's statement teaches a doctrinal truth related to John's preexistence Christology (a view emphasizing the premortality of Jesus) that was effective in teaching others, as will be seen below. For John, however, this episode also served as an opportunity for Jesus to proclaim the truth that he did indeed fulfill the messianic expectation of being the Son of God (2 Samuel 2:14) and came from the unknown location of God's presence. This dualistic language, a type of rhetoric that employs the words of one's opponent to bear witness of the validity of one's own stance, is akin to the dualistic use of language used in other texts from antiquity. John Painter attests that like the Dead Sea Scrolls, "the language [of John's Gospel] reflects the rejection of the rest of Judaism by the community and in exclusive identification of itself with the covenant people of God."[24] Here, Jesus and his apostles begin to separate themselves more fully from the Jerusalem leadership and formulate their own organization, reinforcing their commitment to their message that Jesus is the Christ.

The second confrontation between Jesus and "the Jews" involves questions regarding Jesus's teaching about his impending crucifixion (John 12:32). After Jesus foretells his death, the people (including the Jewish leaders) return to their questions regarding prophecies that the Messiah would endure forever (Psalm 89: 36–37). When Jesus attempted to correct their misguided interpretation concerning the Messiah and even performed miracles as a witness of his messiahship (perhaps as a fulfillment of the words spoken in John 9:31), they "believed not on him" (John 12:37). Though not a successful attempt to bring a correct understanding of the Messiah to the huddled congregation, these events were not fruitless; John later records, "Nevertheless among the chief rulers many believed on him" (John 12:42). These chief rulers, however, fearing they would be expelled from the synagogue, concealed their belief.

This response is nearly identical to that of the parents of the lifelong blind man in John 9. Here, following Jesus's healing the man of his blindness, the parents are asked by the leaders of the synagogue how their son gained the ability to see. Threatened by excommunication from the synagogue, the parents refuse to confess that Jesus is the Christ (John 9:22). It appears that the Fourth Gospel is emphasizing the cost that one must be willing to pay for truly believing in the Messiah. As *Lectures on Faith* attests, "A religion that does not require the sacrifice of all things never has power sufficient to produce the faith necessary [to lead] unto life and salvation."[25] Those who choose to ignore the validity of the Messiah (Jewish opponents of Jesus) or suppress their individual belief in him (chief rulers and blind man's parents) stand in stark opposition to those who fulfill the Fourth Gospel's purpose to persuade individuals to accept Jesus's messiahship. John appears to record these events as an aid to his readers, knowing that belief is an essential component of accepting the Messiah.

As demonstrated above, the author of the Gospel of John is skillfully using the dialogues of the Fourth Gospel to help his readers discern for themselves whether Jesus is the Christ. While the Jews in Jerusalem proved to be unwilling to accept Jesus as the Messiah, they set the stage for others to join in witnessing the validity of Jesus the Christ.

The Woman at the Well and Temple Patrons in Jerusalem (Willingly Altered Messianic Expectations)

One of the primary stumbling blocks that prevented some of the Jews in Jerusalem from accepting Jesus as the Messiah was their belief that they already knew everything about the Messiah. Lacking the humility to be taught caused them to be blinded to the Messiah who was among them. Akin to the Jews in Jerusalem, John presents others who had misconceptions of the Messiah but who were willing to reevaluate their understanding to see "things as they really are" (Jacob 4:13). President Gordon B. Hinckley (1910–2008), fifteenth president of the Church, may have been envisioning just such a group of "converts" when he proclaimed, "Let me say that we appreciate the truth in all churches and the good which they do. We say to the people, in effect, you bring with you all the good that you have, and then let us see if we can add to it."[26] In the Fourth Gospel two such groups fit this category: the temple patrons in Jerusalem who chose to believe in Jesus's teachings in John 7 and the Samaritan woman in John 4.

As was discussed earlier, the confrontation that Jesus has with the Jerusalem Jews at the Feast of Tabernacles in the temple included another group who remained with Jesus to further evaluate his claim to be the Messiah. Choosing to humble themselves, these individuals further inquired into Jesus's messiahship as it pertained to his place of origin and the miracles he had performed. Relying upon the messianic text of Micah 5, this group asked why Jesus would consider himself the Messiah if he was from Galilee and not Bethlehem (Micah 5:2). John emphasizes that these discussions prompted a division among those who remained. While some refused to put aside their previously held interpretation of the Messiah's origins in Bethlehem and joined the Jews in desiring to have him apprehended, *many* proclaimed that he was "the Prophet" and "the Christ" (John 7:40–41).

There may be a host of factors that influenced this group's declaration, but the narrative seems to place the decision on their desire to adhere to Jesus's command as a coupling of their messianic expectations from scripture with belief (John 7:38). I have been impressed that the author of the Fourth Gospel does not combat these inquiries with facts, such as "Well, didn't you know that Jesus was born in Bethlehem!" or "What further miracles would you like to see?" Instead, he records that those who proclaimed him as the Christ did so out of belief, not out of the certainty that those who joined the Jews were seeking. Alma's teaching to the Zoramites rings true for these temple patrons as well: "Even if ye can no more than desire to believe, let this desire work in you, even until ye believe" (Alma 32:27). It appears that the separating factor between those in Jerusalem who listened to and followed Jesus and those who left was belief.

The Samaritan expectations of the Messiah differed from those of the Jews of that period. While the Jews emphasized the words of the Hebrew Bible, the Samaritans relied heavily upon oral traditions. Unfortunately, records about the messianic expectations of the Samaritans are reliant upon records that postdate the Second Temple period by nearly two hundred years.[27] According to these traditions, Samaritans expected the coming of a figure named *Taheb*, a descendant of Jacob and a great prophet-teacher, who would come from the east to Mount Gerizim. To prove his messiahship, he would show the staff of Aaron, produce manna, bring the holy tabernacle back to its residence on Mount Gerizim, and aid in making the Hebrew language universal. Eventually, he would die and be buried with Joseph the son of Jacob.[28]

Allusions to the traditions of *Taheb* are preserved in the dialogue between the Samaritan woman and Jesus in John 4.[29] However, like those in the temple at Jerusalem, the Samaritan woman followed the expression of her understanding of the coming messiah with a listening ear that allowed Jesus to expand her knowledge. It was through this exchange that the woman was truly converted to say, "Come, see a man . . . is not this the Christ" (John 4:29). By choosing to believe that Jesus was the Christ, the Samaritan woman received a personal witness and shared it with her friends and neighbors (John 4:29).

The Fourth Gospel does not attempt to overdramatize the event but shows that while the Samaritan woman and Jesus disagreed at the beginning of their conversation, through an encounter with the Christ, her expectations for the Messiah were changed by belief.

John the Baptist, Andrew, and Martha (Spiritually Received Messianic Belief)

Instead of evaluating the Messiah through reasoning with scriptures and traditions, the Fourth Gospel presents a group of individuals who accept Jesus as the Christ with the spiritual gift of a believing heart (see D&C 46:14). John the Baptist, Andrew, and Martha all make pure proclamations of faith that they believe that Jesus is the Christ that should come, without disputation. This acceptance highlights the Fourth Gospel's incarnation Christology. After spending a day with Jesus, Andrew proclaims, "We have found the Messias, which is, being interpreted, the Christ" (John 1:41). John the Baptist declares to the Jews that he would be one who would bear witness of the Messiah, even in the face of opposition (John 1:20; 3:28). In her extremity following the death of her brother, Martha witnesses her belief that Jesus is the Christ. Her belief comes not after the miracle of the raising of her brother (as it may have for the temple patrons or the Samaritan woman), but prior to it (John 11:27). These characters all manifest the truth taught by President Dallin H. Oaks: "Those who have the gift [to know that Jesus is the Son of God], must give their witness so that those who have the gift to believe on their words can enjoy the benefit of that gift."[30] John the Baptist, Andrew, and Martha share their obtained witness about the Messiah not only with those in their day, but with the later readers of the Fourth Gospel.

Realizing the Messiah through the Gospel of John

Throughout the Gospel of John people converse with one another about the validity of Jesus's claims of being the Messiah. The disparate presentation of messianic expectations in these conversations provides a fruitful backdrop for studying the author's intent to allow readers to choose for themselves to believe in Jesus as the Christ. The final reference to *christos* in the Fourth Gospel serves as a fitting capstone to our discussion. John's concluding proclamation that "these are written, so that you may come to believe that Jesus is the Messiah, the Son of God" (John 20:31 New Revised Standard Version), strategically engages the reader with the ongoing discussions of the Messiah. The Fourth Gospel was not written with the intent to present a portrayal of Jesus's life that convinces the reader of his messiahship through a checklist of scriptural or traditional prophecies. Instead, John desired that the reader would experience and walk with Jesus, like the characters presented throughout the gospel, and come to their own understanding and conclusions that they believe in him as the Christ. Whether they come to believe that Jesus is the Messiah through the gift of a believing heart like John the Baptist, Andrew, and Martha, or they willingly adjust their preconceived messianic expectations like the Samaritan woman or the temple patrons in Jerusalem, the Fourth Gospel is specifically written so that all might "believe that Jesus is the Messiah, the Son of God."

JOSHUA M. MATSON *is a PhD candidate at Florida State University.*

Notes

1. Latter-day Saints adhere to the traditional belief that the Gospel of John was written by John the Revelator/Beloved. See Richard Neitzel Holzapfel, Eric D. Huntsman, and Thomas A. Wayment, *Jesus Christ and the World of the New Testament* (Salt Lake City: Deseret Book, 2006), 126. Some scholars suggest that parts or portions of the text were written

at different times and places. See Urban C. von Wahlde, *The Gospel and Letters of John*, 3 vols. (Grand Rapids: Eerdmans, 2010).

2.   Robin Scott Jensen, Richard E. Turley Jr., and Riley M. Lorimer, eds., *Revelations and Translations Volume 2: Published Revelations*, vol. 2 of the Revelations and Translations series of *The Joseph Smith Papers*, ed. Dean C. Jessee, Ronald K. Esplin, and Richard Lyman Bushman (Salt Lake City: Church Historian's Press, 2011), 346.

3.   James H. Charlesworth, "Introduction: Messianic Ideas in Early Judaism," in *Qumran-Messianism*, ed. James H. Charlesworth, Hermann Lichtenberger, and Gerbern S. Oegema (Tübingen: Mohr Siebeck, 1998), 2.

4.   William Sanday, *The Authorship and Historical Character of the Fourth Gospel* (London: Macmillan, 1872), 124.

5.   Jensen, Turley, and Lorimer, Doctrine and Covenants, 1835, 36, in *JSP*, R2:346.

6.   While there are nineteen references to *christos* in the Gospel of John, two appear as titles attached to the personal name Jesus (John 1:17; 17:3).

7.   Charlesworth, "Introduction: Messianic Ideas in Early Judaism," 2.

8.   John J. Collins, "Jesus, Messianism, and the Dead Sea Scrolls," in *Qumran-Messianism*, ed. James H. Charlesworth, Hermann Lichtenberger, and Gerbern S. Oegema (Tübingen: Mohr Siebeck, 1998), 100–101.

9.   Collins, "Jesus, Messianism, and the Dead Sea Scrolls," 102.

10.   David B. Levenson, "Messianic Movements," in *The Jewish Annotated New Testament*, ed. Amy-Jill Levine and Marc Zvi Brettler (New York: Oxford, 2011), 530.

11.   Richard Baukham, "Messianism according to the Gospel of John," in *Challenging Perspectives of the Gospel of John*, ed. John Lierman (Tübingen: Mohr Siebeck, 2006), 35.

12.   For an exhaustive treatment of the biblical texts attributed to messianism, see John J. Collins, *The Scepter and the Star* (New York: Doubleday, 1995), 49–73.

13.   Craig A. Evans, "Are the 'Son' Texts at Qumran Messianic?" in *Qumran-Messianism*, 141.

14.   Francis J. Moloney, *The Gospel of John*, Sacra Pagina 4 (Collegeville, MN: The Order of St. Benedict, 1998), 355.

15. Bruce K. Waltke, *A Commentary on Micah* (Grand Rapids: Eerdmans, 2017), 294.

16. Sook-Young Kim, *The Warrior Messiah in Scripture and Intertestamental Writings* (Cambridge: Cambridge University Press, 2010), 9.

17. Levenson, "Messianic Movements," 530–31.

18. Debra Scoggins Ballentine, *The Conflict Myth and Biblical Tradition* (New York: Oxford, 2015), 159.

19. Ballentine, *The Conflict Myth*, 159.

20. Martin Abegg Jr., "The Messiah at Qumran: Are We Still Seeing Double?" *Dead Sea Discoveries* 2 (1995): 122–44.

21. Charlesworth, "Introduction: Messianic Ideas in Early Judaism," 5.

22. Dieter F. Uchtdorf, "Be Not Afraid, Only Believe," *Ensign*, November 2015, 78.

23. Moloney, *Gospel of John*, 52.

24. John Painter, *The Quest for the Messiah: The History, Literature, and Theology of the Johannine Community* (Edinburgh: T&T Clark, 1993), 8.

25. Jensen, Turley, and Lorimer, Doctrine and Covenants, 1835, 60, in *JSP*, R2:370.

26. Gordon B. Hinckley, meeting, Nairobi, Kenya, 17 February 1998, quoted in "Excerpts from Recent Addresses of President Gordon B. Hinckley," *Ensign*, August 1998, 72.

27. Ferdinand Dexinger, "Reflections on the Relationship between Qumran and Samaritan Messianology," *Qumran-Messianism*, 83.

28. Dexinger, "Relationship between Qumran and Samaritan Messianology," 85.

29. See John 4:19 ("Thou art a prophet"), John 4:20 (worship on Mount Gerizim), and John 4:25 ("I know that Messias cometh, which is called Christ: when he is come, he will teach us all things").

30. Dallin H. Oaks, "Witnesses of Christ," *Ensign*, October 1999, 29.

11

"Each Person Has a Hymn"
The Creator-Savior Hymns

Thomas A. Wayment

S cholars have long recognized that the New Testament contains what may be a number of fragmentary or even nearly complete early Christian hymns extolling Christ as Savior and Creator.[1] Recovery of these hymns has been difficult because oftentimes the hymns were not written in a consistently discernable meter, or the author who quoted the hymn has disrupted the original meter and wording of the hymn.[2] An additional issue is that the musical notations of these hymns are not noted in early Greek manuscripts of the New Testament.

The most oft-mentioned New Testament hymns are those found in Philippians 2:6–11; Colossians 1:15–20; 1 Timothy 3:16; and portions of John 1:1–18. Since their initial rediscovery, scholars have made great strides in their attempts to recover the hymns, and while there is a general acceptance that the New Testament does contain embedded hymns, there is still a vibrant discussion about them.

With respect to the Colossians hymn, scholars are approaching a near consensus on the structure and general outline of the hymn.[3] Studies on the hymn to the Logos in John 1:1–18 and whether it is a formal hymn or a type of poetic praise to the Logos have not arrived at a consensus.

A full study of the hymns is beyond the scope of a single article, and indeed the discussion surrounding each of these early hymns has generated a sizeable body of secondary literature. Instead of focusing on the question of whether these passages functioned as independent hymns and trying to establish their exact parameters, this paper will consider these passages from a different vantage point. First, this study will accept that Philippians 2:6–11 and John 1:1–18 represent partial hymns that predate the books in which they were recorded. Second, the paper will forego engaging in detail the question of the date and authorship of these hymns in order to look at a related issue: the theology of these hymns. These two early hymns will be discussed and analyzed as evidences of a developing, benevolent Creator-Savior theology that sought both to promote the humanity of Jesus as well as to testify of the continuity between the mortal, earthly Jesus and the premortal Creator.[4] Additionally, early Latter-day Saint hymn-singing practices will be used as evidence that the production of hymns provides a unique opportunity for exploratory theological engagement and development of ideas.

Early Christians, particularly those who knew the historical Jesus from Nazareth, were likely perplexed with embracing the full divinity of Jesus while accepting with equal openness his humanity. The problem became acute for monotheistic Jewish Christians and for gentile Christians who held cultural perceptions of the immortality of the soul that challenged their newfound faith's acceptance of the immortality of the resurrected flesh. This underlying tension is prevalent in the historical sources detailing events from Jesus's life. Those sources—the four Gospels—sought to find balance in the interplay between simultaneously recording the events from the life of the historical Jesus and promoting a belief in the exalted Christ.[5]

The Gospels were fundamentally shaped by the historical progression of Jesus's life—his actions define what events are retold—but in telling the story of the historical Jesus, the Gospel authors established a foundation for belief in Jesus as the exalted and resurrected Christ. Indeed, the New Testament Gospels declare Jesus to be God in three verses on two occasions—John 20:28 and twice in the Prologue (John 1:1, 18).[6] The tension between the humanity and the deity of Jesus Christ, already expressed in a mortal and divine title that functioned later as a name, existed initially among those who knew him both as a person and who believed in him as their Lord.[7] The hymns of the New Testament explore that tension between man and God, but they do not attempt to resolve that conflict. Hymns devoted to illuminating that paradox were a source of spiritual exploration and new understanding.

Early Christian Hymn Singing

The earliest indications of Christian hymn-singing practices following the death of Jesus are the two references to hymns in Ephesians and Colossians and the vivid eyewitness report of the Roman governor Pliny, who saw firsthand the gatherings of early Christians in Bythinia on the southwest shores of the Black Sea in 111–113 CE. He noted in a letter to the emperor, "On a fixed day they meet before dawn and sing a hymn among themselves to Christ, as though he were a god."[8] In the letters of Ephesians and Colossians, the author notes the following about hymn singing: "Speaking to each other in psalms and hymns and spiritual songs, singing and making music in your heart to the Lord" (Ephesians 5:19), and "Let the word of Christ dwell in you richly, teaching and exhorting in all wisdom each another in psalms, hymns, and spiritual songs, singing with grace in your hearts to God" (Colossians 3:16).[9] During Jesus's lifetime, the disciples sang hymns at Passover, as Mark 14:26 records, "when they sang a hymn."[10]

Two important features of the early witnesses to hymn singing are the emphasis on "speaking" or more properly "singing" (Greek, *lalountes*; Latin, *carmen*) and teaching or admonishing (*didaskontes, nouthetountes*) through hymns. From these brief testimonies, it is difficult to ascertain a compellingly complete idea of hymn singing in early Christianity, but several features are important. First, the practice was exclusionary as evidenced by words such as "among themselves" and "admonishing one another" attest. Second, the purpose of the hymn singing was to praise Christ, as phrases such as "to Christ" and "in your hearts to the Lord" clearly demonstrate. Third, Pliny as an outsider conveyed what he perceived to be their intent in singing, "to Christ, *as though he were a god*" (emphasis added). According to Justin Martyr, a Christian author from the second century CE, such hymns were sung to praise God as creator.[11]

Pliny's witness is also important because of what he appears to have assumed, namely that the gathering for the purpose of singing was an intentionally peaceful and ordinary act, which later he asserts when he says, "Not to do some crime, not to commit fraud, theft, or adultery, not to falsify their trust."[12] In other words, the act of singing hymns was a signal to Pliny that early Christian gatherings were harmless and normal. This would indicate that in religious gatherings it would not be unexpected to hear hymns and that to sing to Christ "as though he were a god" was aligned with cultural examples where Greeks might sing to Asclepius or Zeus as though he were a god. For Pliny the only surprise appears to be the object of their singing: Christ.

If Christian hymn singing followed common Greek and Jewish cultural practices, which is the general consensus of recent scholarship, then it is appropriate to draw attention to the fact that singing usually accompanied meals, both religious and celebratory.[13] In connection with early efforts to commemorate Jesus's final meal with his disciples, early Christian communities would sing to Lord Jesus.[14] Clement of Alexandria observed this practice around 200 CE when he noted, "As is fitting, before partaking of food, that we pray to the Creator; so also in drinking it is suitable to sing to him before partaking of his creatures. For the psalm is harmonious and wise. The apostle calls the psalm 'a spiritual hymn.'"[15] Around the same time, Tertullian also noted the practice of singing at Christian meals: "After water for the hands come the lights; and then each, from what he knows of the Holy Scriptures, or from his own heart, is called before the rest to sing to God; so that is a test of how much he has drunk."[16] For Tertullian, the practice of singing counteracted the inclination to drink too much wine, a feature that was also a concern in the letter to Ephesians where excess drinking was connected with singing hymns. "And be not drunk with wine, wherein is excess; but be filled with the Spirit. Speaking to yourselves in psalms and hymns and spiritual songs, singing and making melody in your heart to the Lord" (Ephesians 5:18–19 KJV).

An additional feature of early hymn singing was the inclusion of the responsorial element at the end of hymns, a feature that reveals audience engagement and participation. At the conclusion of a hymn, the congregants would respond by saying or chanting *Hallelujah!*[17] The exclamation means something like "let God be praised," or literally "let Yahweh be praised," and over time it seems to have come to include a general acknowledgment that God is mighty, great, and the object of worship. An early collection of hymns with both Christian and Jewish elements, entitled the *Odes of Solomon*, includes this ending for each of the hymns that were written in the first or second century CE.[18] By singing or chanting *Hallelujah*, Christians joined in the celebratory nature of the hymns and added their voices in praise to God.

To avoid permitting this conversation to become sidetracked in a conversation of early Christian hymn singing, it is important here to draw out the themes that help elucidate the thesis of this study. Christian hymn singing was overtly Christ centered, and the practice of singing is closely, and perhaps exclusively, connected with worship services where meals were eaten. Moreover, Christians sang to Christ as God, which was an intentional move to accept both the mortal and divine Jesus Christ. The New Testament Gospels were reluctant to refer to Jesus as "God," but the hymns were not reluctant to do so. The hymns also encouraged, and may have originally included, an element of audience participation, thus joining cantor and congregant in praising Lord Jesus. Over time, trained choirs emerged, and early Christian sources report boys' and girls' choirs as well as men's and women's choirs.[19] Finally, Tertullian mentions the production of new Christian hymns, likely in Greek, together with the singing of the traditional hymns: the Psalms of the Old Testament.[20]

The Philippians Hymn

Objections to the idea that Philippians 2:6–11 constitutes a preexisting hymn are significant enough that it would be irresponsible not to acknowledge their existence.[21] However, proponents of the hymn have clearly demonstrated a number of important parallels associated with Jewish and Christian hymns. Moreover, the passage contains a number of terms used nowhere else in Paul's letters, "seize," "form," and "to exalt" (*harpagmos, morphē,* and *hyperypsoō*). And the passage discusses themes that are not addressed elsewhere in Paul's letters, thus making it more likely that he has used a source from another author.[22] The question of whether this passage is a hymn cannot be resolved in a study of this length, and at the outset the overriding interest in pursuing the theology of two hymns makes this an issue of secondary importance.[23]

This study now moves with caution into a discussion of the theology of two of the earliest Christian hymns with the acknowledgment that the hymnic origins of the source is partially in doubt. Such concerns are further diminished because the Greek text of these passages is not in question, and therefore many of the conclusions will withstand scrutiny even if these hymns turn out to be didactic poetic narratives. In order to analyze the Philippians hymn more carefully, the hymn must be rendered into modern English that restores the general strophic pattern and sentence structure, while also avoiding some of the infelicities of the King James Version. Verse divisions are noted in parentheses. The final phrase of verse 5, while not technically part of the hymn, provides the subject of the hymn and is therefore included in the translation.

> (5) in Christ Jesus,
> (6)   who was in the form of God,
>   did not suppose that equality with God
>   was a prize to be seized
>
> (7)   but he poured himself out,
>   and took the form of a slave
>   and he was born like human beings.
>
> And he was found in human form,[24]
> (8)   he humbled himself
>   and was obedient to the point of death:
>   death on the cross
>
> (9)   Therefore, God exalted him on high
>   and freely bestowed on him the name
>   that is above every name
>
> (10)   so that in the name of Jesus
>   every knee should bend in worship
>   in the heavens, on earth,
>   and among those who dwell beneath the earth
>
> (11)   and every tongue will confess
>   the Lord Jesus Christ
>   to the glory of God the Father.[25]

The hymn is remarkable in its simple Greek and in its narrow focus on the exaltation of Jesus Christ. The hymn proposes three states of existence: the premortal Christ (Philippians 2:6), the passage through birth and mortality (2:7–8), and exaltation (2:9–10). This structure is paralleled in the prologue hymn: premortality (John

1:1–5), mortality (1:10–12), and exaltation (1:16, 18). Additionally, the Philippians hymn promotes the idea of an exalted mortal existence that lifts up the mortal existence to a higher plane while fundamentally leaving the physical nature of Christ unaltered. In other words, "God exalted him on high," but the hymn does not indicate that any substantive change took place in Jesus's body. He was exalted and given "the name," which refers to both his mortal name, Jesus, and the title, Christ.

These theologically rich statements encourage reflection on the process of and pathway to exaltation.[26] As stated so powerfully in the opening section, the premortal Christ has his own determinative will, and he deliberates or considers his premortal condition. The author offers this powerful reflection, "[He] did not suppose that equality with God was a prize to be seized." While still in a premortal state, the Christ "supposes" that he cannot be fully equal to God, it is a prize that he cannot fully achieve.[27] This thinking, sentient being realizes a shortcoming, and the means of remedy will be birth and mortality.[28] One might critique such a reading of the hymn based on the modern revelation found in Doctrine and Covenants 38:1: "Thus saith the Lord your God, even Jesus Christ, the Great I Am, Alpha and Omega, the beginning and the end, the same which looked upon the wide expanse of eternity, and all the seraphic hosts of heaven, before the world was made." These two differing viewpoints are not mutually exclusive even though the statement from the Doctrine and Covenants represents the work of a fully exalted and divine premortal Christ while Philippians describes a tentative, deliberative premortal Christ who is aware of limitations. Philippians is an exceptionally early reflection of a believing Christian navigating the humanity of Jesus while accepting his divinity. The Doctrine and Covenants is a personal statement of premortal glory given to a prophet who was distantly removed from knowing the mortal Jesus personally.

After realizing or "supposing" a way of achieving or "seizing" equality with God, Christ literally "poured himself out" into a human form like a slave. This describes an active process where Christ lowers himself from one state to another: God does not pour Jesus into a physical body; instead, Jesus takes on a body himself.[29] This new existence is described as a type of slavery (Philippians 2:7), but it is not slavery to God, and Christ chose to seek this state. Although it must remain a conjectural interpretation of the hymn, the language appears to describe the general state of humanity, a state of slavery, a state of subjection to passions and appetites.

The exaltation of Christ is also described vividly in the hymn when the author connects the earthly state of Christ to his exaltation through an act of obedience. He "was obedient to the point of death," which means that he obeyed to the point that he was killed, and "therefore" God raised him up. These verses (8–9) present the culmination of the journey of Christ's soul from the premortal existence, through an obedient mortality, to an exalted postmortal existence. The hymn avoids drawing attention to this journey of the soul as an example for others to follow, but Philippians 2:1–5 clearly frames the hymn with this intent in mind. Christian life should be patterned on the example set forth by Christ, and this seems to summarize Paul's reason for including the hymn in his letter.

Finally, the hymn probes the question of Christ as the Creator, not as premortal Creator but as postmortal steward over all existence. The language of the hymn praises him in the following way, "so that in the name of Jesus every knee should bend in worship in the heavens, on earth, and among those who dwell beneath the earth" (Philippians 8:10). This exploration of the theme of how Christ became the exalted Lord, equal with God, and therefore connected to the creation of the world is achieved through Christ's act of obedience. In the language of the hymn, Christ was appointed to stand above all creation, and all creation was directed to be Christ centered and to show reverence to his name. Modern revelation might not speak of Christ in that way, as the appointed Creator (see Mosiah 3:8; Doctrine and Covenants 38:1), but this hymn represents a developing, nascent faith. In this position, Christ is able to act as Savior. All creation looks to him, and he is uniquely positioned to redeem or save his people.

This type of reading of the Philippians hymn may initially raise questions about contradicting doctrinal statements and disagreement between scriptural sources since Christ is described in the hymn as progressing and yet, for example, in other sources he is proclaimed as the premortal, exalted Lord of creation. To help lessen these objections, the early Latter-day Saint practice of singing hymns will be discussed briefly as a potentially illuminating corollary to the early Christian practice and also to show that early LDS hymns were also experimental in their theological interests. Early Latter-day Saint hymns were exploratory in the doctrines they proposed, they encouraged new ways of thinking about the divine, and they at times went beyond canonical scriptural statements.[30] In this regard, they served a similar purpose for early Christian authors who penned nonbinding hymnic reflections on the nature of Christ. One of the primary examples of this practice was Eliza R. Snow's poem entitled "My Father in Heaven" that was later put to music under the title "O My Father."[31] That hymn contains the famous exploratory refrains, "Truth is reason; truth eternal Tells me I've a mother there" and "Father, Mother, may I meet you In your royal courts on high?"

This hymn is credited with being the first formal declaration of the Latter-day Saint belief in a heavenly mother, and like the Philippians hymn, it probably represented common themes and interests of the day.[32] The hymn "O My Father" also presents an exploratory reflection on the nature of deity that moved beyond canonical statements but simultaneously reflected the sincere faith of the author. Likewise, early Latter-day Saint hymn writing was exceptionally productive during the early years of the Church, and Helen Hanks Macaré has drawn attention to the fact that a remarkable sixteen new Latter-day Saint hymns were composed between 1832 and 1833 alone.[33] These new hymns treated the themes made important in the Restoration such as the redemption of Zion, the restoration of priesthood, and the nearness of the Second Coming.[34]

Although Latter-day Saint hymn authors did not treat the same themes as those found in Philippians, they were extraordinarily prolific in the number of hymns they composed, and there is a close connection between the topics presented in the hymns and those discussed in sermons and publications from the same time period.[35] Such connections may also have existed in Paul's day. The early LDS hymns show an interest in exploring new doctrines or in drawing attention to doctrines that were substantially expanding through the Restoration. This phenomenon may have parallels with the Philippians hymn and may help explain the large number of hymn fragments that remain embedded in the New Testament. Authors seem willing to explore and navigate their belief in ways that were nonbinding but also inspiring to the community of believers. An additional parallel was Latter-day Saint willingness to adapt existing hymns to suit new purposes and interests, a feature that also seems to be prevalent among New Testament authors. W. W. Phelps, like Paul, certainly drew upon the work of another author and adapted it for his own purposes. One of the most radical examples of this was Phelps's adaptation of "Joy to the World," which became a hymn about the spread of the gospel.[36] Here is a stanza from Isaac Watts's original version and Phelps's adaptation:

> He rules the world with truth and grace
> And makes the nations prove
> The glories of his righteousness
> And wonders of his love. (Watts's original)

> Rejoice! Rejoice! in the most High,
> While Israel spreads abroad,
> Like stars that glitter in the sky,
> And ever worship God. (Phelps's adaptation)[37]

The Logos Hymn

There is broad consensus today that John 1:1–18 contains the remnants of an early Christian hymn to the Logos, or to the Word.[38]

Although there is still a significant amount of disagreement over the precise structure and parameters of the hymn, a near consensus exists that these verses preserve a hymn.[39] The hymn speaks of the Logos-Word specifically, but most commentators accept the fact that the author intends the hymn to be read in praise of Jesus Christ.[40] This helps explain why the author of the Gospel of John adds to or comments upon the original hymn by adding narrative explanations such as the following, "There was a man, sent by God, whose name was John." The author of the hymn may not have been the same as the author of the Fourth Gospel, and certain stylistic features suggest that the hymn portions were authored by an earlier writer.[41] The hymn is extremely simple in its wording, but it achieves a certain elegance through the ideas it proposes. The hymn is here reconstructed in a modern language translation with the narrative insertions, those added by the Fourth Evangelist, set off through the use of parentheses.

(1)   In the beginning was the Word,
              and the Word was with God,
              and the Word was God.

(2)   Thus he was in the beginning with God.

(3)   All things were created through him,
              and without him nothing was created.
              What was created (4) in him was life,
              and the life was the light of humanity.

(5)   And the light shines in the darkness,
              but the darkness does not comprehend it.

([6] There was a man, sent by God, whose name was John. [7] He came as a witness in order to testify of the light, so that all might believe through him. [8] He was not the light, but a witness of the light, [9] the true light that lightens all humanity, those who come into the world.)

(10)   He was in the world,
>   and the world was created through him,
>   but the world did not know him.

(11)   He came to his own,
>   but his own did not comprehend him.

(12)   And to all who receive him,
>   to those who believed in his name,
>   he gave them power to become the children of God,

([13] who were born not from blood nor the will of the flesh, but from God. [14] And the word became flesh and lived among us in a body, and we saw his glory, which is the glory of an Only Begotten of the Father, who is full of grace and truth. [15] John testified of him and declared, "This was him of whom I said, 'He who comes after me is greater than me because he was before me.'")

(16)   And from his fullness we have received grace in
>   place of grace.

([17] The law was given through Moses, and grace and truth began as a result of Jesus Christ. [18] No one has ever seen God.)

>   The Only Begotten God,
>   who is in the embrace of the Father,
>   he has declared him.

This following discussion of the Logos hymn will focus on the hymn proper and not on the narrative additions (verses 6–9, 13–15, 17–18a), a detour that would take the discussion unnecessarily too far afield into the theology of the Gospel of John. The hymn's opening line contains a clear echo of Genesis 1:1: "In the beginning God created the heaven and earth."[42] The author of the hymn has borrowed the first two words of the Greek translation of Genesis—the

Septuagint—to initiate a new hymn, although this new hymn is not to God the Father, but to the Logos-Word.[43] Indeed, the parallels to Genesis are quite prevalent through verse 5: creation, darkness, and light, but thereafter the author wholly departs from Genesis. This new composition is therefore not a simple reflection on Genesis that replaces God with Logos, but an entirely new composition with new interests and purposes.[44]

One matter concerning the meaning of the hymn is whether the author intended to say that the Logos-Word is God or divine.[45] Scholars are divided over this issue, which arises from the absence of the definite article "the" before the word "God" in verse 1.[46] The specific issue is whether "and the Word was God" should instead be translated as "and the Word was divine."[47] The grammatical issue is simultaneously easy to describe but impossible to translate unequivocally, and author intent also plays a significant factor in the discussion. The phrase has a clear qualitative, or descriptive, meaning, and without attempting to solve the grammatical debate over the issue, it seems that by stating "the word was God" the author was not saying "the word was God the Father," but "the word was a God" or that he was a God who existed alongside God the Father.[48] The question will remain over whether the author of the hymn proposed that there were two Gods in heaven, a question that cannot be solved here. This study will accept that the intended meaning was close to the idea that the Logos was indeed God because of his ability to bestow the status of "children of God" and the hymn's conclusion that declares "The Only Begotten God, who is in the embrace of the Father" (John 1:18).

With these caveats in place, it is now possible to consider this hymn in light of the Philippians hymn that told of the premortal, mortal, and postmortal states of Christ. The Logos hymn is similar with a premortal Logos, who creates a ministry to "his own" in the world, and a postmortal existence as the exalted "Only Begotten." But the prologue hymn offers a profound reflection on Christ before he lived on earth. Whereas the Philippians hymn proposed a deliberative soul that realized an insufficiency, the prologue sends out reason, the basic meaning of the Greek word *logos*, throughout all creation. God's reason in the person of the Logos, his way of thinking, planning for, and implementing the salvation of humanity, permeates the created world. This appears to be the basic intent of "the Word was with God, and the Word was God." As a spiritual reflection on God, the hymn reports that God's Word was intended to weave itself into the very fabric of existence because that Word "was God." The prologue blurs the lines between God the Son and Father, but in making them nearly synonymous, the author has shown just how fully the fabric of life is interwoven with the reasoning of the Father and Son.

The next major episode of the hymn, apart from the insertion of verses 6–8 that record John the Baptist's witness to the Logos, focuses on the mortal mission of Jesus Christ.[49] The creation that is permeated with light, a "light [that] shines in darkness" (John 1:5), is unable to understand the light, a word that implies that the world can see the light but that they fail to make it their own.[50] Verse 10 highlights the tension between a world that sees the Logos but does not fully understand him when it reports, "He was in the world . . . but the world did not know him." A surprising note follows: "He came to his own, but his own did not comprehend him" (John 1:11). Unlike the Philippians hymn, there is a subtle criticism of believers who also fail to comprehend the Logos.[51] Despite the criticism, some do "receive him," and to them "he gave . . . power to become the children of God."

Verses 5–12 represent the most significant departure from the Philippians hymn because they demonstrate a clear didactic purpose. Two ways of encountering the Logos are presented: incomprehension and reception. And in presenting the way to God in this way, the hymn has prepared the reader for Jesus's later teaching, "I am the way, the truth, and the life: no man cometh unto the Father, but by me" (John 14:6).[52] Thus the context for accepting Jesus Christ as Savior is put forward as a purpose of his mortal existence.

The final portion of the hymn has been the most difficult to reconstruct, in part because it seems to have been the most heavily edited
by the author of the Fourth Gospel. Assuming that verses 13–15 and
17–18a are commentary on the hymn, it is possible to recover some
of the intent of the hymn's closing strophe. After welcoming some
to become the children of God, the final lines of the hymn seem to
address the question of how this was accomplished and how that status as children altered a person's fundamental relationship with God.
Those who receive the Logos will also receive "grace in place of grace,"
a phrase that has become an obstacle for interpreters because it uses a
preposition in an unusual way and appears nowhere else in the New
Testament. Without delving into the many different ways that this
phrase can be interpreted, the translation provided here assumes
that the author is promoting a replacement theology. The first state
of grace would then represent the law of Moses and God's attendant
grace given to the Israelites, whereas the second state of grace represents that brought by the Logos, or the Son of God.[53] This reading of
the hymn would shift the meaning toward the Logos who brings with
him a new day of grace, a period of becoming sons and daughters of
God again that is compared to a previous day of grace.

Finally, the lines at the end of the hymn have triggered a significant amount of discussion because they seem to imply that no one has
seen God at any time (John 1:18). Although the interpretation of the
hymn offered in this study must remain a reasoned conjecture, the
claim that "no one has ever seen God" fits well within the framework
promoted here. If indeed God represents both states of grace, the
law and instructions given in the Old Testament *and* the teachings
of Jesus Christ, then up until that time no one had fully seen God
for who he really was. Each testament bore witness to one part of
God's grace, thus making the final line of the hymn worthy of an
exclamation point: "The Only Begotten God, who is in the embrace
of the Father, he has declared him!" (1:18). Following the reasoning of
the hymn and the comments added to it by the author of the Gospel

of John, the reader can now engage God fully, openly, and in truth because it is through the Son that one can come to know God.

Conclusion

Admittedly, the attempt to reconstruct the meaning of a source without having access to that source in its original language and setting is a difficult endeavor. The hymns examined in this study may have been substantially longer with other clear and even stronger points of emphasis. As this study has demonstrated, the meaning of the hymns will always be partially dependent upon the contexts into which they were copied. With these caveats in place, a couple of unifying features of these hymns emerge as interesting and informative.

The first Christian author to write and have those writings survive in the New Testament was Paul, and fortunately Paul drew upon sources that either were contemporary to him or predated him. This would make the sources that he quoted possibly older than his own writings, and one important example of this is the Philippians hymn. The same is true for the Gospel of John, whose author quoted a potentially earlier hymn to the Logos. Both of these hymns can claim to be among the earliest documents written by a Christian believer. And in an interesting turn of events, both of these hymns bear strong similarities in their contents and the purpose for which they were written.

Both the Logos hymn and the Philippians hymn sing of a premortal Christ who descends to earth and is subsequently exalted on high. While the journey of the soul motif was common in the ancient world, these two hymns give purpose to Christ's journey. He came to earth to save and redeem, and these hymns give purpose to his mortal life. As the Gospels clearly demonstrate, Christ did many miraculous things, but those same authors do little to explain the value of those miracles in light of Jesus's atoning sacrifice: they are connected, they brought people to faith in Jesus, and they generated opposition. But the hymns reflect on these events in a different way: they show descent and mortality as a pathway to exaltation, and they show Christ pouring himself out for others even in his premortal state. The hymns show a greater perspective on the meaning of Jesus Christ's life, and they openly declare him to be God, something that is done only one other time in the Gospels (John 20:28).

Early Latter-day Saint hymn-singing practices provide a corollary to the early Christian practice, and both show a willingness to probe new ideas and beliefs. They capture the interests of their day, and they immortalized those interests in song. Also, the hymns of this dispensation made their way into temple dedications, baptismal services, and sacrament meetings. Likewise, early Christians sang hymns at the meals that were intended to commemorate the Last Supper. They also sang at baptisms and other liturgical events. And in those hymns, they sang to Christ the Lord and openly shared their most profound beliefs in the man from Nazareth who was also God.

THOMAS A. WAYMENT *is a professor of classical studies at Brigham Young University.*

Notes

"Each person has a hymn" is my translation of 1 Corinthians 14:26.

1. The two pioneering works in English on the topic of hymns in the Bible are those of Hermann Gunkel, *The Psalms: A Form-Critical Introduction*, trans. Thomas M. Horner (Philadelphia: Fortress Press, 1967). Hermann Gunkel, *An Introduction to the Psalms: The Genres of the Religious Lyric of Israel*, rev. Joachim Begrich; trans. James D. Nogalski (1926; repr. Macon, GA: Mercer University Press, 1998). These two works published in the early twentieth century seem to have been the impetus for the discussion of psalms in the New Testament. Important for the New Testament hymns are Ethelbert Stauffer, *New Testament Theology*, trans. John Marsh (London: SCM Press, 1955), 338–39, who offers a discussion of twelve

features of hymns, and W. Hulitt Gloer, "Homologies and Hymns in the New Testament: Form, Content and Criteria for Identification," *Perspectives in Religious Studies* 11 (1984): 115–32.

2. This may be due to the fact, among other factors, that the hymns may have been composed in Aramaic and translated into Greek.

3. Notably, N. T. Wright, "Poetry and Theology in Colossians 1:15–20," *New Testament Studies* 36 (1990): 444–68, argues against the consensus.

4. Colossians and 1 Timothy will be excluded because of questions surrounding their date and authorship. E. P. Sanders, "Literary Dependence in Colossians," *Journal of Biblical Literature* 85 (1966): 28–45; I. Howard Marshall and Philip H. Towner, *A Critical and Exegetical Commentary on the Pastoral Epistles* (New York: T&T Clark, 1999), 57–91.

5. The work by Daniel Liderbach, *Christ in the Early Christian Hymns* (New York: Paulist Press, 1998), 34–35, pursues a similar line of inquiry regarding the purpose of the hymns.

6. For a history of this discussion, see B. A. Mastin, "A Neglected Feature of the Christology of the Fourth Gospel," *New Testament Studies* 22 (1975): 36.

7. This approach assumes that the Gospels are at least in part historical reminiscences about Jesus. The effort needed to nuance the discussion to identify how the Gospel authors nuanced and adapted their historical sources lies beyond the scope of this paper.

8. All translations are the author's own, including biblical passages, unless noted otherwise. The Latin text reads, "quod essent soliti stato die ante lucem convenire, carmenque Christo quasi deo" (Pliny, *Epistles* 10.96).

9. The phrase "making music" refers to plucking a stringed instrument, and the author here clearly refers to the practice of using a stringed instrument in accompaniment to singing.

10. The common assumption is that Jesus and his disciples sang the Hallel Psalms 115–18 since the singing of the Hallel Psalms was associated with Passover celebrations.

11. *1 Apology* 13.2.

12. Author's translation of "non in scelus aliquod obstringere, sed ne furta ne latrocinia ne adulteria committerent, ne fidem fallerent" (Pliny, *Epistles* 10.96).

13. Valery Alikin, *The Earliest History of the Christian Gatherings: Origin, Development and Content of the Christian Gathering in the First to Third Centuries* (Leiden: Brill, 2010), 212–14.

14. Tobin thinks that hymns were also sung during the Eucharist or at baptisms. Thomas H. Tobin, "The World of Thought in the Philippians Hymn (Philippians 2:6–11)," in *The New Testament and Early Christian Literature in Greco-Roman Context*, Supplements to Novum Testamentum, ed. M. M. Mitchell and D. P. Moessner (Leiden: Brill, 2006), 92.

15. Clement of Alexandria, *Paed.* 2.2.44.1–2. The reference to the "apostle" is to Paul's statements in Colossians 3:16 and Ephesians 5:19.

16. Tertullian, *Apology* 39.18. Translation from T. R. Glover, *Tertullian: Apology: De Spectaculis* (Cambridge, MA: Harvard University Press, 1984). See also Ignatius, *Romans* 2.2, who mentions Christian choirs.

17. Alikin, *Earliest History of the Christian Gatherings*, 219.

18. James H. Charlesworth, "Odes of Solomon," in *The Old Testament Pseudepigrapha*, ed. James H. Charlesworth (New York: Doubleday: 1985), 2:725–71.

19. Lucian, *Ver. Hist.* 2.15, boys and girls sing in a choir. Aulus Gellius, *NA* 22.1.

20. Tertullian, *Apology* 39.18.

21. Gordon Fee, "Philippians 2:5–11: Hymn or Exalted Pauline Prose?" *Bulletin for Biblical Research* 2 (1992): 29–46, forcefully rejects the notion that this is a hymn.

22. The most readily accessible introduction to the hymn is that of Ralph Martin, *A Hymn of Christ: Philippians 2:5–11 in Recent Interpretation and in the Setting of Early Christian Worship*, 3rd ed. (Downers Grove, IL: Intervarsity, 1997).

23. Adela Yarbro Collins, "Psalms, Philippians 2:6–11, and the Origins of Christology," *Biblical Interpretation* 11 (2003): 361–72, discusses the various possibilities and offers a substantive argument that it is a hymn. My own work is also similar to that of William Furley and Jan Bremer, *Greek Hymns: Selected Cult Songs from the Archaic to the Hellenistic Period* (Tübingen: Mohr Siebeck, 2001), 1:2.

24. The King James Version mistakenly attributes this stanza to verse 8, a result of the Textus Receptus, the foundational Greek text used by the King James Version.

25. Author's translation based on the Nestle-Aland²⁸ edition of the Greek text. There are surprisingly very few textual variants for the hymn. Later manuscripts, represented chiefly by Codex Bezae, omit the definite article in verse 9 so that the translation would be "and freely bestowed on him a name."

26. The hymn does not distinguish between exaltation and salvation.

27. Unlike the other hymns, in Philippians the premortal Creator has self-will and determines to pursue a goal. See Tobin, "World of Thought in the Philippians Hymn," 94.

28. Other scholars interpret the passage to mean that Christ was equal to God, but chose to descend to the lower state of humanity. The Greek is admittedly unclear because of the lack of a finite verb for this clause. See Fee, "Philippians 2:5–11," 30–31.

29. The Greek verb used here, ἐκένωσεν, signifies descent from one state to another, or to render something useless, which in this case is the existing state of Christ before the act of pouring himself out.

30. Michael Hicks, *Mormonism and Music: A History* (Urbana: University of Illinois Press, 1989), 3–4, notes that in upstate New York at the time of the First Vision there were two camps who opposed the public singing of hymns: Baptists and Quakers. He also notes that Methodists were much more accepting of hymn singing and advocated the practice. Presbyterians had choirs, which were viewed with suspicion by Methodists. Lucy Smith may have sung in the Presbyterian choir in Palmyra, and the Smith family sang hymns in the home. The Book of Mormon also mentions singing (see Ether 6:9).

31. The poem was written in Nauvoo in October 1845 and then was published in the *Times and Seasons* 6 (15 November 1845) under the title "Poetry, for the Times and Seasons."

32. See Jill Mulvay Derr, "The Significance of 'O My Father' in the Personal Journal of Eliza R. Snow," *BYU Studies* 36, no. 1 (1996–97): 84–126: David Paulsen and Martin Pulido, "'A Mother There': A Survey of Historical

Teachings about Mother in Heaven," *BYU Studies Quarterly* 50, no. 1 (2011): 70–97.

33. Helen Hanks Macaré, "The Singing Saints: A Study of the Mormon Hymnal, 1835–1950" (PhD diss., UCLA, 1961), 96. The first LDS hymns were published in June 1832 in the initial issue of the *Evening and the Morning Star* under the title "Hymns." The subject of the earliest LDS hymns were persecution, missionary work, revelation, and the last dispensation; and later topics included baptism and sacrament.

34. *Evening and the Morning Star* 2, nos. 15–24 (December 1833–September 1834) contains seven new hymns.

35. Hicks, *Mormonism and Music*, 11, notes the Zion themes of early LDS hymns.

36. Macaré, *Singing Saints*, 94: "Clearly beginning to emerge here (in the first hymnal) is a pattern of altering, adapting, varying, and rewriting old hymns, and of creating new hymns for the use of Zion's children."

37. Another example of this was Phelps's adaptation of John Newton's hymn, "Rock of Ages," which Phelps adapted to "Rock of Enoch." Macaré, *Singing Saints*, 84–85.

38. The Greek word *logos* can be translated as "reason, logic, word, and rational thought." In philosophical thought it can take on a variety of other nuances such as the "animated thought in creation" or even the "deliberative word of god."

39. Ed L. Miller, "The Logic of the Logos Hymn: A New View," *New Testament Studies* 29 (1983): 552–61; Raymond E. Brown, *The Gospel according to John: Introduction, Translation, and Notes*, 2nd ed. (Garden City, NY: Doubleday, 1986), 1:1–42, proposes a much longer hymn.

40. More representative of my approach is Martin Hengel, "The Prologue of the Gospel of John as the Gateway to Christological Truth," in *The Gospel of John and Christian Theology*, ed. Richard Bauckham and Carl Mosser (Grand Rapids, MI: Eerdmans, 2008), 268.

41. Stan Harstine, *A History of the Two-Hundred Year Scholarly Debate about the Purpose of the Prologue to the Gospel of John* (Lewiston, NY: Edwin Mellen, 2015): Stephen Voorwinde, "John's Prologue: Beyond Some Impasses of Twentieth-Century Scholarship," *Westminster Theological Journal* 64 (2002):

15–44: Daniel Boyarin, "The Gospel of the Memra: Jewish Binitarianism and the Prologue to John," *Harvard Theological Review* 94 (2001): 243–84.

42. Boyarin, "Gospel of the *Memra*," 263–67, proposes that the hymn editorializes on the opening chapters of Genesis. For a criticism of this view, see Matthew Gordley, "The Johannine Prologue and Jewish Didactic Hymn Traditions: A New Case for Reading the Prologue as a Hymn," *Journal of Biblical Literature* 128 (2009): 781–802.

43. The opening line of John 1:1 reads, Ἐν ἀρχῇ ἦν ὁ λόγος, whereas the opening line of Genesis 1:1 in Greek reads, Ἐν ἀρχῇ ἐποίησεν ὁ θεός. The parallel position of the Logos and God in these two passages is striking.

44. A similar conclusion is reached by Thomas Tobin, "The Prologue of John and Hellenistic Wisdom Speculation," *Catholic Biblical Quarterly* 52 (1990): 252–69.

45. The Greek word *logos* is complicated to render into English, and context is important when doing so. Philo, a first-century Jewish writer, often referred to the logos as wisdom. See Philo (*Som.* 1:65–66; 2:242–45; *Fug.* 97, 109; *Post.* 122; *Deus* 134–35, but *Her.* 188 where it is similar to Stoic ideals; also *Fug.* 110). Stoic and Platonic philosophers advocated for differing roles of the logos in creation. My own work on the topic favors the idea that the hymn promotes Stoic ideals more closely. See Diogenes Laertius, *D.L.* 7.134: "They [the Stoics] hold that there are two principles in the universe, the active principle and the passive. The passive principle, then, is a substance without quality, that is, matter, whereas the active is the reason (λόγον) inherent in this substance." The word *logos* is not used as a technical term in the Gospel of John despite appearing as the center point of the hymn to Logos in the prologue. Johan Thom, *Cleanthes' Hymn to Zeus: Text, Translation, and Commentary*, Studien und Texte zu Antike und Christentum 33 (Tübingen: Mohr Siebeck, 2005), 495–97.

46. See Philip Harner, "Qualitative Anarthrous Predicate Nouns," *Journal of Biblical Literature* 92 (1973): 75–87.

47. Anarthrous θεός should be translated as "divine," a view first proposed by Origen (*Commentary on John* 2.13–18).

48. Bart Ehrman, *The Orthodox Corruption of Scripture: The Effect of Early Christological Controversies on the Text of the New Testament* (New York: Oxford University Press, 1993), 179–87.

49. Various commentators have attempted to make sense of the insertion of verses 6–9. One of the common views is that the verses were added to reach out to followers of John the Baptist who were hesitant to accept Jesus. Gordley, "Johannine Prologue," 794. The proposal goes back to Rudolf Schnackenburg, *The Gospel according to St. John*, trans. Kevin Smyth, Herder's Theological Commentary on the New Testament (New York: Herder & Herder, 1968), 1:249–53.

50. The Greek word can mean to "seize, make one's own, comprehend, or grasp."

51. The Greek verb is a near synonym to the one used in John 1:5, and in this verse it carries the nuanced meaning of "joining with someone or something." Hengel, "Prologue of the Gospel of John," 277–78, sees this as a reflection on Genesis and the separation of the light from the darkness.

52. Gordley, "Johannine Prologue," 786, has drawn a similar conclusion about the didactic purposes of the hymn.

53. This position is argued for by Ruth Edwards, "ΧΑΡΙΝ ΑΝΤΙ ΧΑΡΙΤΟΣ (John 1.16): Grace and the Law in the Johannine Prologue," *Journal for the Study of the New Testament* 32 (1988): 8–9.

12

The Revelation of Jesus Christ to Paul

Presenting a Deeper, Full Christology

Nicholas J. Frederick and Frank F. Judd Jr.

In any discussion of New Testament Christology, Paul's writings become crucial. His involvement in the Christian movement spanned approximately thirty years. He began as an antagonist toward the followers of the Way, but a divine encounter on the road to Damascus convinced him to fight alongside Jesus rather than against him. He became the first missionary to take the good news outside of Palestine, traveling extensively throughout Asia Minor and into Europe, establishing congregations that he left in the hands of trusted associates. Such extensive traveling required that Paul correspond with his congregants through letters, the standard mode of communication in the ancient world. Over the course of his ministry, Paul composed several such letters, fourteen of which have been canonized in the New Testament.[1] The earliest of these letters, either 1 Thessalonians or Galatians, was likely written around AD 48 or 49, with other letters following soon after. This early writing date places a premium upon Paul's letters, as they are the earliest evidence for what the Christian movement believed, predating even the written composition of the four Gospels.

Significantly, much of Paul's information came through his unique revelatory experience, rather than through oral tradition or discussions he may have had with others. In the opening chapter of Galatians, Paul states, "For I neither received it of man, neither was I taught it, *but by the revelation of Jesus Christ*" (Galatians 1:12; emphasis added). Later, he would assert to those in Corinth that he had received "visions and revelations of the Lord" (2 Corinthians 12:1). While Paul no doubt learned some of what he knew about Jesus from earlier interactions with apostles such as Peter, he also felt that his own revelatory experiences were equal to, if not more important, than what he learned secondhand. This is not to say that Paul's revelatory experiences gave him access to a *more accurate* understanding of Jesus; rather, they helped him to construct a Christology throughout his letters that is built around both the *past* Jesus that he has heard about and the *present* Jesus that he personally encounters. However, one of the challenges in understanding Paul's Christology is that his letters were often written in response to a particular "occasion" occurring in one of his churches, rather than as an attempt to construct a systematic theology (although Romans comes close).[2] Thus, some letters are more pertinent than others, and they often focus on different aspects of Christ's saving work, with none of them providing a complete view of Paul's understanding of Jesus. But if there is one theme that unifies them all, it is a concern for relaying who Jesus is and why his life and death are so relevant for believers.

The basic kerygmatic pattern of Paul's preaching as revealed in his surviving letters gives us a good sense of what he believed about Jesus's identity and purpose. That is, his preaching followed the basic apostolic proclamation (Greek, *kērygma*) that testified that God sent his Son Jesus who then suffered, died, rose again, and ascended to heaven. But to this he also added important information about Jesus in premortality and details about his future, eschatological roles. As a result, we will divide Paul's discussions of Jesus into three phases: The "divine Jesus," the "mortal Jesus," and the "exalted Jesus." The first phase, the "divine Jesus," will explore how Paul conceived of the premortal Jesus: Who was he prior to his incarnation? The second, the "mortal Jesus," will examine how Paul understood Jesus's birth and experiences in mortality, looking specifically at one of Paul's favorite images, the cross. Finally, we will consider Paul's understanding of the "exalted Jesus," namely what Jesus became after his resurrection and how that will affect his interactions with humanity in the future.

The Divine Jesus

There are several places in Paul's letters where he writes of Jesus in a way that suggests he believed Jesus existed prior to his incarnation on earth and that this existence was, somehow, as a divine figure. In this section, we will examine two moves made by Paul in composing this premortal picture of Jesus. First, Paul promotes what has been called a Wisdom Christology, meaning that the Israelite concept of wisdom as a premortal quality or even a personification of the transcendent Israelite God has been appropriated by Christians and applied to Jesus.[3] This appropriation bestows an element of divinity upon Jesus as well as positioning him as the creator and sustainer of the cosmos. Second, Paul promotes a divine identity Christology by identifying Jesus as the same being who in the Hebrew Bible was worshipped as Jehovah.[4]

Wisdom Christology

In Jewish literature prior to the New Testament, particularly in texts such as Proverbs, Job, and the noncanonical Wisdom of Solomon, authors attempted to solve the problem of how a transcendent God could interact in the immanent world by teaching that God possessed an (often feminine) inseparable attribute termed *ḥokmāh* (Greek, *sophia*) or *Wisdom*.[5] It is Wisdom that functions as God's agent in creating the earth and serves as the expression of the divine presence on the earth, a means of interacting with God in this world in a way that didn't breach monotheism.[6] Thus, an association with Wisdom implies an existence that predates creation. For Christian writers such as Paul, the appropriation of Wisdom became useful when attempting to teach that there could be multiple expressions of God while still maintaining some form of monotheism; rather than two separate beings, Jesus could be seen as God because he was in some way inseparably connected with God, perhaps as an attribute or agent of God.[7] This connection between Jesus and Wisdom can perhaps be seen in Paul's epistle to the church at Corinth, where he writes, "But we preach Christ crucified, unto the Jews a stumblingblock, and unto the Greeks foolishness; But unto them which are called, both Jews and Greeks, *Christ the power of God, and the wisdom of God*" (1 Corinthians 1:23–24; emphasis added).[8] However, it is important to remember that just because early Christian writers may have borrowed from the Wisdom tradition in order to form a conceptual background in trying to comprehend Jesus (particularly as a premortal being), they were not necessarily claiming that Jesus *was* Wisdom.[9]

The most explicit statement of this Christology comes from a passage in Philippians 2, several verses of which (namely 2:6–11) appear to be an early Christian hymn that has been embedded in Paul's letter.[10] Beginning in Philippians 2:5, the first part of the hymn reads this way:

> Let this mind be in you,
>> which was also in Christ Jesus:
> Who, being in the form of God,
>> thought it not robbery to be equal with God. (2:5–6)

Here, Paul describes how Jesus, prior to his birth on earth, was in the "form" (Greek, *morphē*) of God and was "equal with God" (Greek, *isa theō*). The implication is that Jesus did not feel that he was somehow robbing God by claiming this equality; rather it was something that was inherently within him. Furthermore, Jesus recognized that his divinity was not something that he need selfishly cling to, something that made him exempt from condescension. Rather, in the words of N. T. Wright, "The pre-existent son regarded equality with God not as excusing him from the task of (redemptive) suffering and death, but actually as uniquely qualifying him for that vocation."[11] Of the importance of the Philippians hymn in understanding how Paul (and likely other Christians) viewed Jesus's preexistent, or premortal, state, Larry Hurtado writes, "All this means, as astonishing as it may be that the idea developed so early, that Philippians 2:6–7 should be read as describing the action of the 'preincarnate' or 'preexistent' Christ."[12]

Concomitant with this Wisdom Christology is the fundamental belief that Jesus, like Wisdom (cf. Proverbs 9:1), is the agent of creation. In a second early Christian hymn embedded into one of his letters, this time Colossians 1:15–20, Paul writes, "For by him were all things created, that are in heaven, and that are in earth, visible and invisible, whether they be thrones, or dominions, or principalities, or powers: all things were created by him, and for him: And he is before all things, and by him all things consist" (Colossians 1:16–17).[13] How, exactly, Jesus performed these creative acts goes unsaid; Paul's point is to emphasize that Jesus is the being who performed it. He stands at creation's head. Yet, somehow, creation was performed *for him*, suggesting that he stands at creation's end as well.

Colossians also asserts that not only did Jesus create the universe, he is also responsible for sustaining it: "He is before all things, and by him all things consist" (Colossians 1:17). The notion that Christ was "before all things" signifies "a continuing stress on the preexistence of Christ and his timeless position of superiority in relation to creation."[14] The Greek verb translated as "consist" (Greek *synistēmi*) means "to hold together" or "cohere."[15] Thus, as one scholar has expressed, "not only is Christ the mediator of the initial creation; he is also the means by which God continues to hold the world in existence."[16] These descriptors recall a revelation to Joseph Smith that describes the power of Jesus Christ, who is "in all and through all things" and whose power is "in all things, which giveth life to all things, which is the law by which all things are governed" (D&C 88:6, 13). The argument of Colossians 1:17 is similar; without Jesus Christ and his light, the universe would fall apart or disintegrate into darkness.

"Divine Identity" Christology

A second way Paul accentuates the premortal, or "preexistent," divinity of Jesus is through what New Testament scholar Richard Bauckham has termed divine identity Christology:

> I shall argue that high Christology was possible within a Jewish monotheistic context, not by applying to Jesus a Jewish category of semi-divine intermediary status, but by identifying Jesus directly with the one God of Israel, including Jesus in the unique identity of this one God. Jewish monotheism clearly distinguished the one God and all other reality, but the ways in which it distinguished the one God from all else did not prevent the early Christians including Jesus in this unique divine identity. While this was a radically novel development, almost unprecedented in Jewish theology, the character of Jewish monotheism was such that this development did not require any repudiation of the ways in which Jewish monotheism understood the uniqueness of God.[17]

What Bauckham argues is, to put it simply, that early Christians such as Paul included Jesus in the "divine identity" of the God *YHWH*, or Jehovah. When they discussed Jesus, they were discussing Jehovah, and vice versa. This is not to say that Paul and other early Christian authors necessarily believed that Jesus was *actually* Jehovah, as Latter-day Saints do today, only that they found value and meaning in discussing Jesus in similar language. The result was that, in Bauckham's words, "the earliest Christology was already the highest Christology."[18] As such, it is related to the Wisdom Christology discussed above, but the focus in this section will be geared toward how

Jesus Christ is specifically linked or included in the identification of *Jehovah*. In other words, stories and passages from the Hebrew Bible dealing with or describing Jehovah begin to be applied to Jesus Christ in a manner that joins the two together and, at least implicitly, gives Jesus an additional element of premortal identity.

In the KJV Old Testament, the word "Lord" in small caps renders the Hebrew divine name YHWH and refers to Jehovah, the God of Israel who revealed himself to Moses: "And God said unto Moses, I am that I am: and he said, Thus shalt thou say unto the children of Israel, I am hath sent me unto you" (Exodus 3:14). This reflected the Jewish practice of reverencing the divine name by replacing it with the Hebrew ʾadōnay for "my Lord" when reciting the text aloud. Similarly, in the process of translating the Hebrew Bible into Greek (the "Septuagint" or LXX), the translators substituted the Greek noun *kyrios*, or "Lord," for YHWH, and this practice was followed by New Testament authors such as Paul, who consistently refers to "the Lord Jesus Christ" beginning with his earliest correspondence (1 Thessalonians 1:1). While the Greek word *kyrios* can technically refer to either Jehovah or a generic lord or master, Paul ascribes to "the Lord Jesus Christ" attributes that Jews reserve for Jehovah.[19]

This application of this Hebrew Bible verse (Exodus 3:14) to Jesus Christ can perhaps be seen most clearly in two passages. The first, Romans 10:1–13, is a lengthy pericope, or passage, in which Paul is arguing that there is only one means of salvation, namely through "the Lord Jesus" (Romans 10:9). Paul's closing remark in 10:13 states: "For whosoever shall call upon the name of the Lord shall be saved." Paul's statement here is a quotation of Joel 2:32: "And it shall come to pass, that whosoever shall call on the name of the Lord shall be delivered." When Joel refers to the Lord, he is speaking of Jehovah. Paul appropriates Joel's language and applies it to Jesus Christ—with the result that now Jesus is filling the role played by Jehovah. This is a critical move by Paul—one he will do again and again—and, in the words of one scholar, "eliminates the possibility of thinking of the God of Israel, YHWH, as apart from the human being Jesus. This unitive relationship is dialectical and hinges in fact on unreserved identification of one with the other as well as on clear differentiation."[20]

A second example returns us to the Christ hymn embedded in Paul's letter to the Philippians. As we saw, the hymn stated that before Christ came to earth "in the likeness of men" he was "equal with God" (Philippians 2:6). And after the mortal Jesus experienced "death of the cross," God "highly exalted" Jesus, restoring him to his former divine status, and gave him "a name which is above every name" (2:8–9). What is this highly exalted name or identity? Paul explained that "at the name of Jesus every knee should bow" and "every tongue should confess that Jesus Christ is Lord" (2:10–11). The hymn's words appear to be an allusion to a passage in Isaiah 45, where Jehovah declared that "unto me every knee shall bow, every tongue shall swear" (Isaiah 45:23). Thus, Paul again identifies Jesus Christ with Jehovah, the one to whom everyone should direct their worship and devotion.[21]

Notably, this type of scriptural application did not just pertain to scriptural passages. Paul was also fond of using biblical narrative to promote this "divine identity." In 1 Corinthians, Paul identified Jesus Christ as the "spiritual Rock that followed" the people of Moses during their journeys in the wilderness of Sinai and who provided for them "spiritual meat" and "spiritual drink" (1 Corinthians 10:3–4). Paul also warned the Corinthians not to "murmur" or "tempt Christ" as the Israelites did long ago "and were destroyed of serpents" (1 Corinthians 10:9–10). These, of course, are events associated with Jehovah in the Old Testament. He miraculously provided life-saving manna and water throughout the wilderness experience, although the children of Israel murmured and rebelled against him before many of them were killed by poisonous snakes.[22]

The Mortality of Jesus

While Paul's letters provide a significant amount of evidence that he understood and taught a premortal Jesus, a divine being who is intricately linked with the Hebrew God Jehovah, the crux of Paul's Christology rests in Jesus's mortal life and his exaltation following his death. For Paul, there are two crucial elements of Jesus's mortal life that must be properly understood. First, Jesus was a *human* being; he was not a spirit who may have looked human, nor was he just a divine being who simply dwelt on earth. Jesus was born of a mortal woman and lived a mortal life, yet he did so as a divine being. Paul relays these two seemingly paradoxical points through a conception Christology and an incarnation Christology. Second, Jesus's suffering and sacrifice were a real event that culminated on the cross, which becomes the most potent symbol of Pauline Christology. We will discuss both of these ideas in this section.

Jesus's Humanity—Conception and Incarnation

Although Paul never explicitly discusses the circumstances surrounding the birth of Jesus in the same way that Matthew and Luke so beautifully do, his epistle to the Galatians contains the earliest documented mention of Jesus's birth:

> But when the fulness of the time was come, God sent forth his Son, *made of a woman*, made under the law, To redeem them that were under the law, that we might receive the adoption of sons. (Galatians 4:4–5; emphasis added)

In this concise summary of Jesus's mortal mission, Paul teaches that God sent his son and that this son was "made of a woman."[23] This statement in itself speaks to the premortal life of Jesus—How could God "send" him if he didn't already exist? When Paul proceeds to explain that this Son was "made," he uses the Greek term *ginomai*, which simply means "born" (cf. Matthew 11:11).[24] The following clause, "made ("born") under the law," suggests that not only did Jesus come into the world in the same *fashion* as everyone else (namely through a woman), but he also came into the same *circumstances* as everyone else—he is as subject to the law as each one of us.[25] Paul will emphasize these same points again in his epistle to the Romans, where in the salutation of the letter he writes, "Concerning his Son Jesus Christ our Lord, *which was made of the seed of David according to the flesh*" (Romans 1:3; cf. 9:4–5; emphasis added). Jesus was a descendant of David the same way we are descendants of our ancestors.[26] The danger of a conception Christology is that some readers could interpret Paul to mean that because Jesus was born and experienced mortality, he was not divine prior to his birth.[27] He was simply exalted by God at his death. Perhaps anticipating this, Paul maintains that Jesus, although human and mortal, was somehow also divine in what is often termed incarnation Christology.[28] This type of Christology suggests that Jesus was, as John puts it, the "word [a divine being] made flesh" (see John 1:14).

Returning again to the Philippians hymn, we saw how this hymn explicitly states that the premortal Jesus was divine, but that he didn't feel that his divinity was something that he needed to selfishly cling to (Philippians 2:6). In the following verse, the hymn relays that Jesus "made himself of no reputation, and took upon him the form of a servant, and was made in the likeness of men" (2:7). The statement that Jesus "made himself of no reputation" is a rather clumsy English translation of the Greek verb *kenoō*, which simply means "to empty," suggesting that Jesus divested himself of some measure of divinity in becoming mortal. The word "likeness" (Greek, *morphē*) is a word brimming with ambiguity that nonetheless "preserves both the similarity of Christ to human beings in his full humanity and the dissimilarity of Christ to fallen humanity in his equality with God and his sinless obedience."[29] While the theological implications of this statement are the topic of much debate, Latter-day Saints can easily see Paul as intending something similar to Nephi's understanding of "the condescension of God," by which divine Jehovah set aside his divinity to become the child of Mary and then proceed forth in the ministry of the man Jesus (see 1 Nephi 11:12–33).

Jesus's Sacrifice—Suffering and the Cross

With Paul's understanding of the premortality and incarnation of Jesus in mind, the imagery and meaning of the cross becomes even more central to understanding Paul's Christology. As James D. G. Dunn has written, "There can be no doubt as to where the centre of gravity of Paul's theology is to be found. It lies in the death and resurrection of Jesus."[30] One of the primary reasons why Paul finds meaning in the cross is that it represented the ultimate scandal— Jesus, the premortal, divine Son of God, sent from heaven to earth, is now nailed to a cross. This scandal, or at least paradox, becomes even clearer in view of the christological title favored by Paul. In his writings and those attributed to him, Paul consistently employed the Greek term *christos* as both a title and as a name to refer to Jesus (i.e., Lord Jesus Christ, Jesus Christ, Christ Jesus, Christ). Meaning "anointed one," *christos* is the equivalent to the Hebrew word *māšîaḥ*, or "messiah." In ancient Israel, different types of individuals were anointed, including prophets (1 Kings 19:16), priests (Exodus 40:13–16), and kings (1 Samuel 16:13). For Paul, Jesus was the fulfillment of God's promises concerning one who would come forth through the lineage of David (Romans 1:3), commissioned to rule Israel in righteousness as the true prophet, priest, and king (2 Samuel 7:12–17). This has a particularly important meaning when we consider Jesus's crucifixion and resurrection. As Larry Hurtado has noted, "It is . . . significant that *Christos* is particularly used in sentences that refer to Jesus' death and resurrection. . . . These statements declare the innovative early Christian claim that the work of *Christos*/Messiah involves his redemptive death and resurrection."[31]

Yet Paul's provocative claim that Jesus was the Messiah—in particular a crucified messiah—conflicted with both Jewish as well as non-Jewish sensibilities during that time period. Although among the Jews of Paul's day there were varied expectations concerning the messiah, many expected a powerful military messiah who would deliver Israel from Roman oppression.[32] Paul seemingly recognized the trouble that much of his audience would have reconciling these messianic expectations with the reality of Jesus's death. To the Corinthians Paul declared that "we preach Christ crucified, unto the Jews a stumblingblock, and unto the Greeks foolishness" (1 Corinthians 1:23). The Greek word translated as "stumblingblock" (*skandalon*) literally means "scandal." It was a scandalous idea to a typical first-century Jewish audience to claim that the Messiah was not powerful but rather died a humiliating death upon the cross at the hands of others.[33] In the Roman world, crucifixion was a gruesome form of execution reserved specifically for noncitizens with no rights. The idea that Christians worshipped a convicted and executed criminal was foolishness to a non-Jewish audience.[34] Believers, on the other hand, understand the true significance of the Messiah's crucifixion, as Paul testified: "The preaching of the cross is to them that perish foolishness; but unto us which are saved it is the power of God" (1 Corinthians 1:18).

So, what was the connection between the cross and the "power of God" that Paul promotes so compellingly? Why would he term his gospel message "the preaching of the cross," as he does in 1 Corinthians 1:18? The answer may well be found in what we term an atonement or sacrificial Christology. First, the cross helped readers focus upon the *suffering* and *sacrifice* of Jesus. To the Romans, Paul described the death of Christ in terms of sacrifice: God sent "his own Son in the likeness of sinful flesh, and for sin" (Romans 8:3)—meaning to be a "sin offering" (NIV). Specifically, as Paul taught the Corinthians, Jesus Christ was a "passover" offering "sacrificed for us" (1 Corinthians 5:7). Just as animals were sacrificed under the law of Moses "to make atonement" for sinners (Leviticus 1:3–5), so also the sacrifice of Jesus Christ was an atonement for sin, described variously by Paul as "for the ungodly" and "for us" (Romans 5:6, 8)—in short, "for all" (2 Corinthians 5:14–15). In addition, the death of Christ has "abolished death, and hath brought life and immortality" to everyone (2 Timothy 1:10). Thus, all humankind is "reconciled to God by the death of his Son" (Romans 5:10). This selfless act of atonement makes Jesus Christ both "the Saviour of all men" (1 Timothy 4:10) who "hath redeemed us from the curse of the law" (Galatians 3:13) and "from all iniquity" (Titus 2:14), as well as the one "mediator between God and men" (1 Timothy 2:5) who "maketh intercession for us" (Romans 8:34). This is Christ's "free gift" of "grace" to a fallen humanity (Romans 5:15). Ultimately, the one who "knew no sin" was made "to be sin for us," so that we through him could be restored (2 Corinthians 5:21).

Second, the cross helps readers focus on the *victory* that is won through the cross. As we mentioned above, many saw the cross as a sign of the scandal of Christianity. Yet for Paul, that is why it becomes the perfect symbol for the movement; only those who have faith can recognize that in the cross the true believer meets the Son of God. It is when we acknowledge, as Paul did, that we all suffer from "a thorn in the flesh," yet recognize that when we are weak, then are we strong (compare 2 Corinthians 12:7, 10). As the Lord told Paul when Paul sought to have his own thorn removed, "My grace is sufficient for thee: for my strength is made perfect in weakness" (2 Corinthians 12:9). Paul's words seem paradoxical on the surface—how can we be strong when we are weak? For Paul, the strength comes through the expression of humility, and this expression of humility brings each of us face-to-face with the crucified Jesus, who was also strongest when he was weakest, who exercised the ultimate humility in condescending to earth and submitting himself to the will of the Father.

Yet there may be something deeper that runs through Paul's words. It is hard for us to understand this, living in a time when the cross carries so much positive religious meaning, but we cannot underestimate "the unspeakable horror and loathing which the very mention or thought of the cross provoked in Paul's day."[35] In fact, the Roman poet and rhetorician Cicero once wrote that he wished that even the name *cross* (Lat. *crux*) would be removed far from the mind and ears of the Roman citizens, such great odium did that word carry.[36] Yet Paul, writing to the Galatians, proudly declares that "God forbid that I should glory, save in the cross of our Lord Jesus Christ, by whom the world is crucified unto me, and I unto the world" (Galatians 6:14). Embracing the cross and all that it represents means a complete repudiation of what the world stands for and turns accepted cultural values upside down. For Paul, acceptance of Jesus means the rejection of the world, both in the sense that Paul rejects the world, but also in the sense that the world rejects him. This radical reassessment of cultural values may have led Paul to one his most evocative images. In Colossians, Paul writes: "Blotting out the handwriting of ordinances that was against us, which was contrary to us, and took it out of the way, nailing it to his cross; And having spoiled principalities and powers, he made a shew of them openly, triumphing over them in it" (Colossians 2:14–15). In the first part of this statement, Jesus takes something akin to an indictment against us for our sins and nails it to his cross, signifying that he has paid our price. Then, even more strikingly, Jesus takes the "principalities and powers" and parades them in front of everyone. Whereas Jesus had been raised upon the cross, hideously murdered and shamed in front of the world, now the triumphant Jesus leads the defeated powers of this world, stripped and exposed, behind him. In the death of Jesus, what was wrong has been set right, and the stage is prepared for the exaltation of the Son of God.

The Exalted Jesus

Having considered how Paul conceived of the premortal and the mortal Jesus, we now turn our attention to the postmortal Jesus, where Paul develops two additional christological ideas. The first is commonly termed resurrection or exaltation Christology.[37] This type of Christology presents Jesus as God's Son through his resurrection from the dead and his being raised up to heaven and reigning from his throne. The second type of Christology Paul develops that centers on the postmortal Jesus is sometimes termed parousia Christology because it focuses upon the glorious appearance (Greek, *parousia*) of

Jesus, when he returns at some point in the future as the glorious King to judge his people and permanently establish his kingdom.[38] This type of Christology may, in fact, be one of the oldest types of Christology in the New Testament because of the recording of the Aramaic phrase *maranā thā*, meaning "Let the Lord come" in 1 Corinthians 16:22.[39]

Resurrection/Exaltation Christology

Paramount for Paul is the belief that Jesus was resurrected from the dead. If there is no resurrection, then belief in Jesus is unwarranted and, quite frankly, useless. Paul repeated one of the earliest creedal summaries of Christian belief to the Corinthians, "that he was buried, and that he rose again the third day according to the scriptures" (1 Corinthians 15:4).[40] As proof of this glorious reality, Paul cited numerous resurrection appearances of Jesus: to Cephas (Peter) and to the twelve (15:5), to a group of more than "five hundred brethren" (15:6), to James (the Lord's brother) and to all of the apostles (15:7), and finally to Paul himself (15:8). Jesus Christ was the first to experience resurrection—becoming "the firstfruits of them that slept" (15:20) and solidifying the hope for all humankind "to be clothed upon with our house which is from heaven" (2 Corinthians 5:2). Thus, for Paul, the fact that Jesus had risen from the dead is of utmost importance for the Christian faith, for "if Christ be not risen, then is our preaching vain, and your faith is also vain" (1 Corinthians 15:14). And if the resurrection of Christ never occurred, Paul asserted, then "we are found [to be] false witnesses of God; because we have testified of God that he raised up Christ" (15:15).

The reality of the resurrection allows Paul to connect Jesus with Adam and present him as a "second Adam."[41] To the Corinthians, Paul offered this comparison between Adam and Jesus: "Since by man came death, by man came also the resurrection of the dead. For as in Adam all die, even so in Christ shall all be made alive" (1 Corinthians 15:21–22). This is a reference to the resurrection of Christ providing the way for all humankind to be resurrected. Later in this same chapter, Paul discussed the difference between mortal bodies and resurrected bodies: "So also is the resurrection of the dead" (15:42). Mortal or natural bodies are sown in corruption, dishonor, and weakness, while resurrected or spiritual bodies are raised in incorruption, glory, and power (see 15:42–44). Thus, extending his comparison of Adam and Christ: "The first man is of the earth, earthy: the second man is the Lord from heaven" (15:47).[42]

The resurrection of Jesus is a sine qua non doctrine for other reasons as well. For Paul, the resurrection demonstrates who Jesus is—his eternal identity. To the Romans, Paul testified very clearly his belief that Jesus was "declared to be the Son of God with power, according to the spirit of holiness, *by the resurrection from the dead*" (Romans 1:4; emphasis added). As the resurrected Son of God, Jesus rules as true king, subjecting all things to himself, who will reign until he has delivered up the kingdom to God his Father (1 Corinthians 15:24–28). As the resurrected Son of God, Jesus is the Savior of humankind, "to redeem them that were under the law" (Galatians 4:5), thus allowing all people to become part of the family of God and cry out with Christ: "Abba, Father" (Galatians 4:6; Romans 8:15).[43]

Perhaps the most vivid picture of Jesus's exaltation comes, again, from the Christ hymn in Philippians 2. Following Jesus's "pouring out" of himself and taking on a mortal form, Paul writes:

> Wherefore God also hath highly exalted him,
>> and given him a name which is above every name:
> That at the name of Jesus every knee should bow,
>> of things in heaven, and things in earth, and things under the earth;
> And that every tongue should confess that Jesus Christ is Lord,
>> to the glory of God the Father. (Philippians 2:9–11)

We already saw that one of the moves Paul makes here is to link Jesus Christ with Jehovah by appropriating language from Isaiah 45 in his description of what will happen "at the name of Jesus." What is pertinent at this point is that God has "highly exalted" Jesus. The Greek verb translated as "exalted" is *hyperhypsoō*, a compound verb that combines the preposition *hyper* ("above") with the verb *hypsoō*, "to lift or raise up." The implication, according to scholar Gordon D. Fee, is that God "exalted him (Jesus) to the highest possible degree."[44] While the exact meaning of this verb and how it is being used is unclear, one scholar writes that it "stresses the incomparable transcendence and absolute majesty of Christ."[45] In other words, Jesus has been lifted up as high as he can go; he is truly the "Lord." In addition to the statement here in Philippians 2:9, Paul also declared to the Colossians that Christ now "sitteth on the right hand of God" (Colossians 3:1) and that God raised Jesus "from the dead, and set him at his own right hand in the heavenly places" (Ephesians 1:20) while putting "all things under his feet" (1:22).[46]

Second Coming, or Parousia, Christology

Paul taught both that the resurrected Jesus would literally return to the earth and that when he did he would judge humanity. In 1 Thessalonians, one of Paul's earliest letters, he reminded his readers that when he originally visited them, he taught the people to "[turn] to God" and to "wait for his Son from heaven, whom he raised from the dead" (1 Thessalonians 1:9–10). Sometime later, it seems that some members of the Thessalonian branch were concerned that those among them who died before the Second Coming may be at a disadvantage when Christ returned. Paul reassured them that "we which are alive and remain unto the coming of the Lord shall not prevent [or "precede"] them which are asleep" (1 Thessalonians 4:15).[47] This is because at the time of the Second Coming "the dead in Christ shall rise first" and return with him (1 Thessalonians 4:16, 14). Then, as Paul further explained, "we which are alive and remain shall be caught up together with them in the clouds, to meet the Lord in the air" (1 Thessalonians 4:17).[48] Paul further warned them to pay attention to the signs of the times because Christ would return "as a thief in the night" (1 Thessalonians 5:2).[49] This, of course, recalls the teaching of

Jesus from his Olivet Discourse that eventually would be recorded in the Gospel of Matthew: "Watch therefore: for ye know not what hour your Lord doth come. But know this, that if the goodman of the house had known in what watch the thief would come, he would have watched" (Matthew 24:42–43).

Paul also taught that the resurrected Jesus would act as final judge of all humankind. Paul warned the church at Rome that God is the ultimate judge of his children on earth and that in the future there would be a "day of wrath and revelation of the righteous judgment of God" (Romans 2:5). But Paul also suggested that Jesus Christ would play a specific and important role in carrying out the will of God at the final judgment. Thus to the Romans Paul explained that there would be a "day when God shall judge the secrets of men by [i.e. through] Jesus Christ" (Romans 2:16). Later in that same letter, Paul declared that "we shall all stand before the judgment seat of Christ" (Romans 14:10), and that at that judgment seat "every one may receive the things done in his body, according to that he hath done, whether it be good or bad" (2 Corinthians 5:10). In Paul's concluding testimony to his beloved associate Timothy, Paul testified: "I charge thee therefore before God, and the Lord Jesus Christ, who shall judge the quick and the dead at his appearing" (2 Timothy 4:1). Thankfully, as Paul taught, God is full of mercy (Ephesians 2:4; 2 Corinthians 1:3) and Jesus Christ "came into the world to save sinners" (1 Timothy 1:15).

Paul's Deeper, Full Understanding of Jesus as "the Christ"

Though occasional in nature and never claiming to be comprehensive treatises on what it meant that Jesus is the Christ, Paul's letters nonetheless provide a very vivid and vibrant depiction of Jesus, revealing him to be the divine Son of God and the vital agent of our salvation. Using multiple Christologies, Paul presented multiple insights into the premortal, divine Jesus; the mortal, human Jesus; and the resurrected, exalted Jesus. Through a Wisdom Christology, he establishes that Jesus had a divine preexistence, or premortal life, where he served as *creator* and *sustainer* of the earth. Through a Christology of divine identity, Paul intricately links Jesus with Jehovah through creative exegesis of scripture and narrative. Through a conception Christology, Paul argues that Jesus was born in a normal, mortal fashion and was just as human as his associates. However, through an incarnation Christology, Paul also demonstrates that Jesus's morality included some level of divinity. It was this unity of mortality and immortality, human and divine, which gave such powerful and efficacious meaning to the cross. Finally, through a resurrection, or exaltation, Christology, Paul argues that Jesus reigns in heaven as a resurrected being, lifted up by the Father himself. The promise that Jesus will one day return and judge humanity is relayed through Paul's parousia Christology. All these christological streams must be studied carefully if readers are to realize the richness of Paul's portrait of Jesus Christ.

Paul's testimony of Jesus Christ, as contained in his many letters to his converts, echoes the solemn witness of modern apostles:

> He was the Great Jehovah of the Old Testament, the Messiah of the New. Under the direction of His Father, He was the creator of the earth. . . . He taught the truths of eternity. . . . He instituted the sacrament as a reminder of His great atoning sacrifice. He was arrested and condemned on spurious charges, convicted to satisfy a mob, and sentenced to die on Calvary's cross. He gave His life to atone for the sins of all mankind. . . . He was the Firstborn of the Father, the Only Begotten Son in the flesh, the Redeemer of the world. He rose from the grave to "become the firstfruits of them that slept." . . . He will someday return to earth. . . . Each of us will stand to be judged of Him according to our works and the desires of our hearts. . . . Jesus is the Living Christ, the immortal Son of God. He is the great King Immanuel, who stands

today on the right hand of His Father. . . . God be thanked for
the matchless gift of His divine Son.⁵⁰

NICHOLAS J. FREDERICK *is an assistant professor of ancient scripture at
Brigham Young University.*

FRANK F. JUDD JR. *is an associate professor of ancient scripture at Brigham
Young University.*

Notes

1. This number of fourteen is correct only if Pauline authorship is accepted
    for all the epistles attributed to Paul. However, scholars remain greatly
    divided on this question. The general consensus is that seven of Paul's letters
    (1 and 2 Corinthians, Romans, Galatians, Philippians, 1 Thessalonians, and
    Philemon) are considered "genuine." Three letters (Ephesians, Colossians,
    and 2 Thessalonians) are considered questionable and have been labeled
    "deutero-Pauline." Pauline authorship of the Pastoral Epistles (1 and
    2 Timothy and Titus) is argued for only by the most conservative schol-
    ars, while the Epistle to the Hebrews is rarely considered, if at all, to be
    authored by Paul. The arguments for and against Pauline authorship tend
    to rely on grammar, word choice, and theology, so differences in grammar
    and word choice should not be interpreted as being indicators of multiple
    authors. Rather, Paul's use of scribes in the composition process could
    be a considerable factor in what grammar and word choice are employed
    throughout a letter. See Lincoln Blumell, "Scribes and Ancient Letters:
    Implications for the Pauline Epistles," in *How the New Testament Came
    to Be: The 35th Annual Sidney B. Sperry Symposium,* ed. Kent P. Jackson
    and Frank F. Judd Jr. (Provo, UT: Religious Studies Center; Salt Lake
    City: Deseret Book, 2006), 208–26. A useful introduction to the issues
    surrounding Paul's epistles can also be found in Luke Timothy Johnson,

The Writings of the New Testament, 3rd ed. (Minneapolis: Fortress Press, 2010), 237–42. In the course of this paper, we will omit the Epistle to the Hebrews but will treat the remaining thirteen letters as if they were written by Paul. For more on the authorship of the Epistle to the Hebrews, see Terrence L. Szink, "Authorship of the Epistle to the Hebrews," in *How the New Testament Came to Be*, 243–59.

2. On the "occasional nature" of Paul's letters, see Eric D. Huntsman, "The Occasional Nature, Composition, and Structure of Paul's Letters," in *How the New Testament Came to Be*, 190–207.

3. For convenience, we will refer to the applicable references in Thomas P. Rausch's short and concise study of New Testament Christology, *Who Is Jesus? An Introduction to Christology* (Collegeville: Liturgical Press, 2003). For Wisdom Christology, see 137–38. The classic (and still very useful) study of Christology is Raymond E. Brown, *An Introduction to New Testament Christology* (New York: Paulist Press, 1994). For Pauline Christology in particular, see Gordon D. Fee, *Pauline Christology: An Exegetical-Theological Study* (Peabody: Hendrickson, 2007).

4. See Rausch, *Who Is Jesus?*, 139–42. We recognize that these two types of Christologies could be reasonably viewed as two sides of the same coin. However, we tease them apart here to try to emphasize, specifically for Latter-day Saints, how the ideas of premortality and the identification of Jesus with Jehovah may have been expressed by Paul.

5. For understandable reasons, the study of Wisdom's relationship to deity has been pursued heavily by feminist scholars. See, for example, Karen Torjesen, "Wisdom, Christology, and Women Prophets," in *Jesus Then and Now: Images of Jesus in History and Christology*, ed. Marvin Meyer and Charles Hughes (Harrisburg: Trinity Press International, 2001), 186–200. For a contrary perspective, see Karen H. Jobes, "Sophia Christology: The Way of Wisdom?," in *Way of Wisdom: Essays in Honor of Bruce K. Waltke*, ed. J. I. Packer and Sven K. Soderlund (Grand Rapids, MI: Zondervan, 2000), 226–50.

6. The classic study of Wisdom literature is Gerhard von Rad's *Wisdom in Israel*, trans. James D. Martin (Harrisburg, Trinity Press International, 1972), although his claim that apocalyptic literature arose from Wisdom

literature has been heavily challenged. For a study of how Wisdom literature was applied to Jesus, see Ben Witherington III, *Jesus the Sage: The Pilgrimage of Wisdom* (Minneapolis: Augsburg Fortress, 2000).

7. An in-depth survey of the arguments for and against the application of a Wisdom Christology to Jesus is found in Aquila H. I. Lee, *From Messiah to Preexistent Son: Jesus' Self-Consciousness and Early Christian Exegesis of Messianic Psalms* (Eugene, OR: Wipf & Stock, 2005), 2–25. For arguments for and against the influence of Wisdom literature on Paul's Christology, see Bruce K. Waltke, *Proverbs 1–15* (Grand Rapids, MI: Eerdmans, 2004), 128–31. For the problem of defining Jewish monotheism and assessing the Christian understanding and reaction to it, see *Early Jewish and Christian Monotheism*, ed. Loren T. Stuckenbruck and Wendy E. S. North, JSNTS 263 (New York: T&T Clark, 2004).

8. The identification of Jesus with wisdom was not limited to Paul among early Christians. In fact, this identification would become a critical point of controversy in the discussions between Arius and Athanasius that led to the formation of the Nicene Creed. The Emperor Constantine's dedication of a church, the Hagia Sophia, to Jesus suggests that he equated the two, and the idea that Jesus is Wisdom incarnate continues to be part of Eastern Orthodox tradition. See discussion in Waltke, *Proverbs 1–15*, 127–28.

9. "It is a mistake to give too much explanatory value to the Wisdom figure in the development of the doctrine of Christ. Personified Wisdom is a way of talking about God's work in the World. But Jesus, as a distinct person, along with the Father and the Spirit, is identified as God." Daniel J. Ebert IV, *Wisdom Christology: How Jesus Became God's Wisdom* (Phillipsburg, NJ: P & R Publishing, 2011), 5. However, see also Elisabeth Schüssler Fiorenza, *Jesus: Miriam's Child, Sophia's Prophet: Critical Issues in Feminist Christology* (New York: T&T Clark, 2015), 161–65.

10. For more on the Philippians hymn, see Thomas A. Wayment, "Each Person Has a Hymn: The Creator-Savior Hymns," 197–202, in this volume.

11. N. T. Wright, *The Climax of the Covenant: Christ and the Law in Pauline Theology* (London: T&T Clark, 2004), 83–84.

12. Larry W. Hurtado, *Lord Jesus Christ: Devotion to Jesus in Earliest Christianity* (Grand Rapids, MI: Eerdmans, 2003), 123.

13. This Colossian Christ-hymn also contributes useful information as to the preexistent, or premortal, divine nature of Jesus, specifically as the "first-born of every creature" (Colossians 1:15).

14. Jerry L. Sumney, *Colossians: A Commentary* (Louisville, KY: Westminster John Knox Press, 2008), 70.

15. "The use of the perfect tense suggests a stative idea: the universe owes its continuing coherence to Christ." Douglas J. Moo, *The Letters to the Colossians and to Philemon* (Grand Rapids, MI: Eerdmans, 2008), 125.

16. Sumney, *Colossians*, 70.

17. Richard Bauckham, *God Crucified: Monotheism and Christology of the New Testament* (Carlisle, UK: Paternoster Press, 1998), 4. More recently, N. T. Wright has written in favor of Bauckham's divine identity Christology and added that "what matters is the pre-Christian Jewish ideas about Israel's God. *Jesus' first followers found themselves not only (as it were) permitted to use God-language for Jesus, but compelled to use Jesus language for the One God*" (emphasis in the original). N. T. Wright, *Paul and the Faithfulness of God* (Minneapolis: Fortress Press, 2013), 655.

18. Bauckham, *God Crucified*, viii.

19. A provocative example of this type of synthesis can be seen in 1 Corinthians 8:6: "But to us there is but one God, the Father, of whom are all things, and we in him; *and one Lord Jesus Christ*, by whom are all things, and we by him" (1 Corinthians 8:6; emphasis added). Here Paul seems to be skating a fine line between monotheism and binitarianism. On one hand, Paul may be intentionally alluding to the *shema* of Deuteronomy 6:4 and aligning "Lord" and "God," both of which refer to Jehovah in Deuteronomy 6:4, with "Jesus Christ" and "the Father." On the other, Paul may have something akin to Abinadi's argument in mind, where Abinadi argues before the priests of King Noah that Jesus is both "the Father" and "the Son" based upon what role or function he is fulfilling (cf. Mosiah 15:1–4; Ether 3:14). If the latter, Paul would be claiming that Jesus as "the Father" was the source of all life, while Jesus as "Lord" was the creator or organizer of all life. Of Paul's theological move, one scholar writes, "The statement of the unique lordship of Jesus Christ is central to Paul's theology in general and to this letter in particular. The 'Christological monotheism' affirmed

here distinguishes the Christian community from both non-Christian Judaism and gentile paganism. Jewish monotheism is affirmed against all forms of pagan polytheism (or atheism), while, against non-Christian Judaism, Christ is understood to participate in God's identity." Roy E. Ciampa and Brian S. Rosner, *The First Letter to the Corinthians* (Grand Rapids, MI: Eerdmans, 2010), 383.

20. C. Kavin Rowe, "Romans 10:13: What Is the Name of the Lord?," *Horizons in Biblical Theology* 22 (2000): 136–37. For a thorough accounting of Pauline passages that describe Jesus through evoking Jehovah, see David B. Capes, *Old Testament Yahweh Texts in Paul's* Christology, WUNT 2, no. 47 (Tübingen: Mohr Siebeck, 1992).

21. Frank F. Judd Jr., "The Condescension of God according to Paul," in *Shedding Light on the New Testament: Acts–Revelation*, ed. Ray L. Huntington, Frank F. Judd Jr., and David M. Whitchurch (Provo, UT: Religious Studies Center, 2009), 171–92.

22. See, for example, Exodus 16:1–31; Numbers 20:1–13; 21:4–9.

23. For more, see Reginald H. Fuller, "The Conception/Birth of Jesus as a Christological Moment," *Journal for the Study of the New Testament* 1 (1978): 37–52.

24. "The expression means to be born as a human being." J. Louis Martyn, *Galatians: A New Translation with Introduction and Commentary* (New Haven: Yale University Press, 2008), 390. However, it should be noted that Paul doesn't use the more common verb for "beget," *gennaō*, although it is safe to say he probably views them synonymously.

25. "The true humanity of the Son and his unity with mankind is underlined by a twofold statement: (a) he was 'born of a woman'—the woman being not only the means of his entrance into the world but also the one from whom he took everything which is proper to mankind (though he knew no sin, 2 Cor. 5:21); (b) he was 'born under the law'—his very birth as man placing him immediately under subjection to the law." Ronald Y. K. Fung, *The Epistle to the Galatians* (Grand Rapids, MI: Eerdmans, 1988), 182.

26. "Here, however, the meaning will be as far as human nature, or perhaps physical descent, is concerned. On the level of flesh, of human life, Jesus really was a descendant of David." Leon Morris, *The Epistle to the Romans*

(Grand Rapids, MI: Eerdmans, 1988), 44. However, this statement should not be interpreted to mean that Paul believed Jesus was descended literally from Joseph: "Paul is using the word *sperma* in the figurative sense, as it often appears in the OT (Gen 12:7; 15:13; 2 Sam 7:12; Ps 89:5), and scarcely in the literal sense of semen." Joseph A. Fitzmyer, *Romans: A New Translation with Introduction and Commentary* (New Haven: Yale University Press, 2008), 234.

27. For the arguments and implications surrounding conception Christology, see Andrew T. Lincoln, *Born of a Virgin? Reconceiving Jesus in the Bible, Tradition, and Theology* (Grand Rapids, MI: Eerdmans, 2013), 266–302.

28. "An incarnation Christology, then, maintains that Christ was a preexistent divine being who became human before returning to God in heaven. Here, Jesus is not understood to be a human who is elevated to divine status; instead, he is a heavenly being who condescends to become temporarily human." Bart D. Ehrman, *How Jesus Became God: The Exaltation of a Jewish Preacher from Galilee* (New York: HarperOne, 2014), 249.

29. G. Walter Hansen, *The Letter to the Philippians* (Grand Rapids, MI: Eerdmans, 2009), 153.

30. James D. G. Dunn, *The Theology of Paul the Apostle* (Grand Rapids, MI: Eerdmans, 1998), 208.

31. Hurtado, *Lord Jesus Christ*, 100–101.

32. See, for example, the plea in the Psalms of Solomon, written approximately in the first century BC: "Raise up for them their king, the son of David, to rule over your servant Israel. . . . And gird him with the strength to destroy the unrighteous rulers, to purge Jerusalem from gentiles . . . to smash the arrogance of sinners like a potter's jar . . . to destroy the unlawful nations with the word of his mouth. . . . And he will be a righteous king over them, taught by God. There will be no unrighteousness among them in his days, for all shall be holy, and their king shall be the Lord Messiah." Psalms of Solomon 17:21–24, 32.

33. Jesus's Jewish disciples may have had similar expectations about the Messiah. After Peter declared Jesus was the Messiah (Matthew 16:16), Jesus then confided to his disciples for the first time that "he must go unto Jerusalem, and suffer many things of the elders and chief priests and

scribes, and be killed" (16:21). In response, Peter protested: "this shall not be unto thee" (16:22). Jesus told Peter that he was relying upon human expectations concerning the messiah, rather than "the things that be of God" (16:23).

34. An example of this attitude is the famous Alexamenos graffito, which was discovered in Rome, dates to around AD 200, and mocks the idea that Jesus was crucified. This image depicts a man worshipping a donkey-headed man being crucified. The Greek inscription below the image reads: "Alexander worships his god."

35. F. F. Bruce, *The Epistle to the Galatians: A Commentary on the Greek Text* (Grand Rapids, MI: Eerdmans, 1982), 271.

36. Cicero, *Pro Rabiro* 16. ("sed tamen in omni calamitate retinetur aliquod vestigium libertatis. mors denique si proponitur, in libertate moriamur, carnifex vero et obductio capitis et nomen ipsum crucis absit non modo a corpore civium Romanorum sed etiam a cogitatione, oculis, auribus").

37. See Rausch, *Who Is Jesus?*, 129–30.

38. See Rausch, *Who Is Jesus?*, 127–29.

39. It is also possible to divide this phrase at a different point, *maran 'athā*, which would be interpreted as "the Lord has come" in the perfect tense. This interpretation, however, makes little sense in the context of 1 Corinthians 16:22, and the majority of scholars go with the imperative "Let the Lord come!" For more, see C. F. D. Moule, "A Reconstruction of the Context of *Maranatha*," *New Testament Studies* 6 (1959/60): 307–10.

40. Paul taught that Jesus was resurrected on the "third day" (1 Corinthians 15:4), allowing for a chronology where Jesus was crucified Friday, in the tomb Saturday, and raised Sunday morning. Other scriptural sources, however, state that Jesus was dead for "three days" (Matthew 26:61; 27:40, 63; Mark 14:58; 15:29; John 2:19–20; Helaman 14:20, 27) or "three days and three nights" (Matthew 12:40). An in-depth discussion and reconciliation of these ideas is beyond the scope of this paper. For more information, see David B. Cummings, "Three Days and Three Nights: Reassessing Jesus's Entombment," *Journal of Book of Mormon Studies* 16, no. 1 (2007): 56–73, 86; and Jeffrey R. Chadwick, "Dating the Death of Jesus Christ," *BYU Studies* 54, no. 4 (2015): 135–91.

41. This comparison between Jesus and Adam that is developed by Paul is often referred to as second Adam or last Adam Christology. What it means, essentially, is that "Adam stands for death, and Jesus stands for life," so "in and by the resurrection, Christ became 'last Adam.'" Dunn, *Theology of Paul the Apostle*, 241. See also Dunn, *Christology in the Making: A New Testament Inquiry into the Origins of the Doctrine of the Incarnation*, 2nd ed. (Grand Rapids, MI: Eerdmans, 1996), 98–128.

42. See the discussion in Gordon D. Fee, *Jesus the Lord according to Paul the Apostle* (Grand Rapids, MI: Baker Academic, 2018), 51–55.

43. King Benjamin similarly taught that when believers make a covenant with Jesus Christ, they become part of a new spiritual family unit: "And now, because of the covenant which ye have made ye shall be called the children of Christ, his sons, and his daughters; for behold, this day he hath spiritually begotten you" (Mosiah 5:7).

44. Fee, *Pauline Christology*, 396.

45. Hansen, *Letter to the Philippians*, 162.

46. This is the way Jesus himself interpreted Psalm 110:1 as recorded in that Gospel of Matthew. In that reference, Jesus asked the Pharisees, "What think ye of Christ? whose son is he?" They answered, "The Son of David" (Matthew 22:42), emphasizing the Messiah as merely a human descendant of King David. Jesus countered by quoting Psalm 110:1, teaching that David's reference to the Messiah as "my Lord" (or "my master") demonstrates that the Messiah was more than just David's human descendant (Matthew 22:43–45). See R. T. France, *The Gospel of Matthew* (Grand Rapids, MI: Eerdmans, 2007), 850–52.

47. It appears that some early Christians, possibly even Paul himself, felt that Christ was going to return very soon—within their own lifetimes. This should not be surprising, for the same seems to be true of early Latter-day Saints. See Grant Underwood, *The Millenarian World of Early Mormonism* (Champaign: University of Illinois Press, 1999). It is interesting that the JST changes "we which are alive" to "they which are alive."

48. The English verb *caught up* comes from the Latin verb *rapiō*, from which other Christians derive the name of the doctrine of the Rapture. It should be noted, however, that even though Latter-day Saints may not refer to

this teaching as the Rapture, they believe the doctrine Paul taught. This doctrine was revealed anew in the latter days (D&C 88:96–98).

49. See the discussion in Gordon D. Fee, *The First and Second Letters to the Thessalonians* (Grand Rapids, MI: Eerdmans, 2009), 164–88.

50. "The Living Christ: The Testimony of the Apostles," *Ensign*, April 2000.

13

"By His Own Blood He Entered in Once into the Holy Place"

Jesus in Hebrews 9

Richard D. Draper

With penetrating and inspired insight, the author of Hebrews bore a powerful witness of the nature and work of Jesus Christ. Unfortunately, history has not preserved who that inspired author was. Though from the second century onward, many attributed the work to the apostle Paul, the epistle itself gives no clear indication as to who wrote it. Because of both the epistle's strikingly different style and treatment of subject matter from that found in Paul's writings, the authorship of Hebrews has been much debated, both anciently and today.[1] Nevertheless, this work, and chapter 9 in particular, presents a commanding christological argument that underscores the work's inspiration and status as scripture. This paper, by taking an in-depth and careful look at Hebrews chapter 9, explores the witness of this author concerning the effect, power, and result of the self-sacrifice of Jesus for the believer.

The Author's Purpose in Writing

Hebrews 9 reveals that the author's purpose in writing was twofold. The first was to fully expose the insufficient nature of the sacrifices of the old covenant to make a change in the worshipper's "conscience" (*syneidēsis*). The Greek noun denotes a sense of moral awareness, but in a broader sense, the word carries the nuance of the pain people sense when they knowingly break a moral law.[2] The author played on this nuance. He insisted that, through participation in the observances of the Mosaic law, each person could be ritually cleansed, *but a cleansing of the conscience did not take place*. An inward uncleanliness remained that caused discomfort among the participants and acted as a barrier between the worshipper and God.[3]

The author's second purpose was to stress that by his obedient sacrifice, Jesus Christ made the all-sufficient atonement through which the believer's conscience could be fully cleansed. To have a cleansed conscience meant being freed from the pain of guilt. The author expanded on this idea and in doing so gave the idea of a cleansed "conscience" an even stronger thrust: the sanctification of the soul. In this way, the cleansing of the conscience provided the way for the disciple to gain access to the transforming power of grace. By that means, the believer was prepared to enter into God's glory. In sum, "Christ's obedience empowers the faithful to live in obedience and in fellowship with God (see [Hebrews] 10:5–10). [Each disciple comes] through him to God's 'throne' in order to find grace for living this life of faithfulness (4:14–16; 10:19–25)."[4]

A High Priest of Good Things to Come

It would appear that the specific audience to which the author directed his epistle were Jewish Christians who, because of the difficulty of belonging to the faith, were tempted to leave the gospel and return to Judaism. The author thus appealed to them on the basis of

Old Testament practices and teachings, but he gave these a decidedly Christian spin.[5]

The epistle states that the Levitical high priest ministered in a holy but earthly tabernacle, "but Christ being come an high priest [ministered in] a more perfect tabernacle, not made with hands" (Hebrews 9:11). The author's use of the phrase "but Christ" presents a sharp contrast between his focus in verses 1–10 that looked at the work of the mortal high priest with his focus in verses 11–14 that looked at the work of the eternal High Priest. The author of Hebrews has shown that the earthly holy place provided no access to heaven, "but Christ" has now opened the way. The emphasis in the first set of verses is on the tabernacle itself,[6] while that of the latter is on the full sufficiency of the Lord's sacrifice that provides complete access to God. In 9:12–14, the author provides his most thorough analysis of Christ's fulfillment of the typological sacrificial rites established by the Mosaic covenant. Throughout the verses the author emphasizes "blood," "self-sacrifice," and "cleansing." He makes it clear in these verses that the reason the Lord was able to enter the heavenly realm and make way for others to do so was because he did what the old covenant failed to do; he purged sins and cleansed the conscience of the worshipper. The author is careful to help his readers see that the whole of the Levitical system was restricted exclusively to external purification. The best it could do was but point to that internal purification so necessary to enter the presence of God.[7]

From an Old Testament perspective, it was a victim's blood that contained a vital force capable of opposing and subduing evil and quashing spiritual death. In instituting the Mosaic rites, Jehovah explained that "the life of the flesh is in the blood, and I have given it to you on the altar to make atonement for your souls; for its blood shall make atonement for the soul" (Leviticus 17:11;[8] compare Deuteronomy 12:23). "But in the sacrifice of Christ, the relationship was reversed: whereas in the Old Testament, it was the blood that gave value to the sacrifices, in the case of Christ, it is his sacrifice that gave value to his blood."[9]

Evidencing the fully sufficient work of Christ is the epistle's note in Hebrews 9:12 that Jesus entered heaven "once for all" (*ephapax*), "a term that excludes both the necessity and the possibility of repetition."[10] The Lord's redeeming work was full, complete, and final—requiring nothing more, forever.[11]

In Hebrews 9:14 the work clearly states the benefits of Christ's atonement. The author first describes what it cleanses: "our conscience" (*syneidēsis*). When God established his covenant with Israel, he also gave them his law. In doing so, he laid down the standard he expected his people to follow. At the same time, he created a condition in which the individual conscience had a standard external to itself. That meant that a person did not decide what was right and what was wrong—the law did. The person, however, could choose to conform to the law or not. The result of choosing not to conform is a transgression (*parabasis*).[12] The word denotes a heavy sin because the person knows the law and the consequences of breaking it and yet chooses to do so. Even so, the atonement of the Lord is so strong that it can reach even those who have broken the law in this manner and redeem them if they will but repent and follow him. This option places the consequences of a person's choice squarely on her or his shoulders.

The effect of the Lord's self-sacrifice was directed not at an outward cleansing as was the old covenant. Instead, it focused on the inward cleansing of "the conscience." The atonement also had the deeper effect of *purifying* it. Both cleansing and purifying "refer to the same reality." Cleansing emphasizes "the removal of sinful pollutions," while purifying refers to "the readiness of the cleansed heart to approach God."[13] Taken together, they denote the "moral transformation of the worshipper."[14]

The term *conscience*, as used by the author, carries much of the same scriptural nuance as does the term *heart* (*kardia*). Both refer to the center of a person's religious life that "embraces the whole person in relationship to God" and where each individual confronts God's holiness.[15] It is on the basis of the conscience and the heart that people decide for themselves if they want to remain with the Father and Son in the heavenly realm (2 Nephi 9:46; Alma 5:15–25; 34:33–34).

The author next states that the conscience is cleansed from "dead works" (*nekrōn ergon*). His reference is likely not to the works of the Mosaic law that, though not fully effective, were able to point the faith-filled follower to Christ. Rather, it refers to the inner state of impurity that the old covenant could not remove—that of an "evil, unbelieving heart" (Hebrews 3:12), which acted as the seat for faithlessness, disobedience, and, all too often, outright rebellion (3:7–4:11), and became an effective barrier between the sinful soul and God. The fault of the Levitical performances was that, though they prepared the worshipper outwardly for temple service, they did not transform the heart such that it became the pure receptacle of faith resulting in obedience. As a result, the worshipper was not freed from propensities that led to misdeeds and the threat of spiritual death.

The author of Hebrews emphasizes that this condition stands opposite the atonement's positive result, namely the worshippers' ability to "serve the living God." With the sinful pollutions removed from the conscience, the soul is cleansed and the barrier between it and God is removed. This cleansing not only delivers the soul from the wrath of God but also enables it to enter the most holy place, God's true sanctuary.[16] But it does more—it acts in mortality to empower the worshipper to follow God's ways and have fellowship with him. Thus, having realized the promise of the atonement, the saints are not only prepared but also anxious to serve him in his way.

Mediator of a New Covenant

In 9:15, Hebrews clearly states how those who transgressed under the old covenant "might receive the promise of eternal life," and in doing so the work intimates that the same is true for those under the new. It was because of the role Christ played. He was the *mesitēs*, which the King James Version translates as "mediator"; however, that translation falls far short of the nuance of the Greek noun. A more accurate understanding would be that of one who stands as a guarantee that promises will be realized. How so? Though the idea of a go-between is an ever-present aspect of the Greek word, the requirements for the salvation of humankind "necessitated that the Mediator should Himself possess the nature and attributes of Him towards whom He acts, and should likewise participate in the nature of those for whom He acts (sin apart); only by being possessed of both deity and humanity could He comprehend the claims of the one and the needs of the other; further, the claims and the needs could be met only by One who, Himself being proved sinless, would offer Himself in expiatory sacrifice on behalf of men."[17] In that way, he became the guarantee of salvation to the faithful. He did so by securing the salvation that could otherwise not be obtained. Thus, as the author states, Jesus is the "surety" (*engous*) of the "better covenant" (*kreittonos diathēkēs*; see Hebrews 7:22; 8:6; 9:15; 12:24) by guaranteeing that the terms of the new covenant would be fully met for his people.

Hebrews 9:15 points out how Christ became the guarantor of the blessings of the new covenant for those who failed in the old—it was because his blameless life made his self-offering acceptable to God. As a result, Jesus was able to redeem those who transgressed because of the weakness inherent in the first covenant. His sacrifice brought to an end all Mosaic sacrifices that could only cleanse "the flesh" (9:10). "Thus, by establishing an effective way of approaching God, [Christ] terminated the Old Covenant as a way of salvation and inaugurated the New that it typified."[18] His sacrifice was, then, one of covenant inauguration. Of its new promise, he became not just the mediator but the guarantor.

Hebrews 9:15 then stresses the result of Jesus becoming the guarantor of the new covenant for those who failed under the old one. The author focuses on "former transgressions" committed under the Mosaic law because the Israelites' redemption from those sins laid the foundation that made the new covenant possible. Their forgiveness made way for the new law to be written on their hearts because they were justified and could, thereby, receive the influence and power of the Holy Ghost (Hebrews 8:10; 10:16; Jeremiah 31:33).[19]

Remarkably, the Lord's sacrifice was retroactive—reaching back to all people of all ages. The author of Hebrews makes a point in line with that of the angel who declared to King Benjamin that Christ's "blood atoneth for the sins of those who have fallen by the transgression of Adam." The angel went on to teach Benjamin that those who lived before the coming of the Lord who believed "that Christ should come, the same might receive remission of their sins, and rejoice with exceedingly great joy, even as though he had already come among them" (Mosiah 3:11–13).

Hebrews refers to those whose conscience has been cleansed as "those who have been called" (hoi keklēmenoi). This group is composed not only of those whose lives are directed by faith and the resultant obedience but also of those who continually persevere in the service of the Master.[20] The author's words do not exclude those who rebelled during the Mosaic era.[21] There is a subtle hint here of vicarious work for the dead through which even those rebellious souls can become "the called" and, with the living, receive the promise of an eternal inheritance (see 1 Peter 3:18–20; 4:6; compare D&C 76:73).

The author's words reveal both the length and width of the Lord's atonement. Its length is vast, covering all those who come to him throughout the entire history of the world. Its width is very narrow, for it excludes all those who do not come to him. The Lord himself made it abundantly clear that all must enter "at the strait gate: for wide is the gate, and broad is the way, that leadeth to destruction, and many there be which go in thereat: Because strait is the gate, and narrow is the way, which leadeth unto life, and few there be that find it" (Matthew 7:13–14; see also 2 Nephi 31:18; 33:9; 3 Nephi 27:33; D&C 132:22).

The epistle makes clear that redemption comes to all only by the means of the Lord's death (Hebrews 9:15). As we look at the substitutionary or ransom model of the atonement used by the author of Hebrews, the question naturally arises: Why would God demand the suffering and death of Jesus as the means of removing the consequences of sin from the Father's other children? Was there no other way the Father could free them except through such a brutal and torturous means? Neither in Hebrews nor in the New Testament as a whole—nor specifically in the recorded words of Jesus—is this question ever addressed. The Lord made it clear that "the Son of Man came not to be served but to serve, and to give his life as a ransom for many" (Mark 10:45). These words are revealing because they show the voluntary nature of the self-sacrifice affected by the Lord. To stress the point, Christ's words emphasize that his atonement was a deliberate, willful act of obedience to God that allowed for a substitution in which one life could be given for others. That life paid the ransom that freed, potentially, all others from the consequences of sin and spiritual death. Hebrews 9:14 clarifies that the ransom is paid to God, allowing him to free others from the demands of justice and, if they will, to come under the power of his mercy (see also 2 Nephi 9:26; Alma 42:13–28).

The author of Hebrews takes this idea for granted. It was "fitting" (*prepō*), he insists, that Christ should suffer and die to redeem his people and make them "perfect [*teleioō*] in respect to conscience" (9:9). Thus, the author never questions why it was necessary for the Father to treat the Son in such a manner. He is satisfied to understand that it was simply necessary for the Lord Jesus to bow to the will of God by giving himself as the ransom. The author's writing, therefore, leaves unexplored the reason behind the divine will.

The same is true regarding the other New Testament writers (compare Matthew 11:25–26; Mark 13:32; 14:35–36; 15:34). We can say that the

> complete subjection to God's will is an integral part of the service which Jesus renders to God. For Jesus, God does not owe anyone, not even the Son, a manifestation of His reasons, let alone a justification of His acts and demands. What God wills and does, He does for reasons which are holy, just and

wise. But this does not mean that He will disclose the reasons. There is a purpose behind God's will; it is not caprice.
But man can know this purpose only if and in so far as God
reveals it to him. What is here revealed to man is that the
death of Jesus is service to God, and that it is a vicarious death
for many in virtue of which they find freedom from sin.[22]

Whatever else the case, Jesus serves as the model for devotion
to God; therefore, what he requires of the rest of us is no more than
what he has given. His obedience is the essence, ground, and revelation of the law of sacrifice we as Christians are asked to follow. *And
no one knows the cost more than does he.*

In Hebrews 9:18 the author makes his point: as with most covenants, the Mosaic law was inaugurated and ratified by the death of
the sacrificial victim and the administration of its blood. Having
validated his position by the use of scripture, the author makes this
point: Blood, and only blood, brings forgiveness. His appeal is to
Jehovah's statement in Leviticus 17:11 that he has given to Israel the
blood "on the altar to make atonement for your souls; for [the sacrifice's] blood shall make atonement for the soul."[23] The Hebrew verb
translated "to atone" (*kpr*) carries the basic meaning to "cover over"
with the extended sense of "atone, make amends."[24] The purpose of
such covering is to put a barrier between a wrongful deed and its ill
effects. When such a deed broke the relationship between persons,
the purpose of the *kaphar* was to expiate the wrongdoing and propiti-
ate or placate the offended party. It was by this means that the offense
was covered over and a good relationship restored.

The purpose of the Mosaic sacrifices was to atone for sin and
thus bring about a reconciliation between the offender and Jehovah.[25]
According to the view of sin during the Mosaic period, committing
a transgression could not simply be forgotten and walked away from.
The only way sin could be forgiven was by one of the expiatory rituals
defined in the law. Jehovah allowed for the transgression to be passed
onto a sacrificial animal and, with its death, the guilt to be removed

from the person (Leviticus 16:20–22; compare 17:11). The act emphasizes that it is God alone who can forgive sins but that this requires an act of atonement.

Hebrews emphasizes that, on the basis of the Mosaic law, no forgiveness could be achieved without the shedding of blood. This fact becomes the ground on which the author will next make his case for the necessity of the Lord's sacrifice. He has carefully shown that both purification and redemption were associated with the new covenant's inauguration. Both old and new covenants required the death of the sacrificial victim. In Hebrews 9:23–28 the author stresses the finality of the Lord's "once for all" cleansing (*ephapax*, Hebrews 10:10) at the time when he inaugurated and put in force the new covenant (9:12). To stress that finality, he contrasts it with both the initiation of the old covenant and the ritual of the Day of Atonement. On the basis of his model, he insists that since everything associated with the first covenant had to be cleansed by sacrificial means so, too, did all corresponding heavenly things.

A Pattern of Things in Heaven

Having made that point, the author of Hebrews presents his definitive evidence for the full effectiveness of the Lord's sacrifice. He boldly affirms that Christ, the High Priest, has entered into the holy place, that is, heaven itself, and proclaims that the all-sufficient sacrifice of the Lord has procured for the disciple an entrance into heaven (Hebrews 9:23–24).

Extrapolating based on tabernacle typology, in Hebrews 9:23 the author uses both the necessity and the method of purification of the tabernacle to explain why there had to be an atonement. As the earthly tabernacle with its furnishings had to be purified and dedicated through the administration of blood, so too did the heavenly tabernacle. He stresses, however, that heavenly purification requires far more than the mere fleshly sacrifices that worked for the temporal order (9:23).

The author's comments that "heavenly things themselves" needed to be cleansed and that what Christ offered were "better sacrifices" brings two questions to mind. First, how is it that "heavenly things" must be cleansed? and second, why does the author denote the Lord's offering as "sacrifices"? To answer, it is best to address the second question first, for it lays down the basis for understanding the first.

Hebrews uses the plural term *sacrifices* to equate what the Savior did with that of the continual offerings the high priest had to administer annually on the Day of Atonement. The author states clearly that the very necessary purification rites associated with the earthly tabernacle typify the need for the same to be done to the true heavenly things themselves. His point is that, by analogy, the way the sacrificial offering cleansed "the pattern" (*typos,* that is, the Mosaic tabernacle and all its furnishing), so Christ cleanses the heavenly. Furthermore, since cleansing the tabernacle was a prerequisite to a priest's entrance into it, the cleansing of the "true" was necessary for entering it. This the Savior accomplished by his one-time sacrifice (9:12) that allowed him, as the eternal High Priest, to enter the heavenly holy place.[26]

So far as the first question is concerned, what polluted the earthly tabernacle was not its location but the sins of the people (Exodus 30:10; Leviticus 16:16, 19). "Their sins formed a barrier that prevented them from coming into God's presence and exposed them to his wrath. If sin erected a barrier forbidding entrance into the earthly sanctuary, how much more did it bar the way into the 'true' Sanctuary in which God dwells."[27] Thus, such defilement was an objective impediment to entrance into God's presence and had to be cleansed.[28]

In sum, it seems likely that Hebrews uses the imagery of the need for a cleansing of the heavenly holy place as a metaphor for the need to cleanse the people in preparation for their entrance into heaven. It is human intransigence that produces an impregnable barrier that threatens the soul with eternal recompense. The cleansing represents Christ's removal of that barrier so that the repentant can enter into the presence of God. In doing what he did, the Lord made it possible for genuine fellowship with the Father to occur.[29] Furthermore, we must stress, a rite of the purification does not necessarily imply the object was previously impure any more than a rededication of a holy site means the first dedication did not work.[30] Even so, there is no doubt that Christ's act was one of both consecration and inauguration.

Hebrews points out clearly that Jesus did what he did in behalf of the saints (9:24). On the basis of the author's temple imagery, entrance into the "true" holy place involves not only the consecration of the place but also the purification of those who would enter. In this way, the work expresses both the subjective and objective significance of the Lord's sacrificial act. The subjects are the individuals within the Christian community and the object is to bring them eternal life by preparing the way.

In Hebrews 9:25 the author points out the vast difference between what the Levitical high priest did and the work that Christ did. In doing so, he sets the stage to showcase the grandeur of the sacrifice the Lord had to effect in order to cleanse heavenly things. He shows that there were three differences: First, the Lord presented himself as the sacrifice, while the high priest presented an animal; second, Christ did not have to perform the sacrifice over and over as did the high priest; and third, he used his own blood, not that of some sacrificial animal like the high priest used.

In 9:26, Hebrews shows that through his sacrifice, Jesus did more than merely weaken or restrain the effects of sin; he brought about their abolishment (*athetēsis*) once for all. He took the entire weight of the consequences of sin—not just the believers' deserved punishment—and bore it away.[31] Doing so enabled him to deliver people from its demands. In other words, the Lord did more than deliver his people from the consequences of sin. He also delivered them from its pollution and domination and thus made way for their total liberation from its demands.[32] Through his self-sacrifice, he annulled the effects of sin, reducing them to nothingness. As a result, sin will never be able to regain its destructive power. In short, Christ vanquished sin with all its consequences "once for all" (Hebrews 10:10). Through that act, he inaugurated the purification of the cosmos (Hebrews 8:10–12). Thus, his atonement, inaugurated in Gethsemane, implemented on Golgotha, and climaxed at the tomb on Sunday, dominates all history from the beginning to the end of time.[33]

Through his work, Jesus provided for humankind the perfect antidote for what has been called the universal human predicament. All face impending death, and, whether they know it or not, they will also face judgment. The latter will become appallingly clear to the ignorant, the denier, and the wicked upon the moment of death. If death has its sting, so much more will be the fear of judgment (Jacob 6:13; Alma 40:11–14; Moses 7:1). Since judgment was a well-known principle among the readers of Hebrews (6:2; compare Alma 12:27), the author's words would have rung abundantly clear.

Jesus was the Father's offering "to bear the sins of many," the author states in Hebrews 9:28. Christ's return will confirm the Father's faith in that offering. The focus of the Son's first coming was on the atonement with the objective of obliterating sin. And it worked for all those who had and would have faith in him. Because of his successful efforts, sin no longer had force and therefore could not determine the final state of its once victims. That work having been accomplished, the Lord has now moved to the work of his second coming. To those who look for him to appear, he shall come to their vindication and bequeath their reward (Revelation 6:9–11; 21:1–4).

RICHARD D. DRAPER *is a professor emeritus of ancient scripture at Brigham Young University.*

Notes

1. For a discussion of this issue from an LDS perspective, see Richard Neitzel Holzapfel, Eric D. Huntsman, and Thomas A. Wayment, *Jesus and the World of the New Testament* (Salt Lake City: Deseret Book, 2006), 254–56. Latter-day Saint scholars are not agreed on this issue. For two examples of those who favor Pauline authorship, see Richard Lloyd Anderson, *Understanding Paul* (Salt Lake City: Deseret Book, 1983), 197; and Terrence L. Szink, "Authorship of the Epistle to the Hebrews," in *How the New Testament Came to Be: The 35th Annual Brigham Young University Sidney B. Sperry Symposium*, ed. Kent P. Jackson and Frank F. Judd Jr. (Salt Lake City: Deseret Book, 2006), 243–59. For an example of those who do not favor Pauline authorship, see Richard Neitzel Holzapfel and Thomas A. Wayment, *Making Sense of the New Testament: Timely Insights and Timeless Messages* (Salt Lake City: Deseret Book, 2010), 446–47.

2. Frederick William Danker, ed., *A Greek-English Lexicon of the New Testament and Other Early Christian Literature*, 3rd ed. (Chicago: University of Chicago Press, 2000), 967–68 (hereafter cited as BDAG). On the moral aspect, see Moisés Silva, ed., *New International Dictionary of New Testament Theology and Exegeses*, 5 vols. (Grand Rapids, MI: Zondervan, 2014), 4:405 (hereafter cited as *NID*).

3. *NID*, 4:402–6.

4. Gareth Lee Cockerill, *The Epistle to the Hebrews*, The New International Commentary on the New Testament (Grand Rapids, MI: Eerdmans, 2012), 386.

5. The greater audience of Hebrews likely included proselytes and God-fearers (gentiles attracted to Judaism) who also came into the Christian fold. See Holzapfel, Huntsman, and Wayment, *World of the New Testament*, 258. The epistle's view that much of the Mosaic law witnessed the work and ministry of the Lord through types and shadows follows the same trajectory as the Book of Mormon (see Mosiah 13:31; 16:14; Alma 25:15–16).

6. Albeit in Hebrews 9:9b–10, the epistle does note that the insufficiency of the sacrifices of the old covenant were the reason access to God could not be obtained.

7. Cockerill, *Epistle*, 397.

8. My translation throughout.

9. Albert Vanhoye, *Letter to the Hebrews: A New Commentary*, trans. Leo Arnold (New York: Paulist Press, 2015), 148.

10. William L. Lane, *Hebrews 9–13*, Word Biblical Commentary 47b (Dallas: Word Books, 1991), 239.

11. Gustav Stählin, *Theological Dictionary of the New Testament*, ed. Gerhard Kittel, trans. Geoffrey W. Bromiley (Grand Rapids, MI: Eerdmans, 1967), 1:383–84 (hereafter cited as *TDNT*).

12. For a study, see Johannes Schneider, *TDNT*, 5:739–40.

13. Cockerill, *Epistle*, 401.

14. Luke Timothy Johnson, *Hebrews: A Commentary* (Louisville, KY: Westminster John Knox, 2006), 238.

15. Lane, *Hebrews 9–13*, 240–41.

16. The main object of the Day of Atonement ritual was to accomplish such a purification. See Johnson, *Hebrews*, 71.

17. "The New Strong's Expanded Dictionary of the Words in the Greek New Testament," in James Strong, *The New Strong's Expanded, Exhaustive Concordance of the Bible* (Nashville: Thomas Nelson, 2001), 161. For additional studies, see Albrecht Oepke, *TDNT*, 4:598–624; *NID*, 3:284–88.

18. Cockerill, *Epistle*, 402.

19. Vanhoye, *Letter*, 151–52.

20. Cockerill, *Epistle*, 403. Those who composed this group may have roots that go back to the premortal existence. See Orson F. Whitney, *Saturday Night Thoughts* (Salt Lake City: Deseret Book, 1921), 129–30, http://gospelink.com/library/contents/620. This applies to those who are called to priesthood authority. As the author of Hebrews states, people do not take this honor upon themselves, but they must be called of God (Hebrews 5:4). Some of those to whom he wrote were members of this group (see Hebrews 3:1). In modern history, the Lord has noted that "many are

called" but because of unfaithfulness do not remain part of this group (D&C 121:40; compare Matthew 24:14).

21. By this means, the author shows that "the called" could include even those who rebelled under Moses if they repented. Johnson, *Hebrews*, 240.

22. Friedrich Büschel, *TDNT*, 4:344.

23. In the LXX, the verb translated as "atonement" is *exilaskomai* and means "to appease" (see BDAG, 350). In its religious but broader context, it portrays the idea that sin causes the gods to become angry and this can bring upon the offending party divine wrath. To appease them, a gift had to be given or some action completed. When such was offered and accepted, then the gods were appeased and good relations restored.

24. Frances Brown, S. R. Driver, and Charles A. Briggs, *A Hebrew and English Lexicon of the Old Testament* (Oxford: Clarendon Press, reprint 1987), 497–98 (hereafter cited as BDB).

25. BDB, 497–98.

26. Cockerill, *Epistle*, 416.

27. Cockerill, *Epistle*, 416.

28. Lane, *Hebrews 9–13*, 247.

29. Cockerill, *Epistle*, 416–17.

30. Paul Ellingworth, *The Epistle to the Hebrews*, The New International Commentary on the New Testament (Grand Rapids, MI: Eerdmans, 2015), 477.

31. The singular here stands in contrast to the plural "sins" used in 1:3; 2:17; 9:28; 10:1 and thereby connotes, with emphasis, "sin" as *the* principle and force that stands between the individual and God. Cockerill, *Epistle*, 422–43, 427.

32. F. F. Bruce, *The Epistle to the Hebrews*, The New International Commentary on the New Testament, rev. ed. (Grand Rapids, MI: Eerdmans, 1990), 232.

33. Cockerill, *Epistle*, 423n22. For the cosmic nature of the Lord's atonement, see D&C 76:23–24.

14

The Paradoxical Lamb and the Christology of John's Apocalypse

Nicholas J. Frederick

With the exception of a few chapters, the book of Revelation is the written record of a magnificent vision beheld by a man identified only as "his servant John" (Revelation 1:1). Over the course of this vision, John is taken to the throne room of God, witnesses a series of bizarre events as the earth descends into chaos, and finally sees the creation of "a new heaven and a new earth" (Revelation 21:1). Central to the book of Revelation's theological project is the introduction and development of its central protagonist, Jesus Christ. While Jesus appears briefly in the very first chapter, over the course of John's lengthy vision Jesus is most often symbolized by a *lamb*, a figure that appears twenty-eight times before the conclusion of the vision. This lamb, in the words of one scholar, is "the leading Christological expression of the book, central for understanding John's rhetorical argument and theology."[1] But this is no ordinary lamb. John's lamb is both victim and leader, one who conquers through his own death and overcomes evil through his own suffering. Achieving victory through vulnerability, the lamb is simultaneously *conquered* and *conqueror*.

The lamb, then, is a paradoxical image brimming with tension, a tension that is not easily resolved but itself leads to a series of questions: What christological understanding is John (and his audience) expected to glean from this lamb imagery? How does John's vision speak to the fundamental nature of Jesus Christ and his mission? What elements of the lamb must we as his disciples develop if we are truly to become his sons and daughters?

It's important to remember that "the book of Revelation is notoriously difficult to interpret, and it is an impossible book to interpret completely."[2] All that readers of the book of Revelation can successfully do is study and analyze John's vision with an eye toward *possible* answers, since the book of Revelation seems almost intended to provoke questions rather than provide answers. With this in mind, exploring the paradox of John's lamb Christology and attempting to alleviate some of its tensions through a close examination of the lamb imagery makes clear the remarkable portrait of Jesus in John's vision. The focus of the paper will be on the sections of Revelation that present the heaviest christological emphasis—namely, chapters 5, 7, 12, 19, and 21.

At this point, it may be useful to further explore how the figure of a lamb was used in Jewish and Christian literature prior to John's writing. The Greek word John uses that is translated in the King James Bible as "lamb" is the Greek term *arnion*, a diminutive of *arēn*.[3] While Jesus is called a "lamb" by other New Testament authors, John the Revelator is the only one to use *arnion*. In 1 Corinthians 5:7, Paul refers to Jesus as "our passover lamb" (Greek, *to pascha hēmōn*), while John the Baptist twice calls Jesus "the Lamb of God" (*ho amnos tou theou*; John 1:29, 36). Notably, the only other place where the Greek term *arnion* appears outside the book of Revelation is in reference to those who believe in Jesus, as in John 21:15 when Jesus tells Peter to feed "my lambs" (*ta arnia mou*). If we look earlier into the Hebrew Bible (the Old Testament), the Hebrew word *keḇeś* appears 130 times, making it the most common Hebrew word referring to lamb.[4] The majority of these references to lamb are in a sacrificial context, specifically the lamb as a burnt offering. In the Septuagint, the Greek translation of the Hebrew Bible, *keḇeś* is normally rendered as *amnos*. When *arnion* (or *arēn*) does appear in the Septuagint, it is primarily in a symbolic or metaphorical context.[5] While semantic discussions are usually hazy and difficult to derive conclusions from, it can safely be said that the book of Revelation is applying to Jesus a christological title unique from other New Testament authors and one that is often applied in symbolic or metaphorical discussions.

Jesus as the "Conquering" Lamb

With this background in mind, let us now turn our attention to the text of John's vision. Revelation 5 finds John the Revelator in the throne room of God, observing a scene that unfolds, as much of the book of Revelation does, rather curiously. God holds in his hand a scroll and seeks one that is worthy to take the scroll and open it.[6] John begins to weep because the book is sealed with seven seals, and "no man in heaven, nor in earth, neither under the earth, was able to open the book, neither to look thereon" (Revelation 5:3).[7] Fortunately, John is assured that someone—a figure described as "the Lion of the tribe of Juda" and "the Root of David" (5:5)— has successfully opened the scroll.

The titles of "Lion of the tribe of Juda" and "Root of David" are familiar from the Hebrew Bible and are titles charged with Jewish messianic expectation. Jacob had likened Judah to a lion ("Judah is a lion's whelp; from the prey, my son, you have gone up. He crouches down, he stretches out like a lion, like a lioness—who dares rouse him up?") and had declared that the "scepter shall not depart from Judah" (Genesis 49:9–10). The latter proved to be true, as the Davidic kings came through Judah's line, as did Jesus. The description of the lion as "the Root of David" alludes to Isaiah 11, where Isaiah prophesies that "a shoot shall come out from the stump of Jesse, and a branch shall grow out of his roots" (Isaiah 11:1). Isaiah's language further links the tribe of Judah with Davidic kingship and points to a future, messianic figure.[8] The choice of the word *conquer* (*enikēsen*) to describe the lion's actions serves to prepare John and his readers for a regal, military figure.

However, what John then sees is something strikingly different. When John looks around for this lion, he sees only a lamb,[9] and not just any lamb, but a lamb that has been slaughtered as a sacrifice (*esphagmenon*).[10] This juxtaposition is potent and forces readers to ask the critical question: Did the elder err in describing the lamb as a lion, or did we as readers err in expecting that Judah's most powerful representative would be anything other than a conquered, bloody, and apparently (previously) dead lamb? As mentioned earlier, in the Hebrew Bible the image of a lamb was often used metaphorically to connote vulnerability.[11] For example, Jeremiah states that "I was like a gentle lamb led to the slaughter" (Jeremiah 11:19) and prophesies that at the arrival of Babylon "the little ones of the flock shall be dragged away" (Jeremiah 50:45). In a passage that may lay behind the application of the lamb imagery to Jesus, Isaiah speaks of the suffering servant as "a lamb that is led to the slaughter." A further possible origin for the usage of lamb imagery in Revelation 5 is that it is meant to evoke the Passover lamb, an image Paul utilizes in 1 Corinthians 5:7.[12] Whether John has in mind Jeremiah's imagery, Isaiah's suffering servant, or the Passover lamb, by promising a lion and then introducing a lamb the throne-room scene in Revelation 5 suggests a critical reversal in Jewish messianic expectations. Rather than a militaristic, warrior messiah (a lion) who will restore the glory of Israel through a physical conquest,[13] the true redemption of Israel will be obtained only through the blood of the lamb, an ultimate victory won through a temporary defeat.[14] It is at this point, then, that readers are introduced to John's "paradoxical lamb," a figure that is at once both dead and alive, victim and victor, one who finds the ultimate expression of life only in death. As one scholar has noted, John employs the image of the lamb in order to "emphasize that it was in an ironic manner that Jesus began to fulfill the OT prophecies of the Messiah's kingdom. Wherever the OT predicts the Messiah's final victory and reign, John's readers are to realize that these goals can begin to be achieved only by the suffering of the cross."[15]

The irony of this scene is further developed through the attribution of "seven horns" and "seven eyes" to the lamb. In Hebrew Bible passages such as Deuteronomy 2:3; Daniel 7:20–21; 1 Samuel 2:1; and Psalm 89:17, "horn" tended to symbolize power and strength.[16] The image appears throughout the Psalms, in passages such as this: "The Lord is my rock, and my fortress, and my deliverer; My God, my strength, in whom I will trust; My buckler, and *the horn of my salvation*, and my high tower" (Psalm 18:2; emphasis added; compare Psalms 75:10; 89:17, 24; 92:10; 112:9).[17] Physically, a horn is typically associated with a ram rather than a sheep, adding an additional level to John's already-complex paradox.[18] The description of the lamb having "seven eyes" is likely an allusion to the lamps of the temple menorah in Zechariah 4:10 (compare Revelation 4:6), while eyes themselves can be viewed as symbolic of knowledge or wisdom.[19] Combined with the presence of the number seven, an indicator of "fullness" elsewhere in the book of Revelation and in biblical literature,[20] John's lamb emerges as a figure who is both *omnipotent* and *omniscient*, qualities one would expect from the Davidic Messiah, the lion from the tribe of Judah. The attribution of these two divine traits to a "slaughtered lamb" only serves to heighten the paradoxical imagery of John's throne-room scene.

The paradoxical juxtaposition of the "messianic lamb" is accentuated through the scene of praise that follows the appearance of the lamb. After the lamb approaches the throne of God and takes the book sealed with seven seals from God's right hand, the four beasts and the twenty-four elders who had been gathered around the throne fall down and begin to praise the lamb. Significantly, the focus of their praise is not the power or knowledge of the lamb, but the fact that the lamb had been slaughtered: "Thou art worthy to take the book, and to open the seals thereof: *for thou wast slain*, and hast redeemed us to God *by thy blood* out of every kindred, and tongue, and people, and nation" (Revelation 5:9; emphasis added). The literal meaning of "redeemed" as "to buy back" appears to be intended here, with the lamb's blood being the "currency" used in the "purchase."[21] The result of this divine transaction is that the lamb "hast made us unto our God kings and priests: and we shall reign on the earth" (5:10).[22] While the "power" and "sight" of the lamb are certainly impressive and noteworthy, John emphasizes that the lamb's worthiness and redemption come through its *vulnerability* and *sacrifice*. Significantly, no mention is made of the lamb *conquering death*—the resurrection is not mentioned as part of the lamb's worthiness. Rather, the focus is upon the lamb's conquering *through* death, an important distinction for John to make.

Jesus as the "Redemptive" Lamb

The blood that flows from the conquering lamb becomes a critical theme in Revelation 7, where John describes what might be termed the "redemptive" lamb. In Revelation 5:9, John had introduced the idea that the blood of the slaughtered lamb acts as a redemptive element for those who follow the lamb. In Revelation 7:14, John further develops the redemptive nature of the lamb's blood through an additional paradoxical image. Here, in Revelation 7, John witnesses the sealing of the 144,000 (12,000 from each tribe). Following the sealing, John notices "a great multitude" standing before God's throne, each "clothed with white robes, and palms in their hands" (Revelation 7:9). When asked by one of the elders for the identity of this party, John responds that he does not know. The elder answers, "These are they which came out of great tribulation, and have washed their robes, and made them white in the blood of the Lamb" (7:14). The idea that "blood" can wash an article of clothing and render it white presents a striking paradox and an additional ironic image for John's readers to grapple with. In the ancient world, one washed one's clothes to remove the dirt, after which a fuller would often bleach the clothing white to remove stains, such as blood. However, the elder's answer is paradoxical, for, as Craig Koester has noted, "even though blood normally stains, here it cleanses."[23] John's imagery of cleansing through blood again highlights Jesus's power. As we sin and thus accumulate spiritual "dirt" or "stain," Jesus offers his cleansing power to those who will receive it.[24] Significantly, we cannot perform this act of cleansing by ourselves—it is his blood, and only he can offer it to us. Understood in this sense, cleansing through blood becomes an act of grace, offered freely to those who have made and kept their covenants and thus "[stand] before the throne" (7:9).[25] Notably, John will return to this imagery later in Revelation, as readers are informed that the devil is overcome "by the blood of the Lamb" (12:11), and the climactic encounter between Jesus Christ and the beasts finds Jesus clothed "with a vesture dipped in blood" (19:13).

The challenge presented by the image of the lamb, particularly throughout the book of Revelation, is how to interpret it. What does the New Testament want us to understand about Jesus and his sacrifice? Front and center is the idea of Jesus Christ as the high priest who offers himself willingly as the true Passover lamb, whose sacrifice will "take away the sin of the world." This conquest of death comes about through slaughtering of the lamb on the cross, as victory over death comes only through submission to it. It is through the violently shed blood of the slaughtered lamb that "sin" is taken away and the "clothing" of those who have faith in his name is made "white."[26] All this leads readers of the New Testament to encounter what one author has termed "the great Christian paradox"—namely, that in order for there to be life, the Son of God must die.[27]

Jesus and the "Parodied" Lamb

At this point in John's vision, the lamb moves to the periphery of events as the focus shifts to other dramatic events and enigmatic characters: the opening of the seventh seal (Revelation 8–9), John's eating of a book (Revelation 10), the slain witnesses (Revelation 11), and the introduction of an unholy trinity, a dragon and two beasts (one from the sea and one from the wilderness). The dragon is identified as the "Devil and Satan, the deceiver of the whole world" (Revelation 12:9), and may also be representative for the chaos that arises as the vision builds toward the creation of a new heaven and earth.[28] The second beast, the one from the land, is described as a prophet who speaks for the beast and promotes worship of the beast (compare Revelation 19:20).[29] It is the first beast, the beast from the sea, that interests us here. Here is how John describes it:

> And I stood upon the sand of the sea, and saw a beast rise up out of the sea, having seven heads and ten horns, and upon his horns ten crowns, and upon his heads the name of blasphemy. And the beast which I saw was like unto a leopard, and his feet were as the feet of a bear, and his mouth as the mouth of a lion: and the dragon gave him his power, and his seat, and great authority. And I saw one of his heads as it were wounded to death; and his deadly wound was healed: and all the world wondered after the beast. And they worshipped the dragon which gave power unto the beast: and they worshipped the beast, saying, Who is like unto the beast? who is able to make war with him? (Revelation 13:1–4)

Like the lamb, the beast receives power and authority from a higher source (God and the dragon). Like the lamb, this beast was wounded in a manner that should have resulted in death, yet miraculously the beast is healed. Like the lamb, the beast receives worship from those who witness it. This beast from the sea, then, represents a *parody* of the true lamb: "Where God's Messiah is Jesus, the slain and living lamb (Rev 5:6), the dragon's . . . vicegerent is the slain and living beast (13:3). Where the death and resurrection of the lamb convey the redemptive power of sacrifice, the purported death and healing of the beast disclose the resilient power of evil. The question for readers is which form of power and authority will claim their loyalty."[30] In this fashion, the book of Revelation sets up its final denouement as being between the potency of the paradoxical lamb and the dragon with his parodied lamb.

Jesus as the "Providing" Lamb

The actual encounter between the lamb and the dragon finally occurs in Revelation 19, but not before John narrates a wedding feast celebrating the union of the lamb and the church. This union introduces a further dimension to the paradoxical lamb—namely, the lamb as "caretaker" or "provider." Typically, sheep require a shepherd to feed and manage the flock. In return, the sheep obey the shepherd and hearken to his voice. Yet in Revelation 19 the lamb is described as a bridegroom ready to wed his bride. In the Hebrew Bible, Hosea speaks of the "marriage" between God and Israel in a very poignant manner: "And I will betroth thee unto me for ever; Yea, I will betroth thee unto me in righteousness, and in judgment, and in lovingkindness, and in mercies. I will even betroth thee unto me in faithfulness: And thou shalt know the Lord" (Hosea 2:19–20).[31] In this sense, it is God (Jehovah) who provides for and loves Israel. The realization of this wedding feast, then, provides a beautiful complexity to the book of Revelation's Christology. Jesus functions as the lamb because he followed the will of his own Shepherd, his Father. But as the lamb takes his place as the Bridegroom, ready to join his bride, who is "arrayed in fine linen, clean and white" (Revelation 19:8), the lamb now becomes the Shepherd, and he will protect and care for those who respond to his name and follow him as if they were his own bride.

The Revelation of the Lamb

It is, finally, at this point that the lamb appears in his true form. The book of Revelation had begun with the promise that what would be revealed was "Jesus Christ" (Revelation 1:1). Until this point, this "unveiling" of Jesus has largely been through paradoxical symbols, but here, finally, readers encounter the revealed Jesus Christ. In a visually impressive description, John states,

> And I saw heaven opened, and behold a white horse; and he
> that sat upon him was called Faithful and True, and in righ-
> teousness he doth judge and make war. His eyes were as a
> flame of fire, and on his head were many crowns; and he had
> a name written, that no man knew, but he himself. And he was
> clothed with a vesture dipped in blood: and his name is called
> The Word of God. And the armies which were in heaven fol-
> lowed him upon white horses, clothed in fine linen, white and
> clean. And out of his mouth goeth a sharp sword, that with
> it he should smite the nations: and he shall rule them with a
> rod of iron: and he treadeth the winepress of the fierceness
> and wrath of Almighty God. And he hath on his vesture and
> on his thigh a name written, King of kings, and Lord of lords.
> (Revelation 19:11–16)

One of the striking characteristics of this description is that John mentions three titles or names for Jesus: "Faithful and True," the "Word of God," and "King of kings, and Lord of lords."

The first, "faithful and true," could refer to Jesus's role as the fulfillment of Jewish messianic expectations.[32] Throughout the Hebrew Bible, prophets such as Isaiah promised that the Lord of Hosts would descend from Mt. Zion and defeat and judge Israel's enemies.[33] In the descent of Jesus from heaven, this promise has been fulfilled; Jesus has been "faithful and true" to his promise.

The title the "Word of God" may suggest to readers a connection with the Gospel of John, which also speaks of Jesus being "the word" (John 1:1). For this reason, this title could be a reference to Jesus's close association with the Father. Jesus is the Logos because he is the Father's agent; the Father expresses his will that an action be brought to pass, and the Logos is the one who fulfills the Father's "words." However, based upon the context, this title is likely describing Jesus's role as judge, since "the rider will judge by means of God's word."[34]

The association of the title the Word of God with judgment is supported by the weapon that Jesus carries. According to Revelation 19:21, Jesus slays his enemies with a sword, specifically a sword that "proceeded out of his mouth." In other words, Jesus's foes are defeated by the weapon of his words—that is, the judgment that he brings upon the wicked.[35]

The final title, "King of kings, and Lord of lords,"[36] is written in a very visible location, on Jesus's "vesture and on his thigh."[37] In verse 12, John had said that Jesus's name was one "that no man knew," but here, in a movement "from concealment to disclosure,"[38] Jesus chooses to reveal his name to everyone.[39]

In addition to the three names, Jesus is also described as having eyes that were "as a flame of fire," a head with "many crowns," and a robe "dipped in blood." The presence of fire speaks directly to Jesus's mission; just as fire both destroys and cleanses, Jesus has arrived to destroy the wicked and cleanse the earth (compare Revelation 1:14; 2:18). The image of a crown carries with it a sense of rule or authority. While kings and monarchs currently upon the earth may have an individual crown, Jesus has "many crowns," suggesting that his authority trumps theirs. Additionally, the dragon and the beast wear a specified number of crowns, but the number of Jesus's crowns remains unspecified. He has authority over not only the human rulers of the earth, but the forces of evil as well.[40] The implication of Revelation 19:12 is that Jesus's name may have been written on the crowns. This would serve as a parallel to both the blasphemous names written on the beast's crowns but also the appearance of the name of the Lord on the Jewish high priest's forehead. Finally, while the robe "dipped in blood" could refer to the blood of Jesus's vanquished enemies,[41] the fact that the robe is dipped in blood prior to the commencement of the battle indicates that the robe was bloody prior to Jesus's arrival. In that case, the presence of blood on his robe would likely be due to his redemptive actions during his mortal ministry—namely, the atonement and crucifixion.[42] Just as those who follow Jesus have their robes "washed white" though his blood (Alma 5:21), Jesus's own robe remains bloodstained.

All these images prepare readers for an additional element of the book of Revelation's Christology—namely, Jesus's function as warrior. The forces of the dragon—namely, the two beasts and the rulers of the earthly kingdoms who have been swayed by the promises of the dragon—have been gathering since chapter 16 in preparation for the battle of Armageddon, which finally takes place in chapter 19. The battle itself, however, unfolds differently than some readers might think. In actuality, there is little that could be termed a battle. Rather, Jesus arrives on the scene and promptly casts the two beasts into "a lake of fire burning with brimstone" (Revelation 19:20). Those who foolishly aligned themselves with the dragon are subsequently slain with the sword of Jesus, a sword that "proceeded out of his mouth" and thus likely refers to an act of preaching and spreading the message of Jesus Christ rather than a literal slaying. While the dragon had boasted of his power and might, all that remains of his forces is a feast for the crows, who "were filled with their flesh" (19:21).

A New Paradox—Jesus as "God"

The remaining chapters, those describing the millennial reign of Jesus and the eventual establishment of a celestial earth, provide the final piece of the book of Revelation's Christology. While Jesus's power and abilities have been alluded to in previous chapters, such as the lamb with seven horns and the seven eyes or the rider upon the white horse, it is in this climactic section that Jesus's association with the Father comes through most vividly. Consider the following passages:

> And I saw no temple therein: for the Lord God Almighty and the Lamb are the temple of it. (Revelation 21:22)
>
> And the city had no need of the sun, neither of the moon, to shine in it: for the glory of God did lighten it, and the Lamb *is* the light thereof. (Revelation 21:23)

> And he shewed me a pure river of water of life, clear as crystal, proceeding out of the throne of God and of the Lamb. (Revelation 22:1)
>
> And there shall be no more curse: but the throne of God and of the Lamb shall be in it; and his servants shall serve him: And they shall see his face; and his name *shall be* in their foreheads. (Revelation 22:3–4)

These statements imply a relationship where the Father and the Son exist as *one* being. Together the Lord God Almighty and the lamb form *one* temple. Both God and the lamb are the "light" of the city. Both God and the lamb share *one* throne. Significantly, those who serve "God and the Lamb" serve "him." Referring specifically to Revelation 22:3, G. K. Beale writes, "That 'they will serve *him*' likely does not refer only to God or only to the Lamb. The two are conceived so much as a unity that the singular pronoun can refer to both. . . . That both are sitting on only one throne and together form one temple (21:22) enhances their perceived unity."[43] This is not to say that Jesus hadn't shared divinity with the Father prior to the creation of the "new heaven and the new earth" or that his divinity was a result of his conquest in Revelation 19, only that this divinity is made explicit through the enthronement scene narrated in Revelation 22. Curiously, the paradoxical Christology of Revelation that appeared to have been resolved in chapter 19 has now returned. How can two beings be one? How can two deities share one throne? These questions have troubled Christian thinkers for two thousand years, and ascertaining exactly what John has in mind in using this language remains a challenge for readers of his text. Perhaps the simplest way to understand these closing chapters is not to try to resolve the paradox but to embrace it, remembering that, ultimately, John leaves little doubt as to who Jesus is—he is God himself.

In summary, what can be said about the Christology of the book of Revelation? Many of the christological elements we would expect as Latter-day Saints are present. First and foremost, Jesus Christ is

God; he is *one* with the Father. He is described as having seven horns and seven eyes, images that suggest a high degree of *power* and *knowledge*. Further, he is a *warrior*. It is he who rides down from heaven and with his sword dispenses justice to the unrepentant. He is also the rightful *ruler* of the earth, the only one who bears the name "King of kings and Lord of lords."

However, one of the most significant messages of the book of Revelation is that Jesus is one with the Father not simply because Jesus is, by nature, divine (although he may be). Rather, the book of Revelation suggests that Jesus's eventual status should be attributed to the personal qualities he demonstrated in the previous chapters. The twenty-four elders do not bow down to the lamb because he is God, but because he is *worthy*. This worth comes through Jesus's *submissiveness* in accepting the book offered by the Father, even though the result was that he became the slaughtered lamb. He suffered and bled and was ultimately crucified. In this action, Jesus also demonstrated a degree of *loyalty*; what the Father asked, he would do, no matter how much anguish he was forced to endure. The result of these experiences was that Jesus became our *Redeemer*; it is his blood that washes our garments white, our sins and pains that leave his garment red. This union between sinner and savior is characterized through the wedding supper of the lamb, where Jesus, as *caretaker*, unites with his bride.

It is this confluence of qualities that perhaps accounts for John's paradoxical Christology. Jesus may now sit enthroned as God, but only because he submitted himself to mortality. Jesus can boast of conquest, but the true sign of his victory was his own vulnerability. As the author of Hebrews poignantly observed, "For we have not an high priest which cannot be touched with the feeling of our infirmities; but was in all points tempted like as *we are*, yet without sin. Let us therefore come boldly unto the throne of grace, that we may obtain mercy, and find grace to help in time of need" (Hebrews 4:15–16; compare Alma 7:11–12). Jesus is the "great high priest" of Hebrews precisely because of the experiences highlighted in the book of Revelation.[44] As

Latter-day Saint readers of the book of Revelation, it is critical that we don't forget or ignore this fundamental element of John's vision—namely, that he has endured our pains and our sufferings *for us*, so that in him we can find the peace, the redemption, and ultimately the salvation that so gracefully he offers us.

NICHOLAS J. FREDERICK *is an assistant professor of ancient scripture at Brigham Young University.*

Notes

1. Laszlo Gallusz, *The Throne Motif in the Book of Revelation* (New York: Bloomsbury T&T Clark, 2014), 142.

2. Richard Neitzel Holzapfel and David Rolph Seely, *My Father's House: Temple Worship and Symbolism in the New Testament* (Salt Lake City: Bookcraft, 1994), 209.

3. ἀρνίον is technically the diminutive form of ἀρήν, though it is unlikely that such detail would have been recognizable enough to carry theological weight by the first century CE. See discussion in *The New International Dictionary of New Testament Theology*, ed. Colin Brown (Grand Rapids, MI: Zondervan, 1976), s.v. "Lamb."

4. According to one scholar, the word *sheep* appears a total of 742 times in the Old Testament. Roy Pinney, *The Animals of the Bible: The Identity and Natural History of All the Animals Mentioned in the Bible* (Philadelphia: Chilton Books: Philadelphia, 1964), 108. See also the lengthy discussion in *Theological Dictionary of the Old Testament*, ed. G. Johannes Botterweck (Grand Rapids, MI: Eerdmans, 1995), 7:43–52.

5. See discussion in Loren L. Johns, *The Lamb Christology of the Apocalypse of John* (Tübingen: Mohr Siebeck, 2003), 28–32.

6. According to D&C 77:6, the scroll contains "the revealed will, mysteries, and the works of God; the hidden things of his economy concerning this

earth during the seven thousand years of its continuance, or its temporal existence."

7. According to D&C 77:7, the seven seals represent temporal periods of the earth's history: "We are to understand that the first seal contains the things of the first thousand years, and the second also of the second thousand years, and so on until the seventh."

8. "The emphases on the tribe of Judah and on Davidic descent together underline one of the crucial qualifications of the Jewish royal Messiah: he must be a descendant of the royal house of David (*Psalms of Solomon* 17:21; Mark 12:35–37; John 7:42), sometimes conceived as David *redivivus* (Jer 23:5; 30:9)." David E. Aune, *Revelation 1–5* (Dallas: Word Books, 1998), 350.

9. It should be noted that the lamb "stood" (ἑστηκὸς). In other words, it did not lie down or limp, as one would expect an animal to do that was wounded. The lamb clearly bears the marks of its wounds but not the effects.

10. "The perfect participle ἐσφαγμένον ("having been slain") expresses an abiding condition as a result of the past act of being slain," with the result that not only does the lamb stand before the throne, he "continues to exist as a *slaughtered* lamb." G. K. Beale, *The Book of Revelation: A Commentary on the Greek Text* (Grand Rapids, MI: Eerdmans, 1999), 352.

11. This vulnerability should not, however, be interpreted as weakness. As Ekkehardt Mueller points out, "The servant of God does not defend himself. No evil is found in him. In him truth resides. He is righteous and yet lives for others and is willing to bear their sin and guilt. *However, the Lamb is not a symbol of weakness. It is a symbol of strength in suffering.* In spite of its vulnerability it is victorious." Ekkehardt Mueller, "Christological Concepts in the Book of Revelation—Part 3: The Lamb Christology," *Journal of the Adventist Theological Society* 22, no. 2 (2011): 45; emphasis added.

12. "There are two different proposals for the background of the 'slain Lamb.' Some prefer to see it as a reference to the OT Passover lamb, while others favor Isa. 53:7: 'he was led as a sheep to the slaughter' (cf. Isa. 53:8ff.). However, neither should be excluded, since both have in common with the metaphorical picture in Rev. 5:6 the central function and significance of the sacrifice of a lamb, which accomplishes redemption and victory for

God's people. The Isaiah 53 background especially highlights the atoning aspect of the lamb's sacrificial death, as well as applying the metaphors of both 'root' (ῥίζα; cf. Isa. 52:2 and Rev. 5:5) and 'lamb' (ἀμνός, LXX) to the sacrificial victim. In fact, 'root' occurs also in Isa. 11:1, 10, alluded to in Rev. 5:5, which may have inspired attraction to the same metaphor in 53:2. The Passover/Isaiah 53 backgrounds are also suggested by the use of ἀρνίον ("lamb"), behind which could lie Aramaic *ṭalia'*, which means not only 'lamb,' but also 'servant' and 'boy.' If that is the case, then ἀρνίον would be a most suitable word to combine the Passover lamb with the servant lamb of Isaiah 53." Beale, *Book of Revelation*, 351.

13. This is not to suggest that all Jewish Messianic expectation centered upon a militant figure. See John J. Collins, *The Scepter and the Star: The Messiahs of the Dead Sea Scrolls and Other Ancient Literature* (New York: Doubleday, 1995).

14. "This scene lies at the theological heart of the Apocalypse. It is specifically designed to communicate the shock, irony, and ethical import of his message that the *Conquering One conquers by being a slain lamb*, not a devouring lion" (Johns, *Lamb Christology*, 159). Of the expectation of seeing a lion and the actual realization of seeing a lamb, David L. Barr writes, "A more complete reversal of value would be hard to imagine." David L. Barr, "Apocalypse as a Symbolic Transformation of the World: A Literary Analysis," *Interpretation* 38 (January 1984): 41.

15. Beale, *Book of Revelation*, 353–54.

16. "The horn was a symbol of power and honor (Pss 89:17, 24; 92:10; 112:9; 1 Sam 2:1; 1QM I, 4) and the ability to save (Ps 18:2; 2 Sam 22:3)." Craig Koester, *Revelation: A New Translation with Introduction and Commentary* (New Haven: Yale University Press, 2014), 377.

17. The attribution of horns to a messianic figure does appear in literature from outside the Hebrew Bible, such as the Dead Sea Scrolls (1Q28b Col. V:26) and the Pseudepigrapha (1 Enoch 90:37). What impact passages such as these may have had upon John's lamb is unknown. Craig Koester writes, "The imagery in Revelation both affirms and transforms earlier connotations. The seven horns affirm Jesus' messianic identity, yet as the Lamb, he saves through his own self-sacrifice" (Koester, *Revelation*, 377). The key

difference, however, is that "the Messiah is never symbolized as a lamb in Judaism, and the special attributes of seven horns and seven eyes together suggest that this composite image is the creation of the author, though the elements are drawn from traditional imagery" (Aune, *Revelation 1–5*, 353–54).

18. "But this lamb had horns, and so we have a fusion of sacrificial lamb and ram features, conveying a deliberate paradox." Ben Witherington III, *Revelation* (Cambridge: Cambridge University Press, 2003), 121.

19. "God was understood to see all things, so no one was exempt from his scrutiny" (Koester, *Revelation*, 377). Witherington calls the eyes "symbols of omniscience" (Witherington, *Revelation*, 120). Compare Revelation 4:5–6, where the four beasts were themselves "full of eyes."

20. "Seven is a symbolic number, denoting wholeness and completeness." Jay A. Parry and Donald W. Parry, *Understanding the Book of Revelation* (Salt Lake City: Deseret Book, 1998), 14.

21. "The verb 'purchase' (*agorazein*) has connotations of the marketplace (Rev 13:17; 18:11), where some people purchased others to be their slaves (*Vita Aesopi* 15; 20). In the divine economy, however, Jesus purchases people for God, which is a redemptive action" (Koester, *Revelation*, 379–80). Compare 1 Corinthians 6:20; 7:23, where the same verb is used in a similar sense.

22. Technically, "kings and priests" (βασιλείαν καὶ ἱερεῖς) should be translated "a kingdom and priests," likely an allusion to Exodus 19:6.

23. Koester, *Revelation*, 422. Additionally, the book of Revelation may be drawing upon the Old Testament imagery of sacrifice with this imagery. Psalm 51:7 contains the injunction "Wash me, and I shall be whiter than snow." Isaiah, in a similar fashion, promises that "though your sins be as scarlet, they shall be as white as snow" (Isaiah 1:18).

24. John may have in mind Isaiah 1:18 or Exodus 19:10–14 here.

25. When John describes the group standing before God's throne who receive "white robes" (Revelation 7:9), he may well have the Abrahamic covenant specifically in mind. As G. K. Beale observes, the phrase "a great multitude, which no man could number," possibly "evokes the promise to Abraham and Jacob that God would multiply their descendants. . . . Therefore, the multitudes in Rev. 7:9 are the consummate fulfillment of the Abrahamic

promise and appear to be another of the manifold ways in which John refers to Christians as Israel" (Beale, *Revelation*, 427).

26. Other New Testament passages add to this imagery. John declares in 1 John 1:7 that "the blood of Jesus Christ his Son cleanseth us from all sin." In two places Paul alludes to this, in Romans 3:25, where he speaks of Jesus's "sacrifice of atonement by his blood" (NRSV), and in Ephesians 1:7, where Paul declares that through his grace we have "redemption through his blood." Finally, the author of Hebrews asserts "without the shedding of blood there is no forgiveness of sins" (Hebrews 9:22 NRSV).

27. Grant R. Osbourne, *Revelation* (Grand Rapids, MI: Baker Academic, 2002), 254.

28. As Koester notes, "In Revelation the dragon has the qualities of a mythic monster. The LXX calls sea monsters (Hebrew, *taninim*) and Leviathan 'dragons' (Ps 74:13–14 [73:13–14 LXX]). Such dragons represented the chaotic forces that needed divine control (Job 7:12; 26:13; 41:1; Ezek 32:2 LXX)" (Koester, *Revelation*, 544).

29. This second beast also hints at the chaos that precedes the new creation through its allusion to Behemoth, another monster described in the Hebrew Bible (compare Job 40:15–24; Revelation 13:11).

30. Koester, *Revelation*, 581. Beale adds, "The expression of Satanic incomparability is an ironic use of OT phraseology applied to Yahweh (cf. esp. Exod. 8:10; 15:11; Deut. 3:24; Isa. 40:18, 25; 44:7; 46:5; Pss. 35:10; 71:19; 86:8; 89:8; 113:5; Mic. 7:18). This is a further attempt at Satanic imitation of God. In all these OT texts Yahweh's incomparability is contrasted polemically with false gods and idols" (Beale, *Revelation*, 694).

31. In the Hebrew Bible, it was common to speak of the covenant as a marriage between God and Israel (compare Ezekiel 16:8; Jeremiah 31:32; Isaiah 54:5). However, the relationship between the Messiah and the Church was rarely, if ever, described in this fashion. In Christian texts, such as Matthew 19:15; John 3:29; and Ephesians 5:28–32, the application of the marriage imagery to the Messiah and the Church became the norm, as reflected here in Revelation 19.

32. "This dual name occurs in Greek only in *3 Macc.* 2:11 (πιστὸς εἶ καὶ ἀληθινός), where it refers to a hope in God's faithfulness, namely that in

answering Israel's prayer God will defend the honor of his name by judging Israel's persecutor (cf. 3 *Macc.* 2:9–14). The verbal identity and similarity of contextual theme indicate that John is probably alluding to 3 *Maccabees* here, and this strengthens the contextual theme of Christ as a divine figure and as the one who executes a just and vindicating judgment" (Beale, *Revelation*, 950).

33. Compare Isaiah 24:21–23; 31:4–5; 34:12.

34. Beale, *Revelation*, 957. Compare Wisdom of Solomon 18:15–16.

35. "To be slain by the sword that projected from the mouth of the warrior on the white steed certainly invites metaphorical interpretation; i.e., the 'sword' must be the words spoken by the warrior." David E. Aune, *Revelation 17–22* (Dallas: Word Books, 1998), 1067.

36. "These titles were ordinarily reserved for God but here are given to Christ, who acts on God's behalf" (Koester, *Revelation*, 766).

37. It is more likely that the name is only written once, on the cloak, with the reference to "his thigh" being appositional or epexegetical, introduced by "and." Understood in this way, the name would have appeared on the cloak but on the part of the cloak that covers the thigh, in other words, where a soldier would carry his sword. See discussion in Koester, *Revelation*, 758. Additionally, in the Old Testament one typically made an oath by placing one's hand underneath the thigh (compare Genesis 24:2; 47:29), an idea that may allude back to the "faithful and true" title in verse 11.

38. Koester, *Revelation*, 754.

39. Concealed names play an important role in the book of Revelation. Believers are given a white stone with a name written on it that remains secret to all but the believer (Revelation 2:17), while the whore in Revelation 17 has a name written that is supposed to remain a mystery, but John reveals it anyway (Revelation 17:5).

40. Coincidentally or not, earlier in the book of Revelation Christians are promised that they will obtain a "crown of life" as a reward for their endurance, while the twenty-four elders who surround the throne of God are also described as wearing "golden crowns." Compare Revelation 2:10; 4:4.

41. This seems to be the implication of Isaiah 63:2–3: "Wherefore art thou red in thine apparel, and thy garments like him that treadeth in the winefat?

I have trodden the winepress alone; and of the people there was none with me: For I will tread them in mine anger, and trample them in my fury; and their blood shall be sprinkled upon my garments, and I will stain all my raiment."

42. As Koester notes, "There are two principal interpretations concerning the source of the blood. The most probable is that this is Christ's own blood" (Koester, *Revelation*, 755).

43. Beale, *Revelation*, 1113. Aune adds, "By sharing the throne of God, the Lamb also shares the sovereignty of God" (Aune, *Revelation 17–22*, 1177).

44. Jesus does appear in language reminiscent of the Jewish high priest in Revelation 1:11–20. Here Jesus is described as being "in the midst of the seven candlesticks," likely implying that he has entered the holy place of the temple.

CHRISTOLOGY AFTER
THE NEW TESTAMENT

15

Preserving or Erasing Jesus's Humanity

Tensions in 1–2 John, Early Christian Writings, and Visual Art

Mark D. Ellison

How do we picture Jesus? To what extent does our belief in Christ's divinity and postresurrection glory influence the way we envision the humanity of Jesus during his mortal ministry? Creators of early Christian literature and visual art grappled with tensions between a desire to affirm Jesus's full humanity and an impulse to minimize or erase it in order to emphasize his divinity. For ancient believers who sought to preserve the teaching that Jesus was both divine and fully human, what was in jeopardy was salvation itself—the whole notion of what it meant that Christ came to earth, was born with a physical body, lived a mortal life, suffered death, and rose again. To deny Jesus's full humanity was to deny that he fully redeemed humanity. New Testament texts and early Christian writings reveal a sustained effort to preserve the doctrine of Jesus's full humanity in the face of counterefforts. This fundamental tension affected the earliest visual portrayals of the crucifixion in narrative art.

It is a history that provides a basis for us, as Latter-day Saint follow-ers of Christ, to think about what is at stake in preserving, minimiz-ing, or erasing Jesus's humanity in our own reading of the Gospels or engagement with visual portrayals of Jesus.

Jesus's Humanity in 1–2 John

In the New Testament, no writing emphasizes Jesus's humanity and its importance in Christian belief to a greater degree than 1–2 John.[1] These texts were written in the late first century, probably at a time of crisis when a group in the church (likely in Asia Minor) had broken off from the rest of the Christian community (1 John 2:18–19, "they went out from us"). One of the defining beliefs of this schismatic group was its denial that Jesus Christ had "come in the flesh":

> For many deceivers are entered into the world, who confess not that Jesus Christ is come in the flesh. This [i.e., any such person] is a deceiver and an antichrist. (2 John 1:7)
>
> Many false prophets are gone out into the world. Hereby know ye the Spirit of God: Every spirit that confesseth that Jesus Christ is come in the flesh is of God: And every spirit that confesseth not that Jesus Christ is come in the flesh is not of God. (1 John 4:1–3)

The schism's refusal to confess that Jesus had come *in the flesh* suggests that it was an early form of a heresy known in other early Christian writings as docetism.[2] In the second and early third cen-turies of Christianity, docetists of various kinds held that deity was incompatible with such human limitations as a material body, limited knowledge, infirmity, and pain. Believing that God was unchangingly immaterial, all-knowing, all-powerful, and impassible (incapable of suffering pain), docetists concluded that if Jesus was the divine Son of God, he could not truly have inhabited a physical body, experi-enced mortal conditions, or endured suffering, but only *seemed* to—the word *docetism* comes from the Greek *dokeō*, "to seem" or "to appear." (For further discussion of this subject, see the chapter by Jason Combs in this volume.)

In apparent response to such claims by the late first-century dissenters, 1 John begins with emphatic testimony that Jesus was no mere apparition, but really lived with a physical body: "[We declare to you] That which was from the beginning, which *we have heard*, which *we have seen with our eyes*, which *we have looked upon*, and *our hands have handled*, [concerning] the Word of life" (1 John 1:1; emphasis added). This echoes the testimony in the prologue of the Gospel of John: "And the Word was made flesh, and dwelt among us" (John 1:14). In its affirmation of a flesh-and-blood Jesus, 1 John gives particular emphasis to the blood of Jesus Christ: Jesus "came by water and blood . . . not by water only, but by water and blood" (1 John 5:6). Scholars debate the exact meaning of this statement but generally agree that it refers to Jesus's humanity (compare John 19:34).[3] The blood of Christ is crucial to redemption: "The blood of Jesus Christ . . . cleanseth us from all sin" (1 John 1:7).

Yet the dissenters appear to have believed that they were without sin, to judge from insistent counterstatements in 1 John: "If we say that we have no sin, we deceive ourselves, and the truth is not in us. . . . If we say that we have not sinned, we make him a liar, and his word is not in us" (1 John 1:8, 10).[4] Believing they were sinless, the dissenters "felt no need of atonement and cleansing by the blood of Jesus" and evidently did not think Jesus's suffering and bodily death had any salvific meaning.[5] Against this, 1 John insists that Jesus is "the atoning sacrifice [KJV 'propitiation'] for our sins" (1 John 2:2 New Revised Standard Version; 4:10).

Some later docetists made a distinction between the divine "Christ" and the human "Jesus"; Christ descended on Jesus at his baptism, but departed before the crucifixion and thus did not suffer.[6] Evidently in response to ideas like this, 1 John refers to liars who deny "that Jesus is the Christ," and defines faithful believers as those who believe "that Jesus is the Christ" and love both God and God's begotten Son Jesus (1 John 2:22; 5:1).

Preserving or Erasing Jesus's Humanity in Other Early Christian Writings

Johannine scholar Robert Kysar observes that the great theological contribution made by 1–2 John lies not just in how these books affirm Jesus's humanity, but also in how they make this affirmation the center of Christian faith, an essential element in "the doctrine [*didachē*] of Christ" (2 John 1:9–10).[7] Indeed, in following decades, other Christian writers adopted this doctrinal position as they argued against docetic teachings along much the same lines as 1–2 John. Early in the second century, for example, Polycarp (AD 69–155), the bishop of Smyrna, wrote to the saints at Philippi, "Everyone who does not confess that Jesus Christ has come in the flesh is antichrist; and whoever does not acknowledge the testimony of the cross is of the devil."[8] Like John, Polycarp saw an essential connection between Jesus's humanity (his coming in the flesh) and redemption of humanity (via the crucifixion).

Even more emphatically, Polycarp's friend Ignatius (c. AD 35–107), bishop of Antioch, addressed the same concerns in seven letters he wrote to churches in Asia Minor while soldiers were taking him through that region en route to his martyrdom in Rome. Throughout his letters Ignatius expresses concerns about divisions, schisms, and false teachings, particularly docetic teachings. Against these, he repeatedly asserts the reality of Jesus's human experiences, including the Savior's bodily suffering and salvific death:

> He is truly of the family of David with respect to human descent, Son of God with respect to the divine will and power, truly born of a virgin, . . . truly nailed in the flesh for us under Pontius Pilate and Herod the tetrarch (from its fruit we derive our existence, that is, from his divinely blessed suffering). . . . For he suffered all these things for our sakes, in order that we might be saved; and he truly suffered just as he truly raised himself—not, as certain unbelievers say, that

he suffered only in appearance [*dokein*]. . . . Avoid such people. . . . Do pay attention, however, to the prophets and especially to the gospel, in which the passion [*pathos*, the suffering of Christ] has been made clear to us and the resurrection has been accomplished.[9]

Some noncanonical early Christian texts provide a glimpse into views like those that 1–2 John, Polycarp, and Ignatius opposed. The second-century Gospel of Peter contains a passage that depicts Christ suffering no pain during the crucifixion: "And they brought two malefactors, and they crucified the Lord between them. But he held his peace, as though having no pain."[10] The Acts of John, written in the second or third century, relates gnostic Christian legends about the apostle John, and portrays Christ in docetic terms. The character "John" in this text states that when he would lay hold on Jesus he would only sometimes feel a material body; at other times he would feel nothing, suggesting Jesus was actually immaterial. When John sees in vision the crucifixion, he sees the Lord in the air above the cross, and the Lord tells him that he is not actually suffering what people would say he suffered in the crucifixion, for he is "God unchangeable, God invincible."[11] Similarly, in the late second/early third-century gnostic Apocalypse of Peter, "Peter" relates teachings given to him by Christ on the day of the crucifixion. Christ tells him that only the physical body of Jesus would undergo arrest and crucifixion, but not the divine Christ, who cannot suffer. "Peter" sees in vision Christ above the cross during the crucifixion, unharmed and laughing at the scene below. This text and others like it reject the idea that Christ suffered as a corporeal being.[12]

In the third and fourth centuries, some Christian teachers continued to oppose docetic and docetic-like teachings in the tradition of 1–2 John, Polycarp, and Ignatius, insisting that the full humanity of Jesus was essential to humanity's redemption. For example, Origen (c. AD 185–254) wrote: "Our Savior and Lord, in his desire to save the human race as he willed to save it, for this reason thus willed to save the body, just as he willed likewise to save also the soul, and willed also to save the rest of the human being: the spirit. For *the whole human being would not have been saved if he had not assumed the whole human being.* They eliminate the salvation of the human body by saying that the body of the Savior is spiritual" (emphasis added).[13] In the Trinitarian debates of the fourth century, Gregory of Nazianzus (c. AD 329–390) adopted Origen's reasoning as he opposed the teachings of Apollinarius of Laodicea (died c. AD 390–392), a heretical bishop who had denied Jesus's full humanity; Gregory famously wrote, "That which Christ has not assumed He has not healed."[14]

Athanasius (c. AD 296–373) also connected Christ's incarnation to salvation, even to human deification: "He was incarnate that we might be made God."[15] However, Athanasius seems to have felt conflicted about affirming the full humanity of Jesus Christ. On one hand, he wrote that Christ took a body like ours, that he died to undo "the law concerning corruption in human beings," that he "became human, . . . possessing a real and not an illusory body," and that "at his death . . . Christ suffered in the body."[16] On the other hand, Athanasius described the incarnation in ways that veered toward formulations used earlier by docetic teachers: Christ's body "was a human body," but "by the coming of the Word into it, it was no longer corruptible," and "became immune from corruption"; "He himself was harmed in no way, being impassible and incorruptible and the very Word and God."[17] As Lincoln Blumell has put it, Athanasius taught an incarnation without condescension.[18]

Athanasius's view of Jesus's qualified humanity prevailed among many Christians. Though the emerging orthodoxy largely rejected the teachings of gnostic Christian groups, elements of docetic thinking left a mark on how believers conceptualized Jesus's humanity and divinity. The creed from the Council of Nicaea (AD 325) that Athanasius championed made use of terminology used earlier by docetists when it rejected any who asserted that the Son of God was subject "to alteration or change" (*hē trepton hē alloiōton*). This echoed the depiction of Christ in the Acts of John as "God unchangeable" (*ametatrepton*), a conception associated with a God invulnerable and impassible.[19] Fourth-century Trinitarian formulations led to fifth-century christological debates over whether the human and divine in Jesus Christ constituted two "persons" or two "natures," or ought to be understood as one undivided nature that was uniquely human and divine. Believers on various sides of the issues felt that they stood to lose either the divinity of Christ or the redemption of humanity in the formulated definitions. It was in this setting that someone produced the earliest surviving artistic portrayal of the crucifixion in a narrative setting.

Jesus's Ambiguous Humanity in the Earliest Depictions of the Crucifixion

Around the years AD 420–430, a skilled artist, perhaps in Rome, carefully carved reliefs on several small ivory panels, producing decorated sides of a box that was probably used to hold a sacred relic or consecrated eucharistic (sacrament) bread. The box's four surviving panels, now called the Maskell Ivories and held in the British Museum, depict scenes from the New Testament passion narratives: Christ carrying his cross, the crucifixion, the empty tomb, and the risen Christ appearing to his disciples. The second panel is the earliest portrayal of the crucifixion in narrative art (see fig. 1).[20]

The scene depicts Christ on the cross, with Mary and John approaching sorrowfully from the left (see John 19:26–27), as a soldier to the right pierces Christ's side with a spear (now missing, though the wound in Christ's side is visible; see John 19:34). Nails are visible in Christ's hands, but his feet appear to be unsupported. A halo encircles his head beneath a plaque inscribed in Latin, *REX IVD[AEORUM]*, "King of the Jews." Christ's eyes are open, looking straight ahead—he is shown alive and alert. His head is held upright. His arms and body do not sag from the nails; they conform to the T-shape of the cross, "as though standing defiantly" against it.[21] He is

Fig. 1. *Ivory panel with relief of the crucifixion, 7.5 x 9.8 cm, c. AD 420–430. The British Museum, London. Photo © The trustees of the British Museum, London / Art Resource.*

a picture of strength, boldness, and triumph and seems "unaffected by the process of his crucifixion."[22] He contrasts sharply with the figure of Judas at the far left. Judas hangs from a leafy tree suspended by a rope around his neck, his head tilted back, his eyes shut, his arms hanging limp at his sides. A bag of coins lies fallen on the ground beneath his feet, open and spilling its contents; the drawstring of the pouch looks almost like a snake crawling toward the tree (see Matthew 27:3–5; Genesis 3:1–15).[23] Viewers may have noticed "the irony of Judas hanging dead on a living tree while the living Christ hanging on a 'dead tree' triumphs over death."[24]

Art historian Felicity Harley-McGowan reads the scene and its accompanying panels as an emphasis of "Jesus's triumph over death" and "the subsequent triumph of the Church." The two images of death—"the suicide of Judas and the crucifixion of Jesus—are pivotal" in the articulation of this theme.[25] But we may note that the image articulates this theme by employing a traditionally docetic motif—that of an impassible Christ who was invulnerable to pain and suffering.

A few years after this ivory panel was created, another workshop artist in Rome carved a different crucifixion scene on one of 28 wood panels for the doors of the basilica of Santa Sabina. The panel is the earliest surviving image of the crucifixion made for public display (see fig. 2).[26] It and the accompanying panels depict various scenes from Christ's life and other biblical narratives. On the crucifixion panel, Christ and the two thieves stand with their arms outstretched against a stone, gabled cityscape (perhaps representing Jerusalem's walls). The figure of Christ is nearly twice as large as the thieves to either side. Only parts of their crosses are visible. All three figures are shown with their eyes open, and rather than hanging from their nailed hands, they are posed as if in the ancient posture of prayer,

Fig. 2. Wooden panel with carved crucifixion scene, Sta. Sabina, Rome, c. AD 432–440. Photo: Art Resource.

with upraised hands (see 1 Kings 8:22; Psalm 28:2; 1 Timothy 2:8).[27] "None of the figures is visibly suffering," observes historian Robin Margaret Jensen.[28]

We should be cautious in assessing the Christology that might be implied in these early images of the crucifixion. There were likely multiple factors that motivated the depiction of a seemingly impassible Christ, including the desire already noted to emphasize resurrection and triumph over death, the inclination to shy away from what is an inherently painful subject for people who love and revere Christ, and the scandal of the crucifixion in the early church (see 1 Corinthians 1:23).[29] Eventually Christian artists explored others ways of depicting the crucifixion in order to highlight Jesus's humanity and convey the pathos of that event.[30] Perhaps the most we can say is that in these early attempts to picture Christ's redemptive death, we see a tendency to avoid depicting his suffering and recognize that this tendency had a long history in Christian conversations about Christ's divinity and his humanity.

Latter-day Saint Reflections

For Latter-day Saints, reflecting on this history is valuable in several respects. For one, it enhances our appreciation of the theological contribution made by key Restoration scriptures. In the Book of Mormon, Nephi's vision describes Christ's birth, mortal ministry, and crucifixion for the sins of the world as manifestations of "the condescension of God" (1 Nephi 11:12–18, 26–33; cf. 2 Nephi 4:26; 9:53; Jacob 4:7). Since Christ "descended below all things," he "comprehended all things, that he might be in all and through all things" (D&C 88:6; compare 122:8). Other important passages describe Jesus's bodily and spiritual suffering as well as the divine empathy and healing resulting from it. Jacob taught that Christ would come into the world to suffer "the pains of every living creature, both men, women, and children" (2 Nephi 9:21). In King Benjamin's words, Christ would "suffer temptations, and pain of body, hunger, thirst, and fatigue," such that "blood cometh from every pore, so great shall be his anguish" (Mosiah 3:7). In the Doctrine and Covenants, Christ states that his suffering caused him, "even God, the greatest of all, to tremble because of pain, and to bleed at every pore, and to suffer both body and spirit" (D&C 19:18). Alma taught that Christ would "go forth, suffering pains and afflictions and temptations of every kind," enduring "the pains and the sicknesses of his people," and then death itself; as a result, Christ would "loose the bands of death," "be filled with mercy," and would "know *according to the flesh* how to succor his people according to their infirmities" (Alma 7:11–12; emphasis added).

These and other passages of Restoration scripture affirm that Jesus, as divine Son, had a fully human experience—he endured real temptations to which he could have succumbed; he was not "unchanging" in the sense of being invulnerable to temptation or pain; he experienced infirmity; and he suffered pain in body and spirit.[31] In these respects latter-day scripture connects us with the early Christian teachings of 1–2 John, Polycarp, Ignatius, Origen, and Gregory of Nazianzus: because Christ fully assumed humanity, he can fully heal humanity.

This history also beckons us to ask ourselves how fully we perceive the humanity of Jesus in our reading of the Gospels or in portrayals of Jesus in art and film. We do not often pause to think critically about images of Jesus, whether they be painted on canvas, chiseled in stone, projected on a screen, or constructed in our own minds. Yet in our increasingly visual culture, thoughtful discipleship and scriptural literacy increasingly require visual literacy.[32]

Artistic portrayals of Christ are not necessarily attempts to represent his likeness—what he really looked like historically—nor do artists necessarily intend to take a conscious stance on fine points of Christology. Nevertheless, images of Christ can influence the way we understand him, so thoughtful viewers should engage those images critically. For example, as Richard Holzapfel has suggested, we might ask ourselves whether a depiction of the Savior represents the mortal Christ or the risen Christ, or perhaps blends the two.[33] Faced with a work of art that retrojects elements of postresurrection glory and perfection onto Jesus in a scene from his mortal life, viewers might recognize a theological statement rather than a historical claim and may ask themselves what limits they should place upon that image as they read the New Testament and construct their own understanding.

Often portrayals of the Savior are made with an understandable reverence dictating that Christ must be depicted with dignity, that the image must transcend the confines of realism and historicity and point to some eternal truth.[34] Yet this aspiration exists in tension with the claim that Christ condescended, lived in a flesh-and-blood body, suffered, and died—and that these factors are central to the whole message of his redemption. Artists wrestle with this tension. For example, LDS artist James C. Christensen described the difficulties he faced as he painted a depiction of Christ suffering in Gethsemane:

> Typical paintings of the Atonement look too serene, too much like evening prayer. They are very unsatisfactory to me. . . . I considered painting the Savior in the most extreme agony. Collapsed, face down, hands in the dirt. Were he to lift up his head, his face would be covered with dust and sweat. But I have not painted that image because he is still our God. It would be unseemly to depict him in an undignified way—even if that image might be historically or pictorially accurate.[35]

LDS artist Walter Rane has taken steps that Christensen did not in several pieces portraying Christ's suffering in Gethsemane. In his etching *Atonement* (see fig. 3), Rane opted not to show Christ's face at all, instead depicting literally the detail found in Matthew that when Jesus prayed in Gethsemane he "fell on his face" (Matthew 26:39) and combining it with the description in Luke: "And there appeared an angel unto him from heaven, strengthening him. And being in an agony he prayed more earnestly" (Luke 22:43–44). This compositional choice makes "the image about the event and not about what [Jesus] looks like,"[36] but more than that, it enables Rane to depict Jesus in an agony far more dramatic and severe than we see in many Gethsemane paintings. Here Christ's suffering is so enormous

Fig. 3. *Walter Rane,* Atonement, *etching. © Walter Rane, used by permission.*

that he does not kneel in evening prayer; he cannot remain upright at all. He lies prostrate upon the ground, his face in the dirt, his hands grasping the earth desperately. Nothing stands between Christ and the world that is crushing him, the world that he is saving. The image makes a "forthright presentation of a heartbreakingly vulnerable Redeemer, something that is almost painful to look upon."[37]

By contrast, some popular depictions of the Savior place him in exquisitely pretty settings, using fine detail and vivid colors. We may appreciate in them intentions to highlight Christ's perfection, perhaps to convey something of the ecstasy of spiritual experience, the breathless beauty of moments when we encounter Christ's trans-forming love. Yet not all viewers may see this. One observer remarked to me that one such painting "looks almost airbrushed, sort of fake." As LDS art historian Richard Oman stated, "Sometimes less detail is more spiritual power. . . . If artists focus only on bright, cheer-ful, well-lit, tightly detailed images of Christ, they may trivialize to an extent the richness and depth of the spiritual experiences that the Savior had in mortality and that we can have, in turn, with him. Great religious art does not always bring a sense of peace. Sometimes it causes us to be uncomfortable."[38]

One viewer, evaluating a highly idealized, vividly colored Geth-semane scene, noted some of its qualities she genuinely appreciated but then told me it felt manipulative to her: "I feel like it's telling me that I'm *supposed* to feel sad." Another observer said she felt like the painting trivialized Jesus's suffering. Pointing to the expression of mild concern on Jesus's face, she remarked, "I feel like that when I lose my car keys." Then, pointing to Walter Rane's *Atonement*, she added, "But there have been a few times in my life when I have felt something like *that*. And it is meaningful to me that the artist has depicted Jesus as one who has felt what I have felt in my most wretched moments."

Do some modern portrayals of Jesus unknowingly embrace a kind of docetism? If a video of Jesus at a wedding feast depicts him sitting somber and detached, unmoved by the festivities, what is that implying about Christ? Was he, is he, really too dignified to smile, laugh, or enjoy people? That contradicts the New Testament witness that one of the main criticisms Jesus faced was that he was *too* jovial, *too* ready to eat and drink, even with those of questionable company.[39] If a film of the crucifixion never portrays Jesus crying out in a loud voice, as he is described as doing in each of the Synoptic Gospels,[40] is reverence rewriting the narrative? What is art suggesting if it portrays a mortal Jesus who does not seem to experience the range of mortal experiences that you and I do, one who neither laughs nor cries out in agony?[41]

Just as salvation was at issue for ancient Christians as they wrote and preserved affirmations of Jesus's full humanity, there may be real, saving significance for viewers of Christian art when they see Jesus portrayed as human, relatable, laughing, crying, feeling pain, feeling joy, rather than continually detached and aloof. There may be hunger for art that conveys the message of Christ's condescension— that he came here and met us where we are, in order to lift us up to where he is. An other-worldly Jesus may give the impression that God is impossibly distant, that we in our human state are hopelessly estranged from him, that the burden rests solely upon us, somehow, to climb to him. But that is not the gospel.

It does not follow that in order to portray Christ's humanity artists must seek out extreme depictions of his suffering, nor is there necessarily any single, preferable approach to portraying the Savior. However, part of our aspiration to be thoughtful followers of Christ is the effort to be aware of how we are visualizing Jesus, informed by scripture, by history, and by an appreciation of the many styles of visual media and the ways they can function. Salvation is at stake, or at least our effectiveness in understanding it and teaching it is, in our choices here. For us, as for our ancient Christian forebears, minimizing Jesus's humanity compromises the reach of his redemption.

MARK D. ELLISON *is an associate professor of ancient scripture at Brigham Young University.*

Notes

1. Robert Kysar, "John, Epistles of," in *The Anchor Bible Dictionary*, ed. David Noel Freedman (New York: Doubleday, 1992), 3:909.

2. So named, for example, in Eusebius, *Ecclesiastical History* 6.12.1–16; for a dissenting opinion, see Urban von Wahlde, *Gnosticism, Docetism, and the Judaisms of the First Century: The Search for the Wider Context of the Johannine Literature and Why It Matters* (London: T&T Clark, 2015).

3. Kysar, "John," 909.

4. For information on use of the contextual method to read 1–2 John (inferring the other side of the "conversation"), see Bart D. Ehrman, *The New Testament: A Historical Introduction to the Early Christian Writings*, 6th ed. (New York: Oxford University Press, 2016), 198–205.

5. I. Howard Marshall, *The Epistles of John*, The New International Commentary on the New Testament (Grand Rapids, MI: Eerdmans, 1978), 15.

6. Irenaeus (c. AD 180) wrote that the late first-century/early second-century heretic Cerinthus held this view; see *Against Heresies* 1.26.1. Irenaeus also recorded that, according to Polycarp, second-century bishop of Smyrna, the apostle John opposed Cerinthus; see *Against Heresies* 3.3.4. But see Marshall, *Epistles of John*, 18, for cautions against simplistically identifying the secessionists of 1–2 John as Cerinthus and his followers.

7. Kysar, "John," 909.

8. Polycarp, *Epistle to the Philippians* 7.1, trans. Michael W. Holmes, *The Apostolic Fathers: Greek Texts and English Translations*, 3rd ed. (Grand Rapids, MI: Baker Academic, 2007), 289.

9. Ignatius, *Epistle to the Smyrnaeans* 1.1–2; 2; 3.1; 7.2, trans. Holmes, *Apostolic Fathers*, 249, 251 [altered "in appearance only" to "only in appearance"], 255. See also Ignatius, *Epistle to the Trallians* 8.1; 9.1–2; 10; Ignatius, *Epistle to the Ephesians* 7.2; Ignatius, *Epistle to the Romans* 6.3; Ignatius, *Epistle to the Magnesians* 11; Ignatius, *Epistle to Polycarp* 3.2.

10. Gospel of Peter 4, trans. J. Armitage Robinson, *Ante-Nicene Fathers* (Buffalo, NY: Christian Literature, 1896), 10:7. Eusebius wrote that this gospel was regarded as heretical, and came from people he and his fellow

Christians called *"Docetae,"* docetists; see Eusebius, *Ecclesiastical History* 6.12.1–16.

11. *Acts of John* 93, 97–104, trans. M. R. James, *The Apocryphal New Testament* (Oxford: Clarendon Press, 1924), 256; according to Eusebius, orthodox believers regarded *Acts of John* as heretical: see *Ecclesiastical History* 3.25.6.

12. Gerard P. Luttikhuizen, "The Suffering Jesus and the Invulnerable Christ in the Gnostic Apocalypse of Peter," in *The Apocalypse of Peter*, ed. Jan N. Bremmer and István Czachesz (Leuven, Belgium: Peeters, 2003), 187–99.

13. Origen, *Dialogue with Heraclides* 7.1–9; emphasis added; trans. Robert J. Daly, Origen, *Treatise on the Passover and Dialogue of Origen with Heraclides and His Fellow Bishops on the Father, the Son, and the Soul*, Ancient Christian Writers 54 (New York: Paulist Press, 1992), 62–63.

14. Gregory of Nazianzus, *Epistle* 101.32; trans. Charles Gordon Browne and James Edward Swallow, *Nicene and Post-Nicene Fathers*, 2nd series, vol. 7, ed. Philip Schaff and Henry Wace (Buffalo, NY: Christian Literature, 1894), 440 (altered, substituting "Christ" for "He"); see discussion of the background on 198–99.

15. Athanasius, *On the Incarnation* 54.3, trans. John Behr, *St. Athanasius the Great of Alexandria, On the Incarnation: Greek Original and English Translation*, Popular Patristics Series, no. 44a (Yonkers, NY: St Vladimir's Seminary Press, 2011), 167.

16. Athanasius, *On the Incarnation* 8.4; 18.1; 19.2, trans. Behr, 67, 89, 91.

17. Athanasius, *On the Incarnation* 20.4; 54.3, trans. Behr, 95, 167.

18. I am indebted to my colleague Lincoln Blumell for this insight, shared in conversation.

19. See the discussion in Lincoln Blumell, "Rereading the Council of Nicaea and Its Creed," in *Standing Apart: Mormon Historical Consciousness and the Concept of Apostasy*, ed. Miranda Wilcox and John D. Young (New York: Oxford University Press, 2014), 196–217 (esp. 206–8).

20. The cross in various forms began to appear in Christian art in the fourth century. The staurogram—a combination of the Greek letters *tau* and *rho* that scribes inserted into the Greek words for "cross" and "crucify" in some third/fourth-century manuscripts—could be said to resemble a man on

a cross, and may represent early attempts to portray the crucifixion visually; see Larry W. Hurtado, *The Earliest Christian Artifacts: Manuscripts
and Christian Origins* (Grand Rapids, MI: Eerdmans, 2006), 135–54.
Two small gemstones inscribed with an image of Christ's crucifixion, one
dating to the late second/early third century and the other to the mid-
fourth century, attest to the use of the image on personal objects used
for amuletic or devotional purposes, and a late second/early third-century
graffito scratched onto the walls of slave quarters of the imperial palace
on Rome's Palatine Hill depicts the crucifixion mockingly; see Felicity
Harley-McGowan, "Picturing the Passion," in *The Routledge Handbook of
Early Christian Art*, ed. Robin M. Jensen and Mark D. Ellison (London:
Routledge, 2018), 290–307.

21. Felicity Harley-McGowan, "Death Is Swallowed Up in Victory: Scenes
of Death in Early Christian Art and the Emergence of Crucifixion Ico-
nography," *Cultural Studies Review* 17, no. 1 (2011): 118.

22. Harley-McGowan, "Death Is Swallowed Up in Victory," 114.

23. Robin M. Jensen, "The Passion in Early Christian Art," in *Perspectives on
the Passion: Encountering the Bible through the Arts*, ed. Christine E. Joynes
(New York: T&T Clark, 2007), 60.

24. Allyson Everingham Sheckler and Mary Joan Winn Leith, "The Crucifixion Conundrum and the Santa Sabina Doors," *Harvard Theological
Review* 103, no. 1 (2010): 80.

25. Harley-McGowan, "Death Is Swallowed Up in Victory," 119.

26. Sheckler and Leith, "Crucifixion Conundrum," 67, 73; but note that the
panel appears at the top of the massive doors, relatively far from
the viewer; it is not known whether the panels now appear in their original
arrangement.

27. Jensen, "Passion in Early Christian Art," 58–59; Sheckler and Leith,
"Crucifixion Conundrum," 80–85; for discussion of the *orans* (praying
figure) in early Christian art, see Robin M. Jensen, *Understanding Early
Christian Art* (London: Routledge, 2000), 35–37.

28. Jensen, "Passion in Early Christian Art," 58.

29. On the relatively late appearance of cross and crucifixion iconogra-
phy, see the discussions in Jensen, *Understanding Early Christian Art*,

130–55; Felicity Harley, "The Crucifixion," in *Picturing the Bible: The Earliest Christian Art*, ed. Jeffrey Spier (New Haven: Yale University Press, 2007), 227–32; and Sheckler and Leith, "Crucifixion Conundrum."

30. See Robin M. Jensen, *The Cross: History, Art, and Controversy* (Cambridge: Harvard University Press, 2017), 92–96, 155–70.

31. For further discussion on Christ's real experience of temptation, see Blumell, "Rereading the Council of Nicaea"; Stephen E. Robinson, *Believing Christ: The Parable of the Bicycle and Other Good News* (Salt Lake City: Deseret Book, 1992), 112–16.

32. See the discussion on this topic in Richard Neitzel Holzapfel, "'That's How I Imagine He Looks': The Perspective of a Professor of Religion," *BYU Studies* 39, no. 3 (2000): 91–99.

33. Holzapfel, "'That's How I Imagine He Looks,'" 93. In the 2001 BBC documentary *Son of God*, Richard Neave drew upon the fields of forensic anthropology and art history to create a model of what a first-century Palestinian Jewish man like Jesus might have looked like: about 5'1" tall, 110 pounds, with short, dark, curly hair (see 1 Corinthians 11:14), dark eyes, a darker, more olive complexion than traditional western art has portrayed, and in Jesus's case he would be somewhat muscular and weatherworn (because of his work as a carpenter/builder); see Mike Fillon, "The Real Face of Jesus," *Popular Mechanics* 179, no. 12 (2002): 68–71; for a more recent study, see Joan E. Taylor, *What Did Jesus Look Like?* (London: Bloomsbury T&T Clark, 2018); see also Richard N. Holzapfel, Eric D. Huntsman, and Thomas A. Wayment, *Jesus Christ and the World of the New Testament* (Salt Lake City: Deseret Book, 2006), 97.

34. Noel A. Carmack, "Images of Christ in Latter-day Saint Visual Culture, 1900–1999," *BYU Studies* 39, no. 3 (2000): 41; Adele Reinhartz, "Jesus in Film," in *The Blackwell Companion to Jesus*, ed. Delbert Burkett (Malden, MA: Wiley-Blackwell, 2011), 521–22.

35. James C. Christensen, "That's Not *My* Jesus: An Artist's Perspective on Images of Christ," *BYU Studies* 39, no. 3 (2000): 13. Though current LDS teaching understands Christ's atonement as encompassing events from Gethsemane to his death on the cross, and culminating in his resurrection (see *True to the Faith: A Gospel Reference* [Salt Lake City: The Church

of Jesus Christ of Latter-day Saints, 2004], 17), LDS artists have often focused on Gethsemane, perhaps seeking a distinctively LDS way to visualize the atonement, perhaps in some cases forgetting the salvific importance of the crucifixion.

36. http://www.mormonartistsgroup.com/Mormon_Artists_Group /Atonement_prospectus.html, accessed 20 January 2013 (page no longer available).

37. http://www.mormonartistsgroup.com/Mormon_Artists_Group /Atonement_prospectus.html , accessed 20 January 2013 (page no longer available).

38. Richard Oman, "'What Think Ye of Christ?' An Art Historian's Perspective," *BYU Studies* 39, no. 3 (2000): 85, 89.

39. For example, see Matthew 9:10–12; 11:19; Luke 7:39; 15:1–2; 19:7.

40. Matthew 27:50; Mark 15:34; Luke 23:46.

41. On humor and sarcasm in Jesus's teaching, see Holzapfel, "That's How I Imagine He Looks," 93–94; Elton Trueblood, *The Humor of Christ* (New York: Harper & Row, 1964).

16

"Christ" after the Apostles

The Humanity and Divinity of the Savior in the Second Century

Jason R. Combs

Late one evening, in the middle of the second century AD, a small group of Christian priests, trained in the philosophy of Plato, met in secret in the back room of a church in Rome. Their goal? To complete the work of transforming the pure doctrine of Christ into a philosophically sound but morally deficient theology. They forged documents and altered scripture to suit their needs.[1] In the end, over the course of that evening, they succeeded in forever altering the true doctrine of the nature of Christ into a fraud that would be propagated throughout the centuries.

The most significant fact about this story is that it never happened. None of it is true; I made it up. Yet Latter-day Saints might be inclined to imagine such a scenario when they read statements from Joseph Smith such as, "all their creeds were an abomination . . . [and] those professors were all corrupt" (Joseph Smith—History 1:19), or "I believe the Bible as it read when it came from the pen of the original writers. Ignorant translators, careless transcribers, or designing and corrupt priests have committed many errors."[2] Notice, however, that neither of these statements implies secret meetings or mass corruption in the ancient Church—in fact, "corrupt priests" is listed as only one out of three possible explanations for "errors" or changes in the biblical texts. And the statement regarding those "professors" of creeds should be understood more specifically as "referring to those ministers . . . with which Joseph Smith was involved," as Robert Millet, professor emeritus of ancient scripture at Brigham Young University, and Elder William Grant Bangerter (1918–2010), a member of the Seventy from 1976 to 1989, have explained.[3]

Sometimes LDS authors have suggested that, in the second century or later, Christians' encounter with Greek language, ideas, and especially philosophy distorted the teachings of Christ found in the New Testament.[4] Yet the spread of Greek culture—a development known as Hellenization—began centuries before any book of the New Testament was written. The Christian authors whom we meet through the New Testament all wrote in Greek and employed Greek styles, genres, and even philosophical thought.[5] To assume that the texts of the New Testament were somehow uninfluenced by Greek or Roman thought would be akin to suggesting that the modern-day writings of N. Scott Momaday or Sherman Alexie show no signs of western European influence because those authors are Native American. What's more, Latter-day Saints should not assume that there is something inherently bad about ancient Greek philosophy.[6] In fact, through the "Statement of the First Presidency regarding God's Love for All Mankind," issued February 15, 1978, the Church affirmed, "Philosophers including Socrates, Plato, and others, received a portion of God's light. Moral truths were given to them by God to enlighten whole nations and to bring a higher level of understanding to individuals."

Rather than imagine early Christians as duplicitous in their efforts to write about and understand their faith, it is more accurate to view them as earnest.[7] The purpose of this essay is to introduce

Latter-day Saints to the origins of the Christian doctrine regarding the nature of Jesus Christ, his humanity and divinity. What we will see are various early Christian authors and groups reading the texts that would one day become the New Testament and laboring to understand their relationship with Jesus Christ as Savior. These second-century Christians were not corrupt. Rather they were earnestly seeking to make sense of sacred texts that could sometimes appear confusing or contradictory. The result of the christological debates of the second century is the shared Christian confession that Jesus Christ is both fully human and fully divine.

Second-Century Christians and Their Christologies

Irenaeus was a Church leader in the late-second century AD in Lugdunum, Gaul—modern-day Lyon, France—part of the Roman Empire where Christians faced persecution.[8] By this time Christianity had grown from a small Jewish movement in Galilee into an empire-wide religion that spanned across modern Europe, North Africa, and the Middle East.[9] As more literate elites converted to Christianity, written communication and interaction between geographically diverse Christian communities also increased. Some Christian leaders realized that the theological diversity that so troubled Paul (1 Corinthians 3:3–4 and Galatians 1:6–9; 2:4) and John (1 John 2:18–19; 2 John 7; and 3 John 9–10) in the first century had continued into the second century. In response, Christians such as Irenaeus wrote treatises aimed at cataloging and refuting "heresies"—in Latter-day Saint parlance today, we might prefer the term *false doctrines* over *heresies*.

I place the terms "heresy," "heretical," and "heretic" inside quotation marks because the very groups that Irenaeus labeled as "heretical" often returned the favor. For instance, the author of the Coptic Apocalypse of Peter describes Irenaeus's brand of Christianity as follows:

> These people oppress their brothers and say to them,
> "Through this fellowship our God has mercy, since salvation
> comes to us alone." . . . And there are others among those out-
> side our number who call themselves bishops and deacons as
> if they have received authority from God. . . . These people are
> dry canals.[10]

Whereas Irenaeus often rhetorically places "heretical" groups outside of what he deems to be official, authoritative Christianity, the
author of the Coptic Apocalypse of Peter claims that Irenaeus's exclusionary rhetoric reveals *him* to be the "heretic." For the author of this
apocalypse, Irenaeus and those like him have no authority from God.[11]

What seems to have most troubled Irenaeus was the fact that
these other Christian groups often appealed to the same traditions
and scriptural authorities but arrived at dramatically different
theological conclusions. Irenaeus insists that the scripture they cite
actually refutes their own theological views.

> The very heretics themselves . . . starting from these [Gospels],
> each one of them endeavours to establish his own peculiar
> doctrine. For the Ebionites, who use Matthew's Gospel only,
> are confuted out of this very same, making false suppositions
> with regard to the Lord. But Marcion, mutilating that accord-
> ing to Luke, is proved to be a blasphemer of the only exist-
> ing God, from those [passages] which he still retains. Those,
> again, who separate Jesus from Christ, alleging that Christ
> remained impassible, but that it was Jesus who suffered, pre-
> ferring the Gospel by Mark, if they read it with a love of truth,
> may have their errors rectified. Those, moreover, who follow
> Valentinus, making copious use of that according to John, to
> illustrate their conjunctions, shall be proved to be totally in
> error by means of this very Gospel.[12]

Throughout the second century, one particular question seems to
have dominated theological discussions: To what extent was Jesus

Christ human or divine? And each of these groups mentioned by Irenaeus—the Ebionites, Marcionites, "those who separate Jesus from Christ," and the Valentinians—arrived at different conclusions about the humanity and divinity of Jesus Christ.

No ancient Christian rejected completely the representations of Jesus Christ's humanity or divinity found in the earliest Christian texts, such as Paul's letters or the Gospels. The problem was that those early texts could be interpreted in different ways. When Paul wrote that Jesus was descended from David and "declared to be the Son of God . . . by the resurrection" (Romans 1:4), did he mean that Jesus was primarily human and a "Son of God" in name only? How about when Paul wrote that Jesus "was made in the likeness of men" (Philippians 2:7)? Did he mean that Jesus only seemed to be human but was actually divine? The second-century debate centered on how to interpret such texts and on how one might understand the humanity and divinity of Jesus Christ represented within them.

This debate was not a purely intellectual pursuit. While early Christians certainly brought all their intellectual resources to bear on these questions, their concern was far from academic. In fact, for them, the salvation of humanity was at stake! Were Jesus Christ not sufficiently *human*, how could he have the ability to rescue *humanity*? Were Jesus Christ not sufficiently *divine*, how could he have *the power* to rescue humanity? The debates about the nature of Jesus Christ were debates about the relationship between humans and God as well as about how humans might be saved and what they might be saved from. The christological debates of the second century represent, in Latter-day Saint terminology, the work of the early Saints to understand the central role of Jesus Christ within the plan of salvation.[13]

Introductory scholarship on the christological debates of the second century typically describes four types of belief about the nature of Jesus Christ: adoptionist, docetist, possessionist/separationist, and incarnation Christologies.[14] An adoptionist Christology emphasizes the humanity of Jesus. He is presented as fully human, conceived through the normal physical union of Joseph and Mary and born in a typical human manner. In this view, the human Jesus is not by nature divine. Yet, due to his righteousness, God chooses him and adopts him to be a son of God. Most commonly this is believed to occur at Jesus's baptism, although some may understand the adoption to occur at resurrection as a reward for Jesus's life of faithfulness.[15]

Docetist Christology could be described as the polar opposite of adoptionism. Whereas adoptionists present Jesus as only human, docetists believe that Jesus is only divine. The term *docetism* comes from the Greek *dokein* which means "to seem" or "to appear." It is an apt description of this Christology because docetists affirm that Jesus Christ only *appears* to be human but is in fact fully divine.[16]

Possessionist or separationist Christology describes Jesus Christ as both human and divine but limits that union to a set time during Jesus's mortal life. This Christology affirms Jesus's humanity in a manner similar to the adoptionists—that is, that Jesus is fully human, conceived through normal human sexual processes. Yet this Christology also affirms that at some point in Jesus's life, he is *possessed* by a preexistent divine being, sometimes called the "Christ." In this state of divine possession, Jesus the Christ performs miracles. Then, at some point prior to his death on the cross, the divinity that *possessed* Jesus *separates* from him—for this reason, the belief is called either possessionist Christology or separationist Christology.[17]

The incarnation Christology that eventually becomes the orthodox position affirms that Jesus Christ is both fully human and fully divine. This Christology differs from possessionist/separationist Christology in the affirmation that Jesus Christ is human and divine from birth, that his conception and birth are miraculous, and that this union of divinity and humanity continues through death and into the resurrection.[18] Like possessionist/separationist Christology, however, incarnation Christology can be understood as occupying a middle ground on a spectrum with adoptionism and docetism as polar opposites.

Latter-day Saints, like other Christians today, would find most of these Christologies to be absurd if not offensive. Likewise, Latter-day Saints and most Christians today may find it difficult to imagine that there was ever a time when some Christians questioned Jesus Christ's complete humanity and divinity. Early Latter-day Saints and the scripture that came through Joseph Smith, such as the Book of Mormon and Doctrine and Covenants, attest to Jesus Christ's humanity and divinity.[19] This is not to suggest that LDS Christology was completely settled from the foundations of Mormonism.[20] For instance, Terryl Givens has noted, "Initially . . . [Joseph] Smith and his colleagues used both titles [Jehovah and Elohim] to refer to God the Father."[21] It is not until 1844, Givens explains, that we find "hints that Smith was beginning to see Elohim as the more proper title for God the Father."[22] Yet, while the understanding of Jesus's identity as Jehovah was only clarified over time for Latter-day Saints, the common Christian affirmation that Jesus Christ is both human and divine was accepted without reservation.[23] And this affirmation has continued to hold sway in the Church. Givens summarizes the LDS view today as follows: "He was truly man and truly God, conceived and born of woman but in some sense progeny of a divine Father."[24] This affirmation is not explicit in the texts of the New Testament but was born out of the christological debates of the second century.

Early Christian history is at least as complex as early Latter-day Saint history. Just as certain aspects of LDS Christology became clear only with the passage of time, so too the very affirmation which became orthodox, incarnation Christology, developed over the course of the second century in dialogue with other Christologies. And those other Christologies were more complex than the categories described above. Those categories—adoptionism, docetism, possessionist/separationist, and incarnation—are heuristically useful, but the descriptions of Jesus Christ that we find in ancient Christian writings often appear as hybrids or combinations of categories. For this reason, we cannot proceed by simply collecting evidence for adoptionism, then docetism, and so forth. It is necessary, instead, to review what specific Christian groups affirmed about Jesus Christ and to use our christological categories as a tool to help us analyze their unique beliefs. In what follows, I adopt Irenaeus's summary of "heretical" groups who preferred one Gospel over another as an organizing principle. I begin therefore with the Christology of the Ebionites, followed by that of Marcion and Valentinus, before concluding with the Christology affirmed by proto-Orthodox Christians.[25]

Ebionites

Ebionites are often described in ancient Christian texts as "Jewish-Christians."[26] Although only fragments of the Ebionites' writings survive, and only in quotations from their theological opponents, we are still able to piece together some of the beliefs of this group. The name Ebionite most likely comes from the Hebrew, 'ebyon, meaning "poor"—as in, "blessed are the poor in spirit" (Matthew 5:3).[27] Irenaeus introduces the Ebionite Christians as follows:

> Those who are called Ebionites agree that the world was made by God; but their opinions with respect to the Lord are similar to those of Cerinthus. . . . They use the Gospel according to Matthew only, and repudiate the Apostle Paul, maintaining that he was an apostate from the law. As to the prophetical writings, they endeavour to expound them in a somewhat singular manner: they practice circumcision, persevere in the observance of those customs which are enjoined by the law, and are so Judaic in their style of life, that they even adore Jerusalem as if it were the house of God.[28]

In this description, the Ebionites' concern for the law of Moses is clear; it is their reason for preferring Matthew over Paul, and it is the reason they continue to practice circumcision as well as other "customs which are enjoined by the law." Irenaeus also emphasizes that they look to Jerusalem "as if it were the house of God," even though by this time the Jerusalem temple had been destroyed and replaced by a Roman temple dedicated to the god Jupiter.

Irenaeus believes that this group emphasizes Jewish customs too much, but he is more concerned about their teaching regarding Jesus.

Here he says only that "their opinions with respect to the Lord are similar to those of Cerinthus." Elsewhere, however, he describes their beliefs in greater detail. Cerinthus, he explains, "represented Jesus as having not been born of a virgin, but as being the son of Joseph and Mary according to the ordinary course of human generation, while he nevertheless was more righteous, prudent, and wise than other men."[29] According to Irenaeus, this is what the Ebionites believe. A point he reiterates again—"The Ebionites . . . assert that [Jesus] was begotten by Joseph"[30]—and again—"Vain also are the Ebionites, who do not receive by faith into their soul the union of God and man, but who remain in the old leaven of [the natural] birth, and who do not choose to understand that the Holy Ghost came upon Mary, and the power of the Most High did overshadow her."[31] According to Irenaeus, Ebionites believe that Jesus was conceived through the normal physical union of Mary and Joseph and was born as naturally as any human being. Jesus was a human being at birth, and nothing more.

One might wonder how the Ebionites, who according to Irenaeus treasured the Gospel of Matthew, could possibly believe that Jesus's birth was normal. What's normal about Mary being "found with child of the Holy Ghost" when she "was espoused to Joseph, before they came together" (Matthew 1:18; see also 1:20)? It may be that the Ebionites' Gospel of Matthew was different from the Gospel that we know today by that name. According to Epiphanius—another chronicler of heresies like Irenaeus, but one who wrote at the end of the fourth century AD—the Ebionites' Gospel was different: "The Gospel of Matthew used by them [was] not in a perfect but in a mutilated and castrated form called the Gospel of the Hebrews."[32] Epiphanius's quotations of the Ebionites' Gospel are more similar to the Gospel of Mark than to the Gospel of Matthew. The Gospel of Mark, of course, does not include a narrative of Jesus's birth.[33] In the Gospel of Mark the only explanation provided for Jesus's divine sonship comes at Jesus's baptism when the heavens part and a voice is heard: "Thou art my beloved Son, in whom I am well pleased" (Mark

1:11). To Jewish-Christians like the Ebionites, this would likely remind them of the divine proclamation to King David in Psalm 2:7, "Thou art my Son; this day have I begotten thee" (see also 2 Samuel 7:14). The Ebionites may have thought that if God could pronounce King David and King Solomon to be his sons without miraculous births, he certainly could do so with Jesus.

In fact, Epiphanius quotes the section of the Ebionites' Gospel that describes the baptism: "Jesus came also and was baptized by John. And as he came up out of the water, the heavens opened, and he saw the Holy Spirit descending in the form of a dove and entering into him. And a voice was heard from heaven, 'You are my beloved son, and in you I am well pleased.' And again, 'This day I have begotten you.'"[34] Here the declaration, "This day I have begotten you," takes on additional meaning because the description of the Holy Spirit's descent includes this statement: "He saw the Holy Spirit . . . *entering into him*" (emphasis added). This supports Irenaeus's claim that the Ebionites' understanding of Christ is similar to that of Cerinthus. Irenaeus's description of Cerinthus's Christology begins with an explanation of Jesus's humanity and then continues by describing Jesus's baptism: "Moreover, after his baptism, Christ descended upon [Jesus] in the form of a dove from the Supreme Ruler, and then he proclaimed the unknown Father, and performed miracles. But at last Christ departed from Jesus, and then Jesus suffered and rose again, while Christ remained impassible, inasmuch as he was a spiritual being."[35] The Gospel quoted by Epiphanius describes the Holy Spirit "entering" Jesus, and here Irenaeus describes the belief that a divine being called "Christ" entered the human Jesus after baptism. The similarity is enough to suggest that one of these views is close to what the Ebionites believed, despite our only sources originating with their theological opponents.[36]

In summary, the Ebionites appear to have believed that Jesus was conceived and born through the normal physical union of Mary and Joseph. Then Jesus was chosen by God, adopted because of his righteousness, and became the vessel for a divine being, called either

Christ or the Holy Spirit. That divine being empowered the human Jesus to perform miracles and to teach about God. Then, prior to Jesus's death on the cross, the divine being departed. Certain aspects of the Ebionites' Christology sound like an adoptionist view, while others seem closer to a separationist/possessionist Christology.

Marcionites

Marcion was born around AD 100 and was raised in Sinope, a Roman port city in the region of Pontus on the southern shore of Black Sea—modern-day Turkey.[37] His father was a Christian bishop, and Marcion became a wealthy shipowner. Around the year AD 139, after Marcion experienced a falling-out with his father, Marcion sailed to Rome. He was, at first, welcomed by Christians there, and he donated 200,000 sesterces to the Church—the purchase price of a nice house in Rome.[38] Eventually Marcion began to develop and preach his own unique theology, so the Roman Church returned his money and excommunicated him.[39]

What did the Church at Rome find so offensive about Marcion's teachings? Marcion taught that the God of the Old Testament, the God worshipped by Jews, was a god of wrath, vengeance, and justice, and was not the God who sent Jesus. For Marcion, the God who sent Jesus was a God of grace, mercy, and love; and Jesus was sent to rescue us from the justice of the Old Testament God.[40] Certainly it is understandable how a Christian might come to this conclusion by reading the Old Testament—some Christians today continue to interpret the Old Testament in this way. But how could Marcion possibly read something like the Gospel of Matthew, the Gospel of John, or the Epistle to the Hebrews and think that Jesus was working against the God of the Old Testament? The answer is that he didn't. That is, in the middle of the second century there was not yet a "New Testament" as we have it today. So Marcion created his own and excluded all of those books. In Marcion's Bible, he included only his own edited version of the Gospel of Luke and a small collection of the apostle Paul's letters—his Bible was "the Gospel" and "the Apostle," and that was it! Nothing from the Old Testament was included.[41] For Marcion, Christianity started with Jesus.

Since, for Marcion, Jesus was not the Creator God of the Old Testament and was not sent by the God of the Old Testament, what did Marcion believe about Jesus? It is difficult to say. As with the Ebionites, our knowledge about Marcion comes entirely from the writings of his theological opponents. In the early third century AD, Tertullian wrote an entire treatise against Marcion.[42] Tertullian was a prolific Latin-writing convert to Christianity from paganism; he lived in the city of Carthage—on the northern shore of Africa in modern-day Tunisia. In his treatise titled *Against Marcion*, he addresses Marcion's Christology as one of the core problems with Marcion's teachings. And Tertullian describes Marcion and his followers as "antichrists" because, he says, "they denied that Christ was come in the flesh."[43] This language about "antichrists" Tertullian borrowed from the Epistles of John; for instance, 2 John 1:7 says, "For many deceivers are entered into the world, who confess not that Jesus Christ is come in the flesh. This is a deceiver and an antichrist."[44] It is not clear whom John was writing about or what precisely they believed, but Tertullian finds in John's words the language to describe Marcion.

Tertullian continues by explaining why Marcion believes that Christ has not come in the flesh. According to Tertullian, Marcion believes that the vengeful god of the Old Testament created this world and that Jesus came to save humanity from that god and from his corrupt material world. "Christ, therefore, in order to avoid . . . the imputation, if possible, of belonging to the Creator, was not what he appeared to be [that is, human]."[45] This idea that Christ only *appeared* to be human even though he was actually fully divine was introduced above as the defining characteristic of docetism.[46]

Tertullian argues that this belief is absurd because if Christ only appeared to be human, then he only appeared to heal people and only appeared to suffer and die, but did not in actuality do any of those things.

> Since however, Christ's being flesh is now discovered to be a lie, it follows that all things which were done by the flesh of Christ were done untruly. . . . If with a touch, or by being touched, He freed any one of a disease, whatever was done by any corporeal act cannot be believed to have been truly done in the absence of all reality in His body itself. . . . On this principle, too, the sufferings of Christ will be found not to warrant faith in Him. For . . . a phantom could not truly suffer. God's entire work, therefore, is subverted. Christ's death, wherein lies the whole weight and fruit of the Christian name, is denied.[47]

For Tertullian, it is absurd that anyone would believe in Marcion's Christ. And it might be tempting to agree with Tertullian, but it's worth remembering that Tertullian is Marcion's theological opponent and as such might not do justice to Marcion's theology. That is, Marcion may not have held a docetic Christology.

Before further analyzing Marcion's Christology, it is worth noting that passages in the writings of Paul—Marcion's favorite apostle—lend themselves to docetic interpretation. For instance, when Paul discusses the challenges of both sin and flesh in this life, he describes Christ's incarnation in a way that could lead someone to believe that Christ was not *incarnated* (literally "in-fleshed") but only appeared to be so: "God sending his own Son in the likeness of sinful flesh" (Romans 8:3). Similarly, in a poetic passage from Paul's letter to the Philippians, Christ is described as only being similar to humans: "But [Christ] made himself of no reputation, and took upon him the form of a servant, and was made in the likeness of men" (Philippians 2:7). Marcion could have read either of these passages and concluded that Jesus's flesh was similar to that of human beings, but not precisely the same. That said, it is not clear that Tertullian's description of Marcion as a docetist accurately captures Marcion's Christology.

We catch a glimpse of the problem with Tertullian's caricature of Marcion's Christology at the very end of his four-volume treatise against Marcion. There he quotes from Marcion's edition of the Gospel of Luke. In the King James Version, the passage reads:

> But they were terrified and affrighted, and supposed that they had seen a spirit. And he said unto them, Why are ye troubled? and why do thoughts arise in your hearts? Behold my hands and my feet, that it is I myself: handle me, and see; for a spirit hath not flesh and bones, as ye see me have. (Luke 24:37–39)

According to Tertullian, Marcion cut many passages out of his version of the Gospel of Luke. Yet, when it comes to this passage, which would seem to contradict a docetic Christology, Tertullian quotes Marcion's Gospel as saying, "Why are ye troubled, and why do thoughts arise in your hearts? See my hands and my feet, that it is I myself; for a spirit hath not bones, as ye see me have." Although this passage does not appear precisely the same as that found in the KJV translation of Luke today—for instance, it omits the command to "handle" Jesus and leaves out the word *flesh*—it, nevertheless, rejects the idea that Jesus was a mere "spirit" after his resurrection and insists that he has "bones."[48] Tertullian is clearly confused by this passage and struggles to make sense of why it appears in Marcion's Gospel. He concludes that "Marcion was unwilling to expunge from his Gospel some statements which [were] even made against him," and he suggests that Marcion only included this passage so that he could "deny that he had expunged anything."[49] Of course, the other possibility is that Marcion did in fact believe that Christ had some form of a tangible body.[50] In fact, Tertullian admits that Marcion's later followers believed that Jesus's body was tangible: "They allow that Christ really had a body. Whence was the material of it, if not from the same sort of thing as that in which He appeared? . . . He borrowed, they say, His flesh from the stars, and from the substances of the higher world."[51] In other words, Marcion seems to have argued that Christ's body looked human but was in reality more divine or was made of more heavenly than earthly material.

How might Marcion have developed the idea that Christ's body was not of this earth but was instead a heavenly body? Once again, Paul uses similar language in his first letter to the Corinthians. In the context of explaining the resurrection, Paul contrasts Adam with Jesus Christ, and thus human beings with the Lord. Referring to Christ as the "last Adam," Paul writes: "There is a natural body, and there is a spiritual body. And so it is written, The first man Adam was made a living soul; the last Adam was made a quickening spirit. . . . The first man is of the earth, earthy: the second man is the Lord from heaven" (1 Corinthians 15:44–45, 47). It is easy to understand how Marcion might have developed from Paul's language in 1 Corinthians 15 the idea that Christ's body was not fully human.

Despite Tertullian's insistence that Marcion was a docetist, Marcion's Christology seems to have been more complex. Rather than insisting that Jesus Christ was a phantasmal being who only appeared to have a tangible body, Marcion actually affirmed that Jesus's body was real and tangible. Yet, for Marcion, this body of Jesus was not made of the evil material that comes from this world. Instead, Jesus's body was comprised of heavenly substance—a concept Marcion likely derived from his reading of Paul.

Valentinians

The story of Valentinus (no relation to the century-later St. Valentine) is similar to that of Marcion. It seems that Valentinus was born in Egypt in the early second century AD and was educated in Alexandria.[52] At some point, Valentinus moves to Rome and begins preaching (c. AD 130–160). Unlike Marcion, Valentinus then becomes so popular that he is almost elected Bishop of Rome.[53] Irenaeus and Tertullian, however, do not think highly of him, and they associate him with other "heretics" such as Marcion. Unlike Marcion, however, Valentinus was not trying to change the beliefs of all Christians in Rome. Instead, Valentinus offered his teaching as an expansion or deeper understanding of the Christian message already taught to the masses—he formed a church within the Church. Irenaeus criticizes, in particular, Valentinus's beliefs about Christ, arguing that he does not place sufficient emphasis on Jesus's humanity.

> And I have proved already, that it is the same thing to say that He appeared merely to outward seeming, and [to affirm] that He received nothing from Mary. For He would not have been one truly possessing flesh and blood, by which He redeemed us, unless He had summed up in Himself the ancient formation of Adam. Vain therefore are the disciples of Valentinus who put forth this opinion, in order that they may exclude the flesh from salvation, and cast aside what God has fashioned.[54]

Irenaeus asserts that Valentinus's Christology is no different than affirming a Jesus who "appeared merely outward seeming," and in this way Irenaeus equates the Christology of Valentinus with docetism. To support this criticism, Irenaeus points to the Valentinian belief that Jesus "received nothing from Mary," and he argues that Christ could not have truly saved humanity (those of "flesh and blood" like "Adam") unless he was also flesh and blood.

Tertullian offers a similar criticism of Valentinus. Likewise focusing on Christ's relationship to his mother, Mary, Tertullian argues that the Valentinians play irresponsibly with the prepositions *through* and *of*: Christ was born *through* Mary, they say, not *of* her. The implication is that Christ did not inherit any particular humanness from Mary.

> [Valentinus's] position being one which must be decided by prepositions; in other words, [Christ] was produced *by means of* a virgin, rather than *of* a virgin! On the ground that, having descended into the virgin rather in the manner of a passage through her than of a birth by her, He came into existence *through* her, not *of* her—not experiencing a mother in her, but nothing more than a way. Upon this same Christ, therefore

(so they say), Jesus descended in the sacrament of baptism, in the likeness of a dove.[55]

Tertullian also mocks the idea of a Christ made of multiple parts (beyond a spirit and a body) by describing the Valentinians as stuffing Christ's body first with "spirit-seed" and "a soul-breath" and later at baptism with this divine being (Jesus), as if the divinity were "seasoning" intended to prevent the other "stuffing" from spoiling.

> I now adduce (what they say) concerning Christ, upon whom some of them engraft Jesus with so much license, that they foist into Him a spirit-seed together with a soul-breath. Indeed, I will not undertake to describe these incongruous crammings, which they have contrived in relation both to their men and their gods. . . . Moreover, there was even in Christ accruing . . . the condiment of a spirit-seed, in order of course to prevent the corruption of all the other stuffing.[56]

Tertullian's mockery, like that of Irenaeus, was intended to disparage the Valentinians' beliefs and portray them as ridiculous. Tertullian concludes by describing the Valentinians as "reducing all things to mere images—Christians themselves being indeed nothing but imaginary beings!" in the thought of Valentinus.[57]

Valentinus's understanding of the world and of Christ's role in it was more logical than his theological opponents allow. And most of his ideas concerning the nature of Christ came from close readings of texts now found in the Bible. For instance, Valentinus's understanding of the nature of Jesus's body seems to have developed in part from his reading of the Gospel of John. Valentinus argued that Jesus's body was special: "He was continent, enduring all things. Jesus digested divinity: he ate and drank in a special way, without excreting his solids. He had such a great capacity for continence that the nourishment within him was not corrupted, for he did not experience corruption."[58] As strange as it may seem that Valentinus would have speculated about the bowel movements of the Savior, it is worth noting that this theory likely originated from his reading of John 6:27. As Bentley Layton explains:

> His exaggerated statement about Jesus' digestion may be based on a New Testament story of Jesus' command to the people of Tiberias in Jn 6:27, playing upon the double meaning of the Greek verb "to labor for," which also means "to digest": "Jesus answered them . . . 'Do not *labor for* (or *digest*) the food which perishes, but for the food which endures to eternal life, which the son of man will give you.'"[59]

As with the other Christian authors we have considered so far, Valentinus is deriving his understanding of Jesus Christ from scripture. In this case, Valentinus is focusing on texts that suggest Jesus's body was unique.

For Valentinus, Jesus's body was different from an average human being's body. In the Gospel of Philip, likely written by one of the disciples of Valentinus, the author explains that Jesus's flesh is the only true flesh.[60]

> [The master] was conceived from what [is imperishable], through God. The [master rose] from the dead, but [he did not come into being as he] was. Rather, his [body] was [completely] perfect. [It was] of flesh, and this [flesh] was true flesh. [Our flesh] is not true flesh, but only an image of the true.[61]

Jesus's flesh is better and more perfect than the flesh of human beings, both because of the way in which he was incarnated and because of the way in which he was resurrected.

For Valentinians, it was necessary that Jesus's flesh be better than that of humanity in order that he might save humanity from a kind of flesh that can get sick and die. In the Gospel of Truth, a work possibly written by Valentinus himself, the flesh of Jesus nailed to the cross becomes the salvific fruit of the tree of life: "He was nailed to a tree and became fruit of the Father's acquaintance. Yet it did not cause ruin because it was eaten. Rather, to those who ate of it, it gave the possibility that whoever he discovered within himself might be joyful in the discovery of him."[62] This tree of the cross becomes for Valentinus "the climactic moment of divine self-revelation," as David Brakke explains.[63] It is through Christ crucified that the Father is revealed and Christians can become acquainted both with God and with their own divine destiny. This tree of the cross of Christ stands in opposition to a tree that would "cause ruin." As Brakke notes, it points back to the forbidden fruit of Eden and forward to the Eucharist—in LDS terminology, the sacrament.[64] Again, Valentinus's love for the Gospel of John shines through as his theology of the cross echoes Jesus's sermon in John about partaking of his life-giving flesh as bread (see John 6:51).

It is not clear whether Valentinus believed that Jesus's material body was comprised of celestial substance, as Marcion taught, or whether Valentinus affirmed that Jesus's body was made of the substance of this world (inherited from his mother, Mary) and redeemed by his own spiritual body that inhabited it.[65] It is clear, however, that the Christology of Valentinus and later Valentinians was more complicated than Tertullian's classification of it as mere docetism. For Valentinus, Jesus Christ was divine and had a body that was crucified and resurrected.

Proto-Orthodox

The Christology that eventually became the orthodox position and continues to be preached by Christians today, including Latter-day Saints, affirms that Jesus Christ is fully human and fully divine. This understanding of Jesus Christ is no more explicit in the New Testament texts from the first century than are the views later promoted by the Ebionites, Marcion, or Valentinus. Rather, during the second century, proto-Orthodox Christians developed and refined their understanding of the nature of Jesus Christ in dialogue with the Christologies of these other groups and authors.[66] As Aloys Grillmeier explains, "The struggle against the Docetists and the Adoptionists gives rise to stronger stress on the Godhead [the divinity] and the manhood in

Christ."[67] We can see the development of this dual emphasis on the full divinity and humanity of Christ in the writings of Irenaeus and Tertullian at the end of the second century.[68]

Irenaeus's arguments against docetism helped him to refine his belief in Jesus Christ's humanity. For instance, Irenaeus argues for Jesus's humanity when he says, "Those, therefore, who allege that He took nothing from the Virgin do greatly err. . . . In that case is His descent into Mary [superfluous]; for why did He come down into her if He were to take nothing of her?"[69] Then, alluding to one of the most common titles Jesus uses for himself in the Gospels, Son of Man, Irenaeus writes, "For if He did not receive the substance of flesh from a human being, He neither was made man nor the Son of man; and if He was not made what we were, He did no great thing in what He suffered and endured." Irenaeus then quotes Galatians 4:4 and Romans 1:3–4 to prove that Christ was "made of woman" and "made of the seed of David according to the flesh."

Irenaeus's arguments against adoptionism helped him to refine his belief in Jesus Christ's divinity. For instance, Irenaeus also quotes the rest of Romans 1:3–4, which continues, "made of the seed of David according to the flesh; And declared to be the Son of God with power, according to the spirit of holiness, by the resurrection from the dead." Since Paul says that it was by his resurrection that he was "declared to be the Son of God," this passage could be read to imply that Jesus became divine by "adoption" through his resurrection but was actually only human. Yet Irenaeus elsewhere argues against those who emphasize Jesus's humanity over his divinity when he writes, "Those who assert that He was simply a mere man, begotten by Joseph . . . are in a state of death having been not as yet joined to the Word of God the Father."[70] With his mention of the "Word of God," Irenaeus alludes to the prologue of the Gospel of John, in which the divine Word is made flesh so that all who receive him might become children of God (John 1:1, 12, 14). The critique, that they have not yet "joined to the Word," has a double meaning. First, they have not accepted the belief that Jesus is fully divine, and second, they have not, Irenaeus suggests, received Christ in such a way that they might be saved. Here, Irenaeus makes an argument similar to Valentinus, that humankind could only be saved by a divine Christ acting to transform humanity's corruptible, mortal nature: "But how could we be joined to incorruptibility and immortality, unless, first, incorruptibility and immortality had become that which we also are, so that the corruptible might be swallowed up by incorruptibility, and the mortal by immortality, that we might receive the adoption of sons?"[71] Of course, Irenaeus argues against Valentinus's view that Christ was more divine than human by insisting that the humanity of Jesus was just as important as his divinity.[72]

In response to these opposing views—that Jesus Christ was more divine than human or that he was more human than divine—Irenaeus insists that both positions are equally true. Grillmeier summarizes Irenaeus's Christology as describing the divine Word, or Logos, "in a living relationship to the flesh he has assumed."[73] In Irenaeus's own words, he affirms:

> For as [Jesus Christ] became man in order to undergo temp-
> tation, so also was He the Word that He might be glorified;
> the Word remaining quiescent, that He might be capable of
> being tempted, dishonoured, crucified, and of suffering death,
> but the human nature being swallowed up in it (the divine),
> when it conquered, and endured [without yielding], and per-
> formed acts of kindness, and rose again, and was received up
> [into heaven]. He therefore, the Son of God, our Lord, being
> the Word of the Father, and the Son of man, since He had
> a generation as to His human nature from Mary—who was
> descended from mankind, and who was herself a human
> being—was made the Son of man.[74]

For Irenaeus, it was necessary that Jesus Christ be both human and divine in order to save humankind.

Tertullian also refined his Christology in dialogue with alternative views and alternative interpretations of scripture. For instance,

the same scriptural passage that docetists might have used to autho-
rize their interpretation of Jesus's difference from humans is used by
Tertullian to affirm Jesus's humanity: "God sending his own Son in
the likeness of sinful flesh" (Romans 8:3). Tertullian explains:

> For in another place also he says that Christ was in the like-
> ness of the flesh of sin: not that he took upon him the likeness
> of flesh, as it were a phantasm of a body and not its reality: but
> the apostle will have us understand by "the likeness of sinful
> flesh" that the flesh of Christ, itself not sinful, was the like of
> that to which sin did belong, and is to be equated with Adam
> in species but not in defect.[75]

In other words, for Tertullian, Paul did not claim that Jesus's body
was only in appearance like that of other humans. For Tertullian,
Jesus's body was comprised of the same flesh as any other human. The
only difference in Tertullian's interpretation of Paul is that Jesus's
flesh was not sinful because Jesus was sinless—therefore, it was in
the "likeness of sinful flesh," but it was nonetheless human flesh.[76]

Tertullian, in response to the Christologies of Marcion and
Valentinus, emphasizes the humanness of Jesus's body. When he
affirms that Jesus was crucified, died, was buried, and was resurrected,
he emphasizes that Jesus's flesh is human: "*I mean* this flesh suffused
with blood, built up with bones, interwoven with nerves, entwined
with veins, *a flesh* which knew how to be born, and how to die,
human without doubt, as born of a human being."[77] For Tertullian,
it is important that Jesus's flesh be exactly the same as human flesh
because it is in part through Jesus's incarnation that he is able to
save human beings: "By clothing himself with our flesh he made it
his own, and by making it his own he made it non-sinful."[78] Notice
how this contrasts with Valentinus's understanding of Christ's flesh.
For Valentinus, Christ's flesh had to be superior to that of humanity
so that through it humans might escape their own sinful flesh. For
Tertullian, however, it is by Christ taking upon himself human flesh
that he is able to redeem that very flesh. Rather than escape from

sinful flesh, in Tertullian's understanding of incarnation, Christ saves flesh from its potential for sinfulness.

For Tertullian, it was necessary that Jesus Christ be both human and divine. In a statement that echoes Irenaeus's affirmation concerning the humanity and divinity of Jesus Christ, Tertullian summarizes his own view:

> Thus the nature of the two substances displayed Him as man and God,—in one respect born, in the other unborn; in one respect fleshly, in the other spiritual; in one sense weak, in the other exceeding strong; in one sense dying, in the other living. This property of the two states—the divine and the human— is distinctly asserted with equal truth of both natures alike, with the same belief both in respect of the Spirit and of the flesh. The powers of the Spirit proved Him to be God, His sufferings attested the flesh of man.[79]

For Tertullian, Jesus Christ was both fully human and fully divine.

This is not the end of the story. While this may have been the first time that the belief in Jesus Christ's two natures was so clearly elucidated, it was not the last. Discussions about the relationship between Jesus Christ's humanity and divinity continued into the middle of the fifth century with the Council at Chalcedon, and beyond.[80] Although Latter-day Saints may now quibble with some of the nuances of the later creeds, we owe a debt of gratitude to the early proto-Orthodox Christians whose Christology we have inherited. Likewise, all Christians owe gratitude to the Ebionites, Marcionites, Valentinians, and others who labored alongside the proto-Orthodox to grow in their understanding of Jesus Christ.

Conclusion

The story of the christological developments of the second century has been told in different ways. Latter-day Saint authors have some-times conveyed this story as though it were a disaster narrative, in which all that is good collapses and is lost or scattered.[81] The orthodox Christian telling of this story is one of heroes and villains, in which authors such as Irenaeus and Tertullian triumph over their heretical rivals.[82] The story that I have related is less dramatic and less triumphalist. It is not the story of a fight for survival and not a story of good versus evil. Rather it is the story of various ancient Christians who worked to understand their relationship with Jesus Christ.

Whereas Latter-day Saints often disagree with Christians of other denominations on the nature of the Trinity, or Godhead in LDS parlance, we find general agreement on the affirmation that Jesus Christ is both fully human and fully divine. Yet this doctrine is not explicitly affirmed by Christians until the end of the second century AD. Latter-day Saints have sometimes ignored or worse disparaged the writings of Christians that came after the texts now compiled in the New Testament. It is sometimes assumed that anything written in the second century AD and beyond must be evidence only of rebellion against God—what we commonly call the Great Apostasy. Yet, as we have seen here, one of the fundamental Christian doctrines, belief in Christ's full humanity and divinity, came into focus over the course of the second century as various Christians worked to understand holy scripture. This is not to deny the LDS doctrine of a Great Apostasy or the concomitant doctrine of the Restoration, but only to suggest that we may not yet fully understand the extent and ramifications of each. For that reason, we should take extra caution when setting limits on whom God might guide and how God might work for the benefit and understanding of humankind. And as Latter-day Saints, we should graciously acknowledge our debt to second-century Christians and be grateful for the understanding of Jesus Christ we have inherited from them.

JASON R. COMBS *is an assistant professor of ancient scripture at Brigham Young University.*

Notes

1. Even though this imagined scenario is not true, some early Christian authors did accuse each other of forgery and of altering scripture; for instance, see Tertullian's criticism of Marcion in Tertullian, *Prescription against Heretics* 38.9. Of course, already in the first century AD, Paul warns that there are forgeries in his name (see 2 Thessalonians 2:2).

2. *History of the Church,* 6:57.

3. Robert Millet quoting Elder William Grant Bangerter, "It's a Two-Way Street," address delivered on 4 August 1985, in *1984–85 BYU Speeches of the Year* (Provo, UT: Brigham Young University Publications, 1985), 161. See Robert L. Millet, "Joseph Smith and 'The Only True and Living Church,'" in *A Witness for the Restoration: Essays in Honor of Robert J. Matthews,* ed. Kent P. Jackson and Andrew C. Skinner (Provo, UT: Religious Studies Center, 2007), 201–31.

4. For instance, see Richard R. Hopkins, *How Greek Philosophy Corrupted the Christian Concept of God,* 2nd ed. (1988; repr., Springville, UT: Horizon Publishers, 2009). Recently, Noel B. Reynolds wrote, "Though the incorporation of Greek philosophy into Christianity was not an original cause of the apostasy, the apostate Christian churches generally reached out to embrace philosophy as a means of bringing common standards and rationality to Christian belief. . . . The Christian tradition that resulted was far different than the one established by Jesus Christ and his apostles in the first century." Reynolds, "What Went Wrong for the Early Christians?," in *Early Christians in Disarray: Contemporary LDS Perspectives on the Christian Apostasy,* ed. Noel B. Reynolds (Provo, UT: BYU Press, 2005), 14.

5. For instance, see David E. Aune, *The New Testament in Its Literary Environment,* Library of Early Christianity (Philadelphia: Westminster, 1987); or Troels Engberg-Pedersen, *Paul and the Stoics* (Louisville, KY: Westminster John Knox Press, 2000). These studies seem to contradict the claim of Daniel W. Graham and James L. Siebach: "It is only in the mid-second century that Christians began to use Greek forums and genres to communicate publicly with the pagan world. They did so at first only to make their case to the secular world and to refute heresies which had

some philosophical inspiration." Graham and Siebach, "The Introduction of Philosophy into Early Christianity," in *Early Christians in Disarray*, 234.

6.   In Colossians 2:8 we read, "Beware lest any man spoil you through philosophy and vain deceit." This is not a critique of philosophy in general. If the word *philosophy* was replaced with *religion* one would not assume that it was a critique of all religion. Rather it would be a critique of anyone who would use religion to lead someone away captive (to "spoil," or better, "despoil" them). Of note, Judaism and Christianity were both understood to be philosophies in the ancient world; see Josephus, *Antiquities* 18.1.2–6; and Justin Martyr, *Dialogue with Trypho* 8.

7.   While it is possible that there were some Christians who were corrupt or who wrote with ulterior motives, the idea of mass corruption and a unified effort, intentional or unintentional, to reshape the earliest teachings of Christianity into something foreign and false is not supported by the extant ancient records—heresiological discourse notwithstanding.

8.   See *The Letter of the Churches of Vienne and Lyons*. On the life of Irenaeus, see Denis Minns, *Irenaeus: An Introduction* (New York: T&T Clark, 2010).

9.   On the growth and spread of Christianity, see Keith Hopkins, "Christian Number and Its Implications," *Journal of Early Christian Studies* 6, no. 2 (1998): 185–226.

10.   The Revelation of Peter 78.31–79.31, in *The Nag Hammadi Scriptures: The Revised and Updated Translation of Sacred Gnostic Texts*, ed. and trans. Marvin Meyer (New York: HarperOne, 2007), 295; ellipses added.

11.   Bart D. Ehrman, *Lost Christianities: The Battles for Scripture and the Faiths We Never Knew* (New York: Oxford University Press, 2003), 185–88.

12.   Irenaeus, *Against Heresies* 3.11.7 (*ANF*). Irenaeus here seems to distinguish the Ebionites' Christology from "those who separate Jesus from Christ." Often the Ebionites have been classified as adoptionists because they believe that Jesus was born of the normal sexual union of Mary and Joseph, then on account of his righteousness was "adopted" by God as son. Yet a close reading of the extant fragments of writing from the Ebionites seems to suggest that they should be grouped with the otherwise anonymous collective of "those who separate Jesus from Christ"—what I call a possessionist/separationist Christology.

13. Although I use the term *debate*, one should not imagine that these various Christian groups ever sat down for a meeting to discuss their opposing views. The earliest theological councils did not take place until the fourth century. Rather I use the term *debate* simply to describe the broad disagreement, the awareness of that disagreement, and the various attempts in writing to affirm one's own view while refuting the alternatives.

14. For instance, Ehrman, *Lost Christianities*. For more detailed treatments of early Christologies, see the foundational work, Aloys Grillmeier, *Christ in the Christian Tradition: From the Apostolic Age to Chalcedon (451)*, 2nd rev. ed., trans. J. Bowden (1965; repr., Atlanta: John Knox, 1975); see also Larry W. Hurtado, *Lord Jesus Christ: Devotion to Jesus in Earliest Christianity* (Grand Rapids, MI: Eerdmans, 2003); and James L. Papandrea, *The Earliest Christologies: Five Images of Christ in the Postapostolic Age* (Downers Grove, IL: IVP Academic, 2016).

15. For more on adoptionism, see Ehrman, *Lost Christianities*, 99–103; Papandrea, *Earliest Christologies*, 23–43.

16. For more on docetism, see Ehrman, *Lost Christianities*, 103–6; Papandrea, *Earliest Christologies*, 45–65; Michael Slusser, "Docetism: A Historical Definition," *Second Century* 1 (1981): 163–72.

17. For more on possessionist/separationist Christology, see Papandrea, *Earliest Christologies*, 23–43, 67–84; Matti Myllykoski, "Cerinthus," in *Companion to Second-Century Christian "Heretics,"* ed. Antti Marjanen and Petri Luomanen (Leiden: Brill, 2005), 224–36.

18. For more on proto-Orthodox Christology, see Papandrea, *Earliest Christologies*, 85–104; Grillmeier, *Christ in the Christian Tradition*, 102–57.

19. For instance, see Mosiah 15:2–4 and D&C 93:4.

20. For the history of LDS Christology, see Terryl Givens, *Wrestling the Angel: The Foundations of Mormon Thought: Cosmos, God, Humanity* (Oxford: Oxford University Press, 2015), 117–23; and Charles R. Harrell, *"This Is My Doctrine": The Development of Mormon Theology* (Salt Lake City: Greg Kofford Books, 2011), 149–84.

21. Givens, *Wrestling the Angel*, 119. See Boyd Kirkland, "Elohim and Jehovah in Mormonism and the Bible," *Dialogue* 19 (1986): 77–93; and Ryan

Conrad Davis and Paul Y. Hoskisson, "Usage of the Title *Elohim*," *Religious Educator* 14, no. 1 (2013): 109–27.

22. Inconsistent and irregular use of the titles Jehovah and Elohim continued throughout the presidencies of both Brigham Young and John Taylor; see Givens, *Wrestling the Angel*, 119.

23. I am not suggesting that early Mormons would have agreed with all the nuances of dyophysitism, for instance, as established in the Chalcedonian Creed; on dyophysitism and Mormonism, see Harrell, *"This Is My Doctrine,"* 160.

24. Givens, *Wrestling the Angel*, 123. Regarding what sense Jesus should be understood as progeny of a divine Father, some LDS leaders have speculated that God the Father impregnated Mary through normal human sexual processes and other LDS leaders have insisted that such speculation should be avoided. For instance, Brigham Young said, "The Father came down and begat him, the same as we do now, and Jesus was the only one"; see *The Complete Discourses of Brigham Young* (Salt Lake City: Signature Books, 2009), 1:321. Harold B. Lee, on the other hand, wrote, "Teachers should not speculate on the manner of Christ's birth. We are very much concerned that some of our church teachers seem to be obsessed of the idea of teaching doctrine which cannot be substantiated and making comments beyond what the Lord has actually said. You asked about . . . the birth of the Savior. Never have I talked about sexual intercourse between Deity and the mother of the Savior. If teachers were wise in speaking of this matter about which the Lord has said but very little, they would rest their discussion on this subject with merely the words which are recorded on this subject in Luke 1:34–35. . . . Remember that the being who was brought about by [Mary's] conception was a divine personage. We need not question His method to accomplish His purposes. Perhaps we would do well to remember the words of Isaiah 55:8–9: 'For my thoughts are not your thoughts, neither are your ways my ways, saith the Lord'"; see Harold B. Lee, *Teachings of Harold B. Lee* (Salt Lake City: Bookcraft, 1996), 14.

25. I do not treat independently "those who separate Jesus from Christ" (possessionist/separationist Christology) because that view is represented by the Ebionites and Cerinthus (see below).

26. For an introduction to the Ebionites, see Ehrman, *Lost Christianities*, 99–103; and Sakari Häkkinen, "Ebionites," in *Companion to Second-Century Christian "Heretics,"* 247–78.

27. Häkkinen, "Ebionites," 247.

28. Irenaeus, *Against Heresies* 1.26.2 (*ANF*).

29. Irenaeus, *Against Heresies* 1.26.1 (*ANF*).

30. Irenaeus, *Against Heresies* 3.21.1 (*ANF*).

31. Irenaeus, *Against Heresies* 5.1.3 (*ANF*); alluding to Luke 1:35.

32. Epiphanius, *Refutation of All Heresies* 30.13; trans. J. K. Elliott, *The Apocryphal New Testament: A Collection of Apocryphal Christian Literature in an English Translation*, rev. ed. (Oxford: Oxford University Press, 1993), adapted.

33. On the Ebionites' Gospel missing an infancy narrative, see Grillmeier, *Christ in the Christian Tradition*, 79.

34. Epiphanius, *Refutation of All Heresies* 30.13; Ebionites frag. 5, trans. Elliott.

35. Irenaeus, *Against Heresies* 1.26.1 (*ANF*, adapted).

36. For comparable Christologies, see Grillmeier, *Christ in the Christian Tradition*, 92–93.

37. For an introduction to Marcion, see Ehrman, *Lost Christianities*, 99–103; and Heikki Räisänen, "Marcion," in *Companion to Second-Century Christian "Heretics,"* 100–124.

38. Martial, 5.35; Pliny, *Epistulae* 6.1; see Peter Lampe, *From Paul to Valentinus: Christians at Rome in the First Two Centuries*, trans. M. D. Johnson (1989; repr., Minneapolis: Fortress Press, 2003), 245.

39. Ehrman, *Lost Christianities*, 108–9; Lampe, *From Paul to Valentinus*, 245.

40. Ehrman, *Lost Christianities*, 104–5; and Räisänen, "Marcion," 105–7.

41. On Marcion's canon and its influence, see Bruce M. Metzger, *The Canon of the New Testament: Its Origin, Development, and Significance* (Oxford: Clarendon, 1987), 90–99.

42. For more on Tertullian's construction of Marcion, see Judith M. Lieu, *Marcion and the Making of a Heretic: God and Scripture in the Second Century* (Cambridge: Cambridge University Press, 2015), 50–85.

43. Tertullian, *Against Marcion* 3.8.1 (*ANF*).

44. See also 1 John 2:18, 22; 4:3.

45. Tertullian, *Against Marcion* 3.8.2 (*ANF*). "Only those souls that had learned his doctrine would attain salvation. The body, on the contrary, since it was taken from the earth, is incapable of sharing in salvation"; Irenaeus, *Against Heresies* 1.27.3; trans. Dominic J. Unger and John J. Dillon, *St Irenaeus of Lyons: Against the Heresies Book 1*, Ancient Christian Writers 55 (New Jersey: Paulist Press, 1992).

46. For an overview of docetic Christologies, see Grillmeier, *Christ in Christian Tradition*, 93–101.

47. Tertullian, *Against Marcion* 3.8.4–5 (*ANF*).

48. Absence of the word *flesh* may be due to Paul's affirmation that flesh and blood cannot inherit the kingdom of God (see 1 Corinthians 15:50).

49. Tertullian, *Against Marcion* 4.43.6–7 (*ANF*).

50. This seems likely; see Lieu, *Marcion and the Making of a Heretic*, 219–21; and David E. Wilhite, "Was Marcion a Docetist? The Body of Evidence vs. Tertullian's Argument," *Vigiliae Christianae* 71, no. 1 (2017): 1–36.

51. Tertullian, *The Flesh of Christ* 6.3 (*ANF*).

52. Based on Epiphanius's comments in the early fourth century, which should be treated with a healthy dose of skepticism; see David Brakke, *The Gnostics: Myth, Ritual, and Diversity in Early Christianity* (Cambridge, MA: Harvard University Press, 2010), 100.

53. Brakke, *Gnostics*, 100.

54. Irenaeus, *Against Heresies* 5.1.2 (*ANF*).

55. Tertullian, *Against the Valentinians* 27 (*ANF*).

56. Tertullian, *Against the Valentinians* 27 (*ANF*, adapted).

57. Tertullian, *Against the Valentinians* 27 (*ANF*).

58. Clement of Alexandria, *Miscellanies* 3.59.3; trans. Bentley Layton, *The Gnostic Scriptures* (New York: Doubleday, 1987), 239.

59. Layton, *Gnostic Scriptures*, 238.

60. For Valentinus, the material world is not real—only God is real; see Brakke, *Gnostics*, 101.

61. Gospel of Philip 68.29–37; trans. Marvin Meyer.

62. Gospel of Truth 17.18–31, in Layton, trans., *Gnostic Scriptures*, 254.

63. Brakke, *Gnostics*, 102.

64. Brakke, *Gnostics*, 102.

65. For a more detailed analysis of Valentinian Christology, see Einar Thomassen, *The Spiritual Seed: The Church of the "Valentinians"* (Leiden: Brill, 2006).

66. In theological terms, Latter-day Saints might describe this as a revelation received line upon line; see 2 Nephi 28:30; D&C 98:12; 128:21. On the relationship of these passages to Isaiah 28:10, 13, see Terry B. Ball, "'Precept upon Precept, Line upon Line': An Approach to Understanding Isaiah 28:7–13," in *Prophets and Prophecies of the Old Testament: The 46th Annual Brigham Young University Sidney B. Sperry Symposium*, ed. Aaron Schade, Brian Hauglid, and Kerry Muhlestein (Provo, UT: Religious Studies Center, 2017), 79–94.

67. Grillmeier, *Christ in Christian Tradition*, 123. Judith Lieu echoes this statement from Grillmeier when she writes, "At every point Tertullian's own convictions and his construction of Marcion play off against each other like a light and the shadows it throws, the sound and its echo." Lieu, *Marcion and the Making of a Heretic*, 84.

68. Prior to Irenaeus and Tertullian, other proto-Orthodox Christians had begun to develop similar ideas regarding Jesus Christ's humanity and divinity: for instance, Ignatius, Justin Martyr, Melito of Sardis, and others. See Papandrea, *The Earliest Christologies*, 91–96; and Grillmeier, *Christ in Christian Tradition*, 102–14. Yet it is in the writings of Irenaeus and Tertullian that we first find the idea of Jesus Christ's dual natures clearly affirmed.

69. Irenaeus, *Against Heresies* 3.22.1–2 (ANF).

70. Irenaeus, *Against Heresies* 3.19.1 (ANF).

71. Irenaeus, *Against Heresies* 3.19.1 (ANF). Irenaeus goes on to write, "For it was for this end that the Word of God was made man, and He who

was the Son of God became the Son of man, that man, having been taken into the Word, and receiving the adoption, might become the son of God" (*Against Heresies* 3.19.1 [ANF]).

72. Both Valentinus and Irenaeus developed this idea from their reading of Paul's letters and the Gospels.

73. Grillmeier, *Christ in Christian Tradition*, 122.

74. Irenaeus, *Against Heresies* 3.19.3. Irenaeus continues by citing Isaiah 7:13–14 as evidence for Jesus's birth from the virgin, Mary. For more on the meaning of Isaiah 7:13–14 in its historical context and in Matthew 1, see Jason R. Combs, "From King Ahaz's Sign to Christ Jesus: The 'Fulfillment' of Isaiah 7:14," in *Prophets and Prophecies of the Old Testament*, 95–122.

75. Tertullian, *The Flesh of Christ* 16.3–5; trans. Ernest Evans, ed., *Tertullian's Treatise on the Incarnation* (London: SPCK, 1956).

76. Tertullian does not here consider the implications of Philippians 2:7.

77. Tertullian, *The Flesh of Christ* 5.5 (ANF).

78. Tertullian, *The Flesh of Christ* 16.5; trans. Evans.

79. Tertullian, *The Flesh of Christ* 5.7 (ANF); cf. Irenaeus, *Against Heresies* 3.19.3.

80. In October AD 451, a council was held at Chalcedon, a city on a small peninsula near the southern mouth of the Bosphorus strait—on the coast opposite Istanbul in modern-day Turkey. There a group of bishops, theologians, and other church leaders crafted a statement to deal with questions regarding whether Christ's divinity absorbed his humanity, whether Christ remained of two natures or whether the two became one, etc.

81. See above, note 4.

82. See Tertullian, *Prescription against Heretics* 29. For a narrative of early Christian history that follows this model, see Eusebius, *Church History*.

Condescension and Fullness

LDS Christology in Conversation
with Historic Christianity

Grant Underwood

Latter-day Saints share with the rest of the Christian world an abiding conviction that the Son of God was divine in the preexistence.[1] They do not, however, share the common Christian belief that he was always so. They believe that he progressed to godhood. Put another way, he was not born or begotten divine. Rather he had to develop the embryonic divinity within him the same as all God's other spirit children. And, here, of course, is another distinctive Mormon doctrine—that literally "we are the offspring of God" (Acts 17:29) and that Christ was literally "the firstborn among many brethren" (Romans 8:29). Latter-day Saints view the human family as the "many begotten" spirit children of God and Christ as the Only Begotten by the Father in the flesh. Although firstborn among many brethren, Christ commenced his preexistent life as a spirit son of God on the same footing as all his spirit brothers and sisters—with the need and opportunity to develop his divine potential. Because of this

different view, historic Christianity and Mormonism frequently mis-
understand and talk past each other rather than engage in beneficial
conversation about our respective beliefs. As will be discussed in this
chapter, LDS similarities and differences with historic Christianity
can be seen in our respective views of Christ's preexistence, his condescension, his mortal nature, the degree to which he progressed on
earth, and how he obtained a fullness of the glory of the Father.

Christ in the Preexistence

To be sure, the Son's development of his divine potential was far more
rapid than that of God's other spirit children. He alone advanced to
godhood in the preexistence. In part, this was a function of his special
position as "Firstborn" (D&C 93:21; Colossians 1:15). Just as not all
children of the same parents are equally intelligent, so LDS scripture
notes: "These two facts do exist, that [where] there are two spirits,
one being more intelligent than the other; there shall be another more
intelligent than they; . . . [and the Son is] more intelligent than they
all" (Abraham 3:19). But his "natural" endowments still had to be
cultivated. "By obedience, by righteousness, through faith, over long
ages and eons," observed Bruce R. McConkie (1915–1985), a member
of the Quorum of the Twelve from 1972 to 1985, the Firstborn "advanced and progressed until he became like unto God in power, in
might, in dominion, and in intelligence." This "ranked him as a God,
as the Lord Omnipotent, while yet in his pre-existent state. As such
he became, under the Father, the Creator of this earth and of worlds
without number."[2]

Still, LDS authorities have not been uniform in their suggestions as to *how* the Firstborn became like the Father. For instance,
noted thinker and LDS apostle James Talmage (1862–1933) believed
that at the appropriate point in the Son's preexistent progress, he was
"invested with the powers and rank of Godship."[3] Laying aside the
unusual choice of "godship" for godhead/godhood, the verb *invest* is
suggestive. It literally means "to clothe"; in other words, "to endue with

attributes, qualities, or a character"; "to install in an office or rank."[4] George Q. Morris (1874–1962), a member of the Twelve from 1954 to 1962, taught in the LDS general conference that the Father "elevated" the Son to the "position" of "the Godhead . . . by divine investiture."[5] To the question of whether the preexistent Son of God was divine by nature or by grace, the Mormon answer appears to be "both."[6]

Given the lack of much clear, authoritative LDS teaching about how the firstborn son of God became God the Son, it is not surprising that nearly everything said about the preexistent Son focuses on his fully divine status. In harmony with the opening lines of the Gospel of John (John 1:1–3), Latter-day Saints extol the Son's virtual equality with the Father. Yet they also agree with those Eastern fathers who, while acknowledging the full deity of the Son and the Spirit, nonetheless accord ontological priority to the Father as the *source* of the divinity of the other two members of the Godhead.[7] In short, the Father is the greatest of the three equally divine persons.[8] The LDS position is similar to that of Origen of Alexandria (c. AD 184–254), an early Greek father, whose description of the Father "as greater than the Son does not refer to any difference of divinity, power, wisdom, or truth [but] to the Father's unique role and character within the Trinity."[9]

This is apparent when Latter-day Saints celebrate the preexistent Son's role as creator of all things both in heaven and on earth. In addition to citing the usual biblical texts that proclaim this reality, such as John 1:3 or Colossians 1:16, they invoke various Book of Mormon passages that refer to Christ as "the Father of heaven and of earth," and sometimes "the very Eternal Father of heaven and of earth."[10] The latter characterization of Christ as "eternal" Father of heaven and earth is explained from the vantage point of Mormonism's nonphilosophical use of the term *eternal*. In 1916 the First Presidency explained Christ's title in this way: "Since His creations are of eternal *quality*, He is very properly called the Eternal Father of heaven and earth."[11] In LDS theology, the one exception to the Son's role as Creator is that he is *not* the creator of human souls, the other spirit children of the Father. Again, the First Presidency is unambiguous on this point: "Jesus Christ is not the Father of the spirits who have taken or yet shall take bodies upon this earth, for He is one of them. He is The Son, as they are sons or daughters of Elohim."[12]

Christ's Incarnation and Condescension

From the early centuries of Christianity, Christ's mortal birth has been known as the "incarnation," a word derived from Latin *incarnāre* that means "becoming flesh" or "investiture or embodiment in flesh." The term has obvious resonance with the famous passage in the Gospel of John: "And the Word was made [became] flesh, and dwelt among us" (John 1:14). For most Christians, how an invisible, immaterial, incorporeal, uncreated Being could encase itself in visible, material, corporeal, created human flesh is a divine "mystery." The early church father Origen wrote that "of the whole number of miracles and marvels attributed to [Christ], there is one which . . . the weakness of mortal understanding can find no way to grasp or to compass. I mean the fact that . . . the very Logos [Word] of the Father . . . in whom all things visible and invisible were created . . . must be believed to have entered a woman's womb, to have been born as a small child, and to have squalled in the manner of crying children."[13]

While both Latter-day Saints and other Christians sometimes refer to the incarnation as the "condescension" of God,[14] the term has particular resonance for Latter-day Saints because of the term's use in a critical passage in the Book of Mormon (see 1 Nephi 11:16).[15] Nevertheless, with his teaching that we are all children of God, Joseph Smith dissolved not only the great ontological divide between Creator and creature but also between the Savior and the saved. As a result, Latter-day Saints almost never refer to the Son taking on "human *nature*" in the incarnation, as is common in other Christologies. Rather, they speak of him taking a human *body*, one that resembles in physical appearance his preexistent spirit body, much as all spirits who come to earth for a mortal experience.

In addition to all the usual soteriological reasons for the Son becoming incarnate, Latter-day Saints add a personal one. Because of their rather unique belief in a corporeal God, the premortal Christ needed to acquire and deify a physical body like his Father. Though the preexistent Christ was God the Son, the Creator of the universe, he did not then possess a divine, physical body. That acquisition required incarnation, resurrection, and glorification. Furthermore, because of the LDS conception of earth life as a spiritual probation, Jehovah, like all God's spirit children, had to be "tested" in a human environment rife with sin and in a body subject to the genetic influences of the fall. LDS scripture quotes God speaking these words with reference to his spirit children: "We will make an earth whereon these may dwell; And we will prove them herewith, to see if they will do all things whatsoever the Lord their God shall command them; And they who keep their first estate [obey divine law in the preexistence] shall be added upon [come to earth and acquire a physical body]; . . . and they who keep their second estate [earth life] shall have glory added upon their heads for ever and ever" (Abraham 3:24–26). Mormon theology expresses no doubt that Christ would "pass" the test, but it also stresses that his earthly "probation" was no sham. Beset by genuine temptation, the Son of God did not succumb; he was sinless (Hebrews 4:15).

Latter-day Saints also share with other Christians the standard understanding that the incarnation enabled Christ to experience the full range of the human condition. In addition to quoting related biblical verses about the purposes of the Son's "humiliation," Latter-day Saints today are fond of quoting this passage from the Book of Mormon: "And he shall go forth, suffering pains and afflictions and temptations of every kind; . . . and he will take upon him their infirmities, that his bowels may be filled with mercy, *according to the flesh*, that he may know *according to the flesh* how to succor his people according to their infirmities. Now the Spirit knoweth all things; nevertheless the Son of God suffereth *according to the flesh* that he might take upon him the sins of his people, that he might blot out their transgressions according to the power of his deliverance" (Alma 7:11–13).[16] Such reflection on the purposes and accomplishments of the incarnation inevitably raises the central christological question about how the earthly Christ was both human *and* divine. Historically, this has been described as the problem of the "two natures," and efforts to understand it spanned the early centuries. Even the famed "Definition of the Faith" set forth in AD 451 at the Fourth Ecumenical Council in Chalcedon did not solve the problem. Debate would continue to the end of the patristic period and beyond.

The early church fathers regarded a complete human nature as including a mind/soul as well as a body. Therefore, they believed that in the incarnation the Son took on *both* a human body *and* a human soul. Because the idea of two souls—the premortal Son's and the one created for the body in Mary's womb—was problematic to some, it was not uncommon in the early centuries to reason that the divine Son or Logos supplied the rational soul for the man Jesus. Although they often held different positions in the great theological debates of their day, figures as diverse as Arius (AD 256–336), Athanasius (c. AD 296–373), and Apollinaris of Laodicea (died AD 382) agreed in their characterization of Jesus Christ as the Son/Logos clothed in flesh. Such a "Logos-flesh" Christology stands in contrast to the ultimately orthodox "Logos-human" Christology, which held that in Jesus the Logos inhabited a full man, complete with his own rational soul. In the twentieth century, Logos-flesh Christology has sometimes been labeled "space-suit Christology." Just as an astronaut dons "an elaborate space-suit which enables him to live and act in a new, unfamiliar environment, so the *Logos* put on a body which enabled him to behave as a human being among human beings."[17] This is similar to the Mormon view that Jesus's physical body was merely the earthly "tabernacle" or "temple" for the Firstborn's preexistent soul/spirit.

In seeking to establish his position that the Logos fulfills the role of, indeed takes the place of, the human mind in Jesus, Apollinaris, who was eager to emphasize Christ's divinity, raised the objection that the idea of a "joint tenancy" of a divine soul *and* a human soul in

Jesus would result in incompatibility. "Either the Logos would simply dominate the human soul and thus destroy the freedom by which it was human, or the human soul would be an independent center of initiative and Jesus would be, in effect, schizophrenic."[18] The persistent rebuttal to Apollinarian Logos-flesh Christology was the idea that whatever the Son did not assume (as in a human soul), he could not redeem. Later, Maximus the Confessor (c. AD 580–662), a Greek monk and theologian from Constantinople, explained that at times Christ exercised the divine will he brought with him from eternity and at other times he acted through the human will that was part of the complete human nature he assumed in the incarnation.

LDS thought has never seriously engaged the possibility of two souls, two wills, or two independent subjects or "principles of action" in the single Christ. Mormon nominalism assumes that two wills, as concrete realities, require two persons. Thus, Latter-day Saints interpret the various New Testament passages in which Christ distinguishes his will from the Father's as proof that the Father and Son are two, separate, volitional beings, not as manifestations of Christ having within him two separate wills—one human and one divine—as would ultimately become the orthodox "two wills" position known as *dyotheletism*.[19] Despite Mormonism's simpler understanding that Christ had a single will, there is widespread acknowledgment among Latter-day Saints that Christ was both human and divine. How Mormons have conceived that interplay in the incarnate Lord differs from many early church fathers, in large part due to the different metaphysical assumptions undergirding their respective Christologies. Since Christ really only has one nature, Mormons do not talk of the Son taking his divine nature with him to earth and conjoining it to a human nature that first materializes in Mary's womb. Instead, they see Christ's preexistent spiritually corporeal body entering his physically corporeal body. Nor do Latter-day Saints feel the need exegetically to tag every expression or action of Jesus as either divine or human. While they do not disavow that the human and the divine coexist in Christ, their metaphysics do not compel them to constantly parse the divine-human grammar. B. H. Roberts (1857–1933), a member of the First Council of the Seventy from 1888 until his death, remarked, "I deplore those [theological] refinements which try to tell us about the humanity of Jesus being separate from the divinity of Jesus. He Himself made no such distinctions. He was divine, spirit and body, and spirit and body was exalted to the throne of His Father, and sits there now with all the powers of the Godhead residing in Him bodily, an immortal, glorified, exalted man!"[20]

Kenosis and the Veil

Joseph Fielding Smith (1876–1972), a long-time member of the Council of the Twelve and president of the LDS Church from 1970 to 1972, declared, "Our Savior was a God before he was born into this world, and he brought with him that same status when he came here. He was as much a God when he was born into the world as he was before. But as far as this life is concerned it appears that he had to start just as all other children do and gain his knowledge line upon line."[21] It is with this final "but" that Mormon thought moves toward what Christian theologians call "kenoticism." Kenoticism is derived from Philippians 2:6–8, where the verb *kenoō* ("to empty") is used in what is considered an early christological hymn to depict the way in which the divine, preexistent Son "in the form of God" took on "the form of a servant" as a human being. Theologically stated, kenoticism encompasses "views of the Incarnation which state that the Word somehow empties himself of—or abstains from the use of all the powers of—one or more of his divine attributes, either functionally or ontologically."[22] Such views have circulated in Christian theology in one form or another since the days of the second-century bishop and apologist Irenaeus (died c. AD 202), who remarked that one aspect of the incarnation was that "the Logos became quiescent so that [Christ] could be tempted and be dishonored and be crucified and die."[23]

Kenotically oriented Christologies vary in how and to what degree they see the Son having relinquished his divine characteristics in the incarnation. Did the Son/Logos turn over to the Father his divine powers or merely turn them off during his earthly sojourn? For some church fathers, either way was unacceptable because withholding the exercise of divine attributes involved change in the divine nature, something neo-Platonic purists could not allow. In Greek philosophy, there was no such thing as partial divinity or growth in divinity. Divinity by definition was complete, perfect, static, and unchangeable, from everlasting to everlasting. Hence the position adopted by the ecumenical council at Chalcedon in AD 451 that the Word's divine nature in Jesus could not be changed or affected by "going along for the ride" with the human nature's experience of temptation, suffering, ignorance, or other human experiences. This led to the complicated christological effort to cordon off the Son's divinity from every ordinary human behavior or expression depicted in the Gospels.

LDS Christology, on the other hand, is noteworthy for rarely attempting to parse the human and the divine in Jesus. Furthermore, in what would have been scandalous to thinkers steeped in Hellenistic philosophy, Mormons understand divinity not as something static and immutable but as something like charity, which can be cultivated, deepened, and increased. At spirit birth, all God's offspring, including Christ, received an embryonic divine nature susceptible to growth and development, as well as stagnation and diminishment. Rather than two categorically different natures, there is only a single nature encompassing a vast range of development. In one sense, then, *human* can be used descriptively rather than ontologically to depict that which tends to one end of a single developmental continuum and *divine* as that which looks to the other end. To be sure, the developmental distance between infinite God and finite earthlings may be, as one scholar put it, the difference between Einstein and a mollusk,[24] but Latter-day Saints do not view the difference as metaphysical, nor do they restrict the possibility of deification to the Son alone.

Thus Mormons do not bifurcate Christ's development, even analytically. Speaking of the trajectory toward divinity, "I, John, saw that [Christ] received not of the fulness at the first, but received grace for grace; And he received not of the fulness at first, *but continued from grace to grace, until he received a fulness*; And thus he was called the Son of God, because he received not of the fulness at the first" (D&C 93:12–14).[25] Elder McConkie considered this passage in the Doctrine and Covenants the best "account known of the mortal progression and achievements of Him who was God before the world was." It shows that "even a God receives not of the fulness of the Father at the first. Even he must be subject to the vicissitudes and trials of mortality; even he must be tried and tested to the full; even he must overcome the world."[26] Another LDS apostle, Orson F. Whitney (1855–1931), put it this way: "By constantly growing in grace and godliness, living from day to day by every word that proceeded forth from the mouth of God, He gradually became entitled to the steadily increasing possession of the Holy Spirit, till finally 'it pleased the Father that in Him should all fullness dwell' [Col 1:19]."[27]

Because historically Mormon doctrine has not known the word *kenosis*, it has described the LDS version of the Son's incarnational "emptying" as a "veiling." For instance, Elder Talmage noted, "Over His mind had fallen the veil of forgetfulness common to all who are born to earth, by which the remembrance of primeval existence is shut off."[28] As a result, his divine omniscience was mitigated. "When Jesus lay in the manger, a helpless infant," remarked Lorenzo Snow (1814–1901), Church president from 1898 to 1901, "He knew not that He was the Son of God, and that formerly He created the earth. When the edict of Herod was issued, He knew nothing of it."[29] The notion of "the veil" received early exposition among Latter-day Saints. Brigham Young (1801–1877), second president of the Church, explained it this way: "The greatest good that could be produced by the all wise Conductor of the universe to His creature, man, was to do just as He has done—bring him forth on the face of the earth, drawing a vail [sic] before his eyes. He has caused us to forget every thing we once knew before our spirits entered within this vail [sic] of flesh. . . . This is right; were it different, where would be the trial of our faith?"[30]

Young's contemporary and fellow apostle Orson Pratt (1811–1881) emphasized a full kenosis of divinity: "All that great and mighty power he possessed, and the great and superior wisdom that was in his bosom, . . . vanished from him as he entered into the infant tabernacle. He was obliged to begin down at the lowest principles of knowledge, and ascend upward by degrees, receiving grace for grace, truth for truth, knowledge for knowledge, until he was filled with all the fulness of the Father, and was capable of ruling, governing, and controlling all things."[31] Joseph Fielding Smith corrected a Church member who wondered if from the outset the veil was "thinner" for Christ, if he was "given more knowledge about his pre-existence as an infant and youth than any other mortal." Smith's answer was: "The Savior was like any other child in the matter of knowledge of his pre-existence."[32] On another occasion, he added, "Without a doubt, Jesus came into the world subject to the same condition as was required of each of us—he forgot everything, and he had to grow from grace to grace. His forgetting, or having his former knowledge taken away, would be requisite just as it is in the case of each of us, to complete the present temporal existence."[33]

Kenoticism and Progression

The kenotic idea that the premortal Christ had set aside his previous divinity opens up the prospect of progression for the mortal Jesus, an idea that seems implicit in Luke's bridging statement following the boy's experience in the temple when twelve years old: "And Jesus increased in wisdom and stature, and in favour with God and man" (Luke 2:52). Joseph Smith also emended the end of Matthew 2 in his New Translation to similarly propose that Jesus progressed in his childhood.[34] Mormons and other Christians who embrace a kenotic Christology and who place the incarnate Son of Man at essentially the same beginning point with the rest of humankind find this doctrine homiletically useful because it provides humanity with a model for spiritual growth. Clement of Alexandria (c. AD 150–250), a theologian from the great catechetical school of Alexandria, wrote, "The Word of God [i.e. Jesus] became man, so that you may learn from man how man may become God."[35] Prominent modern evangelical John G. Stackhouse, in a quotation that bears quotation in full, sees a doctrine of kenosis as particularly critical to this:

> What can we possibly learn about how to live a life of obedience to God, of dependence upon God, and of cooperation with God from a God-man who switches on his divine power-pack whenever he needs to negotiate a difficult situation? To truly serve as an example to us, Jesus has to be like us, seeking to do the will of his Father in heaven and relying moment by moment on the leading and empowering of the Holy Spirit. But how can God possibly be tempted, even if he somehow joins humanity to himself, if he retains his divine powers? Kenotic Christology helps here as well, for in positing a Jesus who could not simply "turn on" his divinity like a lamp to banish sin, this theology upholds a truly useful example for us of a man who did not yield, ever, to sin.[36]

A similar idea is present in Restoration scripture and LDS teaching generally, enabling Latter-day Saints to draw inspiration from the fact that a fully human Jesus had to pursue the same path to glory they do.[37] Asked Joseph F. Smith (1838–1918), sixth president of the Church, "If Jesus, the Son of God, and the Father of the heavens and the earth in which we dwell, received not a fulness at the first, but increased in faith, knowledge, understanding and grace until he received a fulness, is it not possible for all men who are born of women to receive little by little, line upon line, precept upon precept, until they shall receive a fulness, as he has received a fulness, and be exalted with him in the presence of the Father?"[38] A stanza from a popular Mormon hymn proclaims, "He marked the path and led the way, And every point defines; To light and life and endless day Where God's full presence shines."[39] Elder McConkie added that Christ is "the Prototype, the Pattern, the Type, and the Model of salvation.

He is the great Exemplar. He came to earth and worked out his own salvation by worshipping the Father so that all men—as his brethren in the spirit and as his fellow mortals in mortality—could pattern their lives after his and become themselves joint-heirs of God and inheritors with the Son of the fulness of the glory of the Father."[40]

Although expressed in a Mormon idiom, such views have resonance with certain strands of christological thinking from both the ancient Antiochene and Alexandrian perspectives. Antiochene fathers were anxious that their affirmation that Christ was indwelt by the divine Logos in no way detracted from seeing his earth life and path to godliness as fully human, similar to that of other human beings. Theodore of Antioch (c. AD 350–428), the bishop of Mopsuestia who championed the Antiochene school, wrote that "in the period before the cross [Jesus] was being given free room because of the necessity to achieve virtue on our behalf by his own [human] will" even though "he was being stirred on by the Word." Like any human, "he received the cooperative help of God the Word proportionate to his own native will," and in ultimately achieving "the highest peak of virtue," he "provided a type of that life for us also, becoming a path to that goal for us."[41]

Alexandrian scholars, many of whom were inclined toward asceticism and often rejected the physical in favor of the spiritual, arrived at a similar position, notwithstanding their distinctive Christology. As incarnate "Son of man," Jesus practiced askēsis (lit., "training," "exercise"; root of "asceticism"). In so doing, he became the archegos ("leader/pioneer") of [our] salvation (Hebrews 2:10), the lead climber who "marked the path and led the way." For the Alexandrian theologian-ascetic Origen, the eventual "union of the divine and human natures for all Christians depends on the moral progress that makes one worthy of such union . . . by imitation of [Christ's] virtue."[42] All of this implied the possibility of growth and development in Christ's life. The Alexandrian presbyter Arius (AD 256–336) asserted that the incarnate Son experienced prokopē, a word variously translated as "advancement," "improvement," or "progress." Such ideas, however, clashed with strongly held notions of the immutability of the Logos. If Christ "received what he possessed as a reward for his choices," argued Athanasius, if he "obtained it as a result of his virtue and *prokopē*, then he might reasonably be called 'Son' and 'God' [but] he is not 'true God' [the creedal phrase was that the Son was 'true God of true God']."[43] Regarding Philippians 2:9 ("God also hath highly exalted him"), Eusebius of Emesa (c. AD 300–360), a Greek theologian and a student of the more famous Eusebius of Caesarea (c. AD 260–339), rejected the Arian interpretation that the Son was exalted as a "reward for his obedience," stating that Christ was "not somebody who was promoted to being God because of his behavior."[44]

It is one thing to affirm Christ's kenosis and his subsequent *prokopē*; it is another to explain them. Although Latter-day Saints have no official doctrine on these matters, some Church leaders have made suggestive comments.[45] B. H. Roberts described Christ's *prokopē* in part as "the awakening of the Son of God in his earth-life to the consciousness of the really great powers he possessed. . . . He knew not at first whence He came, nor the dignity of His station in heaven. It was only by degrees that He felt the Spirit working within Him and gradually unfolding the sublime idea that He was peculiarly and pre-eminently the Son of God in very deed."[46] In this view, Christ's advancement was a process of overcoming his veil-induced forgetfulness and regaining full consciousness of his divine identity, attributes, and powers.[47] Initially, then, it was more a concealment than a kenosis of his divinity. In the words of Lorenzo Snow (1814–1901), fifth president of the Church, "He grew up to manhood, and during His progress it was revealed unto Him who He was, and for what purpose He was in the world. The glory and power He possessed before He came into the world [were] made known unto Him."[48]

Similarly, other kenotic Christologies claim "that core divine attributes still remain, or else are initially latent but gradually come to consciousness."[49] What is known as "functional kenoticism" posits that the divine traits were always present in Jesus Christ but inaccessible until gradually unlocked—or perhaps unveiled—by the Father.

"Ontological kenoticism," on the other hand, holds that Christ simply did not possess certain divine properties (e.g., omniscience or omnipotence) during his mortal sojourn. Thus, he could not have wielded them even if he desired to do so. One version of this theory differentiates between the Son's essential properties and his accidental/ contingent properties and suggests that only the latter were relinquished during mortality. At times, the LDS emphasis on Christ's humanity is so strong and the emphasis on his needing to grow in grace so robust that it reads like a version of ontological kenoticism, although not one that makes a metaphysical distinction between essential and accidental divine attributes. LDS thought shies away from declaring that Christ's preexistent divinity gave him "a leg up" on human experience.

At the same time, there is also a strand of Mormon thought that emphasizes the "partially full cup" in Christ and acknowledges real difference. "He shall suffer temptations, and pain of body, hunger, thirst, and fatigue, *even more than man can suffer*, except it be unto death," states one Book of Mormon passage (Mosiah 3:7). Elder Talmage describes Christ's earthly experience in this way: "His advancement was from one grace to another, not from gracelessness to grace; from good to greater good, not from evil to good; from favor with God to greater favor, not from estrangement because of sin to reconciliation through repentance and propitiation." Although "Jesus was all that a boy should be," his "development was unretarded by the dragging weight of sin; He loved and obeyed the truth and therefore was free."[50] Christ was peccable (capable of sinning) but lived a sinless life. Although classical Christology tended to add *im*peccability to his sinlessness, Charles Hodge (1797–1878), the famed nineteenth-century champion of Reformed orthodoxy at the Princeton Theological Seminary, reasoned in ways that resonate with Mormon thinking: "If He was a true man He must have been capable of sinning. That He did not sin under the greatest provocation . . . is held up to us as an example. Temptation implies the possibility of sin. If from the constitution of his person it was impossible for Christ to sin, then his temptation was unreal and without effect, and He cannot sympathize with his people."[51] The First Presidency's official Doctrinal Exposition on the Father and the Son in 1916 summarized Jesus's distinctiveness in this fashion: "Let it not be forgotten, that He is essentially greater than any and all others, by reason (1) of His seniority as the oldest or firstborn [among preexistent souls/spirits]; (2) of His unique status in the flesh as the offspring of a mortal mother and of an immortal, or resurrected and glorified, Father; (3) of His selection and foreordination as the one and only Redeemer and Savior of the race; and (4) of His transcendent sinlessness."[52]

The Mormon sense of Christ's distinctiveness began with Joseph Smith, who asked rhetorically, "Why was [Christ] perfect? Because he was the son of God, and had the fulness of the Spirit, and greater power than any man."[53] By the mid-twentieth century, reflection on Christ's nature had progressed to the point that Elder McConkie could write: "In his study and in the learning process he was guided from on high in a way that none other has ever been. Being without sin—being clean and pure and spotless—he was entitled to the constant companionship of the Holy Spirit. . . . Of the Lord Jesus the scripture says: 'God giveth not the Spirit by measure unto him' (John 3:34)." McConkie discusses the impact of the preexistence and the veil drawn at birth in such a way that the veil is hardly to be understood as an intellectual "iron curtain." Christ's earthly knowledge "came to him quickly and easily because he was building—as is the case with all men—upon the foundations laid in preexistence. He brought with him from that eternal world the talents and capacities, the inclinations to conform and obey, and the ability to recognize truth that he had there acquired. . . . Jesus, when yet a child had spiritual talents that no other man in a hundred lifetimes could obtain."[54]

Such talk of Christ's extraordinariness, however, is not intended to diminish his genuine humanity or what he accomplished as a mortal man. In the words of current LDS apostle Jeffrey Holland, "Christ's final triumph and ultimate assumption of godly powers on the right hand of his Father came *not* because he had a divine parent (although that was essential to the victory over death) and *not* because he was given heavenly authority from the beginning (although that was essential to his divine power) but ultimately because he was, in his own mortal probation, perfectly obedient, perfectly submissive, perfectly loyal to the principle that the spiritual in his life must rule over the physical. That was at the heart of his triumph, and that is a lesson for every accountable man, woman, and child who ever lives. It is a lesson [of] spirit over flesh; discipline over temptation; devotion over inclination; 'the will of the Son being swallowed up in the will of the Father' [Mosiah 15:7]."[55]

Obtaining the Fullness of the Father

The LDS affirmation that the incarnate Christ progressed to the point of receiving the "fullness of the Father" raises the question of what Latter-day Saints think Jesus did not possess at first. Was it, for instance, a fullness of the knowledge of what it was like to be human? This is suggested in the Book of Mormon declaration "Now the Spirit knoweth all things; nevertheless the Son of God suffereth according to the flesh" paired with the previous statement "that he may know according to the flesh how to succor his people according to their infirmities" (Alma 7:13, 12). Additional clues are found in Doctrine and Covenants 93, which notes: "He received a fulness of truth, yea, even of all truth" (D&C 93:26); John bore record "that he received a fulness of the glory of the Father; And he received all power, both in heaven and on earth" (93:16–17); and "the glory of God is intelligence, or, in other words, light and truth" (93:36). The LDS understanding of the veil applies to these important concepts and qualities of intelligence, light, truth, channeling Mormon understandings of kenosis along cognitive lines. Apostle Albert Bowen (1875–1953) commented on D&C 93 in these words: "That is to say, when Jesus had attained to, or had received, a fulness of truth, He also received a fulness of glory for the two are one."[56]

Some Mormon thinkers, though, have felt that Christ's growth from grace to grace entailed more. Bruce Hafen, an emeritus member of the Seventy, has reasoned, "His experience shows us also that being free from sin is not quite the same as attaining divine perfection. Jesus lived without sin or blemish, which qualified him in that aspect to perform the Atonement for all mankind. . . . Yet Christ tasted of a central purpose of mortality by learning and growing through his earthly experience, even though he was without sin." As Hafen noted elsewhere, Christ's "life was sinless; hence, he received grace not to compensate for his sins, but to empower his personal growth."[57]

Mormon theologians also vary as to *when* they understand Christ to have received the divine fullness. Those who downplay a sense of kenosis in favor of affirming the divine nature of the incarnate Christ—that is, those who emphasize what the Son brought with him to earth life as a result of preexistent attainments or who focus on the impact of being sired by God the Father—tend to interpret a text like Colossians 2:9 ("in him dwelleth all the fulness of the Godhead bodily") as in some sense true from birth. Representative readings include "this plainly means that Jesus was *like* his Father in his person and in the attributes of his soul," or "Father in heaven was revealed and made manifest in the person of His Son Jesus Christ," or "he received of the fullness of the Father; that is, a fullness of his glory, his power, and dominion, hence Jesus *represented* God in his completeness—'in him dwelleth all the fullness of the Godhead bodily' (Col. 2:9)."[58] Yet, when Christ's kenosis and humanity are emphasized, the principle that he "continued from grace to grace, until he received a fulness" (D&C 93:13) tends to be understood as not being fulfilled until his glorification. Elder B. H. Roberts's statement is typical: "not until after his resurrection" was "he able to come to his disciples and say: 'All power is given unto me in heaven and in earth'" because only then did he receive "all the plenary power of the Godhead."[59] Another strand of LDS thought that parallels some early "adoptionist" Christologies focuses on D&C 93:14–17 to suggest when Christ received the fullness:

He was called the Son of God, because he received not of the fulness at the first. And I, John, bear record, and lo, the heavens were opened, and the Holy Ghost descended upon him in the form of a dove, and sat upon him, and there came a voice out of heaven saying: This is my beloved Son. And I, John, bear record that he received a fulness of the glory of the Father. And he received all power, both in heaven and on earth, and the glory of the Father was with him, for he dwelt in him. (93:14–17)

To Orson Pratt, this passage "informs us of the period when this fulness was granted."[60]

Like other Christians, Latter-day Saints have grappled with the significance and complexity of how Jesus was the Christ—the divine Son of God who shared so much with the Father and was in a real way one with him and yet retained his uniqueness and individual experience. While sharing many of the same conceptions, if not always the same terminology, Restoration scripture and teaching nonetheless have provided distinct ways of understanding Christ's role as the Firstborn, his incarnation, his progression, and his final obtaining of a fullness. This provides Latter-day Saints with a different view of how Jesus of Nazareth was both God and man, and LDS understanding of Jesus's obtaining the fullness of the Father gives us a new way of responding to Jesus's declaration, "And this is life eternal, that they might know thee the only true God, and Jesus Christ, whom thou hast sent" (John 17:3).

GRANT UNDERWOOD *is a professor of history and Richard L. Evans Chair of Religious Understanding at Brigham Young University.*

Notes

1. I am using the term *preexistence* in this paper since it is the standard usage in Christian theological literature in English. I am aware that Latter-day Saint usage has replaced that term with *premortality* or *premortal life.*

2. Bruce R. McConkie, "The Seven Christs," *Ensign*, November 1982, 32; *Mormon Doctrine* (Salt Lake City: Bookcraft, 1966), 121. Neal A. Maxwell (1926–2004), a member of the Twelve from 1981 to 2004, offered this interpretation of the previously quoted statement from Abraham 3:19 that the premortal Christ was "more intelligent than they all": "In *intelligence* and *performance*, He far surpasses the individual *and the composite capacities and achievements of all* who have lived, live now, and will yet live!" Maxwell, "O, Divine Redeemer," *Ensign*, November 1981, 8. Still, because so little is said in LDS scripture or official dogmatic pronouncement about the nature of the preexistence or progress in that realm, several points about the Son's preexistent divinity remain unclear. Did he over time simply develop his essential but embryonic divine traits to a point of full divinity such that his love became perfect, his knowledge omniscient, his powers omnipotent? Or was divinity eventually conferred upon him as a reward for his obedient and loving fidelity to the Father? McConkie's remarks suggest the former.

3. James E. Talmage, *Jesus the Christ* (Salt Lake City: Deseret News, 1915), 10. He refers elsewhere to "His divine investiture" (517). This is not to be confused with repeated references to his "inherent Godship" (602, 626) or his "inherent" power to perform miracles (130, 145, 249, 316, 318, 418), which refer to Christ's incarnate condition, where both divinity and humanity constitute his two "inherent natures."

4. *Oxford English Dictionary*, s.v. "invest."

5. George Q. Morris, in Conference Report, October 1956, 46.

6. Though little is known for certain, it may be that embryonic divinity was developed to mature fruition through both personal effort and gracious assistance from a loving Father, a Father who eventually invested his Firstborn with the divine powers and authority necessary to function as Creator and Redeemer. In philosophical language, whatever the precise relationship between developed "essence" and conferred "accident" in the Son's progress to divinity and membership in the Godhead, the LDS view of divinity diverges significantly from traditional assumptions about its static and immutable nature.

7. The Greek tradition of viewing the Father as the origin of the Trinity and the source of its communion, particularly as articulated by the Cappadocian fathers, is discussed by the influential Orthodox theologian John Zizioulas in his *Being as Communion: Studies in Personhood and the Church* (Crestwood: St Vladimir's Seminary Press, 1997). Previously, Origen was known for teaching that "the Father is the source of the divinity that he communicates to the Son in his eternal and continuous generation and to the Spirit." Henri Crouzel and Emanuela Prinzivalli, "Origen," in *Encyclopedia of Ancient Christianity*, ed. Angelo Di Bernardino and Thomas C. Oden (Downers Grove: Intervarsity Press, 2014), 2:982.

8. Stephen E. Robinson, "God the Father," in *Encyclopedia of Mormonism* (New York: Macmillan, 1992), 2:48–50.

9. Christopher A. Beeley, *The Unity of Christ* (New Haven: Yale University Press, 2012), 26.

10. "Father of heaven and of earth" in 2 Nephi 25:12; Mosiah 3:8; Helaman 14:12. "Eternal Father of heaven and of earth" in Alma 11:39; Mosiah 15:4; Mormon 6:22.

11. "The Father and the Son: A Doctrinal Exposition by The First Presidency and The Twelve," *Improvement Era*, August 1916, 935; emphasis added.

12. "Father and the Son," 942.

13. *On First Principles*, 2.6.2. Cited in Richard A. Norris, *Christological Controversy* (Philadelphia: Fortress Press, 1980), 74–75. The *New Catholic Encyclopedia* describes the incarnation as "the mystery of the Second Person of the Blessed Trinity's becoming man, the mystery of Jesus Christ's being God and man, the mystery of His being the God-Man" (7:373).

14. See, for instance, Thomas Torrance, *Theological Science* (Oxford: Oxford University Press, 1970), 46; and K. Scott Oliphint, *God with Us: Divine Condescension and the Attributes of God* (Wheaton: Crossway, 2012). In LDS scripture, the phrase "condescension of God" appears in the Book of Mormon at 1 Nephi 11:16, 26. It has been regularly referenced and discussed by LDS apostles and prophets. As just one example, Church president Gordon B. Hinckley quoted the passage and remarked, "I suppose none of us can fully understand that—how the great Jehovah should come among men." Gordon B. Hinckley, "Be Not Faithless," *Ensign*, April 1989, 4.

15. Latter-day Saints speak of the incarnation as occurring in the "meridian of time"—the high noon of human history. In this they concur with reformed theologian Karl Barth (1886–1968), who wrote that because Christ lived for all other humans as their representative before God, his life is at once "the center, beginning, and end of all the times of all the lifetimes of all men." *Church Dogmatics* III/2: 440, as cited in Robert Dale Dawson, *The Resurrection in Karl Barth* (Aldershot: Ashgate, 2007), 67.

16. One twentieth-century commentary on the Book of Mormon included this explanation: "The Savior of all mankind condescended to things of lower estate that He might be filled with compassion for the sinner, and help for them that have no other Helper save it be Him." George Reynolds and Janne M. Sjodahl, *Commentary on the Book of Mormon*, edited and arranged by Philip C. Reynolds (Salt Lake City: Deseret Book, 1955–1961), 3:133.

17. R. P. C. Hanson, *Search for the Christian Doctrine of God: The Arian Controversy 318–381* (Edinburgh: T&T Clark, 1988), 448.

18. Norris, *Christological Controversy*, 22. In modern terms, Jesus is not to be understood as analogous to the Sméagol/Gollum character of *The Lord of the Rings*.

19. Not only have no authoritative LDS Church pronouncements been made on this matter, but virtually no General Authorities have addressed the topic in any setting. Even among LDS religious educators, commentary is rare. One BYU religion professor, however, is on record as embracing the idea of two wills in Christ. In the 1980s, Rodney Turner wrote that "begotten of an immortal Father and a mortal mother, Jesus possessed *two natures* (one divine, one human) and, therefore, *two wills* (that of the Father, and that of the Son). He could manifest either nature 'at will.' . . . The atonement required the subjection and sacrifice of the fleshly will of the 'Son' to the spiritual will of the 'Father.' . . . The *Son* willed to let the cup pass; the *Father* willed that it should be drunk to its dregs. . . . In a sense, it was not the Son *as* Son, but the Father *in* the Son who atoned. That is, Jesus not only did the will of his Father *in heaven*, but the will of the Father *in himself*." Rodney Turner, "Two Prophets: Abinadi and Alma," in *Studies*

in Scripture, Vol. 7: 1 Nephi to Alma 29, ed. Kent P. Jackson (Salt Lake City: Deseret Book, 1987), 245.

20. B. H. Roberts, *Seventy's Course in Theology* (Salt Lake City: The Canton Press, 1910), 3:188.

21. Joseph Fielding Smith, *Doctrines of Salvation* (Salt Lake City: Bookcraft, 1998), 1:32.

22. Oliver Crisp, *Divinity and Humanity* (New York: Cambridge University Press, 2007), 122.

23. Irenaeus, *Against Heresies* 3.19.3. Cited in Norris, *Christological Controversy*, 56.

24. Donald Macleod, *The Person of Christ: Contours of Christian Theology* (Downers Grove: IVP Academic, 1998), 210.

25. An influential Doctrine and Covenants commentary ventured that "grace for grace" is better rendered as "grace to grace" and that both phrases mean that "in His life, one grace was bestowed upon Him after another, until His measure was full." Hyrum M. Smith and Janne M. Sjodahl, *Doctrine and Covenants Commentary* (Salt Lake City: Deseret Book, 1951), 591. This agrees with modern English translations of the John 1:16 ("grace for grace" in the KJV) where *charin anti charitos* is rendered "grace upon grace" (NRSV), "one blessing after another" (NIV), or "one gift replacing another" (NJB).

26. Bruce R. McConkie, *The Promised Messiah: The First Coming of Christ* (Salt Lake City: Deseret Book, 1978), 548; McConkie, *The Mortal Messiah* (Salt Lake City: Deseret Book, 1979), 1:299.

27. Orson F. Whitney, "The Gospel of Jesus Christ," in *Scrap Book of Mormon Literature*, ed. Ben E. Rich (Chicago, 1911), 2:500. Although affirming Christ's earthly progression, Joseph Smith reportedly had a very high view of what Jesus had already achieved *even before adolescence*: "When still a boy he had all the intelligence necessary to enable Him to rule and govern the kingdom of the Jews, and could reason with the wisest and most profound doctors of law and divinity, and make their theories and practice to appear like folly compared with the wisdom He possessed." *History of the Church*, 6:608; from instructions given by Joseph Smith on June 27, 1844, in Carthage Jail, Carthage, Illinois; reported by Cyrus H. Wheelock,

in *Teachings of the Presidents of the Church: Joseph Smith*, 56. This statement is consistent with how Smith earlier modified Luke 2:46—"after three days they found him in the temple, sitting in the midst of the doctors, both hearing them, and asking them questions"—to emphasize that the doctors "were hearing *him*, and asking *him* questions." Scott H. Faulring, Robert J. Matthews, and Kent P. Jackson, eds., *Joseph Smith's New Translation of the Bible: Original Manuscripts* (Provo, UT: Religious Studies Center, 2004), 372.

28. Talmage, *Jesus the Christ*, 111. Similar language, with somewhat varying meanings, has been known throughout Christian history. The fifth-century *Tome of Leo*, for instance, paraphrases Philippians 2 in these words: "The Lord of the universe veiled his measureless majesty and took on a servant's form. The God who knew no suffering did not despise becoming a suffering man." Jaroslav Pelikan and Valerie Hotchkiss, *Creeds and Confessions* (New Haven: Yale University Press, 2003), 1:116.

29. General conference address, April 1901, in *Teachings of the Presidents of the Church: Lorenzo Snow* (Salt Lake City: The Church of Jesus Christ of Latter-day Saints, 2012), 279.

30. *Journal of Discourses*, 1:352 (10 July 1853). Young's sentiments were echoed in the twentieth century by apostle-and-future-church-president Joseph Fielding Smith, *Doctrines of Salvation*, 1:33.

31. *Journal of Discourses*, 1:56.

32. Joseph Fielding Smith, *Answers to Gospel Questions* (Salt Lake City: Deseret Book, 1957), 5:165.

33. Smith, *Doctrines of Salvation*, 1:33.

34. And it came to pass that Jesus grew up with his brethren, and waxed strong, and waited upon the Lord for the time of his ministry to come. And he served under his father, and he spake not as other men, neither could he be taught; for he needed not that any man should teach him (Joseph Smith Translation, Matthew 3:24–25); for the manuscript version, see Faulring et al., *Joseph Smith's New Translation of the Bible*, 239.

35. *Protrepticus*, 1.8. Cited in Jens Zimmermann, *Humanism and Religion: A Call for the Renewal of Western Culture* (Oxford: Oxford University Press, 2012), 67.

36. John G. Stackhouse Jr., "Jesus Christ," in *Oxford Handbook of Evangelical Theology*, ed. Gerald McDermott (New York: Oxford University Press, 2010), 151.

37. Bruce R. McConkie, "The Child, the Boy, the Man Few People Knew," *New Era*, December 1980, 7. *Doctrines of the Gospel Teacher Manual*, 10; *The Life and Teachings of Jesus and His Apostles* (Salt Lake City: The Church of Jesus Christ of Latter-day Saints, 1979), 25. Less authoritative but similar statements appear in other LDS sources.

38. Joseph F. Smith, 16 March 1902, *Gospel Doctrine* (1919), 83, cited in *Teachings of the Presidents of the Church: Joseph F. Smith* (Salt Lake City: The Church of Jesus Christ of Latter-day Saints, 1998), 153. See also *Teachings: Joseph F. Smith*, 429, where similar remarks from a 1907 address are reproduced. Church president Wilford Woodruff made the same point. *Journal of Discourses*, 5:51 (22 March 1857); reproduced in *Teachings of the Presidents of the Church: Wilford Woodruff*, 60.

39. Eliza R. Snow, "How Great the Wisdom and the Love," *Hymns*, no. 195.

40. Bruce R. McConkie, *New Witness for the Articles of Faith* (Salt Lake City: Deseret Book, 1985), 381.

41. *On the Incarnation*, as cited in Maurice Wiles and Mark Santer, eds., *Documents in Early Christian Thought* (Cambridge: Cambridge University Press, 1975), 60, 61.

42. Beeley, *Unity of Christ*, 43–44.

43. Cited in Hanson, *Search for the Christian Doctrine of God*, 428. In a longer passage, Athanasius argues that scriptural statements about Christ's exaltation and *prokopē* apply to his human body, not to his indwelling divinity. This, as has been noted, is not a distinction Mormons make when discussing the earthly experience of Jesus Christ.

44. Cited in Hanson, *Search for the Christian Doctrine of God*, 390.

45. Orson Pratt put a unique spin on the Acts 8:33 recension of Isaiah 53:8— "In his humiliation his judgment was taken away"—to describe the veiling of Jesus: "What humiliation?" asked Pratt. "His descending from the presence of God his Father and descending below all things, his judgment was taken away, that is, his remembrance of things that were past, and that knowledge which, while in the presence of his Father, enabled him to

make worlds, and he had to begin at the first principles of knowledge . . . [and grow] up from grace to grace, as the Scriptures say, from one degree to another, until he received a fullness from his Father." See *Journal of Discourses*, 15:245.

46. Roberts, *Seventy's Course in Theology*, 3:132–33.

47. Plato argued that when the human soul learns, it recalls what it knew in the preterrestrial state. Aristotle criticized Plato for this idea.

48. *Teachings: Lorenzo Snow*, 279.

49. Brown, *Divine Humanity*, 21.

50. Talmage, *Jesus the Christ*, 111–12.

51. Charles Hodge, *Systematic Theology* (New York: Charles Scribner, 1872), 2:457, cited in Oliver Crisp, *God Incarnate: Explorations in Christology* (London: T&T Clark, 2009), 123.

52. "Father and the Son," 942.

53. *Times and Seasons* 2 (June 1841): 430.

54. McConkie, *Mortal Messiah*, 1:369.

55. Jeffrey R. Holland, *Christ and the New Covenant* (Salt Lake City: Deseret Book, 1997), 193.

56. *Improvement Era*, June 1935.

57. Hafen, *Broken Heart*, 16, 165; "Beauty for Ashes," *Ensign*, April 1990, 11–12. The same point is made by Marion D. Hanks, "Behold the Man," *New Era*, December 1975, 38: "Though he was without blemish, yet he learned and grew."

58. *Improvement Era*, November 1897; Penrose, "Whom Do Latter-day Saints Worship?," *Improvement Era*, June 1914; Roberts, *Mormon Doctrine of Deity*, 216–17n; emphasis added.

59. B. H. Roberts, "Immortality of Man," *Improvement Era*, March 1907; Roberts, "Answer Given . . . Discourse Delivered in Salt Lake Tabernacle July 10, 1921," *Deseret News*, August 1921. See also McConkie, *New Witness for the Articles of Faith*, 73.

60. *Seer* 1 (August 1853): 120. President Ezra Taft Benson seems to have had a similar understanding. *Ensign*, September 1988. Bruce R. McConkie, however, sees a separation in time between verses 16 and 17: "This same John, looking forward to that day when Jesus would be raised in glorious

immortality to receive that—and more—which was his before the world was, testified: 'And I, John, bear record that he received a fulness of the glory of the Father; And he received all power, both in heaven and on earth, and the glory of the Father was with him, for he dwelt in him'" (McConkie, *Mortal Messiah*, 1:430).

Christology in the Joseph Smith Translation of the Gospels

David A. LeFevre

Christology is fundamentally how scripture portrays Jesus: "A coherent conceptual and theological explanation of Jesus's person, in harmony with the scriptural testimony, which is able to account for his role in its worship and faith."[1] In the case of the four Gospels, there are several common themes in how they portray Jesus but also individual and unique approaches in each book. This study aims to examine the changes in the Joseph Smith Translation of the Bible made by the Prophet between June 1830 and July 1833 and their impact on the christological story told by each author.

In general, the changes to the Gospels in Joseph Smith's New Translation—commonly referred to as the Joseph Smith Translation, or JST[2]—tend to make the Christology higher. That is, they elevate language that in the King James Version (KJV) might be perceived as emphasizing Jesus's mortality, or they add new text that portrays Jesus as divine in nature or acts that are best explained as divinely accomplished. This aligns with the largely high Christology of Joseph Smith's other translations and revelations, as found in the Book of Mormon, the Doctrine and Covenants, and the chapters of the Bible translation in Genesis 1–24, which were translated before he turned to the New Testament in March 1831 (see D&C 45:60–61). But the Joseph Smith Translation does not change each Gospel in the same way.[3] Rather, the Prophet engaged with each book in a manner that respected the original christological approach of the individual writer, enhancing and adding to it in ways that align with each book's character.

These changes potentially speak to Joseph Smith's personal Christology as well. The JST contains a range of textual changes, from highly revelatory passages (such as those in the early chapters of Genesis that end up in the Book of Moses) to purely pedantic grammar and word choice changes.[4] It is impossible to be certain for any passage whether a change was made by revelation, intellect, or both: Joseph Smith called it all a translation, and he seems to have been quite comfortable relying on the inspiration of the Spirit *and* his own intellectual efforts to produce a new biblical text.[5] But knowing that at least some of the JST changes come from Joseph Smith's own learning and understanding of Jesus's identity and eternal role can give insight into his personal understanding of Jesus in the earliest years of the Church.

Mark

Mark's is the shortest of the four Gospels but has many unique characteristics of structure and style. His Christology is the foundation for both Matthew's and Luke's and received the most attention from Joseph Smith as he worked through the Gospels. Examining some of these, especially as they relate to Jesus's own declarations and where the JST raises the Christology of Marcan stories that could be perceived as lower,[6] reveals Joseph Smith's efforts to both harmonize the Christologies of the Gospels and maintain a more consistently high Christology.

Jesus's Indirect Declarations of His Identity

In Mark's Gospel, Jesus does not openly indicate his own identity until the very end of the text. The first verses let us, the readers, view some scenes that portray Jesus's identity: The opening verse declares him to be the Christ or Messiah; the voice from heaven at his baptism declares to Jesus that he is the beloved Son; and angels minister to him in the wilderness (Mark 1:1–13). But after that Jesus only speaks of his own mission and role in the third person, using "Son of man" references, until he stands before the high priest, who pointedly asks him, "Art thou the Christ, the Son of the Blessed?" Jesus answers, "I am: and ye shall see the Son of man sitting on the right hand of power, and coming in the clouds of heaven" (Mark 14:61–62). This statement leads to a charge of blasphemy, which is followed by his crucifixion.[7]

It would have been an easy thing for Joseph Smith to portray Jesus in JST Mark openly declaring his own divinity and power, such as in his other translations and revelations, including 3 Nephi 11:10–14 and Doctrine and Covenants 19:1–4. But that never happens. Instead, Jesus maintains his third-person declarations instead of giving more direct statements about his own identity, and JST Mark even adds several new ones.

For example, in Mark 2:28, which concludes a discussion on the Sabbath, there is a significant JST change that retains the third-person tone of the verse while adding to the point Jesus made in the previous verse about the Sabbath being made for man and not the reverse.

> **Wherefore the sabath was given unto man for a day of rest; & also that man should gloryfy God, & not that man should not eat; for the Son of man made the Sabath day,** therefore the Son of man is Lord also of the Sabath. (JST Mark 2:28)

While declaring the enigmatic Son of man as the creator of the Sabbath, thus equating that title with divinity, the JST maintains the third-person nature of the pronouncement, just as in other KJV Mark passages.

In another verse, responding to the Pharisees seeking a sign from him, KJV Mark 8:12 has Jesus declare that no sign shall be given. The JST harmonizes his answer with similar passages in Matthew and Luke (Matthew 12:39; 16:4; Luke 11:29, adding a comment about the sign of Jonah) and then applies the sign to the "son of man."

> And he sighed deeply in his spirit, & ~~saith~~ **said**, Why doth this generation seek after a sign? Verily I say unto you, there shall no sign be given unto this generation**, save the sign of the Prophet Jonah; for as Jonah was three days & three nights in the Whales belly, so likewise shall the son of man be buried in the bowels of the Earth.** (JST Mark 8:12)

It would have been reasonable to have Jesus apply this added statement directly to himself, since Jesus was already speaking in the first person. But the JST maintains the Marcan pattern of attributing his declarations to the third-person son of man.

A third example from the same chapter is where Jesus declared that if any were ashamed of him and his words, the Son of man would also be ashamed of them when he came in glory (Mark 8:38). The abrupt shift from first person in the first sentence to third person in the rest of the verse is a bit jarring; it's easy to see from this how the disciples might not have fully understood that the Son of man was referring to Jesus himself. The JST adds substantially to the end of the verse, extending the notion of punishment on those who are ashamed of him but promising great blessings to those who sacrifice for Jesus and the gospel.

> Whosoever therefore shall be ashamed of me and of my words in this adulterous and sinful generation; of him also shall the Son of man be ashamed, when he cometh in the glory of his Father with the holy angels. **And they shall not have part in that resurrection when he cometh. For verily I say unto**

> **you, that he shall come; and he that layeth down his life for**
> **my sake and the gospel's, shall come with him, and shall be**
> **clothed with his glory, in the cloud, on the right hand of the**
> **Son of man.** (JST Mark 8:38)

JST Mark here emphasizes switching between first and third person—in fact, adding a new first person right in the middle of the sentence—with Jesus speaking of the disciples taking action directly in Jesus's behalf but promising blessings with the future and unidentified Son of man when he comes in glory.

In a JST change in Mark 3:28, a potential exception to the more veiled references in Mark might be seen, but a careful examination indicates otherwise. Here, a JST addition gives background to Jesus's statement about which sins can be forgiven. "**And then came certain men unto him, accusing him, saying, Why do ye receive sinners, seeing thou makest thyself the Son of God? But he answered them, & said . . .**" In this passage, "certain men," who are clearly confronting Jesus, claim that he is making himself the Son of God. This could imply that he said as much. But there is no record of Jesus saying that, so it cannot necessarily be concluded from this change that he made a direct statement about being the Son of God. Rather, as previous events in Mark are examined, the likely incident from which they would have derived their claim that he made himself a Son of God is found in Mark 2:5–7, where Jesus forgave a paralyzed man his sins. His declaration of forgiveness provoked a strong reaction from the scribes: "Who can forgive sins but God only?" That could naturally lead to a later charge that he was thus making himself the Son of God.

Looking at the other Gospels, the title "Son of man" is only added once each in JST Matthew (25:1) and JST Luke (21:28), even though both accounts also use the title for Jesus (Matthew thirty times and Luke twenty-five times).[8] KJV Mark uses Son of man only fourteen times, so the three additions in the JST are even more significant as a percentage, increasing Jesus's veiled self-declarative statements by 21 percent.

Higher Christology Examples

Mark's christological depiction of Jesus is typically considered the lowest of the four Gospels. That does not mean that Jesus is portrayed without divine characteristics or language that speaks to his divine identity; that is certainly present in Mark's writing. But there are elements in his narrative that can suggest he is more mortal, such as fatigue or hunger, expressions of surprise or wonder, a lack of knowledge, or even depression and insanity,[9] which Matthew and Luke generally edit out when they recount the same stories.

Though most of Mark's low Christology passages are left intact in the JST, a dramatic increase is found in JST Mark 14:32–33, which could be considered one of the top two mortal representations of Jesus, as he commences his experience in the Garden of Gethsemane.

KJV Mark 14:32–33	JST
And they came to a place which was named Gethsemane: and he saith to his disciples, Sit ye here, while I shall pray.	And they came to a place which was named Gethsemane, **which was a garden; and the disciples began to be sore amazed, and to be very heavy, and to complain in their hearts, wondering if this be the Messiah. And Jesus knowing their hearts** he **said** to his disciples, Sit **you** here while I shall pray.
And he taketh with him Peter and James and John, and began to be sore amazed, and to be very heavy;	And he taketh with him Peter and James and John, and **rebuked them,**

This significant christological change shifts the amazement and heaviness—which can be translated as "distressed"[10] and "troubled or in anxiety"[11]—from Jesus to the disciples. This takes one of the major Marcan low Christology passages and changes it to high, because Jesus not only avoids those emotions, but he knows their hearts. In the JST, Jesus perceived their emotions and questions about him supernaturally, then rebuked Peter, James, and John for their doubts while he went off to pray.[12]

Another change to a low Christology passage (Mark 7:24) takes a different approach, but still portrays Jesus with a divine characteristic.

KJV Mark 7:24	JST
And from thence he arose, and went into the borders of Tyre and Sidon, and entered into ~~an~~ house, and would ~~have~~ no man ~~know it~~: but he could not ~~be hid~~.	And from thence he arose, & went into the borders of Tyre & Sidon, & entered into a house, & would **that** no man **should come unto him.** But he could not **deny them, for he had compassion upon all men.**

KJV Mark describes Jesus as ready for some downtime and needing a break from the incessant crowds that surrounded him. But his attempt to get away is thwarted, and the crowds somehow find him. In JST Mark, Jesus is still desiring a break and wanting to be alone for a time, but instead as the crowds come, he is motivated by love and compassion to minister to them, even as it greatly inconveniences him physically. This selfless act raises the Christology of the passage, showing Jesus as making his physical needs subservient to the demands of his calling. It also enhances the transition to the next story about the Syrophenician woman petitioning a blessing from Jesus for her daughter by putting her request in the context of a tired Jesus who nevertheless has compassion and expends what energy he has left on others, including a gentile woman.

A less dramatic but still interesting elevation of Christology that doesn't stem from a low starting point is found in a JST change in Jesus's teaching about humility and surrendering one's will to God, in Mark 9:37.

KJV Mark 9:37	JST
Whosoever shall ~~receive one~~ of ~~such~~ children ~~in my name~~, receiveth me: and whosoever shall receive me, receiveth not me, but him that sent me.	Whosoever shall **humble himself like one** of **these** children, **and** receiveth me, **ye shall receive them in my name.** And whosoever shall receive me, receiveth not me **only,** but him that sent me, **even the father.**

Two changes in the verse elevate the Christology. First, the Greek verb translated "receive" is *dechomai*, which has the meaning of showing hospitality and welcoming.[13] Thus the children are to be welcomed in Jesus's name, which applies authority to the action. Second, the KJV says that this action is equivalent to receiving Jesus and "him that sent [him]," but who sent him is not specified. JST Mark makes explicit who sent Jesus—"the father"—ascribing divine authority to Jesus's actions.

Low Christology

Only one passage seems to have the potential to add to a low Christology in JST Mark, and it is not a strong case. In Mark 8:17, as the disciples were sailing on the lake with Jesus, they discussed something Jesus had said about "the leaven of the Pharisees." In typical Marcan fashion, the disciples misunderstood Jesus's words and believed he said this "because we have no bread" in the ship. In the KJV, Jesus responded after he "knew it," though the text doesn't state how he knew the topic of their conversation; the implication could be that he knew it by divine means. The JST language leans more toward

Jesus merely overhearing them, a more mortal result: "And when **they said this among themselves,** Jesus knew it." Still, either passage could be interpreted as either divinely perceiving or merely overhearing, so it's difficult to assign a christological impact either way.

In summary, Joseph Smith's work on Mark shows a sensitivity to two of the mortal portrayals of Jesus in the book. In Mark 14:32–33, mortal weakness is shifted from Jesus to the disciples, and Jesus's ability to perceive their thoughts and feelings is added. In Mark 7:24, the Prophet changed the passage to portray divine attributes even while retaining the display of Jesus's physical needs. The overall changes still maintain Mark's style, rather than harmonizing it with John or even the other Synoptics, which have higher Christology. One significant enhancement to Mark's stylistic approach is to add three new Son of man passages, which Mark has Jesus use when speaking of his own mission and purpose in a third-person voice.

Matthew

No JST changes in Matthew lower the Christology of the book, but many of them augment it in ways that consistently align with Matthew's pattern and presentation. This section examines two categories of JST changes that enrich the Christology of Matthew while maintaining his tone and approach.

Jesus as the Fulfillment of the Old Testament

Matthew quotes extensively from the Old Testament (often using the Greek Septuagint version instead of the Hebrew text) to demonstrate that Jesus was the fulfillment of prophetic writings, with fourteen fulfillment, or formula, citations (e.g., "that it might be fulfilled which was spoken of the Lord by the prophet," Matthew 1:22) and dozens of other scriptures quoted or paraphrased without direct attribution.[14] It's significant, then, that in JST Matthew, there are nine additional or enhanced formula citations,[15] enlarging this aspect of Matthew's Christology.[16]

- 1:16 "Of whom was born Jesus, **As the Prophets have written**, who is called Christ"
- 1:18 "Now, **as it is written,** the birth of Jesus Christ was on this wise"
- 1:22 "Now all this ~~was done~~ **took place**, that ~~it~~ **all things** might be fulfilled, which was spoken of the Lord, by the Prophets"
- 4:19 "And he ~~saith~~ **said** unto them, **I am he of whom it is written by the Prophets;** follow me"
- 11:3 "Art thou he **of whom it is written in the prophets** that should come, or do we look for an other?"
- 11:13 "For all the Prophets & the law prophecied, **that it should be thus** untill John. **Yea, as many as have prophecied, have foretold of these days.**"
- 13:35 "That it might be fulfilled which was spoken by the ~~people~~ **prophets**"
- 23:39 "**You** shall not see me hence forth, **& know that I am he of whom it is written by the Prophets, until you** shall say, Blessed is he **who** cometh in the name of the Lord"
- 27:11 "And Jesus said unto him, Thou sayest **truly, for thus it is written of me.**"

Mark, Luke, and John also use similar formula citations but not nearly as frequently as Matthew. In the JST, there are two additional such citations in Mark (7:9, 10), three in Luke (3:4; 14:35; 16:16), and only one in John (3:18). Thus, this type of JST change aligns with the original authors' patterns of the use of formula citations.

Divine Authority

Matthew portrays Jesus as having divine authority, using titles such as the Son of God (eight times) and Lord (thirty-nine times applying to Jesus). But he also portrays Jesus's authority from God in other ways. As God did with Moses, Jesus brought people up to the mount and gave them a new law. He is "God with us" when he is born (Matthew 1:23) and until the end of time (Matthew 28:20), who will save his people from their sins. Jesus is the recipient of worship that is only due to God, and he is the one to whom all power is given and who will judge, both in heaven and on earth.[17] This concept of divine authority is substantially enhanced by JST changes, including those below.

Preparation for ministry. At the end of the infancy narrative of Matthew 2 and before the appearance of John the Baptist in chapter 3 is a remarkable addition about Jesus growing up.

> **And it came to pass, that Jesus grew up with his brethren, & waxed strong, & waited upon the Lord for the time of his ministery to come. And he served under his father, & he spake not as other men, neither could he be taught; for he needed not that any man should teach him. And after many years, the hour of his ministery drew nigh.**

Jesus patiently "waited upon the Lord" for the right time to start his ministry. The phrase, "he served under his father" is intriguing, as from the text it cannot be determined if the person referenced is his (step)father, Joseph, or his Father in heaven. If the former, it demonstrates patient preparation for an inevitable ministry under the direction of a mortal mentor; if the latter, it is an additional witness of Jesus acting fully under the authority of God. Given the other content of the addition, the latter interpretation seems likely.

One of the most powerful christological changes in the JST is also in this verse: "He spake not as other men, neither could he be taught; for he needed not that any man should teach him." Throughout the Old Testament, there are records of God teaching his people and people seeking to be taught by the Lord. Moses was promised that he would be taught what to do (Exodus 4:15) and then given the Lord's commandments to teach to Israel (Exodus 18:10; 24:12). Those teachings were passed on to future generations because they came from God (Deuteronomy 4:10; 6:7; 11:19). Numerous psalms implore the Lord to "teach me thy paths" (Psalm 25:4) and "teach me thy way,

O Lord" (Psalm 27:11; 86:11). And Isaiah and Micah proclaim the great day when people will to go the mountain of the Lord, "and he will teach us of his ways" (Isaiah 2:3; Micah 4:2). God himself could not be taught by man (Job 21:22), nor could the power of God's teaching be exceeded (Job 36:22).

In Jesus's ministry, he was consistently a teacher, instructing large crowds, synagogue attendees, and smaller, private groups of disciples. On multiple occasions, the power, authority, and uniqueness of his teaching was noted (Matthew 7:29; Mark 1:22, 27; 6:2; Luke 4:36; 20:2; John 3:2), and his enemies questioned his authority to teach such things (Matthew 21:23; Mark 11:28; John 9:34). But when interrogated by Jewish leaders as to the source of his teaching and authority, Jesus declined to answer (Matthew 21:24; Mark 11:33; Luke 20:8).

In the addition cited above, JST Matthew proclaims that Jesus could not be taught by other men, nor was it needed. Instead, the source of his wisdom and knowledge and later his teaching was divine, as he served under his Father. This matches the language of a promise in 1 John 2:27 that those who follow Christ have an "anointing" received of God, and when that abides in them, "ye need not that any man teach you," because "the same anointing teacheth you of all things, and is truth." The anointing referred to is likely the gift of the Holy Ghost,[18] which Joseph Smith had learned not long before working on his translation of Matthew was "the Comforter, which showeth all things, and teacheth the peaceable things of the kingdom" (D&C 39:6; see also John 14:26). Thus this JST addition can be interpreted to say that Jesus was fully taught and tutored by the Holy Spirit and thus did not need any human teaching, for he had full access to knowledge from above (John 8:23). It does not mean that he did not learn and progress in his mortal experience (as described in D&C 93:10–14), but rather that his progression was not based on mortal understanding or learning. This is a significant addition to Matthew's Christology.

Showing his divine authority. Once Jesus began his ministry, he quickly exhibited divine authority, such as when he got news about

John being imprisoned (Matthew 4:12): "**And** now Jesus **knew** that John was cast into prison, **and he sent angels, and behold, they came & ministered unto him.**" This is the only mention of Jesus sending angels during his mortal ministry, demonstrating both his personal concern for John and his authority to command messengers from heaven. It is worth nothing that in Matthew 4:11, the angels were sent to minister to Jesus at the end of his temptations in the wilderness, but the JST deletes that reference to angels and essentially moves it to the next verse, where Jesus instead sends them to John. In other words, in the JST, Jesus forgoes the blessings of the angels and instead commands that blessing to be given to his forerunner.

Concerning the sending of angels, throughout the scriptures, only God commands and sends angels to teach and bless and sometimes destroy (Genesis 24:7; Exodus 23:20; 32:34; Numbers 20:16; 1 Chronicles 21:27; 2 Chronicles 32:21; Daniel 6:22; Luke 1:19, 26; D&C 38:12). Once sent with authority from above, angels then command men in God's behalf (Judges 2:4; 1 Kings 13:18; Acts 8:26; 1 Nephi 3:29; Helaman 14:9; Alma 9:21). Jesus taught that he had authority to send angels and would do so at a future time (Matthew 13:41; 24:31; Mark 13:27), thus attributing to himself a distinctive divine privilege to command these heavenly beings, which this unique JST change demonstrates was a power he also exercised in his mortal life.

Several other JST Matthew changes declare that Jesus's authority was from God.

- 7:28–29 "the people were astonished at his doctrine; for he taught them as one having authority **from God,** & not as **having authority from** the Scribes."
- 23:10 "Neither be ye called, **Master;** for one is your master, even ~~him~~ **he whom your Heavenly father sent, which is** Christ; **for he hath sent him among you, that ye might have life.**"

+ 12:50 "**I go my way for my father hath sent me, and** whosoever shall do the will of my father . . ."

On other occasions, JST Matthew brings out Jesus's authority by expressing his sanction to judge by virtue of his position in the eternal heavens.

+ 7:22 "**For the day soon cometh, that men shall come before me to Judge ment, to be Judged according to their works.**"
+ 25:34 "**And he shall sit upon his throne, & the twelve apostles with him.**"

In responding to a question from the Pharisees in Matthew 9, Jesus used the metaphor of putting a piece of new cloth on an old garment. However, JST Matthew 9:16 precedes that answer with a substantial addition that has the Pharisees asking Jesus about baptism and obedience to the law of Moses, and Jesus using their question to declare premortal divine authority for himself and to identify himself with the great Jehovah, who spoke to Moses and gave him the law.

> **Then said the Pharicees unto him, Why will ye not receive us with our baptism, seing we keep the whole law? But Jesus said unto them, Ye keep not the law. If ye had kept the law, ye would have received me; for I am he that gave the law. I receive not you with your baptism, because it profiteth you nothing.**

Finally, Jesus spent his life doing the will of the Father, who gave him that authority. In JST Matthew, that effort culminates on the cross in a final expression of total submission, with an added saying not in KJV Matthew 27:50.

> Jesus, when he had cried again with a loud voice, **saying, Father, it is finished; thy will is done,** yielded up the ghost.

KJV John 19:30 also records that Jesus said, "It is finished," but the statement on the cross of God's will being done is unique in all four Gospels. It reflects back to Jesus's prayer in Gethsemane that he would do the Father's will (Matthew 26:42). Thus the passion narrative in Matthew is bracketed at both ends by Jesus committing to do the Father's will and then stating that he had indeed done it; Jesus's absolute obedience to the Father was ultimately the source of his authority (Mosiah 3:18–19).

Luke

The majority of JST changes in Luke could be described as Joseph Smith working like a traditional translator or at least an expert editor; he is updating archaic language, reworking phrases for clarity, adjusting grammar, clarifying pronouns, and providing alternate word choices. There are very few changes that impact Christology, but those made are significant to Luke's presentation of Jesus.[19]

Servant Songs and John the Baptist

One of the characteristics of Luke's Christology is an emphasis on several chapters in Isaiah, often called the "servant songs," including verses from Isaiah 42, 50, and 53.[20] While no JST changes quote from additional servant song passages, there is an addition in John the Baptist's teaching where he speaks of his own mission using Isaiah 40:3–5. Isaiah 40 is the introductory chapter for the entire section that includes all of the servant songs, and Luke uses this passage to declare a number of themes in his Gospel and Acts, including the ministry of the apostles, taking the gospel to the gentiles, the restoration of Israel, and the power of God.

In the JST, an extensive quotation is added in the middle of the Isaiah passage, which quotes "the book of the prophets" and builds on many of Luke's themes of Jesus's ministry.

As it is written in the book of the prophet **Esais; and these are the words** saying the voice of one crying in the willderness, prepare ye the way of the Lord, and make his paths straight. **For behold, and lo, he shall come as it is written in the book of the prophets, to take away the the [sic] sins of the world, and to bring salvation unto the heathen nations; togather together those who are lost, which are of the sheep fold of Israel; yea, even her dispersed and afflicted; and also to prepare the away, and make possable the preaching of the Gospel unto the gentiles. and to be a light unto all who sit in darkness, unto the uttermost parts of the earth; to bring to pass the resurection from the dead, and to asend upon high, to dwell on the right hand of the Father, untils the fulness of time, and the law and the testimony shall be sealed, and the keys of the kingdom shall be delivered up again unto the Father; to administer justice unto all; to come down in judgement upon all, and to convince all the ungodly of their ungodly deeds, which they have committed; and all this in the day that he shall come, for it is a day of power.** (JST Luke 3:4)

The scripture quoted is not found in the Old Testament (KJV or JST) but does have similar language to many existing Old Testament passages.[21] This inspired addition picks up on several of the themes in KJV Luke 3:4–6 (quoting Isaiah 40:3–5) and some additional Lucan themes, especially considering the extension of his Gospel in the book of Acts, including revealing Jesus as

- bringing salvation to all, including the "heathen nations" and "the gentiles";
- gathering "those who are lost" of the house of Israel, who are "dispersed and afflicted";
- being a light unto those in darkness;
- bringing to pass the resurrection;

- ascending on high and taking his place on the right hand of the Father;
- being the one who will "administer justice unto all"; and
- coming in "a day of power" at the Second Coming.

This broad declaration by John the Baptist of Jesus's mission and purpose is a high christological addition that launches Luke's story of Jesus in a powerful way, for both Luke and Acts.

Jesus's Nature

Noted above was the addition of information about Jesus's preparation at the end of Matthew 2. Luke likewise has a less lengthy but informative JST change related to Jesus's preparation period that adds to our understanding of this time in his life. The story of Jesus in the temple at the age of twelve is well known (Luke 2:41–52). In the KJV, Mary and Joseph find Jesus in the temple hearing the "doctors" there and asking questions. The JST change is subtle but significant in its description of Jesus as one who has divine knowledge.

> and it came to pass, after three days they found him in the Temple, sitting in the midst of the Doctors, ~~both hearing them and asking them questions~~ **and they were** hearing **him**, and asking **him** questions. (JST Luke 2:46)

As the JST manuscript demonstrates, the scribe first wrote the verse exactly as in the KJV and nothing else, then immediately crossed out the last phrase of the verse and wrote the change,[22] which is a reversal of the KJV: the doctors were hearing Jesus and querying him. Their reaction in the next verse is unchanged in the JST: "All who heard him were astonished at his understanding and answers" (Luke 2:47). While the change in verse 46 does serve to bring the two verses into better alignment,[23] the more profound impact on Luke's Christology is that Jesus at twelve was exhibiting what Matthew said, that "he needed not that any man should teach him" (JST Matthew 2:23) but that he instead was the teacher.

A second passage that speaks to Jesus's godliness is Luke 12:9–10, which in the KJV is a general statement that those who deny Jesus shall likewise be denied before angels. The JST change gives the reason Jesus made the statement and applies it very specifically to his disciples.

> but he ~~that~~ **who** denyeth me before men, shall be denied before the angels of God. ~~and whosoever shall speak~~ **Now his disciples knew that he said this, because they had spoken evil against him before the people; for they were affraid to confess him before men. And they reasoned among themselves, saying,** ~~he~~ **He knoweth our hearts, and he speaketh to our condemnation, and we shall not be forgiven.** (JST Luke 12:9)

The words struck through in the JST are the first words of verse 10; the scribe started to write that verse as is but was interrupted before the phrase was even finished and immediately wrote new text that was inserted between the verses. In the addition, the disciples had "spoken evil" against Jesus, which is then qualified as "they were affraid to confess him before men." They had evidently done this out of earshot of Jesus, so they took his preceding words about denying him as a divine recognition of what was in their hearts and feared not only that he was condemning them but that forgiveness might not be possible. Their reasoning is an interesting conflict of high (Jesus knows their hearts) and low Christology (Jesus may not forgive them, a potentially mortal reaction on his part, if true). However, verse 10 resolves their concern and ends up making the whole passage high.

> **But he answered them, and** **said unto them,** Whosoever shall speak a word against the son of man, **and repenteth,** it shall be forgiven him; but unto him ~~that~~ **who** blasphemeth against the holy Ghost, it shall not be forgiven **him.** (JST Luke 12:10)

Jesus assured his fearful disciples that their sin was forgivable upon repentance.[24] Though not stated here, two passages in Luke point to Jesus's ability to forgive sins, including the second unique to Luke, emphasizing that divine ability (Luke 5:20–24; 7:47–49). This passage thus provides a third example of Jesus demonstrating the power and authority to forgive sins, and only in JST Luke.

John

John has the highest Christology of the four Gospels, taking the christological themes in the other three and greatly developing them in length and depth. Since the JST work results in higher Christology in the Synoptic Gospels, the already high Christology of John may have required fewer changes. Indeed, JST John includes very few christological changes, and not many of significance.[25] One is discussed here because the KJV passages are very well known while the JST modifications are not.

John 1 is a beautiful, lyrical opening to the book that takes the reader back to "the beginning," a clear reference to Genesis 1:1 and the creation of the world. John's premise is that "the Word" was there from the beginning, both with God and as God himself. He created everything, life is in him, and he is the light of men that shines in darkness. The same Word—of whom John testified—came to earth but was not known by the world, though he was its creator.

The JST makes several changes in this chapter; the theme of the changes is making the identification of "the Word" unambiguous: he is "the Son of God."

KJV John 1:1, 7, 10, 15, 16	JST
In the beginning was the Word, and the Word was with God, and the ~~Word~~ was God.	In the begining was the **gospel preached through the son. And the gospel was the** word, and the word was with **the Son, and the son was with** God, and the **Son** was **of** God.
The same came for a witness, to bear witness of the Light, ~~that~~ all *men* through him might believe.	The same came **into the world** for a wittness, to bear wittness of the light, **to bear record of the gospel through the son, unto all, that** through him **men** might beleive.
He was in the world, and the world was made by him, and the world knew him not.	**Even the Son of God.** He **who** was in the world, and the world was made by him, and the world knew him not.
John bare witness of him, and cried, saying, This ~~was~~ he of whom I spake, He ~~that~~ cometh after me is preferred before me: for he was before me.	John bear wittness of him, and cried, saying; This is he of whom I spake; he **who** cometh after me, is prefered before me; for he was before me. **For in the begining was the word, even the son, who is made flesh, and sent unto us by the will of the Father.**
And of his fulness have all we received, and grace ~~for grace~~.	And **as many as beleive on his name shall receive** of his fullness. **And of his fullness** have all we received, **even imortality** and eternal life, through his grace.

JST John 1 raises the Christology of this already high passage through its multiple and unambiguous designations of Jesus as Son of God, declaring that he is "sent unto us by the will of the Father" and that his promised "fullness" is "imortality and eternal life" to mankind, which can only come "through his grace."

In the Gospel of John, the phrase "the Word" is only found in John 1, and verses 14–18 transition that title to Jesus, but the changes in JST John 1 draw out that transition across the entire section, intermingling "the Word" and "the Son" in a beautiful, expressive work that confirms that Jesus was there from the beginning and came to earth by the will of the Father so all people might have immortality and eternal life through his grace, which is wrought by his selfless atoning sacrifice. There may perhaps be no high Christology passage in all the Gospels that more thoroughly describes Jesus's entire mission.

Conclusion

Each of the four Gospels displays unique information about Jesus Christ and his purpose. Their individual characteristics, stories, and language represent their christological approach. Joseph Smith made a number of changes in the JST of these books that impact Christology. He showed sensitivity to low Christology passages, giving them close attention and often elevating Jesus's portrayal in them. He modified other verses to speak of Christ's nature, though such a topic wasn't initially in the verse in the KJV. This type of high Christology approach would be natural to him, given that it is the tone of the Book of Mormon and many of the revelations in the Doctrine and Covenants, as well as the early chapters of Genesis, which he translated before starting his work on the New Testament.

However, tempering his general raising of Christology, the changes the Prophet made are in line with the approach and style of each author in telling the story of Jesus and teaching about his nature. The individual voice and characteristics of each Gospel author are maintained, rather than all being raised to a uniform, single, high Christology voice. Such an effort speaks to both the inspiration and careful study of Joseph Smith in much of the work he did on the Bible, especially when it came to the identity of Jesus Christ.

DAVID A. LeFEVRE *is an independent scholar in the Seattle, Washington, area.*

Appendix: A Sample of Additional JST Changes That Impact Christology by Topic

Power over the Devils, Sickness, and Sin

+ **Matthew 4:5** not only is his purpose to "be with" and commune with God (JST Matthew 4:1–2), but Spirit carries him around, not the devil (also Matthew 4:8)
+ **Matthew 4:23** people are healed because they believed on his name
+ **Matthew 5:2** those who believe on Jesus will receive a remission of their sins
+ **Matthew 12:31** forgiveness to those who receive him and repent

Commissions Others to Preach His Message

+ **Matthew 5:2** "Blessed are they who believe on your words"
+ **Matthew 6:25** "Go ye into the world teaching"
+ **Matthew 7:1** the words Jesus taught his disciples to teach others

- Matthew 7:4 "Go thou and say unto them, you are children of corruption"
- Matthew 7:6 "Go ye into the world, saying repent"

Priesthood

- Luke 8:1 the twelve were ordained by Jesus (a physical act not mentioned elsewhere, showing Jesus's authority in the priesthood)
- Luke 9:25 to be saved, we must receive him "whom God hath ordained," both clarifying Jesus's role in our salvation and the source of his authority (ties back to 8:1)

Salvation

- Matthew 19:13 Jesus said children will be saved (disciples quoting Jesus)
- Luke 9:34 not just lose your life to save it, but lose it for Jesus's sake
- Luke 11:41 keep Jesus's commandments and "your inward parts" will be clean
- John 1:18 no man can be saved except through Jesus
- John 3:36 those who believe on Jesus will receive of his fullness
- John 5:29 all will be judged by the Son of man

Jesus's Identity

- Matthew 21:46 "I am the stone," "the head of the corner"
- Mark 14:8 woman's anointing will be remembered in generations to come
- Luke 9:31 speaks not just of his death, but "also his resurrection."

- **Luke 14:33** Moses and prophets testified of Christ, which was their purpose; Jesus is sent to give life
- **Luke 16:17** Jesus was sent by the Father to fulfill the law
- **Luke 21:25, 28, 36** makes clear that the signs Jesus is discussing relate to the Second Coming
- **John 3:34** Jesus has a fullness of the Spirit given him by God
- **John 5:30** Jesus does the will of the Father only, unable to anything of his own will
- **John 6:44** the Father bears record of Jesus, and who does the Father's will will be raised up by Jesus in the resurrection of the just

Notes

1. Alan J. Spence, *Christology: A Guide for the Perplexed* (London: Bloomsbury, 2015), chap. 1, Kindle.

2. For simplicity, this paper consistently refers to the work as the Joseph Smith Translation, or JST, though it can also rightly be called the New Translation (e.g., D&C 124:89). All JST quotations herein are from New Testament Manuscript 2 on the Joseph Smith Papers website (JosephSmithPapers.org/paper-summary/new-testament-revision-2), unless otherwise noted. Original spelling and punctuation are retained, though later insertions, marked in the manuscripts with brackets, are included without indication. JST changes when compared to the KJV are highlighted in bold text, whether in side-by-side comparisons (when there are KJV deletions) or singly (when the JST change is a pure addition or there are no KJV deletions). The interested reader is encouraged to also consult transcriptions of the manuscripts, available in printed form, in Scott H. Faulring, Kent P. Jackson, and Robert J. Matthews, *Joseph Smith's New Translation of the Bible: Original Manuscripts* (Provo, UT: Religious

Studies Center, 2004). See also Thomas A. Wayment, *The Complete Joseph Smith Translation of the New Testament* (Salt Lake City: Deseret Book, 2005), which presents the KJV and JST side by side with changes indicated in bold, though Wayment has additionally edited the JST text to standardize spelling and grammar.

3.   The maintenance of separate Gospel personalities in JST changes has been discussed in Robert L. Millet, "The JST and the Synoptic Gospels: Literary Style," in *The Joseph Smith Translation: The Restoration of Plain and Precious Truths*, ed. Monte S. Nyman and Robert L. Millet (Provo, UT: Religious Studies Center, 1985), 147–62.

4.   Various classifications of JST changes have been proposed. Faulring, Jackson, and Matthews proposed five types: (1) restoration of original text, (2) restoration of original words or actions never recorded, (3) editing to improve modern understanding, (4) editing to harmonize with other scriptures or revelations, and (5) changes to teach modern readers. They acknowledge that "it is difficult to know with certainty the nature or origin of any particular change" (Faulring, Jackson, and Matthews, *Joseph Smith's New Translation*, 8–10). In an interesting study, one scholar analyzed several examples of biblical variants and JST changes, concluding that the restoration element could not generally be supported textually but that "assimilation to better known wording, harmonization of contradictions, and doctrinal clarification of problematic texts" were the best explanations for most JST changes. Kevin L Barney, "The Joseph Smith Translation and Ancient Texts of the Bible," *Dialogue* 19, no. 3 (1987): 100. I have argued that the most significant reason for the JST effort was as a doctrinal and leadership tutorial for Joseph Smith. David A. LeFevre, "The Education of a Prophet: The Role of the New Translation of the Bible in the Life of Joseph Smith," in *Foundations of the Restoration: The 45th Annual Brigham Young University Sidney B. Sperry Symposium*, ed. Craig James Ostler, Michael Hubbard MacKay, and Barbara Morgan Gardner (Provo, UT: Religious Studies Center, 2016), 99–120, which Robert Matthews also wrote of as the ultimate purpose of the work. Robert J. Matthews, *"A Plainer Translation": Joseph Smith's Translation of the Bible, A History and Commentary* (Provo, UT: Brigham Young University Press, 1975), 53–54.

5. This is the thrust of Doctrine and Covenants 9:7–9—that to "study it out in your mind" is to exert personal, intellectual effort on an issue and to "ask if it be right" through prayer and revelation. It was perhaps the combination of the two that produced the translation of the Book of Mormon, which D&C 9 may reference, but especially Joseph's other translations and revelations, including the JST.

6. Though not addressed in the text of her commentary, see an excellent study on JST changes in Mark enhancing that Gospel's unique style in appendix 9, "The Joseph Smith Translation," in Julie M. Smith, *The Gospel of Mark* (Provo, UT: BYU Studies, forthcoming). This book also explores in great detail the relationship between the Synoptics, especially the influence of Mark on Matthew and Luke.

7. For a valuable discussion on Son of man references in Mark and the other Gospels, see Larry W. Hurtado, *Lord Jesus Christ: Devotion to Jesus in Earliest Christianity* (Grand Rapids, MI: Eerdmans, 2003), 283–306.

8. There is another addition of Son of man in Matthew 26:50, but only in the first New Testament manuscript; the phrase was not retained in the second translation of that chapter in New Testament 2; see Wayment, *The Complete Joseph Smith Translation of the New Testament*, 84; Kent P. Jackson and Peter M. Jasinski, "The Process of Inspired Translation: Two Passages Translated Twice in the Joseph Smith Translation of the Bible," *BYU Studies* 42, no. 2 (2003): 35–64.

9. Examples include Mark 3:5 and 10:14, where Jesus is angry; 3:21, where his family believes he is insane; 11:12, where he is hungry; 13:32, where he doesn't know the day or hour of his own future coming; and 14:33–34, where he is amazed and depressed.

10. Frederick William Danker, *A Greek-English Lexicon of the New Testament and Other Early Christian Literature*, 3rd ed. (Chicago: University of Chicago Press, 2000), s.v. "ekthambeō."

11. Danker, *Greek-English Lexicon of the New Testament*, s.v. "adēmoneō."

12. Julie Smith identifies ten instances where the disciples are portrayed more negatively in JST Mark than in KJV Mark; see Smith, *Gospel of Mark*, appendix 9.

13. Danker, *Greek-English Lexicon of the New Testament*, 221; Timothy Friberg, Barbara Friberg, Neva F. Miller, *Analytical Lexicon of the Greek New Testament* (Victoria, BC: Trafford, 2005), 6107; "dechomai" in Bibleworks 10.

14. Robert L. Millet, "The Testimony of Matthew," in *Studies in Scripture, Volume Five: The Gospels*, ed. Kent P. Jackson and Robert L. Millet (Salt Lake City: Deseret Book, 1986), 55–57; for a full list, see Craig Blomberg, "Matthew," in *Commentary on the New Testament Use of the Old Testament*, ed. G. K. Beale and D. A. Carson (Grand Rapids, MI: Baker Academic, 2007), 1–109.

15. With potentially a tenth one, though the formula isn't quite the same. When Herod heard of the child who the wise men said was the new king, he asked his scribes in the JST, "Where is the place that is written of by the Prophets in which christ should be born?" The king sought an answer from the scriptures.

16. None of these JST additions quote scriptures directly but affirm that prophets have spoken of the event being presented. Two merely add emphasis to the citation by changing the singular "prophet" to the plural "prophets."

17. Joel B. Green, ed., *Dictionary of Jesus and the Gospels* (Downers Grove, IL: IVP Academic, 2013), s.v. "Christology," Kindle.

18. Richard Neitzel Holzapfel and Thomas A. Wayment, *Making Sense of the New Testament* (Salt Lake City: Deseret Book, 2010), 483; also Raymond E. Brown, *An Introduction to the New Testament* (New York: Doubleday, 1997), 386.

19. See S. Kent Brown, *The Testimony of Luke* (Provo, UT: BYU Studies, 2015). This in-depth study of the Gospel incorporates insight about JST changes throughout the commentary.

20. John N. Oswalt, *The Book of Isaiah: Chapters 40–66* (Grand Rapids, MI: Eerdmans, 1998), 107–9; Tremper Longman III and David E. Garland, eds., *The Expositor's Bible Commentary, Vol. 6, Proverbs—Isaiah* (Grand Rapids, MI: Zondervan, 2008), 456–58.

21. Compare Psalm 98:2; Isaiah 9:2; Psalm 68:18; Isaiah 41:13; Isaiah 8:16; Psalm 110:3.

22. This is similar to the Prophet's experience with John 5:29, where they wrote the verse just as it is in the KJV, and then had it "given" unto them to change, which "caused [them] to marvel, for it was given unto us of the Spirit" (D&C 76:15–18). This change follows the same pattern of writing the KJV and then immediately changing it, which potentially means it was a similar experience of inspiration to change just a few words with significant impact.

23. Kent Brown notes that the JST "changes the scene to accord with the next verse [v. 47] so that it is Jesus who is the teacher, becoming a Rabbi of sorts" (Brown, *Testimony of Luke*, 165).

24. As Brown wrote, "This expressed fear [of not being forgiven], that underlies their response to Jesus's words about denying him, opens the occasion for Jesus then to affirm" forgiveness (Brown, *Testimony of Luke*, 609).

25. It's also significant to the number of changes in John that the first five chapters have dramatically more JST changes than the rest of the book. This is because starting at John 6, Joseph Smith changed the way his scribes recorded the Bible translation results. Instead of writing out every word of every verse as they had been doing since the start of the effort in June 1830, even if there was no change from the KJV, from John 6 forward they only wrote changes in the manuscript and indicated the placement of the changes with marks in Joseph's Bible. (Though the exact date of the method change is not known, Doctrine and Covenants 76 was recorded on 16 February 1832, tied to the translation of John 5:29, near the end of that chapter. John 6 was likely done very shortly after that date, as Joseph and his scribe for this part of the text, Sidney Rigdon, were heavily engaged in the work at this time.) The result is that there are far fewer changes of a more pedantic nature—grammar, word choice or order, modernization, and the like. The changes captured going forward are generally more significant doctrinally or textually, which is why the number decreases so dramatically not only for John but for the rest of the New Testament and the Old Testament when they return to that work in July 1832. See the letter to William W. Phelps dated 31 July 1832, wherein the Prophet wrote, "We have finished the translation of the New testament great and marvilous glorious things are revealed, we are making rapid strides in the old

book"; Matthew C. Godfrey, Mark Ashurst-McGee, Grant Underwood, Robert J. Woodford, and William G. Hartley, eds., *Documents, Volume 2: July 1831–January 1833*, vol. 2 of the Documents series of *The Joseph Smith Papers*, ed. Dean C. Jessee, Ronald K. Esplin, Richard Lyman Bushman, and Matthew J. Grow (Salt Lake City: Church Historian's Press, 2013), 267. The "old book" is the Old Testament, showing that by the end of July they had completed the work through the end of the New Testament and were back in Genesis 24 working on the Old Testament, where they had left off in March 1831; see D&C 45:60–62.

Appendix
Principal Christological Titles
in the New Testament

The frequencies of the most important titles for Jesus in the New Testament are suggestive of their relative importance for how New Testament authors understood his identity, roles, and functions. They are also interesting given that common patterns in Latter-day Saint parlance—such as a pronounced preference for referring to Jesus as "the Savior" or "the Redeemer" rather than by his personal name—seem to be a result of the usage of these titles in Restoration scripture rather than the pattern in the New Testament.

The following chart presents seven names and titles in order of their frequency in the New Testament. The Gospels, which recount the mortal ministry of Jesus Christ, overwhelming refer to the Lord by his given name "Jesus" (see boldface 625). Note, however, the pronounced Pauline preference for "Christ" (406) and to a lesser extent "Lord" (276). Notice also that the Johannine corpus—in this case the Gospel of John (29) and 1 John (23)—produces the greatest numbers of references for "Son of God" and the only New Testament references to "Only Begotten" (see the entry below for the translation of *monogenēs*).

	Jesus	Lord[a]	Christ	Son of God	Savior	Only Begotten	Redeemer[b]
Gospels							
Matthew	172	48	15	15			
Mark	97	19	8	7			
Luke	100	83	16	13	2		
John	256	43	21	**29**	1	4	
Gospels total	**625**	193	60	64	3	4	0
Acts	68	109	31	7	2	0	0
Pauline Letters							
Romans	38	45	68	6			
1 Corinthians	27	67	69	2			
2 Corinthians	20	29	49	1			
Galatians	17	6	41	4			
Ephesians	21	25	46	1	1		
Philippians	22	15	38		1		
Colossians	8	13	26				
1 Thessalonians	17	25	14	1			

	Jesus	Lord	Christ	Son of God	Savior	Only Begotten	Redeemer
2 Thessalonians	12	19	13				
1 Timothy	14	8	16				
2 Timothy	14	17	15		1		
Titus	4	1	4		3		
Philemon	7	6	7				
Pauline total	221	276	406	15	6	0	0
Hebrews	14	17	13	12			
James	2	15	2				
1 Peter	11	6	21	1			
2 Peter	9	15	8		5		
1 John	12		10	23	1	1	
2 John	2	1	4	2			
3 John							
Jude	5	7	5				
Revelation	14	23	11	1			
	69	84	74	40	6	1	0
New Testament total[c]	983	662	571	125	17	5	0

	Jesus	Lord	Christ	Son of God	Savior	Only Begotten	Redeemer
Book of Mormon	187	1573	388	59	12	9	41
Doctrine and Covenants	103	735	132	27	21	13	22
Pearl of Great Price	13	202	16	6	6	25	1
Restoration scripture	303	2510	536	92	39	47	64

a. All New Testament occurrences of "Lord" in this chart refer to Jesus Christ (or, by extension, to deity more generally) and do not include instances in which the term is used for a temporal master, owner, teacher, or ruler.

b. For details on the surprising absence of the title "Redeemer" in the New Testament, see the entry below.

c. New Testament statistics are by physical count.

The following entries provide detailed breakdowns for these and other christological titles in the New Testament arranged alphabetically.

Christ (571)

Literally the Greek *christos*, like the Hebrew *māšîaḥ*, means "the anointed one." Early Israelite kings and priests were regularly anointed, and in some instances prophets were as well (e.g., Elisha in 1 Kings 19:16). In the intertestamental period, various messianic expectations arose, usually centering in a looked-for Davidic king or sometimes a legitimate Aaronide priest who would restore the kingdom and right worship. Early Christians saw Jesus as the Messiah or chosen one, increasingly in a spiritually salvific sense but also linked with actual kingship in connection with his promised eschatological return, judgment, and rule.

"Christ" appears in the New Testament 571 times. Particularly in the Gospels, it serves as a title. Sometimes it functions as an attributive title in the formulation "Christ Jesus," but most often in the rest of the New Testament it serves as part of the proper name "Jesus Christ," or, frequently, as a name by itself.

CHRIST USED AS A TITLE, USUALLY AS A PREDICATE AS IN "JESUS IS THE CHRIST" (48)

Matthew (9): 1:16; 2:4; 16:16, 20; 22:42; 26:63, 68; 27:17, 22

Mark (4): 8:9; 13:6, 21; 14:61

Luke (13): 2:26; 3:15; 4:41 (2x); 9:20; 20:41; 22:67; 23:2, 35, 39

John (14): 1:20, 25, 41; 3:28; 4:25, 29, 42; 6:69; 7:26, 41; 9:22; 10:24; 11:27; 20:31

Acts (6) 2:26; 4:26; 9:22; 17:3; 18:5, 28

1 John (2) 1:22; 5:1

CHRIST AS AN ATTRIBUTIVE TITLE WITH THE NAME "JESUS" IN THE FORMULATION "CHRIST JESUS" (58; 54 TIMES IN THE PAULINE LETTERS)

Acts (1): 19:4

Romans (6): 3:24; 8:1, 2, 39; 15:5; 16:3

1 Corinthians (5): 1:2, 30; 4:15; 15:31; 16:24

2 Corinthians (1): 4:5

Galatians (5): 2:4; 3:26, 28; 4:14; 6:15

Ephesians (7): 1:1; 2:6,7, 10, 13; 3:11, 21

Philippians (9): 1:1; 2:5; 3:3, 8, 12, 14; 4:7, 19, 21

Colossians (3): 1:4, 28; 2:6

1 Thessalonians (2): 2:14; 5:18

1 Timothy (6) 1:12, 14, 15; 2:5; 3:13; 6:13

2 Timothy (8): 1:1, 2, 9, 13; 2:1, 10; 3:12, 15

Philemon (2): 1:6, 23

Hebrews (1): 3:1

1 Peter (2): 5:10, 14

CHRIST AS A NAME (THE PRONOMINAL USE; 264; 219 IN THE PAULINE LETTERS)

Matthew (4): 1:17; 11:2, 23:8, 10

Mark (3): 9:41; 12:35; 15:32

John (5): 7:27, 31, 41, 42; 12:34

Acts (8): 2:30, 31; 3:18; 8:5; 9:20; 17:3; 24:24; 26:23

Romans (35): 1:16; 5:6, 8; 6:4, 8, 9; 7:4; 8:9, 11, 17, 34, 35; 9:1, 3, 5; 10:4, 6, 7; 12:5; 14:9, 10, 15, 18; 15:3, 7, 18, 20, 29; 16:5, 7, 9, 10, 16

1 Corinthians (47): 1:6, 12, 13, 17 (2x), 23, 24; 2:16; 3:1, 11 (2x); 4:1, 10 (2x), 15, 17; 5:7; 6:15 (2x); 7:22; 8:11, 12; 9:12, 18, 21; 10:4, 9, 16 (2x); 11:1, 3 (2x); 12:12, 27; 15:3, 12, 13, 14, 15, 16, 17, 18, 19, 20, 22, 23 (2x)

2 Corinthians (38): 1:5 (2x), 21; 2:10, 12, 14, 15, 17; 3:3, 4. 14; 4:4; 5:10, 14, 16, 17, 19, 20 (2x); 6:15; 8:23; 9:13; 10:1, 5, 7 (x3), 14; 11:2, 3, 10, 13, 23; 12:2, 9, 10; 13:3

Galatians (25): 1:6, 7, 10, 22; 2:16, 17 (2x), 20 (2x), 21; 3:13, 16, 17 (2x), 29; 4:7, 19; 5:1, 2, 4, 24; 6:2, 12

Ephesians (27): 1:3, 10, 12, 20; 2:5, 12, 13; 3:4, 6, 8, 17, 19; 4:7, 12, 13, 15, 20, 32; 5:2, 5, 14, 23, 25, 32; 6:5, 6

Philippians (18): 1:10, 13, 15, 16, 19, 20, 21, 23, 27, 29; 2:1, 16, 30; 3:7, 8, 9, 18; 4:13

Colossians (20): 1:2, 7, 24, 27; 3:1 (2x), 3, 4, 11, 13, 16, 24; 2:2, 5, 8, 11, 17, 20; 4:3, 12

1 Thessalonians (3): 2:6; 3:2; 4:16

2 Thessalonians (2): 2:2; 3:5

1 Timothy (2): 2:7; 5:11

2 Timothy (1): 2:19

Philemon (1): 1:8

Hebrews (9): 3:6, 14; 5:5; 6:1; 19:11, 14, 24, 28; 11:26

1 Peter (10): 1:11 (2x), 19; 2:21; 3:16, 18; 4:11, 13, 14; 5:1

2 John (2): 1:9 (2x)

Revelation (4) 11:15; 12:15; 20:4, 6

Christ (excluding "Jesus Christ") in Restoration scripture: Book of Mormon (312), Doctrine and Covenants (41), Pearl of Great Price (7)

TOGETHER WITH "JESUS" AS THE COMPOUND, PROPER NAME "JESUS CHRIST" (201)

Matthew (2): 1:1, 18

Mark (1): 1:1

Luke (3): 2:11; 24:26, 46

John (2): 1:17; 17:3

Acts (16): 2:38; 3:6, 20; 4:10; 5:42; 8:12, 37; 9:34; 10:36; 11:17; 15:11, 26; 16:18, 31; 20:21; 28:28

Romans (27): 1:1, 3, 6, 7, 8; 2:16; 3:22; 5:1, 11, 15, 17, 21; 6:3, 11, 23; 7:25; 13:14; 15:6, 8, 16, 17, 30; 16:18, 20, 24, 25, 27

1 Corinthians (17): 1:1, 2, 3, 4, 7, 8, 9, 10; 2:2; 3:11; 5:4 (2x); 8:6; 9:1; 15:57; 16:22, 2.3

2 Corinthians (10): 1:1–3, 19; 4:5; 5:18; 8:9; 11:31; 13:5, 14

Galatians (11): 1:1, 3, 12; 2:16 (2x); 3:1, 14, 21; 5:6; 6:14, 18

Ephesians (12): 1:1–3, 5, 17; 2:20; 3:1, 9, 14; 5:20; 6:23,24

Philippians (11): 1:1–2, 6, 8, 11, 19, 26; 2:11, 21; 3:20; 4:23

Colossians (3): 1:1, 2, 3

1 Thessalonians (9): 1:2 (2x), 3; 2:19; 3:11, 13; 5:9, 23, 28

2 Thessalonians (11): 1:1–2, 8, 12 (2x); 2:1, 14, 16; 3:6, 12, 18

1 Timothy (9): 1:1 (2x), 2, 16; 4:6; 6:3, 14; 5:2.1

2 Timothy (6): 1:2, 10; 2:3, 8; 4:1, 22

Titus (4): 1:1, 4; 2:13; 3:6

Philemon (4): 1:1, 3, 9, 25

Hebrew (3): 10:10; 13:8, 21

James (2): 1:1; 2:1

1 Peter (9): 1:1, 2, 3 (2x), 7, 13; 2:5; 3:21; 4:11

2 Peter (8): 1:1 (2x), 8, 11, 14, 16; 2:20; 3:18

1 John (8): 1:3, 7; 2:1; 3:23; 4:2–3; 5:6, 20

2 John (2): 1:3, 7

Jude (4): 1:1 (2x), 4, 17, 21

Revelation (7): 1:1, 2, 5, 9 (2x); 12:17; 2:21

Jesus Christ *in Restoration scripture: Book of Mormon (68), Doctrine and Covenants (84), Pearl of Great Price (8)*

High Priest (11)

Unique to the book of Hebrews is the explicit identification of Jesus as a high priest, although Revelation 1:10–20 presents Jesus in the guise of a heavenly high priest who stands in the midst of seven candles that are reminiscent of the temple menorah. Some scholars have also seen the reference to Jesus's inner tunic that was "without seam" (John 19:23) as a sign that John meant to present Jesus as a priest so that he was not only the sacrifice but also the sacrificer.

Hebrews (11): 2:17; 3:11; 4:14, 15; 5:5, 10; 6:20; 7:26; 8:11; 9:11; 10:21

Lamb (28)

Several New Testaments writers present Jesus either as a sacrificial lamb or more specifically as the Lamb of God. While only the Gospel of John explicitly describes Jesus this way twice in its beginning (1:29, 36), this imagery informs its passion narrative, which presents Jesus as the ultimate paschal lamb.

Acts (1): 8:32

1 Peter (1): 1:19

Revelation (21): 5:8, 13; 6:1, 16; 7:9, 10, 14, 17; 12:11; 14:4 (2x), 10; 15:3; 17:14 (2x); 19:7, 9; 21:9, 14, 22, 24

LAMB OF GOD (2)

John (2): 1:29, 36

LAMB WHO WAS SLAIN (3)

Revelation (3): 5:6, 12; 13:8

Lord (662)

The use of the Greek term *kyrios* is broad, having as many as four possible meanings. These include its simple use for "master" or "owner"; as a form of polite address, meaning simply "sir"; in a courtly sense when used of a social superior; and, significantly, as a Greek translation of the Hebrew term *'adōnay*, which was regularly used to substitute for the divine name YHWH, or "Jehovah."

FOR YHWH, THE GOD OF ISRAEL, WHETHER THE FATHER OR THE PREMORTAL JESUS CHRIST; LORD GOD; LORD OUR GOD (162)

Matthew (18): 1:20, 22, 24; 2:13, 15, 19; 3:3; 4:7, 10; 5:33; 9:38; 11:25; 21:9, 42; 22:37, 44; 23:39; 28:2

Mark (9): 1:3; 11:9, 10; 12:11, 29 (2x), 30, 36; 13:20

Luke (42): 1:6, 9, 11, 15, 16, 17, 25, 28, 32, 38, 43, 45, 46, 58, 66, 68, 76; Luke 2:9 (2x), 15, 22, 23 (2x), 24, 26, 29, 38, 39; 3:4; 4:8, 12, 18, 19; 5:17; 10:2, 27, 41; 12:37; 13:35; 19:38; 20:37; 20:42

John (4): 1:23; 12:13, 38 (2x)

Acts (37): 1:24; 2:20, 25, 34, 39; 3:22; 4:24, 26, 29; 5:9, 19; 7:30, 31, 33, 37, 39, 59; 8:24, 26, 39; 9:39; 12:7, 11, 17, 23; 13:2, 10, 11, 47; 14:43; 17:24; 18:25 (2x); 20:19; 21:14, 20; 22:16

Romans (9): 4:8; 9:28, 29; 10:16; 11:3, 34; 12:19; 14:11; 15:11

1 Corinthians (1): 14:21

2 Corinthians (2): 6:17, 18

Hebrews (13): 1:20; 7:21; 8:2, 8, 9, 10, 11; 10:16, 30 (2x); 12:5, 6; 12:5, 6; 13:6

James (5): 4:10; 5:4, 10, 11 (2x)

1 Peter (3): 2:3; 3:23, 15

2 Peter (1): 3:8

Jude (3): 1:4, 5, 9

Revelation (15): 4:8, 11; 11:15, 17; 15:3, 4; 16:5, 7, 10; 18:8; 19:1, 6; 21:22; 22:5, 6

LORD FOR THE MORTAL JESUS

Used as a polite form of address for Jesus (21)

Matthew (9): 8:2, 6, 8; 9:28; 15:22, 25, 27; 17:15; 20:30, 31, 33

Mark (2): 7:28; 10:51

Luke (7): 5:12; 7:6; 9:57, 59, 61; 18:41; 19:8

John (3): 6:34; 8:11; 9:36

When used with special meaning for the Lordship of Jesus, especially by his disciples (69)

Matthew (21): 7:21 (2x), 22 (2x); 8:21, 25; 12:8; 13:51; 14:28, 30; 16:22; 17:4; 18:21; 21:3; 22:43, 44, 45; 24:42; 26:22; 27:20; 28:6

Mark (6): 2:28; 5:19; 9:24; 11:3; 12:36, 37

Luke (18): 5:8; 6:5, 46 (2x); 9:54; 10:17, 40; 11:1; 12:41; 13:23; 17:37; 19:34; 20:42, 44; 22:33, 38, 49; 23:42

John (22): 6:68; 9:38; 11:3, 12, 21, 27, 32, 34, 39; 13:6, 9, 13, 14, 25, 36, 37; 14:5, 8, 22; 20:2, 13; 21:20

Acts (2): 2:34; 10:36

LORD FOR THE RESURRECTED, GLORIFIED JESUS

After-the-fact references by evangelists as post-Easter narrators (17)

Luke (13): 7:13, [31]; 10:1; 11:39; 12:42; 13:15; 17:5, 6; 18:6; 19:8; 22:31, 61 (2x)

John (4): 4:1; 6:23; 11:2; 20:20

Encounters with the "Risen Lord" (include evangelists as a postresurrection narrators (25)

[Mark, long ending (2): 16:19, 20]

Luke (2): 24:3, 34

John (10): 20:18, 25, 28; 21:7 (2x), 12, 15, 16, 17, 21

Acts (10): 1:6; 9:5 (2x), 6 (2x), 10 (2x), 11, 13, 15

Revelation (1): 1:8

References to the "Lord Jesus," "Jesus our Lord" (30)

Acts (13): 1:21; 4:33; 7:59; 8:16; 9:29;
  11:20; 19:5, 10, 13, 17; 20:24, 35;
  21:13
Romans (3): 4:24; 10:9; 14:11
1 Corinthians (1): 11:23
2 Corinthians (3): 1:14; 4:10, 14
Galatians (1): 6:17
Philippians (1): 2:19

Colossians (1): 3:17
1 Thessalonians (2): 4:1, 2
2 Thessalonians (1): 1:7
Philemon (1): 1:5
Hebrews (1): 13:20
2 Peter (1): 1:2
Revelation (1): 22:20

References to "Christ the Lord," "Lord Christ" (2)

Luke (1): 2:11

Colossians (1): 3:24

References to the "Lord Jesus Christ," "Christ Jesus our Lord," "Jesus Christ our Lord" (99)

Acts (6): 11:17; 15:11, 26; 16:31;
  20:21; 28:31
Romans (13): 1:3, 7; 5:1, 11; 6:11, 23;
  7:25; 13:14; 15:6, 30; 16:18, 20, 24
1 Corinthians (13): 1:2, 3, 7, 8, 9, 10;
  5:4 (2x), 5; 6:11; 8:6; 16:22, 23
2 Corinthians (4): 1:2, 3; 11:31; 13:14
Galatians (3): 1:3; 6:14, 18
Ephesians (9): 1:2, 3, 15, 17; 3:11, 14;
  5:20; 6:23, 24
Philippians (3): 1:2; 3:20; 4:23
Colossians (2): 1:2, 3
1 Thessalonians (9): 1:1 (2x), 3; 2:19;
  3:11, 13; 5:9, 23, 28

2 Thessalonians (11): 1:1, 2, 8, 12
  (2x); 2:1, 14, 16; 3:6, 12, 18
1 Timothy (6): 1:1, 2, 12; 6:3, 14; 5:21
2 Timothy (3): 1:2; 4:1, 22
Titus (1): 1:4
Philemon (2): 1:3, 25
James (2): 1:1; 2:1
1 Peter (1): 1:3
2 Peter (6): 1:8, 11, 14, 16; 2:20; 3:18
2 John (1): 1:3
Jude (3): 1:4, 17, 21
Revelation (1): 22:21

References to "the Lord" alone (likely of Jesus by context and usage; 237)

Acts (41): 2:21, 36, 47; 3:19; 5:14;
8:25; 9:1, 17, 27, 35, 42; 10:4, 14,
36, 48; 11:8, 16, 21 (2x), 23, 24;
13:12, 48, 49; 15:17 (2x), 35, 36;
16:10, 14, 15, 32; 18:8, 9; 20:21;
22:8, 10 (2x); 19; 23:11; 26:15

Romans (20): 5:21; 8:39; 10:12, 13;
12:11; 14:6 (x4), 8 (x3), 9; 16:2, 8,
11, 12 (2x), 13, 22

1 Corinthians (52): 1:31; 2:8, 16; 3:5,
20; 4:4, 5, 17, 19; 6:13 (2x), 14, 17;
7:10, 12, 17, 22 (2x), 25, 32 (2x),
34, 35, 39; 9:1 (2x), 2, 5, 14; 10:21
(2x), 22, 26, 28; 11:11, 20, 23, 26,
27 (2x), 29, 32; 12:3, 5; 15:31, 47,
57, 58 (2x); 16:7, 10, 19

2 Corinthians (20): 2:12; 3:16, 17
(2x), 18; 4:5; 5:6, 8, 11; 8:5, 9, 19,
21; 10:8, 17, 18; 11:17; 12:1, 8;
13:10

Galatians (2): 1:19; 5:10

Ephesians (16): 2:21; 4:1, 5, 17; 5:8,
10, 17, 19, 22, 29; 6:1, 4, 7, 8, 10, 21

Philippians (11): 1:14; 2:11, 24, 29;
3:1, 8; 4:1, 2, 4, 5, 10

Colossians (9): 1:20; 2:6; 3:16, 18, 20,
23, 24; 4:7, 17.

1 Thessalonians (14): 1:6, 8; 2:15; 3:8,
12; 4:6, 15 (2x), 16, 17 (2x); 5:2,
12, 27

2 Thessalonians (7): 1:9; 2:8, 13: 3:1,
3, 4, 5

1 Timothy (2): 1:14; 6:15

2 Timothy (14): 1:8, 16, 18 (2x); 2:7,
14, 19, 22, 24; 3:11; 4:8, 14, 17, 18

Philemon (3): 1:16, 20 (2x)

Hebrews (3): 2:3; 7:14; 12:14

James (8): 1:7, 12; 2:1; 4:15; 5:7, 8,
14, 15

1 Peter (2): 1:25; 2:13

2 Peter (7): 2:1, 9, 11; 3:2, 9, 10, 15

Jude (1): 1:14

Revelation (5): 1:10; 11:18; 14:3; 17:4;
19:16

Lord as a temporal master, owner, teacher, or ruler (60 additional New Testament occurrences)

Lord in Restoration scripture: Book of Mormon (1,570), Doctrine and Covenants (720), Pearl of Great Price (199).

Only Begotten, Only Begotten Son (5)

The KJV rendering of the Greek *monogenēs* as "Only Begotten" is probably better translated "one and only," "uniquely begotten," or even "one of a kind." Still, the traditional rendering has parallels in Restoration scripture and underscores the fact that Jesus was the literal, and only, begotten of the Father in the flesh.

John (4): 1:14, 18; 3:16, 18   1 John (1): 4:9

Only Begotten *in Restoration scripture: Book of Mormon (9), Doctrine and Covenants (13), Pearl of Great Price (26)*

Redeemer (0)

While Redeemer is not a title that appears in the New Testament, the concept of God or his servant as being a personal and national redeemer was an important promise in the Old Testament, especially in the later writings of Isaiah (Job 19:25; Psalms 19:14; 78:35; Proverbs 23:11; Isaiah 41:14; 43:14; 44:6, 24; 47:4; 48:17; 49:7, 26; 54:5, 8; 59:20; 60:16; 63:16; Jeremiah 50:34).

Redeemer in the Old Testament (18)
Redeemer *in Restoration scripture: Book of Mormon (41); Doctrine and Covenants (22), Pearl of Great Price (1)*

While not used in the New Testament, the concept can be seen in the use of the verb *redeem* and the noun *redemption*.

Redeem (9)

Luke (2): 1:68; 24:21   1 Peter (1): 1:18
Galatians (2): 3:13; 4:5   Revelation (3): 5:9; 14:3, 4
Titus (1): 2:14

Redeem in the Old Testament (88)

Redeem in Restoration scripture: Book of Mormon (59), Doctrine and Covenants (26), Pearl of Great Price (2)

REDEMPTION (11)

Luke (2): 2:38; 21:28

Romans (2): 3:24; 8:23

1 Corinthians (1): 1:30

Ephesians (3): 1:7, 14; 4:30

Colossians (1): 1:14

Hebrews (2): 9:12, 15

Redemption in the Old Testament (9)

Redemption in Restoration scripture: Book of Mormon (51), Doctrine and Covenants (39), Pearl of Great Price (2)

Savior (17)

The title "Savior," or "deliverer" (Hebrew, *môšîāʿ*; Greek, *sōtēr*), was one frequently used of God in the Old Testament (2 Samuel 22:3; Psalm 106:21; Isaiah 19:20; 43:3, 11; 45:15, 21; 49:26; 60:16; 63:8; Jeremiah 14:8; Hosea 13:4). Understood in a Jewish context as a national and perhaps spiritual deliverer, it was also a term that appeared frequently in Hellenistic and Roman imperial propaganda of rulers who were benefactors to their subjects, bringing peace, security, and prosperity.

Nevertheless, "Savior" is a fairly rare title in the New Testament, occurring only three times in the Gospels and some of the other instances in the New Testament actually applying to God the Father. Relatively speaking, it is much more frequent in Restoration scripture.

Savior used of Jesus (17)

Luke (2): 1:47; 2:11

John (1): 4:42

Acts (2): 5:31; 13:23

Ephesians (1): 5:23

Philippians (1): 3:20

2 Timothy (1): 1:10

Titus (3): 1:4; 2:13; 36

2 Peter (5): 1:1, 11; 2:20; 3:2, 18

1 John (1): 4:14

Savior in the Old Testament (16)

Savior *in Restoration scripture: Book of Mormon (12), Doctrine and Covenants (19), Pearl of Great Price (4)*

Used in letters where the subject is most likely God the Father (6)

1 Timothy (3): 1:1; 2:3; 4:10

Titus (2): 1:3; 2:10

Jude (1): 1:25

Son of David (20)

Son of David, David's Son (16 [17])

Matthew (9): 1:1; 9:27; 12:23; 15:22; 20:30, 31; 21:9, 15, 42

Matthew [1]: 1:20 (for Joseph, Mary's husband)

Mark (3): 10:47, 48; 12:35

Luke (4): 3:31; 18:38, 39; 20:41 (David's son)

His father David (1)

Luke (1): 1:32

SEED OF DAVID (3)

John (1): 7:42   2 Timothy (1): 2:8
Romans (1): 1:13

Son of God (125)

Perhaps the most important christological title, Son of God is most
common in the Johannine corpus, where forms of it appear 33 times
in the Gospel of John, 24 times in 1 John, and 2 times in 2 John.

SON OF GOD, SON OF THE MOST HIGH GOD, SON OF THE HIGHEST,
SON OF THE LIVING GOD, SON OF THE FATHER, SON OF THE
BLESSED (53)

Matthew (9): 4:3, 6; 8:29; 14:33;   2 Corinthians (1): 1:19
  16:16; 26:63; 27:40, 43, 54   Galatians (1): 2:20
Mark (5): 1:1; 3:11; 5:7; 14:61; 15:39.   Ephesians (1): 4:13
Luke (8): 1:32, 35, 38; 4:3, 9, 41; 8:29; Hebrews (4): 4:14; 6:6; 7:3; 10:29
  22:70   1 John (8): 3:8; 4:15; 5:5, 10, 12, 13
John (11): 1:34, 49; 3:18; 5:25; 6:69;   (2x), 20
  9:35; 10:36; 11:4, 27; 19:7; 20:31   2 John (1): 1:3
Acts (2): 8:37; 9:20   Revelation (1): 2:8
Romans (1): 1:4

Son of God in *Restoration scripture: Book of Mormon (51), Doctrine and Covenants
(21), Pearl of Great Price (6)*

HIS SON, HIS SON JESUS CHRIST, MY SON, THY SON (30)

John (3): 3:17; 17:1 (2x)   Galatians (3): 1:16; 4:4, 6
Acts (3): 3:13, 26, 33   1 Thessalonians (1): 1:10
Romans (5): 1:3, 9; 5:10; 8:3, 29   Hebrews (5): 1:2, 5 (2x); 3:6; 5:5
1 Corinthians (1): 1:9   1 John (9): 1:3, 7; 3:23; 4:9, 10; 5:9,
                                             10, 11, 20

His Holy Child, Thy Holy Child (2)

Acts (2): 4:27, 30

The Son, the Son of the Father (33)

Matthew (4): 11:27 (x3); 28:19
Luke (3): 10:22 (x3)
John (15): 3:35, 36 (2x); 5:19 (2x), 20, 21, 22, 23 (2x), 26; 6:40; 8:35, 36; 14:13

1 Corinthians (1): 15:28
Hebrews (3): 1:8; 5:8; 7:28
1 John (6): 2:22, 23 (2x), 24; 4:14; 5:12
2 John (1): 1:9

My Beloved Son (7)

In the Synoptics, God uses this address at the baptism and transfiguration of Jesus; 2 Peter 1:17 also refers to the transfiguration.

Matthew (2): 3:17; 17:5
Mark (2): 1:11; 9:7

Luke (2): 3:22; 9:35
2 Peter (1): 1:17

Son of Man (89)

The title "Son of Man" appears eighty-five times in the Gospels, almost always in the mouth of Jesus as the most common title for himself, and four other times later in the New Testament (Acts 7:56; Hebrews 2:6 [quoting Psalms 8:4]; and Revelation 1:13; 14:14). Latter-day Saints, because of the insights of Restoration scripture (Moses 6:57; see D&C 78:20; 95:17), tend to interpret this title as a way of referencing Jesus as the Son of God, who himself is known as "Man of Holiness." In the Old Testament, however, it most commonly was used to refer to a mortal being (e.g., Psalm 8:4; Isaiah 51:12; and Ezekiel passim). The book of Daniel introduced the term in reference to an eschatological figure who would come with power and glory (Daniel 7:13; 8:17), and this was the use that became prevalent in the intertestamental period.

While this eschatological use may have been how people at the time of Jesus would likely have understood the term, all three uses may obtain in the Gospels according to context. Accordingly, some passages emphasize the mortality of Jesus, as in the passion predictions; others clearly refer to his second coming; and others view this term as a sign of his divine authority to teach and act.

IN A MORTAL OR AMBIGUOUS CONTEXT (9)

Matthew (4): 8:20; 11:19; 13:37; 16:13   Hebrews (1): 2:6 (Psalm 8:4)
Luke (4): 6:22; 7:34; 9:58; 11:30

EMPHASIZING MORTALITY IN A PASSION CONTEXT (32)

Matthew (10): 12:40; 17:9, 12, 22;   Luke (6): 9:22, 44; 18:31; 22:22, 48;
    20:18, 28; 26:2, 24 (2x), 45.   24:7.
Mark (9): 8:31; 9:9, 12, 31; 10:33, 45;   John (7): 3:14; 6:53; 8:28; 12:23, 34
    14:21 (2x), 41.   (2x); 13:31.

EMPHASIZING JESUS'S DIVINE AUTHORITY (17)

Matthew (4): 9:6; 12:8, 32; 18:11   John (5): 1:51; 3:13; 5:27; 6:27, 62
Mark (2): 2:10, 28   Revelation (1): 1:13
Luke (5): 5:24; 6:5; 9:56; 12:10; 19:10

EMPHASIZING AN ESCHATOLOGICAL ROLE (31)

Matthew (14): 10:23; 13:41; 16:27, 28;   Acts (1): 7:56
    19:28; 24:27, 30 (2x), 37, 39, 44;   Revelation (1): 14:14
    25:13, 31; 26:64
Mark (4): 8:38; 13:26, 34; 24:62
Luke (11): 9:26; 12:8, 40; 17:22, 24,
    26, 30; 18:8; 21:27, 36; 22:69

Glossary

As noted in the introduction, President Spencer W. Kimball encouraged students and scholars to become bilingual in the languages of scholarship and faith. Because the study of Christology sometimes involves terms that may be unfamiliar to some readers, this glossary provides brief definitions and summaries that we hope will help readers navigate some of the essays in this volume.

adoptionist Christology (or adoptionism): In ancient Israel, the anointed kings were seen as being adopted or proclaimed sons of YHWH, or the God of Israel, upon their coronation (see Psalm 2:7). By analogy, some early Christians saw the Father's proclamation that Jesus was his Son at the baptism (Mark 1:11) as a form of adoptionism, though this view was later declared heretical by the proto-Orthodox. *See* Ebionites; proto-Orthodox.

Anointed One (Hebrew, *māšîaḥ*; Greek, *christos*): In the Hebrew Bible kings, priests, and on occasion prophets were anointed as a sign of divine appointment and empowerment. In the intertestamental period, different expectations developed regarding a coming Messiah who would redeem Israel and restore it to glory, and early Christians saw Jesus as the realization of their Messianic hopes. For Latter-day Saints, the premortal Jesus Christ was chosen and appointed in the premortal council as the Savior of humanity and the central figure in the Father's plan of salvation for his children.

atonement or redemption Christology (also known as "lamb Christology" by some scholars): Building upon the psalms featuring a suffering servant (e.g., Psalm 22) and the servant song prophecies of Isaiah (e.g., Isaiah 42:1–9; 49:1–7; 50:4–9; and 52:13–53:12), this Christology saw the work of God's Chosen One as including being despised and rejected as part of his bearing his people's griefs, sorrows, and transgressions. Jesus's passion predictions (Mark 8:31–33; 9:30–32; 10:32–34; and parallels) reveal his focus on this part of his mission. *See* sacrificial Christology.

Colossians Christ hymn: An early poem or liturgical fragment preserved in Colossians 1:15–20 that stresses Jesus Christ's role in creation and in the reconciliation, or redemption, of that creation.

conception Christology: Jesus became God's Son when Mary became pregnant with him following the annunciation. Examples of passages that teach this include Romans 1:3; Matthew 1:20–25; and Luke 1:26–38. For Latter-day Saints, the Firstborn of the Father became the Only Begotten when he was divinely conceived and miraculously born.

condescension: Literally meaning "coming down to be with" us, condescension refers to both God (Heavenly Father) becoming the Father of the mortal Jesus Christ and especially the premortal Christ setting aside his glory, power, and knowledge to be born as the Babe of Bethlehem. The pivotal text for Latter-day Saints is 1 Nephi 11:12–33, which also applies it to his humble, healing ministry and his willing, sacrificial death. See *kenosis*.

divine identity Christology: Equating or identifying Jesus with YHWH, or Jehovah, the God of Israel. Examples include Jesus as the Creator and Sustainer of the universe (John 1:3; Colossians 1:15–17; Hebrews 1:2) or as the Lord and Guide of his people (e.g., 1 Corinthians 10:1–4). Latter-day Saints regularly see the premortal Jesus as the Jehovah of the Old Testament and the Lord most frequently referred to in the Book of Mormon. *See also* preexistence Christology; YHWH.

docetic Christology (or docetism): This term is derived from the Greek *dokeō*, meaning "to seem" or "to appear," and it describes the belief that Jesus Christ only seemed or appeared to be human. Docetists affirm that Christ is fully divine but not human. They may have appealed to Romans 8:3 or Philippians 2:7 to support the idea that Christ appeared only in the "likeness" of human beings. Certain passages in the Gospel of John appear to specifically refute this belief (see John 1:14; 19:34–35), and it is denounced in the Epistles of John (see 1 John 4:1–3; 2 John 1:7) and was declared heretical by later proto-Orthodox Christians.

Ebionites: A group of Jewish-Christians first identified by this title in the second century AD. The name Ebionite most likely comes from the Hebrew, *'ebyon*, meaning "poor"—as in, "blessed are the poor in spirit" (Matthew 5:3). Although they accepted Jesus as the Messiah, they continued to observe much of the law of Moses and believed that Jesus was the natural son of Mary and Joseph. Jesus was then adopted by God at baptism on account of his righteousness. *See* adoptionism; possessionist/separationist Christology.

exaltation Christology: Closely associated with resurrection and second coming Christologies, this approach sees Jesus as becoming more fully divine with his resurrection and ascension into heaven when he becomes the reigning Lord. An important example is the Philippians Christ hymn, the second stanza of which speaks of God exalting Christ Jesus, at whose name every tongue will confess and every knee bow (Philippians 2:9–11).

high Christology: An approach to the person and work of Jesus that begins with his implicit godhood and attributes the highest degree of divinity to him, such as preexistence and divine identity Christologies. High Christology thus stresses Jesus's divinity over his humanity. Latter-day Saints particularly resonate with this Christology because of the high Christology of the Book of Mormon and the revealed insights of Joseph Smith and subsequent leaders of the Church.

incarnation Christology (or Logos Christology): The belief that the divine Jehovah, the preexistent Logos or Word of God, was clothed in flesh (John 1:14; Philippians 2:7). Such a christology emphasizes both the divinity and the humanity of Jesus Christ. The Book of Mormon strongly testifies of the incarnation, for instance, in the powerful testimony of Benjamin in Mosiah 3:5–8. *See also* condescension; divine identity Christology; Wisdom Christology.

judgment Christology: Focuses on the future role of the exalted Jesus, to whom the Father has entrusted the responsibility to judge the world (see John 5:22–29).

kenosis **(from Greek,** *kenō,* **"to empty")**: As suggested in the Philippians Christ hymn, the premortal Christ, who was in the form of God, "emptied himself" (KJV, "made himself of no reputation"), setting aside his divinity at the incarnation. *See also* condescension.

kenotic (also "veiling") Christology: Approaching the nature of Jesus by seeing his divinity as being set aside through *kenosis* or kept in abeyance, or set aside, during mortality. For Latter-day Saints, the idea that Jesus Christ's premortal glory, power, and knowledge was restored "grace for grace" is taught by passages such as D&C 93:12–14. *See also* condescension; preexistence Christology.

kērygma (Greek, "proclamation"): The basic apostolic testimony that God sent his Son, who went about doing good, suffered, died, rose again, ascended into heaven, and will return again in glory (e.g., Acts 10:34–43).

kyrios (Greek, "lord, master"; KJV, "Lord"): Meaning everything from "sir" to "master," the Greek term *kyrios* was also used for the Hebrew *'adōnay*, or "my Lord." This, in turn, was the standard respectful substitution for the divine name YHWH. *See* divine identity Christology; YHWH.

Logos hymn: Possibly antedating the rest of the Gospel of John, this poetic prologue (John 1:1–18 with prose interruptions about the Baptist) presents preexistent, divine identity, and incarnation Christologies with Christ as the Divine Word that becomes Flesh.

low Christology: Belief regarding the nature of Jesus Christ that begins with or emphasizes his humanity. Like *adoptionism*, it can focus its understanding of Jesus's position as Son of God as a position that was achieved or declared. Low Christologies tend to stress Jesus's humanity over his divinity.

Marcionites: A group named for its founder, Marcion of Sinope (born c. AD 100), a wealthy and influential Christian who was eventually excommunicated from the Roman Church for promoting ideas considered heretical. Marcion affirmed that the creator God of the Old Testament was evil and vengeful and that Jesus came to save us from that God of wrath. Since the creator God was evil, creation was evil. Therefore, Marcion reasoned, Jesus's body was not made of the evil material stuff of this world, but his body was divine. *See also* docetic Christology.

narrative Christology: This approach seeks to understand the person and work of Jesus by looking at what Jesus says and does in the context of the narrative and the actions of others. Arguing that Jesus can be grasped only within the narrative, proponents carefully study plot, narrative structure, actions, and dialogues to see what they reveal about Jesus's identity, character, and purpose.

New Translation (or Joseph Smith Translation): The prophet's inspired revision, expansion, and commentary of much of the Bible.

Philippians Christ hymn: An early poem or liturgical fragment preserved in Philippians 2:6–11 that confesses Jesus Christ's *kenosis* or condescension and his subsequent exaltation.

possessionist or separationist Christology: The belief that the human Jesus was "possessed" by the divine Christ for a certain time during his life, typically beginning at his baptism. This divine being then abandoned Jesus prior to his death so that he could die (see Mark 15:34 or Matthew 27:46). First John 2:22 appears to specifically refute this Christology, and it was declared heretical by proto-Orthodox Christians.

preexistence Christology: Belief about the nature of Christ that focuses on his premortality or existence and activity before his birth as the Babe of Bethlehem. For Latter-day Saints, an understanding that the premortal Jesus Christ was the Firstborn of the Father bearing the divine title Jehovah is an important tenet of the Restoration. *See* incarnation Christology; Wisdom Christology.

proto-Orthodox: Term used by scholars to identify those second- and third-century Christians who became the forerunners of the Orthodox Christianity established in the fourth century and beyond. Its positions were strongly argued by figures such as Justin Martyr, Irenaeus of Lyons, and Tertullian of Carthage. Although the term can be helpful in distinguishing broad trends in the early history of Christianity, some proto-Orthodox Christians shared more in common with contemporary "heretics" than with the later Orthodox Christians who claimed them as their own. Proto-Orthodox Christians affirmed a divine incarnation Christology as a way of understanding that Jesus was both fully human and divine.

prokopē (**Greek, "advancement, progression"**): Understanding Jesus's development or progression, usually in mortality. Restoration scripture confirms that in mortality Jesus indeed "received not of the fulness at the first, but received grace for grace" (see D&C 93:12–14).

royal Christology: The Davidic covenant (see 2 Samuel 7:12–16) had promised that there would always be a descendant of the house of David to reign in Israel. With the lapse of the Davidic dynasty in Zedekiah's time, the hope that a descendant of the royal house would arise to be the anointed king who would restore Israel fueled much intertestamental and New Testament messianic expectation. To this end, the Synoptic Gospels, especially Matthew, often used the title "Son of David" to identify Jesus as the fulfiller of this Davidic hope.

resurrection Christology: Understanding that Jesus became God's Son or Chosen Servant most fully through the resurrection (e.g., Romans 1:4). Without disputing that Jesus was already God's Son in premortality and became his Only Begotten at his conception and birth, Latter-day Saints can see statements such as Jesus's revision of Matthew 5:48 in 3 Nephi 12:48 (adding "ye should be perfect *as I*, or your Father who is in heaven is perfect"; emphasis added) as an indication that he became even more like his Father through the resurrection.

sacrificial Christology: Focusing on the salvific work of Jesus, this approach understands Jesus's identity in terms of his fitness as the sinless, eternal Son of God to be a sacrifice and his willingness to offer himself to reconcile man to God. *See* atonement or redemption Christology.

second coming (or *parousia*) Christology: Belief about the nature and role of Christ that focuses upon his return as Judge of all the Earth and on the restoration of Israel and the world as a whole to a millennial state of peace. The hope for this is represented in the prayers for Christ to come quickly in passages such as 1 Corinthians 16:22 and Revelation 22:20. *See also* judgment Christology.

Son of Man: This title appears eighty-five times in the Gospels, almost always in the mouth of Jesus as the most common title for himself, and four other times later in the New Testament (Acts 7:56; Hebrews 2:6 [quoting Psalms 8:4]; and Revelation 1:13; 14:14). Latter-day Saints, because of the insights of Restoration scripture (Moses 6:57; see D&C 78:20; 95:17), tend to interpret this title as a way of referencing Jesus as the Son of God, who himself is known as "Man of Holiness." In the Old Testament, however, it most commonly was used to refer to a mortal being (e.g., Psalm 8:4; Isaiah 51:12; and Ezekiel passim). The book of Daniel introduced the term in reference to an eschatological figure who would come with power and glory (Daniel 7:13; 8:17), and this was the use that became prevalent in the intertestamental period. While this eschatological application may have been how people at the time of Jesus would likely have understood the term, all three uses may pertain in the Gospels according to context. Accordingly, some passages emphasize the mortality of Jesus, as in the passion predictions; others clearly refer to his second coming; and others view this term as a sign of his divine authority to teach and act.

Valentinians: This group was named after its founder, Valentinus. Born in Egypt in the early-second century AD and educated in Alexandria, Valentinus became a popular Christian theologian in Rome (c. AD 130–160). For Valentinus, the material world was an error, created by a lesser deity who turned from God. Whatever this world or humanity lacks, however, is made up for by God through his Word, Jesus Christ, whose body was more divine than human. Jesus's more patent divinity revealed the divinity that exists within all humans. Later proto-Orthodox Christians declared Valentinus a heretic and labeled him docetic. *See* docetic Christology.

Wisdom Christology: Borrowing from the late Jewish concept that wisdom (Hebrew, *ḥokmāh*) was an attribute of God and an agent in the creative process, as seen in Proverbs 8, Christians began to speak of Jesus in similar language, a move that allowed them to maintain a monotheistic position while also speaking of two divine beings.

YHWH (Hebrew, "The one who exists, causes to be"; KJV, "Jehovah"): The Tetragrammaton, or four-letter, Hebrew name of God. Deriving from the verb "to be," it includes the meanings "the one who was, is, and will be" with the idea of "the one who causes to be." Because it was unvoweled in surviving texts, its original pronunciation is unknown, though it is commonly rendered as *Yahweh*. Too sacred to pronounce in normal circumstances, ancient Israelites and modern Jews usually substituted the term *'adōnay*, or "my Lord," which the King James translators rendered in small caps as LORD. For today's Latter-day Saints, the Lord in the Old Testament generally refers to the premortal Jesus Christ.

Index